The Stephen Cobb
User's Guide
to
FileMaker®

Stephen Cobb
Chey Romfo

Windcrest®/McGraw-Hill

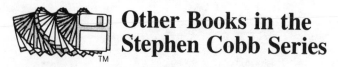

Other Books in the Stephen Cobb Series

The Stephen Cobb User's Handbook to Lotus 1-2-3, Release 3.0
The Stephen Cobb Complete Book of PC and LAN Security
The Stephen Cobb User's Handbook to Excel for the IBM PC

FIRST EDITION
SECOND PRINTING

© 1991 by **Windcrest Books**, an imprint of TAB Books.
TAB Books is a division of McGraw-Hill, Inc.
The name ''Windcrest'' is a registered trademark of TAB Books.

Library of Congress Cataloging-in-Publication Data

Cobb, Stephen, 1952-
   The Stephen Cobb user's guide to FileMaker II / Stephen Cobb, Chey
Romfo.
     p.   cm.
   ISBN 0-8306-3411-8
   1. Data base management. 2. FileMaker II (Computer program)
3. Macintosh (Computer)—Programming. I. Romfo, Chey. II. Title.
III. Title: User's guide to FileMaker II.
   QA76.9.D3C623   1990
   005.75—dc20
                                     89-48114
                                         CIP

TAB Books offers software for sale. For information and a catalog, please contact
TAB Software Department, Blue Ridge Summit, PA 17294-0850.

Director of Acquisitions: Ron Powers
Technical Editor: Sandra L. Johnson
Production: Katherine G. Brown
Series Design: Jaclyn J. Boone
Cobb Associates trademark is used by permission.
                                                 SCS

Acknowledgment

The authors wish to acknowledge
the assistance, examples, and advice
provided by:

MacAcademy:
Professional workshops for FileMaker users
in Florida and around the country.

Florida Marketing International, Inc.
477 S. Nova Rd.
Ormond Beach, FL 32174
(904) 677-1918

Contents

About This Book

THIS BOOK WILL SHOW YOU how to make use of and benefit from the features and abilities of FileMaker, the leading data management program for the Apple Macintosh. The book is designed to help you better access the power of the FileMaker program than you can from the manuals alone. Throughout this book, you will find tips and techniques that have been collected from many users and from a variety of sources. Some of the techniques you will read about in this book are not documented elsewhere. Many are not immediately obvious from the existing documentation, or they are simply things that users have discovered while putting the program through its paces. Of course, there are always more uses to a program than can be documented in the program manuals, and it was our job to ferret these out for you.

ABOUT FILEMAKER

How do you know if you can benefit from FileMaker? Take this simple test: Do you spend your workday making lists, keeping records, sorting out facts, compiling proposals, tracking numbers, or updating files? If you have answered "Yes" to at least one of these duties, then you do indeed need FileMaker to help!

In today's office place, the average employee is often forced to deal with information overload. It does not matter if you are administrative, management, or executive in status, and the size of the office or company makes no difference—you can be a member of a multi-national conglomeration, or just starting out in your own business at home. You are still forced to deal with certain obstacles in managing your information and data. The worse-case scenario is one in which all the information is there that is needed to run the business efficiently and profitably, but there is no way to control that information.

One obvious solution to this problem is a computer equipped with good information management software, such as FileMaker. This dynamic combination can take the tedium out of record keeping, put information into order, and allow you to more clearly weed through the chaff to find the kernels of vital information. You might be surprised to know that many Fortune 500 companies use FileMaker. Although they might have spent a lot of money on large mainframe computers, they have also seen the wisdom of providing an easy but powerful microcomputer application for the day-to-day needs of their workers.

In this book, we assume that you already obtained your Mac, or at least are strongly considering one, and now are in need of a database management application. You have decided on FileMaker, one of the easiest and most effective tools you can buy to help with your business. We should point out that FileMaker, like most professional software, has been through several revisions, or upgrades. While we simply are using the term FileMaker, this book is actually based on the version known as FileMaker II. For more about the different versions of FileMaker, see Chapter 1.

WHAT FILEMAKER CAN DO

FileMaker gives you a powerful tool for distilling the piles of information encountered in your day-to-day business activities: mailing lists, marketing data, sales orders, personnel records, and so on. Managing that data means being able to sort it and find the information you need. It also means being able to present your data with visual impact needed for effective communications. With FileMaker, you can arrange your data, and also create professional-looking data entry screens, business forms, form letters, columnar reports, multi-column directories, free-form reports, and last but not least, the much dreaded but most essential mailing label. FileMaker's ability to dress up information and present it in an interesting way makes the program more than just a database manager. It has broken new ground and is more aptly referred to as a "database publishing" tool.

Not everything you create in FileMaker will be perfect the first time, much the same way the letter you have just composed and sent to word processing is always in need of changes before it is finally sent out. With FileMaker, you can change your mind about any aspect of your files. You can experiment with different ways to organize information and use new arrangements to take advantage of better ideas.

As you grow more familiar with the program, you'll also discover ways to reduce your workload by having FileMaker automatically enter information for you, look up something from another file, or copy data from another source like a spreadsheet or a word-processed document. FileMaker also has the capability of simplifying repetitive tasks in automated steps called *scripts*, sometimes referred to in other applications as macros.

The appearance of your reports, forms, and other printed materials is very important in today's information society. You can have all the right information in all the right places, but if it doesn't look good, it won't receive the recognition it deserves. You don't need to be an artist to enhance the appearance of the forms, reports, and other documents you need to produce for your business. In any file, you can start with a preset layout, then move things around, paste in a logo or a chart, change fonts, add explanatory text, place boxes and other graphics; all the things that might have been too time consuming or expensive to do before FileMaker. Included in the program are templates and sample files for your immediate usage or customizing.

Another important feature is being able to share your information with others in your workplace on a network. FileMaker comes with multi-user capabilities already built in, so each person in your work group can have access to the information he or she needs even while others are using the same file. One person can be creating a new report layout, while others are entering records, and someone else is analyzing the results of a calculation. Sensitive information is easily protected with passwords and other features. All you need for data sharing is your Macintosh, FileMaker, and a network. If you have a separate file server, FileMaker can also take advantage of its special capabilities.

WHO THIS BOOK IS FOR

This book is for anyone who needs to know more about FileMaker than they already do. But each person's need for increase documentation and/or training is different, so the goal of this book is to cover all aspects and features of the program in order to meet the needs of a wide range of readers. This book is a multi-purpose learning guide and reference book, aimed at beginning, intermediate, and advanced users.

If you are new to the world of computers, the simplicity of FileMaker, plus the tips and comments in this book, will enable you to move quickly and confidently into the amazing world of information processing and database publishing.

If you are new to FileMaker but have used other database programs, this book will help you discover the similarities and differences, and allow you to customize your operations more easily.

If you have already started using FileMaker, the tips, techniques, and extensive examples will increase your effective and productive use of the program's features.

Many examples in the book can be followed keystroke-by-keystroke in order to reinforce the learning process and your comfort level with the program. As the book progresses, the emphasis will shift to the practical considerations of your applications and will show you how to create very complex computations and summaries that were probably previously handled by your spreadsheet program.

USING THIS BOOK

This book is divided into three parts, each of which explores FileMaker from a different level of user's experience or expertise. You might be able to skip some chapters if you are already familiar with the program. However, bear in mind that if you are a self-taught user, you might have missed some of the basics, and so you might just want to start at the beginning and work your way through.

The first part covers the basics of FileMaker. It gives you everything you need to know to begin managing data. You can take a quick tour of the program's commands, screens, and features to give you an idea of the possibilities available to you as you progress.

The second part covers practical features of FileMaker. It shows you how to use the more complicated and useful features that make FileMaker a semirelational database through the use of the lookup features. You'll also be given information on how to import and export data from other programs, as well as learning how to create calculations and summaries for quicker analysis of the information.

The third part shows you how to add power to FileMaker. It provides the real-world applications of FileMaker as well as tips and techniques for improving database designs and operations. You'll also be given information on managing FileMaker on your network with such features as passwords, confidential layouts, bridges, and zones. You'll also be given some unconventional database management examples to encourage you to apply your creativity to the power of FileMaker. The final chapter of the book covers enhancements available in FileMaker Pro.

CONVENTIONS AND ASSUMPTIONS

Notes to you are indicated by the pen-in-hand icon to the left of the text. These can be notes of interest or importance.

Tips are indicated by the pointing-hand icon to the left. These tips should help you use FileMaker.

In writing this book, we have assumed that you already know how to operate a Macintosh computer. By the word "operate," we do not mean that you know how to customize the operating system using ResEdit, or even that you know what INITs and CDEVs are. We simply assume that you can click on objects with the mouse, use the mouse to pull down menus and make selections, and enter and edit text in dialog boxes. If you have already been through the introductory disk that comes with every Macintosh, you will have mastered these skills. For example, you will know what the word *drag* means in the context of the Mac.

If you have not achieved this level of familiarity with the Mac, do not despair. Learning the basics of Mac operation does not take long, and you will find useful definitions in the Glossary.

We trust this book will help you get the most from FileMaker and will find a permanent place in your computer library or the desk next to your Mac. In addition to providing insight into how the program works, this book should also make using it fun!

1
An Overview

THIS CHAPTER PROVIDES you with an overview of FileMaker, what the program can do, and how you can get it running on your Macintosh. The various versions of FileMaker are discussed. We begin with the requirements for running FileMaker and move on to examine FileMaker in relation to other database software.

REQUIREMENTS FOR RUNNING FILEMAKER

FileMaker is a versatile Macintosh program that can be used on most Macs. In Fig. 1-1, FileMaker is starting on a Mac II that is running under the Finder.

Note the list of files and folders together with several command buttons. This is the dialog box that FileMaker presents when you double click on the FileMaker program file or icon. To start FileMaker, you must either Open an existing database or create a New database.

Normally when you use the Finder, only one program is running at a time—in this case FileMaker. You can use FileMaker on any of the following systems:

Macintosh Plus
Macintosh SE
Macintosh SE/30
Macintosh II or later, provided that the system has either two 800K disk drives or
    a hard disk with an 800K disk drive, and 1 megabyte of RAM.

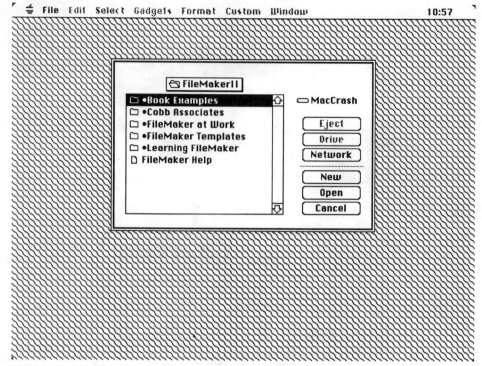

Fig. 1-1. Opening screen on a Mac II.

Hardware Qualifications

Although some people might tell you that FileMaker will work on any 512K Enhanced machine (which is supposedly the rough equivalent of a Mac Plus), that is not necessarily the case. There have been problems when running FileMaker with some third-party memory upgrades, and so we can't recommend running this program on anything less than a "real" Mac Plus. Of course, all of the above systems come with a minimum of one megabyte (1Mb) of memory. This is the minimum amount required for the effective use of FileMaker. You probably do not need us to tell you that having more memory is advantageous. Basically, the more memory you have, the more you will be able to do with FileMaker and with your Mac in general.

One technical note on adding memory to your Mac: Any memory units or SIMMS that you purchase to upgrade your Mac must be installed correctly. Your SIMMS must be inserted in the proper configuration, or you will not receive the amount of memory you had anticipated. Mixing your SIMMS is a bit like mixing radials and bias ply tires on your car!

Printers

FileMaker supports any of Apple's impact printers such as the ImageWriter or laser printers such as the LaserWriter. You can also use compatible models like the

General Computer Personal Laser Printer. To print from FileMaker make sure that the printing resource or driver for your printer is located in your System folder. What's a printing resource, you say? It is easily identified as a Chooser document, and its icon appears when you pick Chooser from the Apple menu. You can see the LaserWriter resource being selected in the Chooser in Fig. 1-2. More information on printers and their appropriate drivers can be found in Chapter 8.

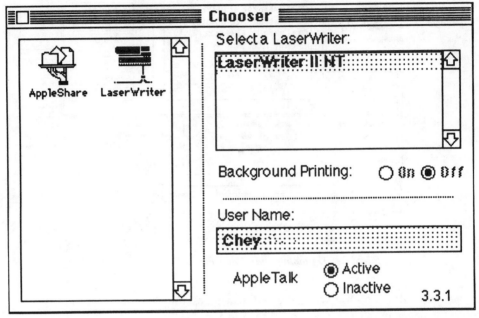

Fig. 1-2. LaserWriter resource in Chooser.

RUNNING FILEMAKER WITH MULTIFINDER

MultiFinder is the multi-tasking feature of the Mac operating system. Running FileMaker with MultiFinder allows you to use more than one application at the same time. You can see FileMaker being started under MultiFinder in Fig. 1-3.

Note that there are several windows in the background behind the FileMaker II dialog box. These include a MacDraw II document and an Excel spreadsheet. Also note the *F* in the top right of the screen. This is the FileMaker II icon under Multi-Finder, showing you that FileMaker is the currently active program.

Before running FileMaker with MultiFinder, check to make sure that you have enough memory to do so. FileMaker requires a memory allocation under MultiFinder of at least 512K of memory, but by allocating more memory to FileMaker under MultiFinder, some FileMaker tasks operate faster.

You can increase the memory allocation of a program under MultiFinder. To do this, you first make sure that you are running under MultiFinder, and then select File-Maker II from the desktop, *but do not launch it*. Select Get Info from the File menu on

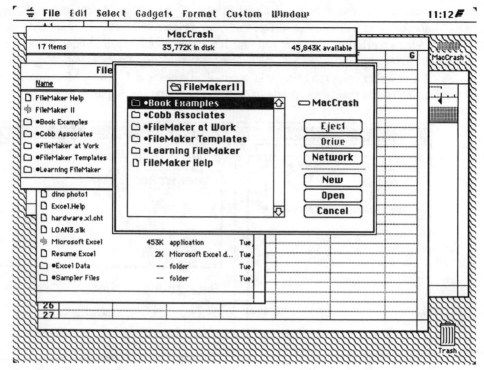

Fig. 1-3. FileMaker II running under MultiFinder.

the desktop. You will get a box that gives you the release version, Claris address, phone number, and so on, as seen in Fig. 1-4.

In the lower right-hand corner is the Suggested Memory Size and, below that, an insert point where you type in the amount of memory to allocate to the program. Enter the desired amount and press Return.

Increasing the Application Memory Size for FileMaker can sometimes make the program run a little faster under MultiFinder. Getting the right amount of memory is usually achieved by the famous trial-and-error method of computer management. Just make sure that you don't give FileMaker so much memory that the other programs poop out. *Never* decrease the amount of memory below 512K, as that is the absolute minimum amount of memory needed by FileMaker to operate under MultiFinder.

The advantages to running FileMaker with MultiFinder include:

- Letting FileMaker finish finding, sorting, printing, and other tasks while you work in another application, without closing files or quitting FileMaker.

- Copying data from another application and pasting it into your FileMaker file, without closing files or quitting either application. This is very handy when you are creating images in a draw program to be used as graphics or pictures in a FileMaker file.

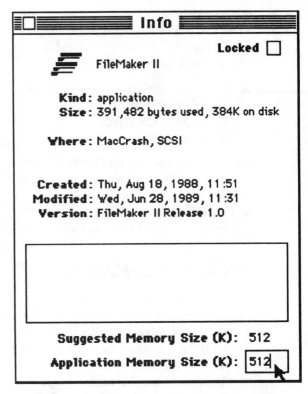

*Fig. 1-4. The Get Info
dialog box.*

The main disadvantage to running FileMaker with MultiFinder is the possibility of conflicts between programs. These can result in system errors. These inter-program incompatibilities under MultiFinder generally relate to the order in which applications are loaded. For example, we have found that it is best to load word processing and spreadsheet programs *before* FileMaker, or system crashes are more likely to happen. You have to beware, though, of other programs that recommend that they be loaded last, or these programs might fight for your attention by causing those nasty little bombs to appear. Look for upgrades to the Macintosh System software to resolve these conflicts.

PRODUCT SUPPORT

We would be negligent if we did not mention that all FileMaker users should be registered users. The advantages of becoming a registered user include access to the FileMaker Customer Support Hot Line provided by Claris, early notification of upgrades, and discounts on new versions.

In the early days of FileMaker, there had been some criticisms concerning technical support for the product, and rightfully so. There was no toll-free number, and you sometimes had quite a long wait on hold until you finally spoke to a human being. Claris became aware of these problems and has worked hard to speed up their support call response time. Although there is still no toll-free number to contact, we have found that calls are handled faster and more efficiently these days.

To register your copy of FileMaker and other Claris products, you can contact Claris at their new location:

Claris
5201 Patrick Henry Drive
Santa Clara, CA 95052
(408) 987-7000

FileMaker is not copy protected. This means you should have no problem making backup copies of your program disks, something you should always do before installing the software on your Mac. However, pay close attention to the software licensing agreement that describes what you can and cannot do with copies. See Chapter 9 if you need to run FileMaker on more than one machine at one time.

A SHORT FILEMAKER HISTORY

Some confusion surrounds the product name FileMaker. This book is based on FileMaker II. You might wonder about the difference between FileMaker 4 and File-Maker II, and FileMaker Pro. Does this program belong to Apple, Nashoba, or Claris? Is this a result of the constant company mergers that one hears about in Silicon Valley? The answer is a definite maybe.

The first incarnation of this program was simply called FileMaker. The software was developed as a simple but graphically oriented database manager that made the most of the power and simplicity of the Mac. FileMaker was first marketed through the software company Nashoba, with strong ties to Apple.

Not long after FileMaker came FileMaker Plus, which added features to the original program. FileMaker Plus still had some severe limitations, and Nashoba quickly upgraded the program and renamed it FileMaker 4. This is when its real strengths and advantages became apparent. (Nashoba also realized that a program this powerful and this much fun must have a decent manual, and they produced a beautiful hardbound manual with an index that was exceptionally good for a computer manual. However, for all its innovation, the manual lacked an intuitive flow and didn't have many hard-core examples.)

More recently, Apple absorbed Nashoba. A single company, Claris, was formed to handle all of Apple's application software. The Nashoba people were merged into Claris. Almost all the people who were involved with FileMaker from its inception have stayed with the program, and are now working with it under Claris.

Shortly after Claris was formed, FileMaker 4 was again enhanced and renamed FileMaker II. Now, if that doesn't make the Confusing Software Names Hall of Fame, we don't know what does. (A likely explanation is that Claris wanted a name that follows the same vein as their other products MacDraw II, MacWrite II, and MacPaint II.) For all intents and purposes, FileMaker 4 and FileMaker II are the same creature. Now a later version exists: FileMaker Pro.

Whatever version of FileMaker you are working with, this book will be about 97 percent accurate. However, you might want to contact Claris for your upgrade, because it is usually a good idea to work with the latest version. We simply use the name FileMaker throughout the rest of the book without distinguishing different versions unless there are major differences.

Once you have installed FileMaker II, any file created under FileMaker 4 will work. As soon as you open the FileMaker 4 file, it will automatically be changed to a FileMaker II file. When you open a FileMaker II file with FileMaker Pro, it is converted to FileMaker Pro.

WHAT A DATABASE IS

We have been tossing around the term "database" without really explaining what it means. A *database* is a collection of information organized in a meaningful manner. A typical example is the telephone directory. Here the data (the names, addresses, and phone numbers) are organized alphabetically in columns. This type of arrangement can be called a *columnar database*. Each row of the database table is a different record. Each column is a different piece of information about that record. These categories of information are called *fields*, so each column represents a different field.

The same type of information can be arranged differently. A card file of names, addresses, and phone numbers offers the same type of information as a phone book. However, the card file is a *form-oriented database*. Each entry or record occupies a new card. The fields are laid out on the card to separate the different categories of information. You can see the two types of database arrangement diagrammed in Fig. 1-5.

Tabular database

Name	Address	Phone

Form-oriented database

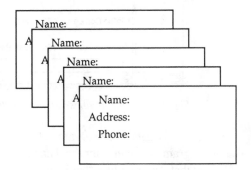

Fig. 1-5. Two methods of arranging data.

FileMaker is a form-oriented database. You enter information in fields laid out on records that are presented as separate forms or cards. A simple FileMaker database for names and addresses might look like the one in Fig. 1-6.

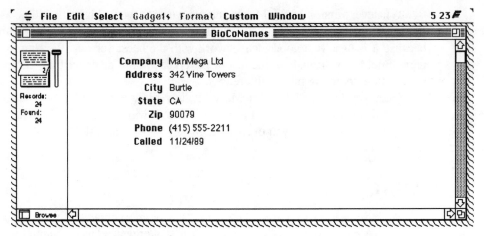

Fig. 1-6. Simple FileMaker database.

However, information stored in a FileMaker database can be laid out in many different ways. In Fig. 1-7, you can see a name and address report that is arranged in a list format, as a table.

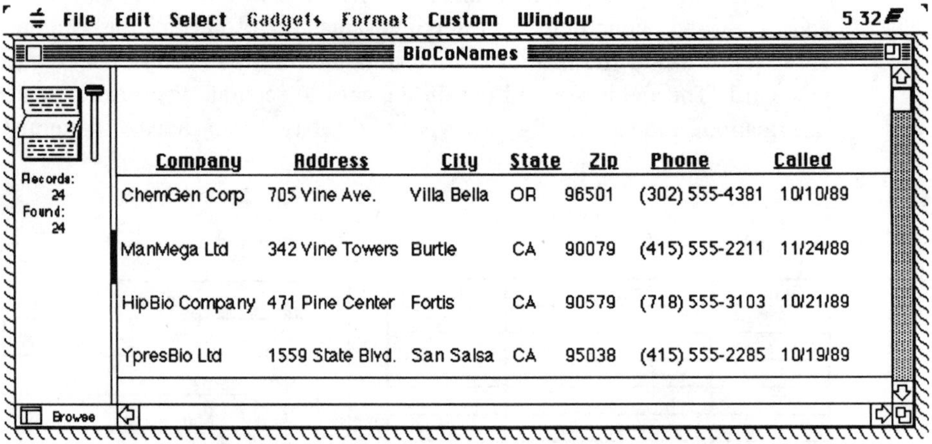

Fig. 1-7. Simple database laid out as list.

A database program helps you manage information or data. With a database program, you can enter the data you wish to keep, store it in various ways, and manipulate that data in a way that is meaningful to you. A database program will simplify record keeping and many other tasks that are often repetitive and/or time consuming. The card file at your local library is an example of the old style of a database that is both time consuming in its data search (let your fingers do the walking) and not very flexible.

FileMaker is a *database management program*. It is also, to use one of Claris' favorite terms, a *database publisher*. The "publisher" part of FileMaker means you can make very sophisticated files and reports without getting too many headaches, and you don't need a degree in mechanical drawing in order to make your reports look professional. For example, the document displayed in Fig. 1-8 is actually a FileMaker database report.

Country Guest Houses of Europe

Inverdale

Peebleshire   Scotland

Tweedale Road
Near Peebles
Peebleshire
SCOTLAND,
ML13 2RT

U.K. 0721-34234

Fax/Telex   0721-43456

Season

Open early April to late
November

A delightful place from which to explore the Border region of Scotland, rich in history and folklore. The rooms are small but well-appointed with showers in most. The proprietor, Mr. Burns, is an amiable host and very attentive. Book early as this is a very popular venue, particularly during the Edinburgh Festival in late September thru early October.

How to get there:

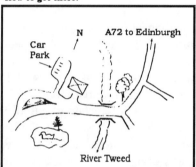

Rates

40-50 per person per night
(Pounds Sterling)
VISA/MC

Pets	✗
Meals	✔
Kids	✔
Parking	✔
Pool	✗
Camping	✗
Sports	✔
Laundry	✔

Scotland   Page 33

Fig. 1-8. Example of database publishing.

Much of the information we deal with on a daily basis comes from a database. As we have said, a phone book is an example of a database. Personnel records, customer accounts, and sales figures can be considered databases.

Let's take the personnel records example for a moment, and look at the different ways in which this information can be used. Suppose you work for the plastics company, Tuff Stuff. Obviously, the personnel database would have all the vital statistics on you, the employee. This would include such things as your address, your position, perhaps your department head, pay scale, hire date, evaluations, attendance, and possibly such things as your educational background, family size, insurance benefits, and ethnic background.

Based on the data in these records, the personnel department could generate all of the following reports—all originating from the same source:

- Employee phone lists.
- Organizational charts.
- Form letters with distribution lists.
- Welcome letters to new hires.
- Congratulatory letters on your anniversary hire date.
- Lists of prospects for new position openings, based on educational background and job performance.
- Insurance reports.
- Company racial mix, for meeting federal guidelines.
- Daycare evaluation, based on the number of employees with young children, combined with the number of sick days taken in a given year.
- Departmental budgets.
- Incentive program evaluation, based on performance, salaries, and daily work attendance by departments.

That's a lot of reports to come from one file!

The old method of information gathering was for the boss to come to you with stacks of files at 5:00 P.M. and tell you that he'd like a report on his desk at 9:00 A.M. Let's suppose that he wants a list of all employees born in odd-numbered years and in cities that have more than three syllables. If you had all this information in a database, all you would have to do is to sort out the data you need, put it in a report layout that looks attractive, and put it on his desk. That is a lot better than pulling an all-nighter, complete with cold coffee and take-out food!

Suppose that your boss is reluctant to put all this information about employees into a database, because he doesn't want you, the lowly employee, to see certain data? With FileMaker, this is no problem. He can simply lock you out of confidential data with password security or provide you with a password that only allows access to specific levels of data. FileMaker can do that and more! With FileMaker you can find specific or global data in any field, record, or file. You can also group and analyze that data, summarize it, throw it into a ready-made template, and print the results. Now, what about the raise you wanted?

ELEMENTAL, MY DEAR

A database consists of the three basic elements of fields, records, and files. This is also the basic FileMaker structure. These elements allow you to organize your data to make the best use of it. A simple analogy is to think of fields as leaves, the records as branches, and a file as a tree. The file (tree) is the biggest part of the whole. The records (branches) subdivide the whole. The fields (leaves) are the smallest part. One branch or leaf does not make an entire tree, nor is the tree complete without both the branches and the leaves.

DATABASE TYPES

A number of database management programs are available, and they differ widely in their capabilities. The two very broad categories of database managers are *flat-file databases* and *relational databases*. FileMaker falls into a gray area between these two categories.

Flat-File Databases

The flat-file databases are also called *simple* databases and keep all their data in one file. This is an electronic version of the traditional card-file approach to managing data. To get the information you need, the computer literally reshuffles the cards every time you need your data in a different manner. This type of database has many limitations, the biggest of which is that the data you need is frequently not all held entirely within one database, but is scattered throughout several databases.

Relational Databases

A *relational database* can relate several separate files to one another by linking information that each has in common. A purchase order file, for example, probably contains some of the same information that is in the customer file as well. The ability to relate the two files allows automatic entry of a customer's name, address, and customer number in the purchase order without having to look up this information manually. Some database programs of this type are quite large and powerful, using their own programming languages in order to link the files to one another. Two widely-used relational databases that are sold for the Mac are Oracle and 4th Dimension. Both are fine examples of this type of database, but the learning curve associated with these is quite steep, relatively speaking.

FileMaker is something of a mixture of the two types of database. It emulates a relational database in the sense in that it has the ability to link certain files through the use of its Lookup Files command. An excellent illustration of this is included in the examples disk that comes with the FileMaker II software package. In the example called Orders, you'll find an order form for furniture. This is customized shelving for entertainment systems (television, VCR, stereo, and so on). One of the fields in Orders shows an actual picture of the system being purchased. This picture field is linked to another file called Models. When you type the name of the model in the correct field, FileMaker "looks up" the information in the Models file and automatically places the correct picture of your system in the Order, as well as the appropriate pricing. Check the sample files that come with your FileMaker software. This book gives you examples of links or *lookups* in Chapter 6.

FileMaker offers you the simplicity of a flat-file database and so does not require complex programming to create lookups. However, it is limited in its relational capabilities in that you are restricted to one lookup at a time. In a more complex relational database, the linkages can be more extensive.

Another difference between FileMaker and other databases is the way the fields are *indexed*. With most other database programs, as you set up your database, you have to choose how your fields will be organized and which of the fields will be indexed so that data can be found. That's a pretty overwhelming task when you're new to databases and are not sure what you will need to index. However, FileMaker does this for you automatically by indexing not only every field, but every word! There are no complicated formulas to worry about either.

THE FILEMAKER MODES

As described, a database has three basic elements: fields, records, and files. File-Maker also gives you the added flexibility of looking at your data in almost innumerable different views. Each database can be arranged in many different *layouts*. These are used for browsing and reporting data. Each layout can be viewed from one of several *modes*.

FileMaker modes allow you to view your data in different ways. Each mode is a different screen, accessed by a simple command or keystroke. This might lead to a certain amount of confusion when you first begin working with FileMaker. After a short time, changing among the modes will become almost second nature. These modes are Browse, Layout, and Find. The uses and features of these modes will be described in further detail in the next few chapters. For now we'll give you a preview of the screens and the various icons.

Browse Mode

Easily 80 percent of what you will be doing in FileMaker will be in the Browse mode. An annotated diagram of this mode is shown in Fig. 1-9.

In the Browse mode, you can add new records, edit information in existing records, and delete unwanted records. Claris probably could have thought up of a better name for this mode, but that's not very likely to change now, and you'll get used to it quickly.

In Fig. 1-9, you can see a database entitled YGH CLIENT LIST. This is a collection of information about clients of the advertising firm of Yiu, Gotda-Havvitt. The record displayed in Fig. 1-9 is for the companys Frerra's Jackets. This is record 2 out of a total of 11 records. Note that the screen is divided by a vertical line on the left side. The area on the left of this line is referred to as the *status area*.

At the top of the status area, you can see the book icon and the slide control icon. Both of these are used to show you how many records are in your file and in which file you are currently working. Your records are in a stack that you can flip through. If you click on the lower page of the open book, you are shown the next record down in the stack. Click on the upper page, and the record above the current one is displayed. Drag the slide control handle to move more quickly between records. Dragging the handle to the top reveals the first record. To get to the last record, drag the handle to the bottom.

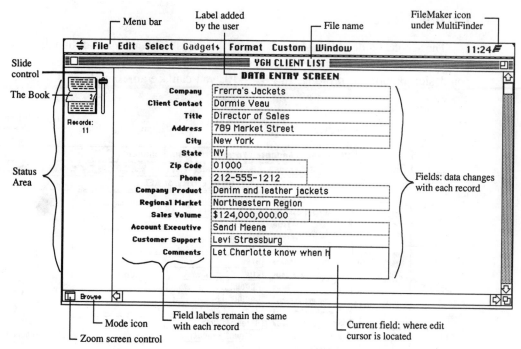

Fig. 1-9. Browse mode.

In the lower left of the screen in Fig. 1-9 is a box with the word "Browse" next to it. This tells you that you are in the Browse mode. You can edit the current record in this mode or move to view a different record. The funny rectangular shape is the screen width screen zoom control. When you click on this rectangle, FileMaker *zooms* in the screen's main screen area, placing the status area in limbo so you can view the record undistracted by the information on the left.

In the center of the screen are the fields, or field boxes in which to enter data, and next to those field boxes are the *field labels*. The FileMaker manual refers to these labels as *objects*, but we refer to them as field labels for clarity. Note that the field box next to Comments is solid, while the others are dotted lines. The solid line indicates that particular field box is *active*, and that the insertion point is located in that field box. If you were to move to one of the other field boxes, Comments would become a dotted line box, and the box you moved to would become a solid line box.

On the menu line, you can see typical Apple menu items such as File and Edit. Note the Select option, which is central to the way FileMaker operates. Also note that the command Gadgets is grayed out and is inactive in this mode. All the other commands are active in the Browse mode. All the parts of the screen to the right of the status area in Browse mode are *static*. This means that the parts cannot be moved to a different area of the screen. If you want to change the appearance of the screen in Browse mode, you go to the next mode, which is aptly called the Layout mode.

Layout Mode

The second mode of FileMaker is Layout, and this is where you'll design the various formats in which the data will be shown in the Browse mode. This is also where you design reports for printing. In Fig. 1-10, you can see an example of the Layout mode.

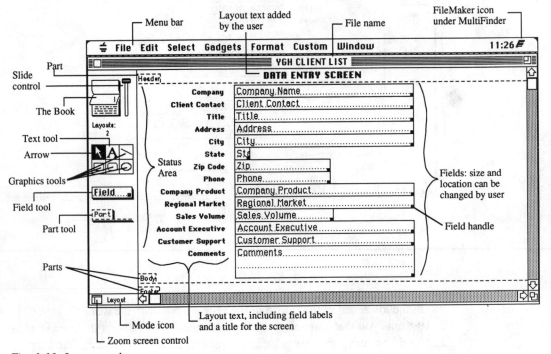

Fig. 1-10. Layout mode.

This particular arrangement of fields, one below another, is basically the one that FileMaker uses unless you request a different one. We refer to this as the *default* layout. A good tip is to design your layouts on paper before changing them from the default format used in FileMaker.

At first glance, the Layout mode looks similar to the Browse mode in that the status area to the left has the book icon and slide control. However, you cannot enter data or view records through the Layout mode. You can create multiple layouts for the same data, and you can switch between these layouts by using the book or slide control. While you are in Layout mode, the pages of the book take you to different layouts rather than to different records as they do in the Browse mode.

The Toolbox in the status area is used to manipulate the objects in the layout. You can move objects by using the arrow tool. You can add text such as the title DATA ENTRY SCREEN with the text tool. You can draw lines, boxes, rounded boxes, and circles with the graphics tools. Using the tools in the Layout mode, you can dramati-

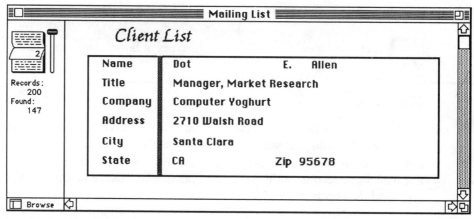

Fig. 1-11. Enhanced database.

cally change the way your data appears in the Browse mode. Even the simple database shown earlier in the chapter looks quite impressive in Fig. 1-11.

Below the Toolbox is the field tool. This tool is used for adding to the layout fields that have already been defined. Completely new fields, that is, fields not yet defined, are added using the Select Define command and will be described in Chapter 3 in the section about adding or deleting fields. (Even the most experienced database planner can forget to include a field or two at the outset.)

The last item in the status area is the part tool. Notice that the main area of the screen has dotted line divisions entitled Header, Body, and Footer. These are just some of the parts that can be used in any given layout, although they are not always vital to every layout. The only part that is constant is the body.

The main screen area of the Layout mode is similar to what you saw in the Browse mode. The difference is that you now see the name of the field in the field box rather than a blank field box awaiting data input. In this example, the field names just happen to be the same as the field labels, but it is not critical that they be the same. In fact, many times the field name will bear little resemblance to the label that you attach to that field.

In the Layout mode, you can size and shape the field boxes by dragging the handles on each box. When we first created this example, the State field was the same size as the surrounding fields. We made it smaller to demonstrate how fields can be resized. All these fields and labels can be moved and placed anywhere on the screen. Then, when you return to the Browse mode, the changes are reflected in that view.

Last, but not least, note that each field has a dotted line running through it. This is called a *base line* and serves two purposes. First, it shows you where the data will be placed in the box when entered. Secondly, the base line is used as an alignment aid when the position of the field is changed to be on the same line or level as another.

The design of the screen in the Layout mode reflects how your records will be printed. Organizing the information is as important as presenting it in a legible form, and is a crucial part of any database program. FileMaker provides you with basic layout formats: the *standard* layout, the *columnar* layout, the *label* layout, and the *blank* layout. There are, however, no limits to the types of layouts you can create with File-Maker.

Find Mode

In FileMaker, the Find mode, as shown in Fig. 1-12, is a separate screen, or another way of looking at your data. In most database programs, "find" would be a command or a formula. For example, rather than have you quit out of data entry to find a duplicate record, in FileMaker you can quickly change modes to find what you need, and then get back to data entry.

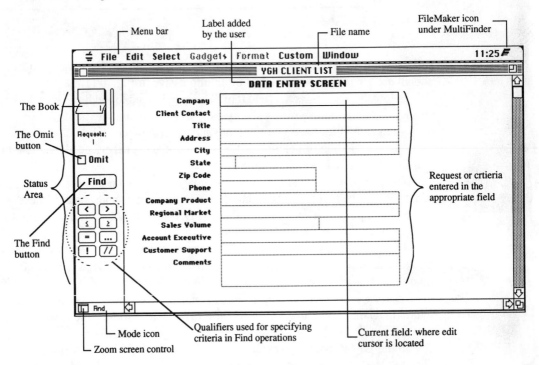

Fig. 1-12. The Find mode.

Once again, in the Find mode, you will notice the status area. The book icon or slide control are used when you have more than one request at a time, and they are frequently used in an "either/or" situation. The Find mode is used by entering criteria into the appropriate field for the data search.

Notice the word Omit with a box next to it. This is used when you want to find everything *except* the criteria you've entered. For example, if you had entered San Francisco in the City field, then checked the Omit box, FileMaker would search for all the records except the ones that have San Francisco in that field.

The next button is Find which is, in effect, the command button. After the criteria for the search has been entered, you click the Find button to begin the search.

At the bottom of the status area are the *operator symbols*. These are explained in detail in Chapter 6. Basically, the operator symbols are used to assist FileMaker in being more specific in its searches. Each of these operators work slightly differently in their search, depending on the type of field in which they are used.

In the main part of the screen are all the fields in which you can specify your criteria for your search or searches. You will use the Find mode quite frequently as you become more familiar with the program. It is one of the easiest find commands we have seen in any database program.

CONCLUSION

To review, FileMaker allows you to complete the following data management tasks without the need for extensive experience with databases:

- Organize your data.
- Sort and update your data.
- Retrieve needed groups of data or specific records.
- Calculate data.
- Analyze your data.
- Prepare professional printed documents, including the ability to fill out complex, preprinted forms.

In the next chapter, you will build a simple customer database and begin to appreciate how easily FileMaker can be learned.

2
Going with FileMaker

IN THIS CHAPTER, you will create a simple database so you can get a feel for File-Maker. Because most companies and professionals need to keep track of clients in order to do promotional mailings and to provide detailed information to your support and sales staff, we look at a typical client database as our first example.

STARTING UP

Prior to creating any database, it is best to start with a rough outline of the list of items that you would like to include in the database. This list of items will be your fields and the backbone of your database. Simply put, if the data isn't in your database, you can't have access to it.

A Basic Example

For example, in a database of clients, two obvious field choices would be the name of the client and the client's phone number. Any database can be as simple as that and would be just as effective as a more complex database. The whole concept revolves around your specific needs.

In our first example, we create a simple client database for the advertising firm of Yiu, Gotda-Havvitt, or YGH for short. This firm needs to build a database that includes their client's company name, client contact, phone numbers, address, company product, regional market, and sales and support persons assigned to that account.

Defining Fields

With FileMaker properly installed, first double click on its program icon to start the application. If this is the first time you have started the FileMaker application, a licensing screen will appear. You are supposed to type in your name and your company name. In fact, you cannot proceed without filling out this screen. Click OK after you have finished, and the application will then launch. The licensing screen is a step that only occurs once with each machine on which the program is installed and does not affect the master disk. For example, if you were to sell your current computer and then install FileMaker on your new computer, you would again have to start with this licensing screen.

Now you must either open an existing file or create a new one. Click once on New to create a new file and type in the title YGH CLIENT LIST, then tap Return. The next screen presented to you is the Define screen, and this is where you set up your field names, along with the corresponding field types. Collectively this information then forms the database's field definitions. After you enter a field name into the Field name box, you select the Field type. Then tap Return or click OK and proceed to define the next field. The definition you have just created will then appear in the Field Definition box. After the first few fields for this example, the screen will appear something like the one shown in Fig. 2-1.

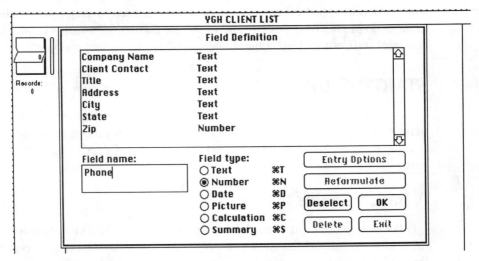

Fig. 2-1. Field definition.

For this example, type in the field names listed below, tapping Return and clicking OK after each entry.

Company Name   Text
Client Contact   Text
Title   Text
Address   Text

City	Text
State	Text
Zip	Number
Phone	Number
Company Product	Text
Regional Market	Text
Sales Volume	Number
Account Executive	Text
Customer Support	Text
Comments	Text

Next to each field name in the above list is the appropriate field type. You select the Field type by either clicking the button next to the Field type, or by using the keyboard shortcut shown next to the Field type. For example on the Phone field shown in Fig. 2-1, you first type Phone in the Field name box and then click on Number, or use the keyboard shortcut of Command−N to select Number as the Field type.

 The keystroke Command−N in FileMaker departs from other Mac applications in that it is *not* the command for New file. In FileMaker, Command−N has a different purpose in different screens or modes.

You should now have fourteen fields, all of which will make up one record as completed. Each Field type is either Text or Number. (The other field types of Date, Picture, Calculation, and Summary will be used in later chapters of this book.)

Now check to see that the Zip and Phone and Sales Volume fields are listed in the Field definition box as Number fields. You might have entered these as Text fields by mistake. If any fields are not correctly defined, select the incorrect entry by clicking on it once in the Field Definition box, then click once on the correct radio button for Field type, and tap Return. When you change the type for a field, FileMaker warns you with a dialog box that asks you if you want to proceed. This warning box is important in certain situations, but for now you can ignore it and click OK to accept the change.

After you have defined all of the fields correctly, click the Exit button and you will be placed into FileMaker's Browse mode with an empty record appearing, complete with all your newly created fields. The screen will appear like the one shown in Fig. 2-2, except that there will be no boxes next to the field names.

Many databases can be quite restrictive when it comes to creating fields, but not so with FileMaker. The only limits for the field name is a maximum of 63 characters, and most of the other restrictions are those created by your system configuration; namely, disk space. FileMaker can accept a maximum of 32,000 characters in any text field, roughly equivalent to 16 pages of text. However, it is highly unlikely that you would ever need that much space for one field.

 An alternative method of moving from the Field definition screen to the Browse mode is to choose Browse from the Select menu. The shortcut for this is Command−L.

Entering the First Data

Now that you are in the Browse mode, click once in the blank area to the right of the Company Name. You will see that boxes appear next to all of the field names, as shown in Fig. 2-2. These are the actual boxes in which you will enter the data for a client record. The active field shows up as a box with a black solid outline and a blinking insertion point, while the other boxes will show as light gray dotted-line boxes.

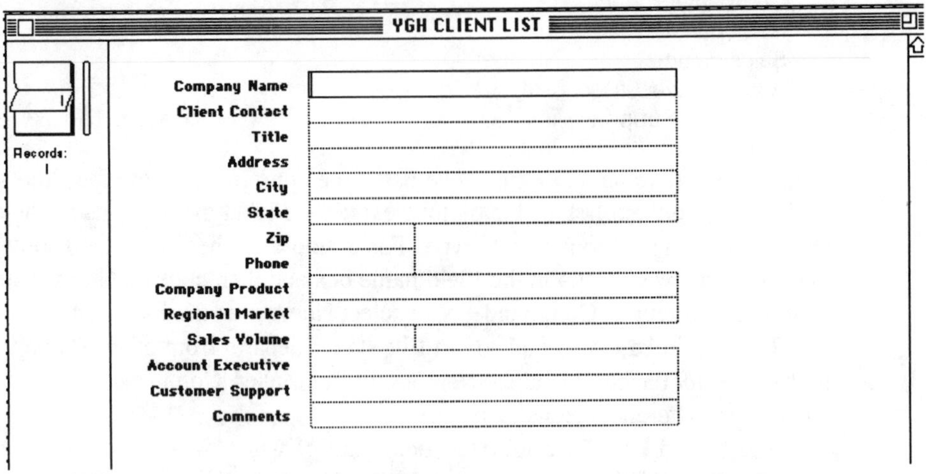

Fig. 2-2. Blank record in Browse mode.

In each of the fields, enter the following data. You can move from field to field by tapping the Tab key after each entry. To go back to a previous field, use Shift – Tab or Option – Tab.

Company Name	Mountain Foods
Client Contact	Monty Mountback
Title	Director of Marketing
Address	1234 Summit Heights
City	San Francisco
State	CA
Zip	90000
Phone	415-555-1212
Company Product	Coffee
Regional Market	Western Region
Sales Volume	$4,000,000.00
Account Executive	Garrison Clymer
Customer Service	Sheila Doosit
Comments	Network spots and local print media

If, after filling in one of the fields, you tap the Return key by accident instead of the Tab key, you will note that you do not move to the next field, but enlarge the field box that you are in. To correct this, you tap the Delete key or the Backspace key until you are back on the first line. Although the box still looks larger, it will go back to its original size once you tab past it. If you do not Backspace or Delete in this field in its enlarged state, the next time you select it, it will show up as an enlarged field until you use the Backspace or Delete key.

These enlarged text field boxes are created because when you press Return, File-Maker thinks that you want a second line of text. While a large field box will not affect the data in that field, it is best to return it to normal size.

 This field enlargement only occurs with text fields; it does not apply with number fields. When you tap Return while in a number field box, instead of tapping Tab, File-Maker will just beep at you.

You have now completed your first record in your database. The record will look something like the one shown in Fig. 2-3, except that there will be boxes around your entries.

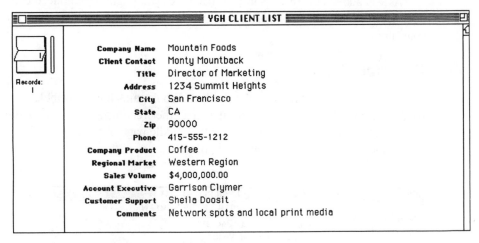

Fig. 2-3. Sample record.

If you notice a question mark in the phone field, or that part of the sales volume figure is truncated, do not worry. These anomalies will be explained in the next section.

Once this record is complete, go to the Edit command and select New Record (Command−N). Continue adding new records, making them up as you go, perhaps using addresses of friends and relatives. (You can use the record shown in Fig. 2-4 as your second record if you like.)

Note that you do not have to make an entry in every field of a record. Simply press Tab to skip the field if you do not want to enter anything in it. Create several records so that you become well acquainted with the process, remembering to press Command−N after each record is completed.

Saving Data

As you increase the size of your database, you might worry about the fact that you have not yet issued a Save instruction. With FileMaker this is no problem. FileMaker has no Save command in the File menu, nor is there a keyboard shortcut of Command−S for Save. This is due to the fact that FileMaker *automatically* saves your records as you work. You occasionally hear a whirring sound while you work that indicates that your disk is running and your work is being saved. As a precaution, we do suggest that you make frequent copies of real work you do with FileMaker, storing the copy on a separate disk in the event of some mechanical failure on the part of your computer. The Save a copy command is under the File menu and is discussed in more detail at the end of this chapter.

WHAT'S GOING ON HERE?

As you added new records to your database, you might have noticed that both the book icon and the slide control change. We now examine how Filemaker is handling your input.

Browsing Records

When you make your second record, the book gains little "scribbles" on the top page, as seen in Fig. 2-4. This indicates that other records are present, and the number of the current record will appear on the middle page of the book. Below the book is the number of records in total in this file.

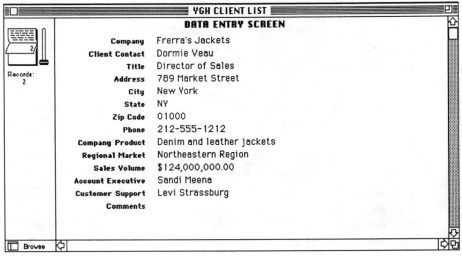

Fig. 2-4. Second sample record.

The slide control knob moves down from the top position to indicate the position of the current record within the stack. As you add new records at the end of a database, the knob is in the bottom position, as shown in Fig. 2-4. When additional records are below the current one, you will notice scribbles on both the top and bottom pages, as seen in Fig. 2-5.

The slide control knob shows the relative position of the current record.

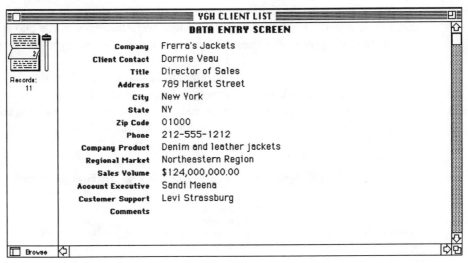

Fig. 2-5. Record 2 of 11.

You have four methods to use when you want to flip through the records you have created:

- Click on the pages of the book to move through the records one at a time. The top page moves you to the previous record and the bottom page moves you to the next record.

- Click on the page number on the middle page of the book. Type the page you wish to move to, and hit Return.

- Drag the slide control knob up or down to the record you are looking for. Note that, as you move the slide control knob, the page numbers on the book icon change to indicate which record is at that point. When you release, that record will appear.

- Use the keyboard shortcut of Command−Tab which moves you from one record to the next.

Default Settings

Let's go back to the first record for the moment, Mountain Foods, and take a look at some of the peculiarities of FileMaker's default settings and how you can change them to suit your needs. Remember that in computer talk, the term *default* means what the program does unless you tell it to do differently.

As you have been creating records by entering data into the fields you have defined, the field boxes have remained active. This means that the outlines of the boxes are visible. Locate the Mountain Foods record and move the mouse pointer arrow to the left of the word Company Name. Now click once. The boxes around the fields will disappear but the data you have entered remains. This is how the record will appear when printed. The field boxes will not be shown.

When you make the field boxes inactive like this, you might see a difference in some of your data. A question mark (?) might be in the place of the phone number, and the last two zeros in the Sales Volume might not be completely visible as shown in Fig. 2-6.

These anomalies are due to the fact that there was more data in that field than the default field size allowed. FileMaker responds by giving you a question mark, indicating that there is a change to be made here. In fact, if you were to print that record, the printed form would appear just as it is on the screen in Fig. 2-6. Fortunately, it is easy to overcome this problem by using the Layout mode.

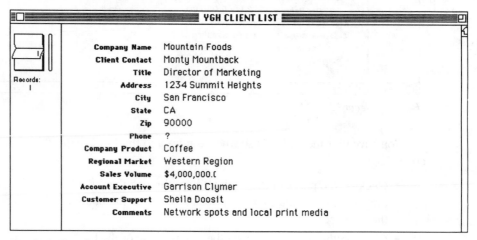

Fig. 2-6. Completed record.

LAYOUT MODE

Most databases require you to specify the length of each data field before that field can be used for data. This tends to overcomplicate the process of setting up a database. FileMaker takes a different approach, assigning default sizes to all fields.

Field Size

FileMaker does not set field size in terms of the number of characters per field, but in measurement in inches. For example, the default size for a Text field is roughly $3^1/_2$" long and the default for a Number field is almost 1" long. Likewise, the default size for a Date field is about $1^5/_8$", a Picture field is 2", and both a Calculation and a Summary field measure 1" each. That is not to say, however, that these are the sizes that you have to keep. FileMaker allows for easy changes to your field sizes in its Layout mode.

Field Arrangement

Layouts in FileMaker can range from very simple to extremely complex and exact in measurements. All layouts in FileMaker are easily created and changed. That in itself is one of FileMaker's strong points. How many times have you labored long hours over the layout of a form only to have your boss come back and say he or she hates it? Doing it over usually meant more tedious hours hunched over your desk and probably ranked right next to doing dishes as one of your favorite things to do. File-Maker's Layout mode allows for quick and easy changes with the minimum amount of skill.

The Layout mode is, simply put, another way of looking at your data and presenting it without actually changing the data itself. In the Layout mode, you can change the size and shape of your fields, add titles, instructions, change fonts, add pictures and boxes, include counters and page numbers, and endless other changes. You are not limited in the number of layouts you create for any particular database; you can create as many layouts as you have disk space to store. Your only limit is the physical paper size. The largest layout you can create in FileMaker II is 36 " by 36 ", in File-Maker Pro it is 112 " by 112 ".

Altering the Arrangement

As soon as you define the fields in a new file, such as the YGH CLIENT LIST you have created, FileMaker creates a layout referred to as the *Standard layout*. This is the default layout and is intended for the quick and easy entry of simple data. The *Standard layout* is great for its intended purpose and as a starting point.

To alter the layout of your form, you need to get to Layout mode. From the menu bar, pull down the Select menu. Note that the command, Browse, currently has a check-mark next to it indicating that you are presently in the Browse mode. Drag your arrow down to the Layout command and release. Your screen should now resemble Fig. 2-7, and the book icon in the lower left portion of your screen should now have the word Layout next to it, instead of Records.

One of the first things you'll notice about this new screen, or mode, is that the fields now show the field name in them, instead of the data that you had entered while in the Browse mode. That field name is what you had named the field when you defined that field in the Field definition screen at the beginning of this exercise.

 If you need to change the definition of a field and cannot remember what you named that field, go to the Layout mode and the name of that field is shown in the Field box. This is particularly helpful when you start using calculations and summaries where the names given to a certain field are sometimes less than obvious, or if you are given to creating cryptic codes for your field names rather than an obvious name.

LAYOUT TEXT

When you first define a database, the field boxes and their titles are placed in what is called the *Standard layout*. In the Standard layout, FileMaker automatically places some text on the left of the field boxes. This text acts as a field description. Any text entered as part of a layout is called *layout text*.

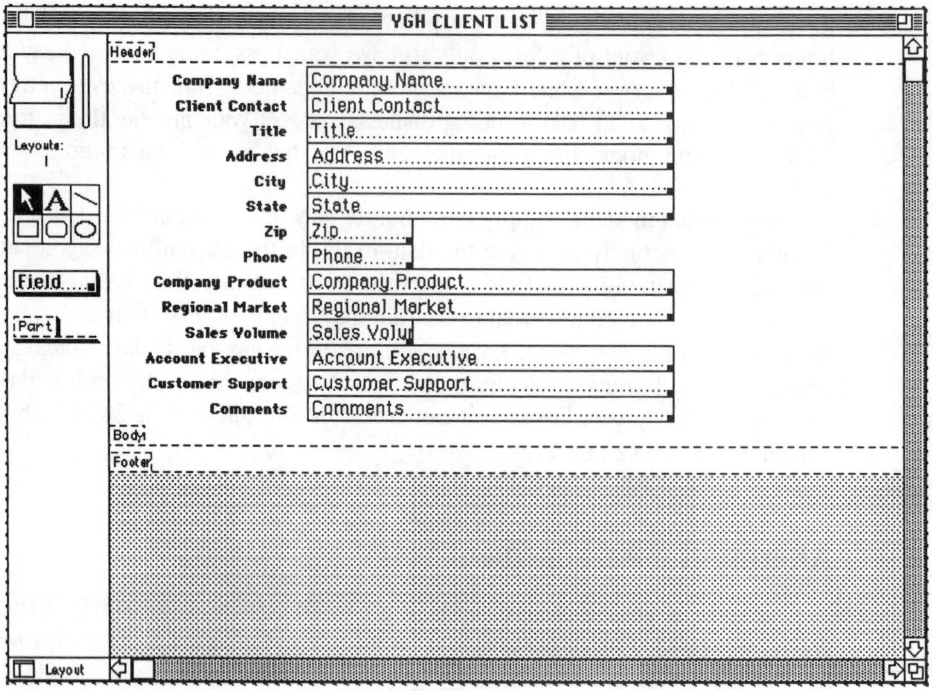

Fig. 2-7. Layout mode.

Field Labels

When you first create a database with FileMaker, the program automatically assigns layout text that matches the name of each field. While this text is initially the same as the field name, it can be changed to anything you prefer. We use the term of *field label* for this particular usage of text on the layout, in that it more accurately identifies the text associated with a field. For all other text used on a layout, we use the term *layout text* and hopefully avoid any confusion. Unless you are creating a new layout with the field tool described in Chapter 4, FileMaker matches field labels to the field name.

Using Layout Text

The layout text that forms the field labels is not "attached" to any of the fields. The text can be moved independently of any field or object on the layout. You can change the layout text size and font. You can add further text as instructions on a form or as further labels for the form. The changes you make to any layout text or field labels does nothing to alter the actual field names as field names are only changed in the field definition.

Some layouts might not need text at all. A good example of that is a mailing label that is simply an address. For such a mailing label, all you would need are the actual fields to be printed on the label and not the field label. However, you could design a mailing label that included a return address. In this case, the return address would be made up of layout text. Other layouts might have dozens of different types and sizes of layout text, particularly where there are a lot of descriptions or explanations to the layout.

Any piece of text you type on the layout will be one item, or *object* as far as File-Maker is concerned. This is true for all text entered at once, whether it is one line or several lines produced by carriage returns. For example, although your field label Company Name is two words, it is one object and the words would have to be separated manually by using the text tool to erase one word, type the other word somewhere else on the layout, and then lining the two of them up again. Such a procedure would be redundant in this case, but there might be times that you will not want all of your text to be one object. For more on the subject of layouts and annotating forms, see Chapter 4.

Changing Layout Text

To add text to a layout, you use the text tool located in the status area to the left of the layout area. The text tool is indicated by the letter A in the box next to the arrow tool. Just remember that any text you add on the layout will appear while in the Browse screen.

Altering the Example

Let's try a few things with the text to your layout of your YGH CLIENT LIST. First, click on the text tool (the letter A in the Toolbox) to activate it. The tool will indicate that it is active by becoming black and the pointer will become an I-beam. Next, move the I-beam to the area above the dotted line marked Header and click once just under the letter Y in the file name or title line. Now type DATA ENTRY SCREEN. Do not tap Return after you have finished typing, simply select the entire text line by clicking and dragging the I-beam across the text. It will appear as a gray selected area when you release the mouse button. With the text selected, go to the Format menu and select Style and a submenu will appear with the various styles available. Select Bold and release. You now have a bold header entitled DATA ENTRY SCREEN.

Now place your I-beam to the right of the e in the field label Company Name and tap Delete or Backspace until the word Name is gone. One more change, and we're done for the moment. Place the I-beam next to the field label Zip and type a space and then the word Code. Your layout should now resemble Fig. 2-8.

To see what difference your changes make to the actual appearance of the data entry form, change to the Browse mode (Command−B or choose Select then Browse). After you have viewed these changes, go back to the Layout mode (Command−L or choose Select, Layout) to continue with this section. Note that changing the label Zip to Zip Code does not change the name of the field, which remains Zip.

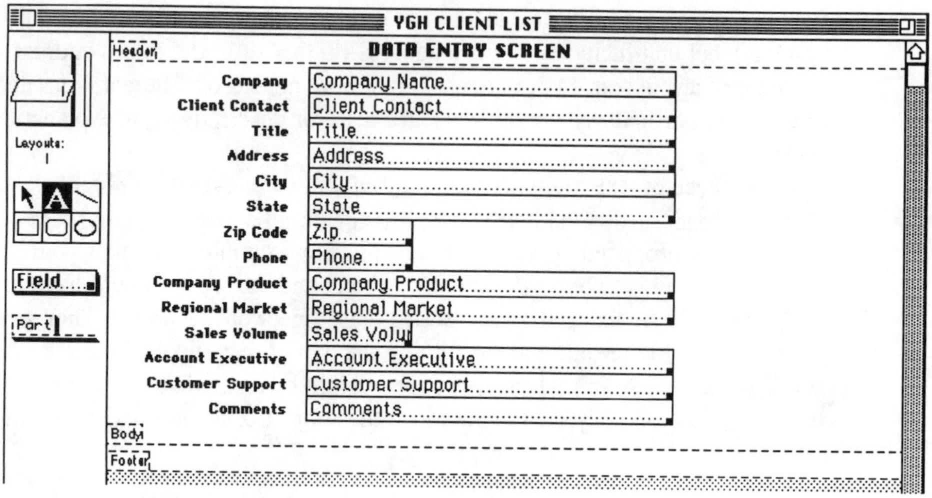

Fig. 2-8. Changes in layout text.

WHAT'S THAT LINE?

You've been looking at them and asking yourself this question for a few minutes now, right? What are those funny dotted lines in the fields? The dotted lines running through the fields are called *base lines*, and they have two purposes: To indicate where your text will appear in relation to the size and shape of the box and to be used as an alignment tool.

The base line is one of those things that is easier to explain visually than verbally. To illustrate this, first click on the arrow tool in the Toolbox and then place your arrow on the Zip field and drag it around the screen. The field becomes a light gray box with light gray base lines radiating horizontally from each side. Now, release the mouse button and the Zip field has been moved to where you left it and the base line returns to a dotted line inside of the field box. To put it back where it was, go to the Edit menu and select Undo and the Zip field will zap back to its previous position.

To use the base line as an alignment tool, select the Zip field once again, and move the field up to the State field. Note that the lines radiating from the Zip field run straight through the State field. When the light gray line from the Zip field lines up exactly with the dotted base line in the State field, release the mouse button. The Zip field is now exactly in line with the State field. To put the Zip field back in its original position, go to the Select menu and choose Undo or use the keyboard shortcut of Command−Z.

SIZING YOUR FIELDS

As we had mentioned earlier, the phone number in the Phone field was not appearing in its entirety in the Browse mode because the default field size for a number field is too small. Because the number of characters exceeded the physical size of the field, FileMaker assigned a question mark to that field when in the Browse mode, with the fields unselected. As there is no way to change the default sizes of any particular field type, FileMaker does make allowances by making it very easy to change the field sizes in the Layout mode. Once you have changed the size of that field, it will stay that size in all records until you change the size again.

Using the Handles

Note that each field box in the Layout mode has a small black handle on the lower right-hand corner of the box. By dragging that handle, you can resize any field at any time, but only in the Layout mode. You cannot change the size of fields while in the Browse mode or in the field definitions.

To make the phone number in the Phone field appear in its entirety, grab the handle to the Phone field and drag it to the right of your screen until it is roughly half the size of the State field above it. If you were to now go back to the Browse mode for a moment, you would see that the entire phone number is visible. If you were to then click in the Phone field while in the Browse mode, you would see the new boundaries of that field. You should always make your field sizes just a bit larger than your largest anticipated entry as that reduces the possibility of having to change it later to accommodate large entries. Go back to the Layout mode, and we'll make some more changes to a few of the field sizes.

Looking at your other number fields, you realize that they, too, might have to be enlarged. The amount $4,000,000.00 does not quite fit in a number field of the default size. Because many zip codes now have nine numbers, and ten characters if you include the hyphen, those extra characters will need extra space. Grab the handle now for the Zip field and move it to the right to about the same size as the Phone field. If you alter the size too much, you can Undo your move and start over, or simply grab the handle and move the field to a better position. If you move the field down (vertically) instead of to the side, you may cause your Zip field to overlap the Phone field.

 Because fields can be enlarged horizontally as well as vertically, sometimes you can inadvertently overlap your fields. To control the vertical or horizontal movement of a field when you move it with the handle, hold down the Option key as you move. This will keep your field movement on an even line.

All About Zip Codes

A few words are in order on the subject of zip codes since they are an inescapable part of address type databases. We have heard from more than one contributor to this book that they have had problems in using the nine-digit zip codes on mail. It seems that if the last four digits are in error, your mail can spend days in mailroom limbo, and even end up coming back to you. And that's even with the first five digits correct! Therefore, we are using the expanded zip field only as an example. Whether you or your company subscribes to including the last four digits or not is entirely up to you; we make no recommendations in that area.

Another question that hangs over zip codes is whether or not they should be handled by number fields or by text fields. This question is important in two areas of File-Maker: sorting records, and exporting data to other programs. Sorting is discussed in Chapter 7, and exporting is discussed in Chapter 8. Users in Europe will need to consider their own alternative to a zip field, something that can accommodate British postal codes, which are alphanumeric and not consistent in length (you can have ML12 6JD, or CV4 7AU).

More Size Changes

Now that the Zip field has been resized, let's now change the size of the State field. If you will only be using the two-letter code for each state, you will not need all the space allotted to that field by FileMaker. Grab the handle of the State field and move it to the left until just the first three or four letters of the word State are visible. That should be more than enough room for that field. You'll also notice that if you try to move that field too far to the left, FileMaker will override your decision and leave the field size as it was. In this case, you cannot make the field much smaller than you have done.

The last field we will change in this section is the Comments field. The Comments field is basically free-form. That is, several notes can be put in that field, or nothing at all. In some cases, comments on a client can be quite extensive, so that field should have more space. Grab the handle and move the Comments field down. What? It won't go down past the dotted line entitled Footer! How do you make that field larger then?

The dotted line entitled Body is referred to as a *Part*, and it controls the physical size of the single record on the screen. To give yourself some more room to maneuver you'll have to adjust the size of the record, or the body. We'll go more into the various parts you see on your screen in a moment, but for now click on the word Body and drag that line down a couple of inches to give yourself some more space. (We're not going for absolute accuracy at this point, so don't go scrambling for a ruler to measure two inches.)

After you have moved the body, you will be able to move the Comments field down. Move it at this point so that there are about five of the base lines (dotted lines) showing in the Comments field. Figure 2-9 shows what your screen should look like at this point.

One important note: Do not move the Comments field past the body and into the area marked Footer. If you move *any* field into the Footer, any data entered in that area of the layout will be handled as a footer—which, without going into enormous detail now, is akin to putting it in a street gutter. It's still there, and it's going to show up somewhere else later on! The manipulation and usage of parts effectively are handled in detail in Chapters 4 and 5.

Now that we have finished making changes to this layout, let's go back to the Browse mode for a moment to see what we've done, and maybe take the time to enter a few more records. If, when you've gone back to the Browse mode and found that some of your fields are still not exactly as you want them, simply go back to the Lay-

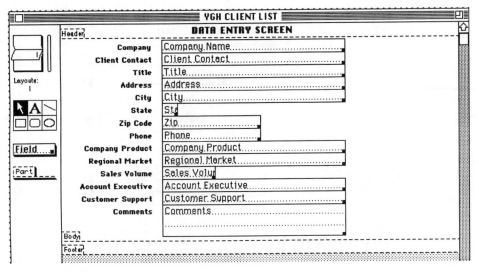

Fig. 2-9. Layout with resized fields.

out mode to make your changes. After you are finished with this area, we'll go on to create a label layout for your mailing list.

LABEL LAYOUT

You have, up to this point, been utilizing FileMaker's Standard layout for data entry in your YGH CLIENT LIST database. In addition to FileMaker's Standard layout, there are three other layout options in FileMaker: Columnar Report layout, Label layout, and Blank layout. FileMaker allows you to create as many layouts as you need, and again, the only restriction is the amount of disk space you have to store your layouts.

Once you have created more than one layout, you flip through the layouts the same way you do as in the Browse mode, that is, by using the book icon, slide control, or the keyboard shortcut of Command–Z. FileMaker II numbers the layouts sequentially, in the order in which they were created. FileMaker Pro allows you to give names to layouts in order to distinguish them. Simply use the Layout Options from the Layout menu and edit the name in the Name box, or assign a name when a new layout is created.

A Mailing Label Example

For our next example, we will show you how easy it is to make labels with File-Maker. Although FileMaker's labels are not foolproof, they are still the best we have seen in any program, including many programs that were developed exclusively to handle this task.

First, make sure you are still in the Layout mode and then select New Layout from the Edit menu or use the keyboard shortcut of Command–N. You will receive a dialog

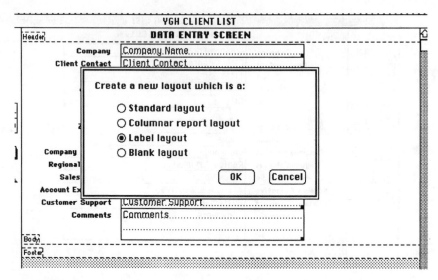

Fig. 2-10. Layout dialog box.

box asking for the layout type: Standard, Columnar report, Label, or Blank as shown in Fig. 2-10. FileMaker Pro adds a further type: envelope.

Select Label by clicking in the radio button next to it and select OK. Next you will get a Page setup dialog box asking for the page size, number of labels across, and the label size as shown in Fig. 2-11.

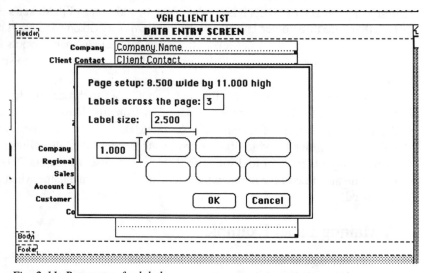

Fig. 2-11. Page setup for labels.

The default settings are a page size of $8^1/2$ " by 11 ", three-across labels, and a label size of $2^1/2$ " wide by 1 " tall. (There is a difference in the Page setup between laser printers and dot matrix printers, and you might need to check that you have the correct printer selected in the Chooser document. For more information on printers, consult Chapter 8.) You can accept the default setting for now by clicking OK.

The next dialog box wants to know which fields to put on your labels and in which order. This is a perfectly valid question because FileMaker wants to know exactly as possible how you do your work. You can see the Field List and Field Order dialog boxes in Fig. 2-12.

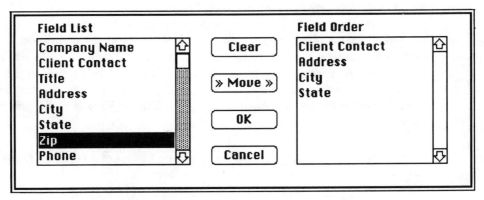

Fig. 2-12. Field list and field order for the Label layout.

Note that the left box is entitled Field List, while the right-side box is entitled Field Order. What FileMaker is asking for at this point is: What fields do you want on your labels, and in what order do you want them presented? You select the fields you want on your labels either by selecting the field and clicking on Move, or by double clicking on the field you need. You cannot use Shift—click to select all the fields at one time; they have to be chosen one by one. In any case, you will see the fields appear, one by one, in the Field Order box to the right.

Some Restrictions

There is one small restriction in FileMaker as far as setting up the fields for your labels: You are initially limited to only five fields. FileMaker does not take into account the way you have resized any of the fields in any of the previous layouts, so it sets the fields up on the label layout as all the same size. This is not a problem, because the field sizes can be changed, and more fields can be added after the label layout has initially been created.

The restriction in our example is that FileMaker won't let us put the Company, Client Contact, Title, Address, City, State, and Zip on the label all in one fell swoop. Unfortunately, that's seven fields, two fields too many for FileMaker to handle at this point. So for the moment, we'll select five fields and add two later on. Select and move the following fields in this order:

Client Contact
Address

City
State
Zip

Your screen should now resemble Fig. 2-12. Remember, we can only move five fields at this juncture, but we will add some after adjusting the sizes of the fields on our labels. Once you have moved all your fields, click OK or hit Return, and you'll be placed in the label layout as shown in Fig. 2-13.

You are now presented with the complete layout for your labels. As in Fig. 2-13, you should have a blank header, one white area with your fields in order, and two similar-sized areas which are shadowed. Notice that this layout has no footer. The left (white) label is representative of all the records that will be printed on the labels. You'll also notice that, below the book icon, is the number 2, indicating that there are now two layouts for your database. If you go back to the Browse mode, you will see one of your records set up for a mailing label.

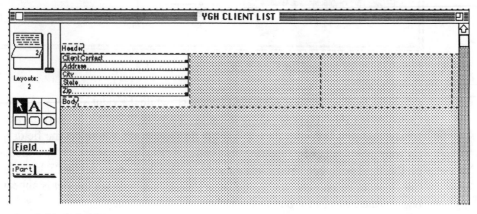

Fig. 2-13. Label layout.

The Preview Mode

You might be concerned that there is only one label showing in the Browse mode! What happens to all the other records? Will they only print one to a page? How do you know this will work? Don't panic. At this stage, you are only viewing one record at a time in FileMaker. The program will be printing all of the records as labels, and you can preview your labels to see how they will look in printed form by going to the File menu and selecting Preview (Command − U). The results will appear something like Fig. 2-14. In FileMaker Pro, Preview is on the Select menu.

While in the Preview screen, take a minute to play around with its views. As you are in a full page setting at first, select Reduced by clicking once in the box. You will see what all the records you have entered will look like on the printed page. If you were very ambitious and entered enough records to go onto a second page, click on Next Page to preview it. To exit this screen, simply click once on Exit, and you will be back in your label layout.

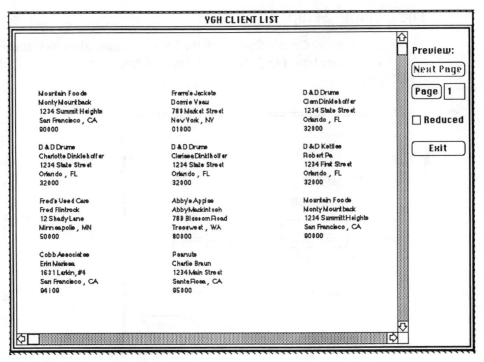

Fig. 2-14. The Preview screen.

USING GADGETS

FileMaker does a number of things automatically when a label layout is created. Go back to the Layout mode and look at the menu called Gadgets. You can see this menu is Fig. 2-15. In FileMaker Pro, Gadgets are found on the Layout menu.

Gadgets are exclusive to the Layout mode. For now, notice that there are check marks next to the menu items Column Setup and Slide Objects. These are two of the things that FileMaker automatically selected for you when you created this label layout.

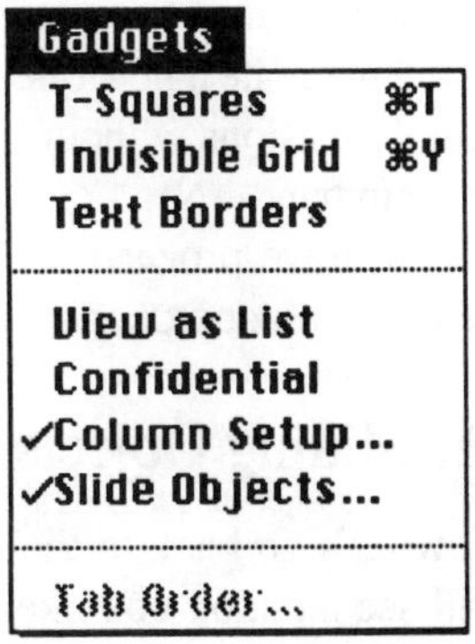

Fig. 2-15. The Gadgets menu.

The Column Setup

When you choose Column Setup from the Gadgets menu, take a look at the dialog box. As you can see from Fig. 2-16, the option Print records in 3 columns is selected, as well as Across first.

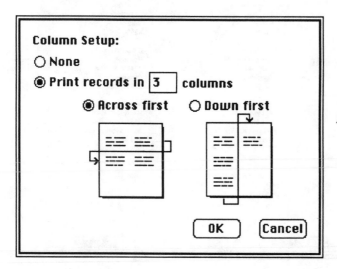

Fig. 2-16. The Column setup.

You can change these choices by simply clicking in the radio buttons and/or changing the number in the number of columns box.

Let's look at how FileMaker handles the number of columns across for a moment. Suppose that you wanted two-across labels instead of three-across. Choose Column Setup from the Gadgets menu (there is no keyboard shortcut). If the number 3 is not highlighted, double click on it to select it. Then type in the number 2 and click OK. You are then placed back in the layout. Notice that the white label area has expanded, but the size of the fields has not. If you now go to Preview under the File menu (Command−U), you will see that there are now two columns across instead of three. It is important to remember, however, that the *size* of the labels has not been changed.

If you ever have to change the size of labels, it is best not to change an existing layout, but to create a new one. This is due to the fact that there is no way to change the the label dimensions without first going to the New Layout command (Select/New Layout or Command−N). For this exercise, let's return to the default of three labels across before we proceed. Choose Column Setup from the Gadgets menu and then change the Print records in # across to 3 then click OK.

About Sliding Objects

Now let's go back to the Gadgets menu for a moment and select Slide Objects. You will see a dialog box like the one in Fig. 2-17.

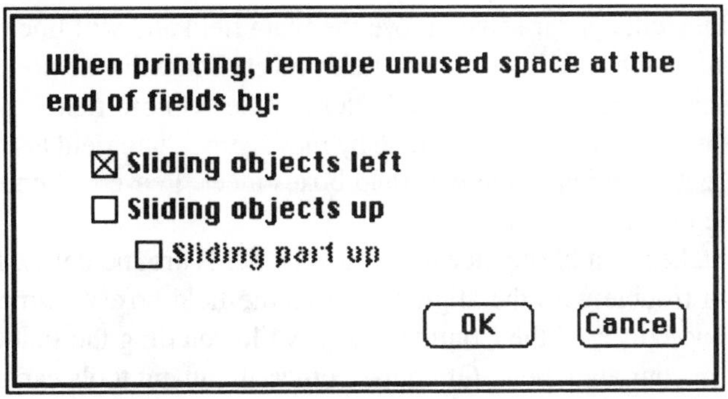

```
┌─────────────────────────────────────────────┐
│ ┌─────────────────────────────────────────┐ │
│ │                                         │ │
│ │ When printing, remove unused space at the│ │
│ │ end of fields by:                        │ │
│ │                                         │ │
│ │   ☒ Sliding objects left                │ │
│ │   ☐ Sliding objects up                  │ │
│ │      ☐ Sliding part up                  │ │
│ │                                         │ │
│ │              ┌────────┐  ┌────────┐     │ │
│ │              │   OK   │  │ Cancel │     │ │
│ │              └────────┘  └────────┘     │ │
│ └─────────────────────────────────────────┘ │
└─────────────────────────────────────────────┘
```

Fig. 2-17. Working with sliding objects.

One of the most difficult and irritating problems in most database reports and layouts is getting the program to eliminate blank space. Usually you just have to accept the fact that, if you had placed the city and the state on the same line in the mailing label, the state will always stay in the same place, regardless of how much space the city actually takes up. FileMaker gives you the option of choosing Sliding objects left in order to fill up any unused or blank space when printing.

Another problem with labels is moving data upwards from the bottom of the label to fill the blank lines. Suppose you had a number of companies in your database with no title. The average label program would just leave that area blank on the label—a dead giveaway that you used computer-generated labels. In the event that one of the fields placed on your label layout in FileMaker has no data, the program can automatically fill in that gap by shifting the next line up to fill the space above if you have chosen the Sliding objects up option in the Slide object dialog box. This feature is very handy for those who create many different mailing lists requiring labels.

The third option in Slide Objects is Sliding part up. Although you normally would not have additional parts in a label layout, you might well come across a situation one day when printing a report where not all pages of your layout have the same parts. To avoid large blank spots on a page, FileMaker will move the next part, or page, up to fill in the space to create a more attractive report.

Sliding into Action

To see how the sliding of objects works, let's now work on changing the label layout a bit. First, make sure you are in the Layout mode with the three-across labels. In this layout, you will notice that FileMaker has automatically placed all the fields you had selected to be placed on the label underneath one another. Note that they are all the same field width as well. This results in the State appearing below the City and the Zip appearing below the State.

First, we will resize the City and State fields and then place them on the same line. To do this, grab the handle on the City field, hold the Option key (to control horizontal movement), and drag the field to the left to make it approximately $3/4$ of its original size. Next, select the State field and drag the State field up to meet the City field. Your base line will appear as you move the State field and will line up exactly with the City field when the base lines of both fields meet. You will also notice, that when these two fields are properly aligned, the bottom of the Address field box will seemingly merge with the State field box. Continue by moving the State field to the left, towards the City field, but do not have the two field boxes meet. Leave just enough space between the two fields for one character.

It takes a bit of practice to move your fields around deftly. If you are experiencing a bit of trouble with the alignment, like the field boxes "jumping" up and down, or right and left, hold the Command key while you drag the field. This will temporarily assist in your alignment. Of course, other alignment tools can assist you, and they are further explained and demonstrated to you in Chapter 4.

Now you should have the City field and the State field on the same line, but the State field should be extending into the gray area of the next label. There is no present danger in leaving the State field that way but, for practice, we will resize it to fit into the white layout area. Use Option—drag to move the State field by its handle to the left.

Next we will resize the Zip field by grabbing the handle and (Option—drag) dragging it to the left until it is just large enough to hold the zip code. You can check the field width for accuracy by returning to the Browse mode and clicking on the zip code. The boxes will then appear around your fields, and you can determine whether or not your field is the correct size. When you have gotten the Zip field the correct width, drag the field up so that the top of the Zip field aligns with the bottom of the City field.

Now that you have some extra space to work with, you can add another field. As you remember, FileMaker would only let us put five fields in the label when we first started working on it. But, now that you have moved a few things around, you will find that there is more space for an extra field or two. In this case, we add the Company Name field. We start by going to the Edit menu and picking Select All (Command—A). All the field boxes should now be black (selected). Drag all the fields down until the Zip field is almost on the part marked Body. Now that there is more space at the top of the label, you can bring in another field. You bring in another field by dragging the field tool from the status area to the area within the layout that you want the field to appear. Do this now by dragging the field tool to the space above Client Contact. As soon as you release the mouse button, a dialog box with all the fields in it will appear as shown in Fig. 2-18.

In this instance, we select the field Company Name to go in the label layout. Select the Company Name field by clicking on it twice, or click once to select and then click on OK. You should now have the Company Name field at the top of your label layout and the field should be a bit smaller than the Address field below it. Resize the Company Name field to the same size as the Address field by using its handle. Again, if you have trouble with the field not sizing correctly, or it is jumping about, use the Command—drag process to assist in aligning it properly.

All that remains now is to fill in the small blank space between the City field and the State field. We had you leave that area blank for a purpose. Because FileMaker will slide the data in the City and State fields to the left in order to fill up any blank

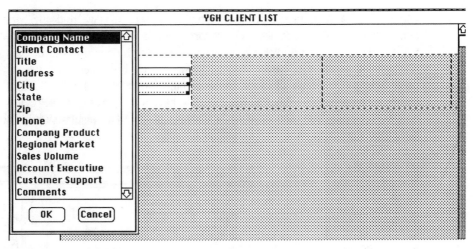

Fig. 2-18. List of fields.

spaces, there will be no separator between the two. For example, FileMaker would give you Tampa FL in the label instead of Tampa, FL. There are two ways to handle this, one of which is to create a new field called Comma that has nothing in it except a comma. The other way to put a comma in between two fields is to use the text tool to place a comma between the fields. As the second way is the easier of the two, that is what we describe here.

Select the text tool by clicking on the A in the toolbox in the status area and your cursor will become an I-beam. Place the I-beam in between the City field and the State field and click once. Now type a single comma and go back and click on the pointer tool in the Toolbox so we can position the comma correctly. It is important to note at this point that when you have the option of Sliding objects left selected, *all* objects must be aligned exactly the same on the top line in order for the sliding to work. (There is a tip in Chapter 4 for doing this.) Your screen should now look like Fig. 2-19.

Click on your comma, and place it so that the top of the object is aligned with the bottom line of the Address field. If you have trouble placing it exactly, use Com-

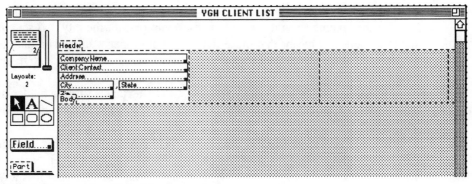

Fig. 2-19. Completed Label layout.

mand—drag to help in the placement. To check to see how we're doing, first go back to the Browse mode to see how your records look in the label layout. Note that the text has *not* slid to the left and that the comma seems to be hanging out in the middle of nowhere. Remember, however, that the Browse mode is not necessarily a good indicator of how your records will look in the printed form. To get a more accurate view of how your labels will look when printed, you have to look at them in Preview. Do that now by selecting Edit then Preview or Command—U. The results should look something like Fig. 2-20.

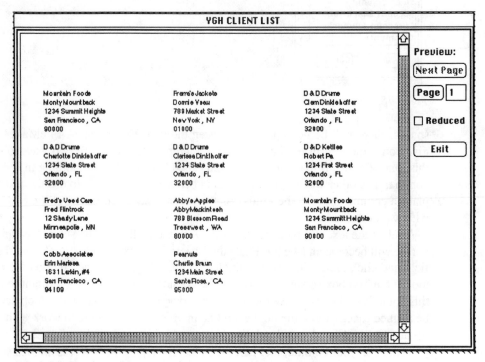

Fig. 2-20. Results in Preview mode.

In the Preview, you should see that the city and state have indeed slid to the left and that the comma separates them. If, for some reason, the city and state *have not* slid to the left, that means that those fields are not properly aligned on the same line. To correct that, Exit from the Preview and go back to the Layout mode to re-align your fields.

All that is left now is to print your labels. Printing labels varies a bit depending on whether you are using a laser printer or a dot matrix printer. You can find more information on printers in Chapter 8.

One small tip about printing your labels is to always do a dry run on plain paper first, then you can compare the plain paper printout with your label stock to see if it will all line up on the labels correctly. If things do not line up, then it is a relatively easy task to go back to your layout to make any corrections needed.

That's it! You have successfully created a database with two layouts: one for data entry and one for labels. You are ready now to save your work and quit the program.

SAVING AND QUITTING

FileMaker automatically saves to disk any changes you make to your file—any additions, deletions, or editing. This saving occurs during the short lulls in your keyboard activity. This means that there is no need for a separate Save command. This is very helpful when a system error icon suddenly appears and you have to restart, because even your latest change has been saved.

The automatic save feature is not so good when you inadvertently start changing the wrong record or layout and your changes have been saved over the original. There are ways to protect your records from being changed, and these methods will be discussed in Chapter 4. Also note that there is an Undo (Command–Z) command in the Edit menu. Many times using Undo will suffice to correct the error if FileMaker has not had a chance to save your most recent changes.

While FileMaker's Save system is different from the normal Macintosh interface, the Quit command follows the universal Mac standard of Command–Q or File then Quit. When you quit from FileMaker, you will not be asked if you want to save the changes or not, because FileMaker has already assumed that you would want to save those changes and has already done it. It must be noted, however, that FileMaker places a "bookmark" of sorts, based on the last layout in use, when you close or quit the file. For example, if you were in the label layout when you quit, then when you reopen that file you would be in the Browse mode with the label layout you were working on. Likewise, if you were working on purchase orders layout when you quit, the purchase orders would be what you see when you reopen the file.

FileMaker will never bring you back in to the Layout mode when you open a file, it will always bring you into the Browse mode. For an example, let's go to the Layout mode, and select the first layout. This was the DATA ENTRY SCREEN. Now select Quit from the File menu. When you reopen this file, you will be in the Browse mode. The current layout will be the DATA ENTRY SCREEN.

CONCLUSION

In this chapter, you have learned enough to design and build your own database with multiple layouts. You have seen just a fraction of the possibilities for customization that are available with FileMaker. In the next chapter, we go into greater detail on the subject of fields. In addition to the descriptions and examples of various fields, we show you how to speed up data entry through the use of FileMaker's Entry options for data.

3
FileMaker Fields Forever

IF YOU HAVE NEVER used a database before, the number of questions to be answered before starting can be quite intimidating. You might wonder, "How much information should I put in one field?" or, "Should I have separate fields for both the street number and for the street name?" Although many questions are ahead of you, don't let that keep you from experimenting with your fields. As with most programs, anything you do incorrectly *can* be fixed. If you forget to include certain fields in the beginning, you can add those later. If you made the mistake of defining a field type as text when it should be number, that too can be changed. Do expect, however, to put in a good amount of time on the design of your database before you start using it for serious work. Remember that the time you put into the planning will be well appreciated later when you have a database that works quickly and efficiently and is a pleasure to use.

WHERE DO YOU START?

There are three very important steps to follow before you actually sit down to begin building your database. These steps are outlined in the next three sections.

Think Small

Make a list of every conceivable piece of data in the smallest of possible sections. For example, instead of creating one field for Name, you might want to create three fields: First Name, Middle Initial, and Last Name. While it is true that you can use calculations to separate out the first name or last name from a single field, it is much easier to create a calculation that combines those fields.

Sometimes simple omissions such as this can create big headaches later on. The worst-case scenario is wasted hours spent reentering data that should have been there in the first place. (*Please note*: The Client Contact field in Chapter 2 was designed for simplicity, and not necessarily for accuracy.)

Think Ahead

Make a list of every possible use for your database. In keeping with this step, you might discover that there are additional fields to be included that you had not considered. For example, if you are creating a database for mailing labels, you might want to use those same names in a form letter for direct mailing at a later stage. If that is the case, then you can define a field Salutation that can be used in the letters later.

In an actual situation, a company sponsoring a convention used a database on-site to mail out invitations for their show. As the RSVPs came in, the company entered the number of persons from each company who would be attending. What they forgot to include was the actual names of the attendees. Later, they decided to use that same database to print the badges on-site, only to discover that the database was next to useless in this case because they did not have the names of the attendees for those badges.

Think Paper

Make a rough draft of what you'd like your data entry screens and reports to look like. You need not be an artist to do this because it is a rough draft for your reference only. Doing this accomplishes three things: it is helpful in creating a logical flow in the way fields are placed; it gives you an idea of the paper size you will need to use along with the size restrictions, and you might also discover the other fields that need to be added. We once spent days designing a special form only to discover, when we went to print it, that the form was 2″ too long!

If you are still having trouble deciding what fields to include, remember this: If you think you'll need it later, include it now. It is easier to deal with too many fields than not enough and any superfluous fields can always be deleted at a later date.

The Index Question

Your next question is probably, "How does FileMaker know how to find the information I'm looking for if I don't create a separate field for every word or character?" That does seem to be a bit of a challenge, doesn't it? Actually, FileMaker automatically creates an index of every word and character that you enter. It then uses this index as a reference in every sort of search that you execute. In many database programs, you have to decide at the beginning which fields are to be indexed and how. FileMaker makes it much easier by assuming that everything you enter should be indexed.

THE FIELDS

As you saw in Chapter 2, you begin creating any database by first defining each field to be used. There are, in total, six possible field types in FileMaker: Text, Number, Date, Picture, Calculation, and Summary. In this chapter, we first give you definitions and explanations of the various fields and their effects on data. We then proceed to the working examples. The sections below give you the characteristics of the field types. Most explanations are fairly straightforward but, because calculations and summaries can be both confusing and intimidating, they are handled in greater detail in Chapter 6.

Text

A text field will accept anything you can type from your keyboard. The information entered in a text field can be as simple as one character or as complex as many lines of data. As you type information in a text field, it will automatically word wrap as in word processor programs.

FileMaker automatically indexes every word and character typed in a text field, and it can find every occurrence of that word or character when instructed to do so.

You can sort text fields in alphabetical order, and reverse alphabetical order. The Sort command approaches a text field by looking at the first letter or character in the field. If two records are found that begin with the same letter, FileMaker then looks at the second letter, third letter, and so on, to put text in proper order. For example, if you are sorting on Last Name and have records with Brown, Braun, and Browning in that field, FileMaker puts those names in the proper alphabetical order: Braun, Brown, Browning.

Text fields can be used in calculations and summaries. For example, you can create a calculation that takes the data in the fields Salutation, Title, and Last Name to come up with Dear Mr. Smith from your records.

You are able to format text fields with any font, size, or style. You do this with the Format command in Layout mode. You are only limited by the fonts you have installed in your system. Additionally, you can format text placement in a text field, aligning to the left, middle, or right within the field.

Number

A number field will also accept anything you can type from a keyboard, but you are limited to one line of data in the field itself. The information you type will not word wrap, and, if you tap the Return key, FileMaker will give you a warning sound.

FileMaker indexes the number fields as well, but it will only index numbers or values, not any other characters or text. For example, perhaps you had included an extension number in a phone number field like 212-555-1212, ext.479, and now you need to find that number. If you ask FileMaker to find the characters ext. in a number field, the program will tell you that you have entered an invalid request.

Numbers can be sorted in ascending or descending order, and they can be formatted in a number of ways. In addition to being able to format the font, style and size of numbers, you can also format numbers with commas, dollar signs, percentage symbols, and a specific number of digits to the right of a decimal point. You do this with the Format command in Layout mode.

Date

When you specify a field as being a date field type, the date must be entered as mm-dd-yy or mm/dd/yy. For example, you can enter 12/4/88 or even 12-4-88, but not Dec 4, 88. You can use any date between 01/01/0001 and 12/31/3000. However, while you are restricted in the way you enter dates in a FileMaker date field, you have more options when it comes to displaying the date. You can choose one of the following five date formats:

```
7/22/88
Jul 22, 1988
July 22, 1988
Fri, Jul 22, 1988
Friday, July 22, 1988
```

You do this with the Format command in Layout mode. Dates simply entered as mm/dd/yy and displayed without formatting are considered "unformatted" dates by FileMaker. If you need to have a date field that shows the date field in a format other than one of the above formats accepted by FileMaker (like Sunday, May 7, for example), you must change the date field to a text field to accept a date entered in that manner.

Date fields can be used in calculations or in summaries. For example, you can create a formula to give you the number of days between the current date and the day you were born. Or, in a more serious application, you can find all the invoices that are more than 90 days overdue on payment.

Picture

A picture field allows you to paste graphics within a field in your records. There is a distinct difference between a graphic image pasted on a layout and a graphic that appears in a picture field. A graphic image that has been pasted on a layout might be your company logo or an elaborate border. In this case, the graphic image will be displayed on all records, and it remains the same. In a picture field, you have the ability to change the image from record to record. One example of this could be purchase orders or invoices that have the individual pictures of each item ordered. Not everyone will be ordering the same items, so not every record will have the same pictures.

As FileMaker has a limited capability to draw graphics, pictures are best created in a graphics program and then brought in through the Cut then Paste or Copy then Paste options under the Edit menu. Picture fields will also accept scanned images.

Although picture fields in themselves cannot be sorted, you can create an additional field to be used as a description or a caption of the picture. The description or caption will be indexed by FileMaker and then can be found and sorted.

Calculation

As calculations can be quite complex and for some, intimidating, the complete subject matter is handled in more detail in Chapter 6. You can name a calculation field as you name any other field; that is, in a manner that is meaningful to you. It is important to note, however, certain symbols and words should not be used as part of a calculation field name. If you do incorporate any of the following symbols or words in your calculation field name, FileMaker will interpret them as part of your calculation and your result will be wrong. Do not use these words and symbols in a calculation field name:

```
+     −     *       /
 ^     &     =       !
 >     <     ≥       ≤
 (     )     "     and
or    not   today
```

You do not actually enter any data in a calculation field, because the data shown in that field is the result of the other fields included in the formula. A calculation field tells FileMaker to compute the contents through the use of a formula. The formula is created by you and it uses values in other fields within a record to provide the answer you are seeking. (A complete table of formulas are given in Chapter 6.) The answer is referred to as a *calculation result*.

For example, you can create a calculation field to compute the outstanding balance due on an invoice. A calculation field cannot, however, be used to compute the outstanding balance on *all* invoices. That sort of a calculation is considered a summary by FileMaker.

The computed figure or calculation result can be text, as in the example of Your Account Is Overdue. The result can also be a number or a date. If you use a number or date field as a calculation result, the resulting date or number can be formatted in any of the forms previously mentioned. If you change a value in one of the fields used in the formula, the calculation result is automatically updated. An index of the calculation field is kept so you can find and sort as you would in a text field.

Summary

In addition to being somewhat confusing, summaries are affected by the "parts" of the layout. For more information on the summary field and its related parts, please refer to Chapter 5.

A summary field is a field that contains a numeric summary of all the values of a given field *over a group of records*. Calculation fields are more appropriately linked to individual records. For example, you might have a calculation field in a record to compute the sales production figures for a particular salesperson. However, if you needed to calculate the sales production figures for *all* salespersons, you would use a summary field.

Another difference between the calculation field and the summary field is that the summary field has preset formulas, whereas the calculation field does not. The basic summary formulas are: Total, Average, Count, Maximum, Minimum, Standard Deviation, and Fractional Total. You can specify variations within the summary formulas, but you cannot create new ones.

Like the calculation field, you do not enter information directly in a summary field because the summary formula controls what appears in the summary. One aspect of summary fields that differs greatly from all other field types is that the result indicated depends on where you place the summary field on the layout, and whether or not the records are sorted. This is due to the fact that the result of a summary field is calculated on all the records currently being browsed. Therefore, you can have a summary field that will give you one amount on *all* payments overdue when all records are being browsed. That same summary field will give you a different figure when browsing only the records that are more than 60 days overdue.

LET'S GET TO WORK

You've been given the job of creating a database for Way to Go Travel (WTGT). The manager of WTGT wants a database that will do a number of things. She wants a way to track how many clients her agency has traveling on any certain tour, or in any given period. She wants to be able to use this database for future mailings, and she wants to be able to check the productivity of her staff. She also wants to come up with an orders database to be able to give the client written confirmation of that trip. Lastly, the agency will need to pick out the pricing information in order to generate invoices if needed.

Given those determining factors, we can come up with a number of fields to be included in this database, even without knowing much about the company or its business. We know that there will have to be certain client information such as the name, address, and phone. We know that there will need to be certain tour information that could possibly be linked to the pricing information. For the client, we might want to give them the date they booked, their travel dates, the salesperson they worked with, and a customer number for future reference. And, because there is pricing information to consider, we might want to include information on the form of payment the customer will be using.

In this first example, we use only three types of fields: text, number, and date. Using the criteria previously discussed, we start by selecting New from the File menu in order to create a new file entitled Tour Orders. After you have entered the file name, the Field Definition screen appears in which you are to enter your field names and field types. Enter the following fields as shown:

Field Name	Field Type
Name	Text
First Name	Text

Last Name	Text
Address	Text
City	Text
State	Text
Zip	Number
Customer Number	Text
Tour Number	Number
Tour Description	Text
Departure Date	Date
Return Date	Date
Total Number of Days	Number
Form of Payment	Text
Tour Cost	Number
Deposit	Number
Total Amount Due	Number

If you make a mistake while typing in the field names, either click the Deselect button to start over again on that field name, or make use of the standard Macintosh editing techniques to correct your error. Please note that the field names are not limited to the length of characters shown here. The maximum number of characters for a field name is 63 characters.

After you have entered all the fields shown above, click Exit on the screen and you will be placed in the Browse mode in the default (Standard) layout. Note that the Standard layout places all the fields in a vertical line in the order that you defined them. The field labels are also placed to the left of each field. Accept this layout for now and make changes to it later.

ADDING, DELETING, AND CHANGING FIELDS

As you look through these fields, you recognize the error of your ways and realize that you goofed! There are so many errors that you don't know where to begin. First off, you forgot some fields altogether: the Date, Salesperson, and Phone fields are missing and will have to be added. Then you also notice a superfluous field called Name that duplicates the two fields of First Name and Last Name. The Name field will have to be deleted. You also suspect that you incorrectly defined your Customer Number field as a text field instead of a number field. You'll have to check on that to see if it needs to be changed.

You cannot tell by looking at the fields in the Browse mode whether or not they have the correct definitions. In order to double check your field definitions, you have to go back to the Field Definition screen. In order to make these amendments to your database by changing or editing your fields, first pick Define from the Select menu. In FileMaker Pro, use Shift−Command−D as a shortcut. You will be placed in the Field Definition screen, which includes your previously defined fields.

First, let's add the missing fields of Salesperson (Text) and Date (Date) and Phone (Number). Those three fields will be added to the bottom of the list in the Field Definition screen. Now we make changes to the Name field by clicking once on the word

Name to select it. Once you select Name, notice that Name now appears in the smaller box on the lower left, and is highlighted. Three of the buttons to the right are also now active, where they were previously grayed out. Those buttons are: Entry Options, Deselect, and Delete. See Chapter 11 for details of FileMaker Pro buttons.

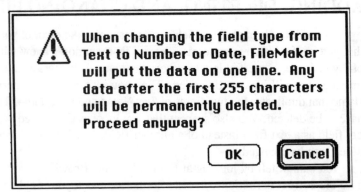

When you create new fields, FileMaker will add those fields to the bottom of the current layout and to any new layouts you create, but it will not add the new fields to any previously existing layouts. In order to add new fields to a previously existing layout, you have to bring those fields in with the field tool, and you will have to label those new fields yourself using the text tool.

Click the Delete button, and you will be given a warning dialog which indicates that all the contents of this field will be deleted if you continue. If you had made use of this field by entering data in it, all the data in that field would be banished to computer never-never land when you delete the field. The default button is Cancel, to prevent you from inadvertently deleting a field and its contents. Now click OK, and you will return to the Field Definition screen. Name is now deleted from the field definition window, and it has also been removed from the layout.

Next you'll want to change the Customer Number field from a text field to a number field. Select Customer Number by clicking once, and it will appear in the box in the lower left. Once Customer Number is listed in the box, either click the radio button next to Number, or use the keyboard shortcut of Command−N. Then click the OK button to accept the change, or hit Return.

What you will now receive is a warning dialog as shown in Fig. 3-1 stating that when you change a Text field to a Number or Date field, FileMaker will put the data that has already been input onto one line, and it will delete any characters after the first 255 characters.

Fig. 3-1. Warning dialog box in field definitions.

This message appears because, although FileMaker can accept pages and pages of data in a text field, a number or date field cannot accept that much data. Number and date fields are restricted in both the number of lines of data it can accept (try tapping the Return key when you are entering data in a Number field, and you will receive an error sound), and there is a maximum number of characters that these fields will accept.

For example, suppose that you have a text field entitled Comments. As you entered the data in the Comments field, the text either word wrapped in the box, or you hit Return, thus creating more than one line of data. Now you decide to change the Comments field to a different field called Number of Guests, and you want to change the field type from Text to Number. Once you complete this change, you will find that all your data is not on many lines, but just one. Also, any data after the first 255 characters is now gone. When you return to the Browse mode, FileMaker is completely confused and responds with a question mark next to Number of Guests. If, while in the Browse mode, you click in the Number of Guests field, your previously entered data will appear, but once you click outside of the boxes the question mark reappears. You would eventually have to change the data in this field to match the requirements of a number field.

After you have finished with your changes, click Exit and you will return to the Browse mode. Note that your added fields appear at the bottom of the page, in the order that you added them. The body size has also changed in size to accommodate the new fields.

FUN WITH FORMATS

Now that you have all your fields properly defined, let's go on to format some of them. Just what exactly is formatting? Is formatting the opposite of backmatting? Simply put, *formatting* is a way in which to change the look of your data. Formats can be applied to either fields or layout text (including what we refer to as field labels). The format you assign to a field or layout text controls the font, font size, and size, as well as the alignment of those items.

There are any number of reasons to format certain items within a layout. Formatting can control the consistency of your data by making sure it looks the same in all records. You can format for multiple values in a given field, and you can format to help you save time. One example of formatting to save time would be formatting a number to include the dollar sign, commas, and decimal point. There would be no need for the data entry person to include those symbols in that particular field because FileMaker would automatically enter them.

Fonts, Sizes, and Styles

When you create a database and use FileMaker's Standard layout or Columnar layout, the fields you create and define are shown in a certain default format. FileMaker's defaults for the layout text are Helvetica, 9 point, bold, and the default format for the field contents are Helvetica, 12 point, plain text. Of course, this is assuming that you have Helvetica installed in your System File. If that is not the case, then Geneva would be the default font.

In our Tour Order example, let's start by changing the fields to a different font and size. First, let's select all the fields on the layout and exclude the layout text (field labels). This can be done in one of two ways. The first way is to Shift—click on the fields, one at a time, until all are selected. The second method is to drag your pointer across the fields, and is called drag–select. When you use your pointer to drag–select these objects, any object partially or completely within the rectangle it creates will be selected when you release the mouse button.

Once you have the fields selected, go to the Format menu and select Font. A submenu will appear in which all the fonts currently available on your current startup disk's System file are shown. Please note that FileMaker's submenus are not the "sticky" sort that will stay on your screen after you release the mouse button. In File-Maker, you will have to perfect your "submenu slide" technique or you'll constantly be losing your submenus. Go ahead now and pick a new font of your choosing, and all the fields you have selected will change to the font you have chosen. That new font will be reflected in the field when you go back to your layout. Once you have chosen the font from the Font submenu, a check mark will appear to the left of the font you have chosen. In FileMaker Pro, the fonts will appear "in format" for you.

 When you change the font and/or the font size in a field, the changes are immediately reflected in that particular field. If the new font or font size is smaller than the original, the field box will change its size in proportion to the new format.

Deselect your fields now and select the field labels. Try your hand at changing the font size by selecting the Fontsize command from the Format menu. The largest font size available in FileMaker is 72 points, but it is rare that you would ever use a font size that large. If you do happen to pick a font or a font size that is too large for the layout space you are working with, you'll receive a warning like the one in Fig. 3-2, telling you that what you have chosen to do cannot be done, and you'll have to move things around or use a smaller font size.

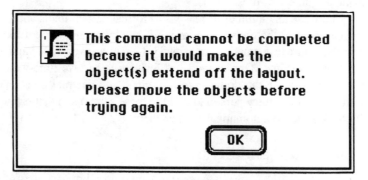

Fig. 3-2. Warning dialog box from Format menu.

But beware! Once you click OK on this warning, FileMaker can still make those changes to some of the fields or objects. The result of this is usually a mess of overlapping fields and/or layout text.

The next option is your font style. The FileMaker default style is Plain text for fields and Bold for the field labels. Often though, you'll want to emphasize certain fields over others by choosing Bold or Italic, for example. Select your field labels by using either the Shift–click method or drag–select. Then go to the Format menu and select Style, and your submenu will appear with the choices of Plain text, Bold, Italic, Underline, Outline, and Shadow. Again, check marks will appear to the left of the style or styles you have chosen. As with most Mac programs, you are able to use a combination of styles in any given font. For example, you may want the First Name and Last Name fields to be Bold Italic and the Form of Payment field to be Italic Outline. Give yourself some time now to experiment. Try changing the field labels as well as your fields.

Although the keyboard shortcuts are not shown in the Style submenu, they do exist. The keyboard shortcuts are:

Plain Text	Command – Shift – P
Bold	Command – Shift – B
Italic	Command – Shift – I
Underline	Command – Shift – U

In FileMaker Pro, Outline and Shadow have similar shortcuts.

In our example, you have been making changes to the fields while in the Layout mode. When you make changes to your fields in the Layout mode, these changes are reflected in *all* records when you return to the Browse mode. The reverse is not true, however. While you can use the Font, FontSize, and Style commands while in the Browse mode, those changes will be recorded *for that record only*, and not all records. If you want to emphasize a field or a word in a single record, you can make the change while in the Browse mode. If you want to emphasize a field in all records, you need to make that change in the Layout mode.

Alignment

The next choice available in the Format menu is Align. Your alignment choices are Left, Middle, and Right. The Align command is not available in the Browse mode. Align is used to position the data *within* the field box but does not align the data in relationship to the layout page. For example, you might want a row of number fields to Align Right so they will create a column of numbers that are easier to read. When you change a field's alignment, the change is again reflected in the field box in the Layout mode. To illustrate this, select the Customer Number field and choose Align from the Format menu. Drag over to the submenu and select Middle. After you release the mouse button, the field name Customer Number will align itself to the middle of the field box. If you reduce or enlarge that field box, the field name will move to the center of the field box. When you return to the Browse mode, you'll notice that the alignment is reflected there as well when data is entered in that field.

When you use the Align command on layout text, FileMaker moves the layout text relative to the area of the layout text boundary. For example, all of your field labels in the Standard layout are positioned to Align Right in order to keep the labels close to their corresponding fields. If you were to change your field label Date to Booking Date you would select the text tool, place the I-beam to the left of the word Date, and then type in Booking. As you type the word Booking, the text would move to the left in order to maintain the right alignment. Another use for the Align Right format would be to keep a row of numbers in alignment, thus making them easier to read.

One important thing to keep in mind when using the Align command is that it can affect the Slide Objects option. When you are in a layout where you have chosen the Slide Objects option, all the fields in that layout must be left aligned in order for them to slide. Conversely, if you have a layout where you want some fields to slide, but not others, change the alignment of the fields you don't want to slide to Middle or Right. Say, for example, you have a label layout with the City, State, and Zip fields all on the same line and you have opted for these fields to slide left to close up the space. When you print your labels, or preview them, you would see that the City, State, and Zip have all slid to the left to close up the empty spaces. But what if you don't want the Zip to slide? If you change the alignment of the Zip field to Middle or Right alignment, the Zip field will not slide left.

If you are not sure of a field's format, or the layout text's format, simply select that field or text and go to the Format menu. The font, font size, and alignment will be indicated by check marks for that particular object.

Some keyboard shortcuts can be used for alignment, although they are not apparent. Those shortcuts are Command–Shift–L for Left alignment, Command––Shift–M for Middle alignment, and Command–Shift–R for Right alignment.

Picture fields can be aligned as well. For more information see the following sub-section on Formatting Pictures.

Formatting Example

Before we move on to the next section in formatting, create a new Tour Order layout and change the placement of the fields and layout text to replicate Fig. 3-3. We are changing this layout because some of the changes we will make in formatting will conflict with the placement of the fields in your standard layout of the Tour Order. There is no need to be exact in creating this new layout; a rough equivalent will suffice. Remember, if you have difficulty placing your fields and/or text where you want, you can use Command–drag to eliminate the "jumping motion" of the objects.

Once you have created a new layout for Tour Order, make sure you are in the Layout mode, and go to the Format menu. Note that the second section of that menu is separated by a line and that there are ellipses (. . .) next to the commands rather than an arrow pointing to the right. In FileMaker, an arrow indicates that there is a submenu to follow and the ellipsis indicates that there will be a dialog box that follows, rather than a submenu. Your first choice in this section of the Format menu is Format number, followed by Format Date, Format Picture, and Repeat. We'll now look at these in order.

FORMATS FOR NUMBERS

One of the most frequent uses of number fields in any database is for indicating a series of numbers, as in a customer number for example, or for counting a series of

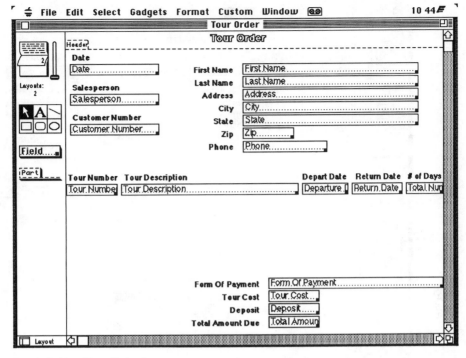

Fig. 3-3. New Tour Order layout.

items or fields. Number fields are also used for recording values such as prices or costs. Number fields are commonly used in calculations and summaries.

Selecting a Number Format

On any layout, you can choose a format in which to view and print number fields. The format of the number does not change the data within that field, but rather changes the way it is displayed on your screen and the way it is printed. For example, you can format a number so that commas are automatically added, thus saving you the time of counting digits in order to insert the commas into a number like 7893759237845. Formatting a number can also be used to show percentages, add dollar signs and decimal points, and to round numbers up or down. Formatting a number in a calculation or summary is most often used to increase accuracy and legibility.

There are eight number fields in your Tour Order layout. Select the Tour Cost field and go to the Format menu and select Format Number. You are now presented with the dialog box as shown in Fig. 3-4.

This box indicates that the selected field, Tour Cost, is unformatted at present, but may be formatted in a number of ways: Commas, Notation (Dollar and Percent), Fixed number of decimal digits, and Yes/No.

Because the chance of a tour cost being over a thousand dollars is pretty good, we'll format this number to show it correctly when browsing and printing. Click in the

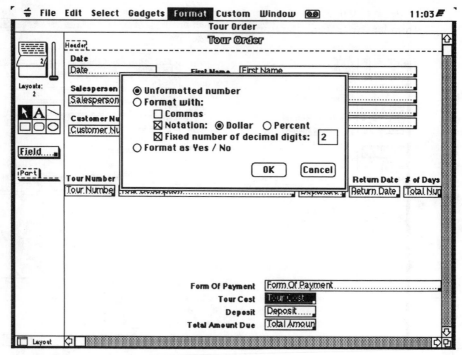

Fig. 3-4. Dialog box for Format Number.

radio button next to Format with and choose Commas, Dollar notation, and the Fixed number of decimal digits of 2; then click OK.

 There is no fail-safe or double-check for the Format Number command. If you forget to select a field before you choose Format Number, you have not formatted any field on your layout, but you have selected the format for the *next* number field you bring in with the field tool. You can also select all the various options for formatting your number, but if you forget to click on Format with before you exit, none of your formatting changes will take effect.

Back in the Layout mode, there is no change to the Tour Cost field that is visible at this point. Because formatting a field in this manner affects the actual viewing, or browsing of that particular field, as well as the printing of it, you have to print or browse a record with that field in order to see the changes. Go to the Browse mode for your new Tour Order layout, and we will illustrate how this number format will work.

Click in the Tour Cost field in your record to make it active and type in the number 98765. Type this without dollar signs, commas, and so on. Tab to or click in the Deposit field and enter 1000. So far, nothing new, huh? Now click *outside* the Tour Cost field so that the fields in this record are inactive and, amazingly, the Tour Cost is now presented as $98,765.00 while the Deposit field remains plain old 1000 because that field is unformatted. If you click in one of those fields again to activate them, the numbers will again appear just as you had entered them—without notation, commas, or decimal point. In this instance, formatting the number is a time saver as it saves you from having to enter additional data.

Go back to the Layout mode and change both the Deposit and Total Amount Due fields formats as you did with Tour Cost. When you come back to your record, the 1000 in Deposit will appear as $1,000.00. Also note that the numbers are not lined up by the decimal. To adjust the alignment of those fields, go back to the layout, select those fields and format them to Align Right. They should then appear in a column row when you go back to the Browse mode.

Number fields can sometimes be strange creatures. If you enter text in an *unformatted* number field, the text will appear on the screen and when printed. But, if you enter text in a *formatted* number field, the text will not appear when printed or browsed; it will only appear when that particular field is active. For example, if you format a number field with dollar notation and then enter $3.00 each in the field, the word each will not appear when printed or when viewing a record in the Browse mode. If you click in that field to make it active while in the Browse mode, the word each will reappear. It will disappear once again when you click outside of the field box.

Decimal Points of Detail

When you formatted your costing fields, you specified a fixed number of decimal points, in this case two decimal points. Just what does that affect, if anything? To illustrate, let's go back to the Browse mode and look at the Tour Cost field. The number in this field does not appear as $987.65 because your selected option of Fixed number of decimal digits has *added* the two zeros to the end of your entry. Go back to the Tour Cost field, and edit your number to read 98.765. When you click outside of the field box, the number now appears as $98.77. Again, the two decimal places have overridden your entry and it has also *rounded the number up*. That is perhaps unexpected, but it is one of the functions of specifying how many decimal points.

FileMaker reads the decimal places instruction as "round up or down" to the nearest x number of decimal places. FileMaker's default number of decimal places is 2, but that can be changed to any number between 0 and 30. For example, if you specify 2 decimal places and enter the number 928.645, FileMaker will display that number as 928.65. If you specify no decimal points by entering 0 as the number of digits, the number 928.645 would appear as the number 929.

You can also have FileMaker round your numbers to the nearest ten by specifying − 1 as the number of decimal places. In that case, the number 928.645 would appear as the number 930. If you use − 2 to round up to the nearest hundred, that same number would appear as 900. What FileMaker does in this case is look at the number of the digits to the *left* of the last digit to determine how much to round up or to round down by.

If you use a formatted number field in a calculation where the number has been rounded up or down, the calculation will use the actual number entered and not the rounded number. (If you want to use a rounded number for calculations and summaries, there is a Round function in the calculation formulas.)

If you need to print special symbols in a number field associated with currency such as the yen symbol (¥) or the pounds sterling symbol (£), you must leave that number unformatted, and you will have to enter the special symbol, commas, and decimal point manually. Use Decimal Options for this in FileMaker Pro.

In addition to the notations we've mentioned, FileMaker will display any number entered in a number field formatted as Percent by multiplying that number by 100, followed by a percentage (%) sign. For example, a number entered as .10 will be displayed as 10%. A number entered as 1.15 would be displayed as 115%. This notation is very useful when working service charges, loans, and taxes.

Last, but not least, a number field can be formatted to Yes/No. The Yes/No format works as follows: If you enter any number greater than 0 in a number field formatted as Yes/No, Yes will appear instead of the number entered. If, on the other hand, you enter 0 (zero) in that field, the resulting display will be No. For example, suppose you had a database set up for the parts departments of an automotive repair center. The database in this case keeps track of all stock on hand. A calculation can be set up that will count the available stock on hand and give the staff the appropriate response in a field entitled Available?. If the number of items on hand is greater than zero, Available will indicate Yes.

FORMATTING DATES

A date field is probably one field that you would not necessarily think of as requiring a format. However, there are a number of date formats available in File-Maker. Many database programs limit your display of dates to simply the number of the month, day, and year. Others give you some abbreviations of month names and year numbers. FileMaker gives you those options, and two more which include the day of the week as well.

 If you enter just the last two digits of the year, FileMaker assumes you refer to the year as being in this century. For years other than those in the twentieth century, you must use the entire year in your entry, for example, 1876 or 2001.

FileMaker considers an *unformatted* date as one entered as either mm-dd-yy or mm/dd/yy. You cannot enter a date as Jul 22, 1989 in a date field and have it accepted as a valid date. If you do enter a date in this manner, you will get a warning similar to the one shown in Fig. 3-5.

Additionally, even when you have formatted a date, your data entry must follow this same entry method, or that too will result in an error warning. This might be a bit confusing in the beginning, but after two or three records worth of warnings, you quickly get the message.

Let's format the dates on the Tour Order file and get a look at how the various formats differ. From the layout mode, select the Date field and then select Format followed by Format Date. The dialog box appears like the one in Fig. 3-6, in which you are given six different ways in entering a date, including Unformatted.

Select the fifth option Fri, Jul 22, 1988, and click OK. Again, you must make sure that the field you want to format is selected before you choose the format, or your

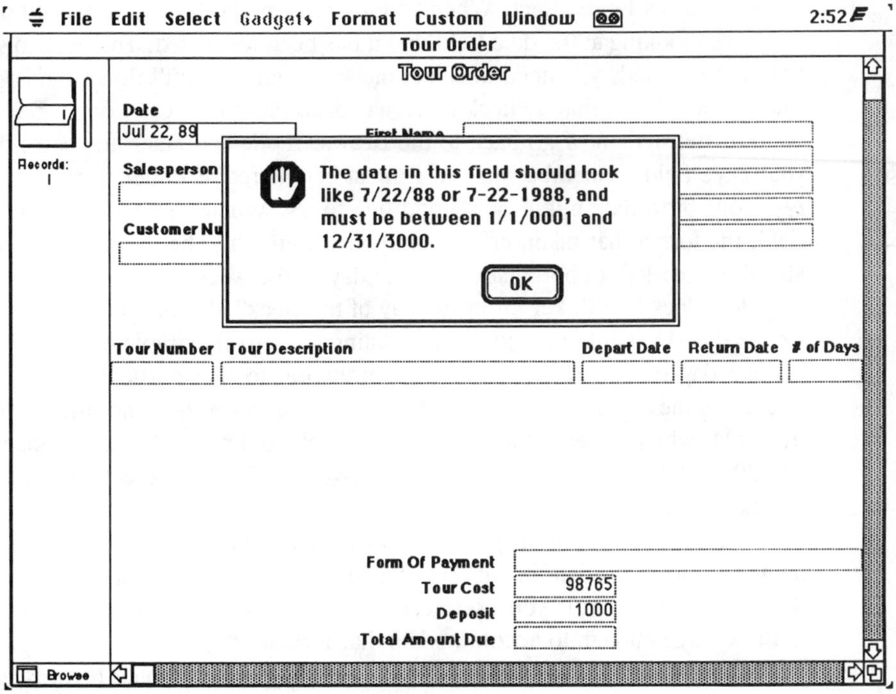

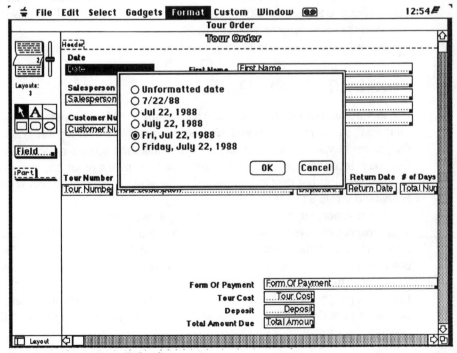

Fig. 3-5. Incorrect date entry warning.

Fig. 3-6. Format Date dialog box.

change will not be in affect. When you are back in the layout, you will not be able to tell just by looking at the date field that it has been formatted. To check to see if a date field is formatted, you need to select the field and then pull down the Format menu. There you will see that a check mark has been placed next to Format Date.

For fun, let's now go back to the Browse mode and enter any date you please in your Date field, remembering that it must be entered as either mm-dd-yy or mm/dd /yy. Your birth date might be a good one to try. When you click outside of the date field, the format has taken effect, and you see not only the month, day, and year, but also the three-letter abbreviation for the day of the week.

How does FileMaker know the day of the week? The program does this by refer- ring to the Mac's internal clock and running a relatively simple computation to figure out the day of the week. There is a limitation to this particular format, however (including the day of the week). The computation can go back no further than January 01, 1904 (which is Year One to the Mac's clock) and no further ahead than December 31, 2039. Obviously the makers of FileMaker, Claris, expect the program to be around at least that long.

In a more serious vein, your date format should conform to its function. There is no need to format a date in the longer forms if a shorter form of the date will suffice. Remember, too, that if you use the longer forms of a formatted date, the date field must be large enough to accommodate that format.

 If you would like the current date to appear on your printed records, use the text tool to type the characters // (two forward slashes) on the appropriate area of the lay- out. (In the body part, if you want it on all records printed, or in the Header or Footer, if you want it to appear once on a page.) The current date symbol (//) can also be for- matted in the same manner as a date field.

For information on date fields in calculations, refer to Chapter 6.

FORMATTING PICTURES

Pictures and picture fields can add a lot to any FileMaker report. Pictures are any- thing that you can cut or copy and then paste onto a FileMaker layout. When you paste the picture in your layout, that picture will remain the same for each page or report that you print or browse. But what if you want to prepare a report that has many differ- ent pictures in it, but they are all placed in the same space in different records. Then you would create a picture field.

For instance, suppose you are preparing a database for a real estate office to use with prospective buyers. You could easily create a For Sale file with separate records for each house on the market. In addition to the statistics on each house for sale, you could insert a picture of the house in each record. Because each picture would vary from record to record, you would need to create a picture field in the layout so that the individual pictures of the houses could change from record to record. Then, when you browse or print the records, you would have the correct house appear with the corres- ponding statistics.

An excellent example of picture fields that change from record to record can be found in the FileMaker example disk called "Orders." There is also more information on pictures and picture fields in Chapter 10.

The purpose of this section is not to explain the differences between pictures and picture fields, however. In this section, we simply explain how to format your picture fields. When you format a picture field, you change the way the pictures are shown within a picture field. Basically, you have two choices, as shown by the dialog box in Fig. 3-7.

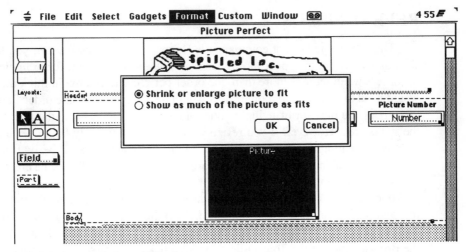

Fig. 3-7. Format Picture dialog box.

To format your picture, select the Picture field you want to format and then choose Format Picture from the Format menu. Then you are given the two choices: Shrink or enlarge picture to fit and Show as much of the picture that fits.

Let's tackle the first command first, Shrink or enlarge. . . . What does that command mean? It means, that if the picture you place in that field is larger or smaller than the field itself, FileMaker will resize the picture to fit the space you have allowed for it to appear in. The only drawbacks to that command are that the picture might not necessarily be shown in proportion, or you might lose the detail in a large picture made small. On the other hand, if you select Show as much. . ., you might see only a small portion of your picture; perhaps none of it at all, if the picture has a lot of white space in it. The best way to get around the distortion this command may cause is to make sure that your picture and your picture field are approximately the same size. For example, if you are planning a computerized database of houses for sale, give some thought to the size of the pictures you will be using when designing the picture fields.

Another small difference between Format Picture and the other format commands is that there isn't really such a thing as an "unformatted" picture field. As soon as you create a picture field, FileMaker applies the default format of Shrink or enlarge. . . to any picture field.

In addition to formatting your picture fields, you can align the picture to the left, middle, or right of the field, just as you would set the alignment on any other field in FileMaker. When you change the alignment of a picture field, the picture is displayed in that area of the field box. If your picture field is relatively small, however, and your pictures are larger than the field, such an alignment change might not be necessarily noticeable.

REPEAT FIELDS

The last of the Format commands is Repeat, which is used when you have one field that you want to appear more than one time on your layout, for example, a field for orders when there is more than one order per record. You might think that all you would need to do to create more orders would be to expand a single order field, either by resizing the field, or bringing in more of the same field by using the field tool from the status area. However, if you resize your field, you still only have one field and if you do calculations on that field, the calculation may not work properly. If you bring in extra fields with the field tool, these are copies, and you will only be creating more fields with the same data.

For example, go to the Layout mode in your Tour Orders model, grab the field tool and place it under the Tour Number field. When the list of fields comes up, select Tour Number and another Tour Number field will be placed in your layout. Then go to the Browse mode of the Tour Orders model, click in the first Tour Number field, and enter the figure 102. When you tab past the first Tour Number field, the same number, 102, will appear in the second Tour Number field. What you have done is to just create another field with the same value. This illustrates the basic difference between adding the same field on a layout versus using the Repeat command to create the same field *with more than one value*. To remove the extra Tour Number field, go back go the Layout mode, select the second Tour Number field, and then choose Clear from the Edit menu.

Let's use the Repeat command on the following fields: Tour Number, Tour Description, Depart Date, Return Date, and # of Days. First, select all these fields by either dragging across them with the pointer or by doing a Shift—click on each one. Once you have all these fields selected, go to the Format menu and choose Repeat. You will then receive a dialog box asking you how many times to repeat these fields to show separate values, as shown in Fig. 3-8.

Change the number in the Values box to 5, and either tap Return or click OK. You will then be returned to your layout, and all five fields will have been repeated five times. Because those fields were all of the same size and alignment in relation to one another before you chose Repeat, they retain their size and position alignment after they have been repeated.

Also note that the field handle remains in the first (topmost) box of each field. If you resize the first box in any way, the repeating fields will resize in exactly the same

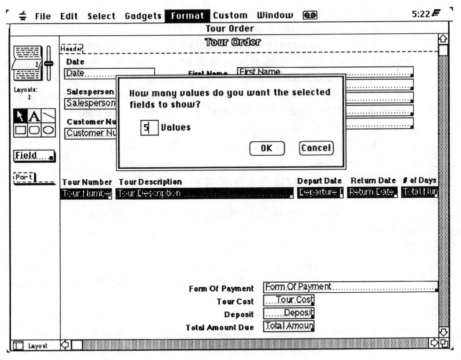

Fig. 3-8. Using the Repeat command.

size and manner. The same holds true the other way around. If the field you wanted to repeat had been resized to include four lines before you chose Repeat, the Repeat command adds the additional fields with four lines each. There is not a definite maximum number of times you can format a field to repeat. The limit is only in the amount of disk space you have.

Now that you have your fields repeated, go back to the Browse mode and fill in one record to see how the Repeat format worked. Click or tab to the first Tour Number field and enter the data shown in Table 3-1.

This person certainly has a lot of vacation time, doesn't he? Actually, this exercise is just to prove a point. By formatting these fields to repeat, those fields can now show more than one value, rather than the one value you were previously restricted to. If you want to make your layout of these fields appear a bit neater, you can change the alignment of some of these fields to the middle or the left.

Table 3-1. Sample Data.

Tour Number	Tour Description	Depart Date	Return Date	# of Days
387	Hawaiian Holiday II	6-22-89	6-29-89	7
199	Daytona Firecracker 400	7-1-89	7-5-89	4
102	Ski Vacation at Jackson Hole	12-23-89	12-30-89	7

If you use repeating fields in your Sort command, FileMaker will sort on the information or data in the first (topmost) field only. Repeating fields can also be used in calculations. You can create a calculation that will even separate the values in each of the repeated fields. When repeating fields are used in calculations, all the field values are used in the calculation, even if the field is not visible. If you format a field to repeat, enter more than one line of data, and then change the format back to one field instead of "x" amount, FileMaker will continue to store all the data, even though those fields are no longer visible on your layout. There is more information on calculations and their effects on repeating fields in Chapter 6.

CHANGING THE TAB ORDER

As you know by now, FileMaker uses the Tab key to move from one field to another. One of FileMaker's little quirks is that it has its own way of keeping tabs on the Tabs you issue. It does not matter to FileMaker in which order the fields were defined, it simply begins tabbing at the top of the layout, from left to right, top to bottom. The order in which FileMaker tabs through a layout is referred to as the *tab order*.

When we first defined our fields for the Tour Order, FileMaker placed those fields in a straight line, top to bottom. At that point, it was both readable and efficient to leave the tab order as it was. So now that we've changed the layout completely from the original standard layout, FileMaker does some funny tabbing.

Try tabbing now with a Tour Order record, and you'll find that you start with the Date field, then you tab to the other fields in this order: First Name, Last Name, Address, Salesperson, City, State, Customer Number, Zip, and so on. Skipping all over the place is not a very efficient way to enter data in this layout. To improve matters, we are going to change the tab order by creating tab *groups*. This will tell File-Maker to tab through one group before tabbing through another group, thus making it easier on you to enter data.

First, you need to go to the Layout mode in your Tour Order file. There we are going to be using a command under the Gadgets menu called Tab Order. (For more information on the other commands under the Gadgets menu refer to Chapter 4.) Notice that when you look at the Tab Order command, it is grayed out and inactive. The particular command will not work until you have selected a field or fields for which to set up a Tab order. Let's start by selecting all the fields in the top right part of the layout: those fields which include the name, address, zip, and so on. Once you have those fields selected, go to the Gadgets menu and select Tab Order. You will be given a dialog box as shown in Fig. 3-9.

FileMaker is saying that it will group these particular fields together so that, when you are in the Browse mode, you can tab through them as a group before going on to another group. Click OK and then select the Date and Salesperson fields and create a tab group for them in the same manner.

Once you have finished, you can go back to the Browse mode to see how the new tab order has worked. Even though you selected the name and address fields first in

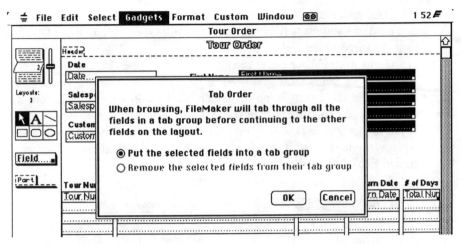

Fig. 3-9. Tab Order dialog box.

the tab order, FileMaker will still start with the field that is in the top left-hand corner to begin tabbing from. Now you'll see that you begin tabbing with the Date field but, instead of going next to the First Name field, you tab next to the Salesperson field. Those two fields were put together in Tab Order, and they are in the upper left, so FileMaker starts with them first. Next you'll tab to the name and address fields, all the way through, before going back to the Customer Number field. The remaining tab groups remain the same because you have not changed them.

If you are not happy with the way you have set up your tab groups, or if you change the layout and want to change the tab group again, simply go back to the Tab Order command after you have selected your fields and remove the Tab Order by clicking the button next to Remove the selected fields from their tab group and click OK. This command does not become active until you have selected a group of fields that have already been grouped.

You can set up your tab orders in any order that you please. You can even instruct FileMaker to jump all over the layout by selecting fields from different areas of the layout. It is usually much better, though, to keep your fields in the tab groups that are most logical for data entry.

 To see which fields are grouped together in a tab group, go to the layout, select one field, and then tap the Tab key. The entire tab group will then be selected.

MAKING LIFE, AND DATA ENTRY, EASIER

Up to now, we have been working with the basics of fields involving how they are set up to accept and display data. We will now go a step further to explain how fields can be set up to enter their own data automatically to ensure accuracy and consistency, and to avoid typographical errors in data entry. These changes are referred to as Entry Options and are selected in the Field Definition screen as they are, in fact, an extension of the definition of a field. You may add Entry Options to any field that you can type

data into: text, number, date, and picture. You cannot use Entry Options on a calculation field or a summary field because you don't type data into those fields; they derive
their data from other fields.

Going to your Tour Order model, let's make some changes to the Entry Options in
some of your fields. You first need to get to the Field Definition screen by selecting
Define from the Select menu. This can be done in either the Layout mode or the
Browse mode. The first field in which we will change Entry Options is the Date field.
If you do not see the Date field on your screen, use the elevator box to scroll down the
window until you see it. Once you select the Date field on the screen, the button
named Entry Options becomes active as shown in Fig. 3-10.

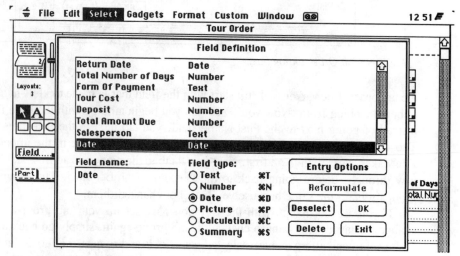

Fig. 3-10. Field Definition screen.

After you have clicked on the Entry Options button, you are then placed in another
screen or dialog box, shown in Fig. 3-11.

In this box, you specify which options you want for this particular field. Notice
that the field you are working on is named in quotation marks at the top of the box.
Your first choice of Entry Options is to Auto-enter in each new record:. Take note of that
word *new*. FileMaker will only use this auto-entry option in each *new* record. Therefore, any records you have created before changing the definition of the Date field with
Entry Options will not have the Date field's data automatically entered in them. For
those previously created records you still will have to enter the data in the Date field
manually.

There are three types of auto-entry that you can choose from. You can choose
only one of these types because to choose more than one would create a conflict
amongst the commands. FileMaker does not give you an error warning in the event
you choose more than one of these types, but what it will do is decide arbitrarily
which of these commands to use. More often than not it will pick the Data: command.
Notice that in this case, the New Serial Number type is grayed out. That's because

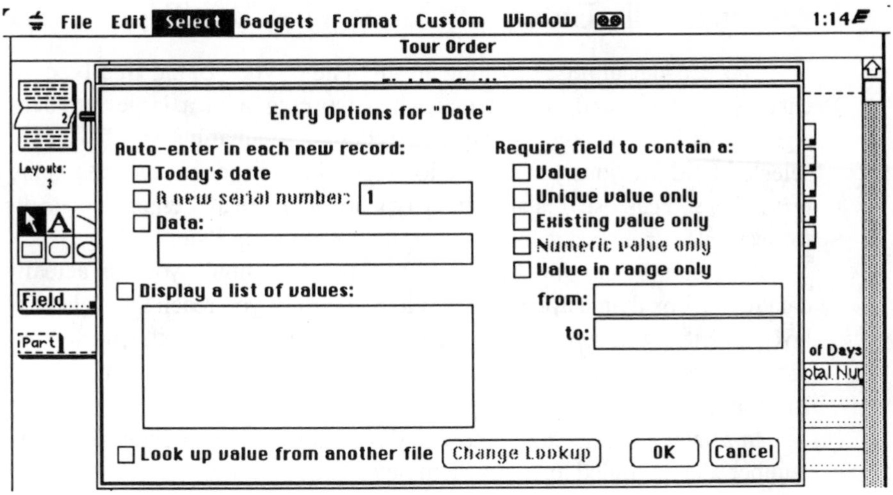

Fig. 3-11. Entry Options screen.

FileMaker looks at the first definition of the field, in this case it is a date field, and then decides what restrictions to place against that field type.

FileMaker will not let you auto-enter a number in a date field, nor will it let you auto-enter a date in a number field. There are no such restrictions placed against a text field, however. In a text field, you have all three choices available to you. To further explain the characteristics of each of these types, let's look at them one by one.

Automatically Entering the Date

When this type auto-entry is chosen, FileMaker looks to your Mac's internal clock to insert today's date in the date field, but only in each *new* record. This is a handy little device to use for those of us who can never remember what the date is! If the date is formatted, it will appear on your screen in the Browse mode in the format you selected. You can use this auto-entry type in a date or a text field, but not in a number field.

Automatically Entering a Serial Number

This auto-entry type is used when you want to number records in sequence automatically as you create them (invoices, for example). This type can be used in a text field or a number field, but it cannot be used in a date field. You select which number you want FileMaker to start with in the next *new* record and from that point on, File-Maker will automatically enter a new number in every record. If you had already manually entered the first 599 records, then you would want FileMaker to start from the next number, 600, on the new record.

Automatically Enter Any Value That You Type

You can put almost anything in this entry type. Using this type of auto entry ensures accuracy and consistency when working with a large number of records. Again, this is applicable to only new records, so anything you have entered in your selected field previously will have to be checked to see that the data is the same. In a text field, you can use this auto entry type to automatically enter a salesperson's name, for example, or even a standard paragraph for a form letter.

Although the box for the data to be typed in is small, you can actually type more data in that box than it appears it would hold. Once you reach the right edge of the data box, your text will scroll off to the left until you are finished. You will not be able to view this text in its entirety without going back to a record and viewing it in the Browse mode.

In a number field, this auto entry type allows you to enter the minimum of one number and unlimited text. An example of this might be 1 each OR @ 2.99 each. This does not mean that you must have a combination of number and text. No, you can use this when you want the same number to appear in all new records, like a mandatory $100.00 deposit, for example. The same is basically true when using this auto entry type for a text field. You can enter anything that you can type from your keyboard in the data box.

 If you use the data type auto-entry for a date field (if you want a particular date to appear rather than the current date, for example), the date you put in the data box must follow the FileMaker date entry guidelines of mm/dd/yy. If you type in Monday, for example, FileMaker will accept it as a valid Field Definition and you will be able to exit from the Field Definition screen. Then when you tab to the date field, Monday will appear in the date field. But, when you try to tab past the date field, FileMaker will give an error warning to the effect that the date entered in that field does not follow the correct format. If you want a field to display a date in a format other than those formats allowed by FileMaker (like Monday, June 5th for example), you must change that field type from a date field to a text field for FileMaker to be able to accept that entry.

Adding Entry Options

Back in your example, let's have FileMaker automatically enter the date in each of your new records by clicking in the Today's date box. An X will appear in the box you have selected to indicate that your entry option is active. Click OK or tap Return, and you will be placed once again in the Field Definition box. There you will see that your Date field has the additional definition of Auto Enter Today displayed in the box. Don't click on Exit just yet, as we want to add Entry Options to two other fields before we show how these fields have been affected by the additional definitions.

In the Field Definition screen, select the Customer Number field and then click Entry Options. You will then be given the Entry Options dialog box for the field Customer Number. We want a different number to appear in this field for each new record, so this time we will choose the A new serial number option. Click once in the box, and then type the number 1000 in the box. In doing this, you are telling File-Maker to put the number 1000 in the next *new* record, and FileMaker will sequentially number each record after that.

Click OK to accept this change and then select the Salesperson field and click Entry Options. In this field, we want a list of names to appear when we tab to that box, and we do that by selecting Display a list of values. Once you click in the box next to Display a list of values, the insertion point appears in the box directly below. As we want the various salespersons' names to appear in that field, type in the following names. Tap Return after typing each name:

    Christopher
    Maryanne
    Joseph
    David

After you have typed in these names, click OK and return to the Field Definition screen. Note that the field Salesperson now has the definition of List next to it in the definitions box.

The List auto-entry command is useful as a time-saving step. You can have your field display such things as all the two-letter codes for the state, the various credit cards used for payment, all the branch offices, or any other list of things that otherwise would have to be typed from memory. It is really quite a versatile command and in addition to being a time saver, it also helps to ensure consistency and helps to avoid typographical errors. This command can be used on a date, number, or text field. It must be noted that, if your field is formatted to accept data in a certain format, the data inserted in the list of values box must match that format exactly in order for it to be accepted by FileMaker.

Now that we have made the changes to the fields we wanted, let's go back and create a new record to see how it works. Click Exit to leave the Field Definition screen, go to the Browse mode, and create a new record. The first thing you should notice in your new record is that today's date magically appears in the Date field and the number 1000 appears in the Customer Number field. If you create another new record, the same date appears and the Customer Number is then 1001. If you had formatted your date field to one of the longer formats, once you click outside of the fields in the record, your date will appear as you had formatted it.

In a blank record, tab to the Salesperson field, or click in the field once. Voila! Your list of salespersons appears for you to choose from as shown in Fig. 3-12.

You must then choose one name from this list as the data to be entered. You can make your selection in any one of three different ways: Double click on your selection, click once and tap Return, or Down arrow to your selection and tap Return.

Once you have selected one of the names, the name you picked will be inserted into the Salesperson field, the list of names will disappear, and the cursor will move to the next field. We must make note at this point that, even though you have selected Auto Entry for certain fields, that does not mean that you cannot enter any other data in those fields. You can edit or change the data in a given field by clicking in that field and using whatever editing techniques you choose to make the change. In a field with

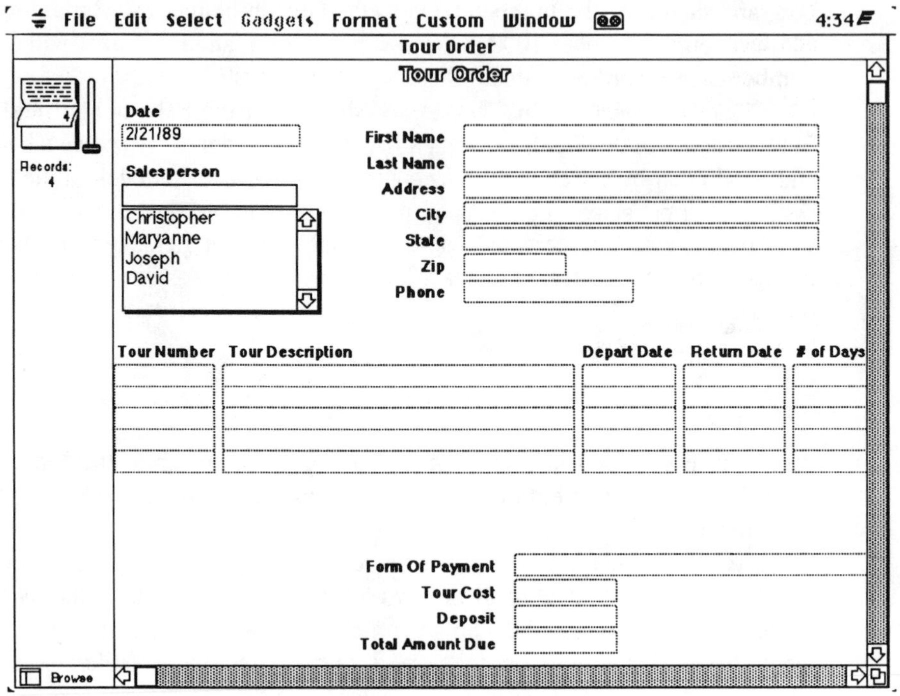

Fig. 3-12. Auto-Enter list.

an auto-entry list, however, the list will again appear. If you wish to change the data to something else that is included in the list, simply make your selection and FileMaker will insert the new selection from the list.

You are not limited to the items on the list and can enter other data by double-clicking in that field. If you double-click quickly, the field will be highlighted, and you can tap Delete and type in your new entry. If you click once so that the list appears, and then click once again, the insertion point will be placed at the end of the entry. You can then use Delete, Cut, Paste, or any of the other Mac editing commands.

ACCURACY IN DATA ENTRY

Entry Options are used to speed up data entry and to provide some means of controlling the accuracy of the data being input. But what's to keep you from tabbing past a field and not entering anything, or inadvertently using the same invoice number again? The answer to that is also in Entry Options under the Require field to contain a section. To use this option, let's redefine a few fields.

In the Field Definition screen, again choose the Date field and click Entry Options. We want to make sure that every record has a date and, to ensure that no date field is left blank, we will tell FileMaker that the Date field is required to contain a value. Value in this sense does not refer to a number or a cost. In FileMaker's mind, every bit of data in a field is also referred to as a *value*. Click to put an X next to Value, and then click OK.

Before you Exit the Field Definition screen, note that the field definition for the Date field now reads Auto-enter Today, ... The ellipsis means that there is more to the field definition now than just auto-enter. In any field that is defined thus, you cannot read the entire definition in the Field Definition screen, but must go into the area where the definition was expanded; in this case it is Entry Options.

Once you have exited the Field Definition screen, we want you to make a small change. Because the date is auto-entered into the Date field, we want you to remove the date (double-click and then Delete), and then try to create a new record or move to another record. What you receive is a warning dialog box like the one in Fig. 3-13.

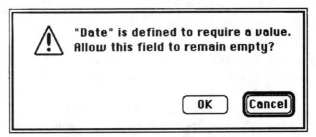

Fig. 3-13. Required Value warning dialog.

You can Tab past the Date field, and FileMaker will not give you a warning. It's just when FileMaker thinks you are finished with that record that it will respond with an error warning.

You still have the option of leaving the Date field empty by simply clicking OK on the warning box. If you click Cancel, however, you must manually enter something in that field to be able to go on to work other records.

In addition to the Entry Option of requiring a value, there are other options available to you to assist in ensuring against blank fields and accuracy. The following section is for your reference.

Require a Field to Contain a Value

When you require a field to contain a value, you are telling FileMaker that it cannot remain blank. This is useful in making sure that the current date and the operator's name are included in each record. You can also use it to make sure that a car's registration number is included in an insurance record, for example.

Require a Field to Contain a Unique Value Only

This option makes sure that not only the field contains a value, or data, the data must also be *unique*. This option is to be used when you want to make sure that each invoice is a different number, for example. When you choose this option, FileMaker looks at the same field in all the other records you have created and compares all the other data in those fields. If it finds another record with the same data, you will receive a warning that asks you if it is okay to have this duplicate or not.

Selecting this option also helps you when using the Entry Option to look up a value in another file (see Lookups, later in this chapter). When you use this option, File-Maker checks all the records in the file you are working in, as well as the file used in the lookup feature to make sure that the data is unique. This option is very useful when working with files that might look up a Social Security number, or a driver's license number, or any other thoroughly unique value.

Require a Field to Contain an Existing Value Only

This option is the complete opposite of the previous two others. In the others, we were checking to see that a field contains a value that is only used once and once only. With this option, you are having FileMaker run a check against the other records to make sure that they are all the same. An example of this might be a check to make sure that a certain paragraph is the same in all form letters, or that the two-letter state abbreviation matches one of the codes entered in a list or another file with the state codes. If you then tried to leave a record with the code FA for example, FileMaker would alert you with a warning box that tells you that code does not conform to the others. Again, you would not receive this warning until you tried to leave the record, and once you do get the warning, you have the option of leaving it the way it is.

When FileMaker makes this check on a text field it is not case sensitive, and File-Maker ignores such things as punctuation and the order in which the words are placed. Therefore, if you are entering data in a text field like Secretary of State, welfare and education and your existing value is actually Secretary of State, Education, and Welfare, FileMaker would not catch the difference and would allow the first entry as valid. But, if you enter Director, Sales/Marketing and the existing value is Director/ Sales, Marketing, FileMaker would sound the alarm because the slash (/) is not a punctuation mark and its position would be checked.

Require a Field to Contain a Numeric Value Only

Using this option tells FileMaker that only a number can be used in this field, even if that field is a text field. A date field, however, cannot be used for this option, and FileMaker will prevent you from doing so by graying out this option when you have chosen a date field. The only minor exception is that one decimal point and one minus sign ($-$) might be included in a number since that constitutes a valid number format. This option would be useful in working with invoices where a reference to a P.O. number is required to receive payment. It is also a check for accuracy in that it will not allow a lowercase letter "l" to be used instead of the number "1", and a lowercase "o" cannot be inadvertently used as a zero.

Require a Field to Contain a Value in a Range

If you want to control the numbering on your purchase orders, for example, and don't want the numbers to go beyond the number 9999, then you would use this option to exert that control. In choosing this option, you give FileMaker your range by typing the beginning number in the from: box and the ending number in the to: box (don't forget to select this option first by clicking in the box next to Value in a range).

Once your field number reaches the maximum, FileMaker would make a decision as to what to do, depending on the other options you might have chosen in concert with this range. If you have selected to have a serial number auto-entered, that command will take priority over the range command. FileMaker would continue with the next number in the series, even if that is beyond your range.

The opposite would be true if you had selected the range, but had *not* specified that this field needs to have a number in it by selecting the Value option. In that event, FileMaker would simply stop numbering altogether; it does not start over at the beginning of the range. If you had chosen your field to require a Value as well as a Value in a Range, then when FileMaker reaches the end of that range it won't tell you that you have reached the end of the range, but it will alert you to the fact that a value is required in that field, and do you want to leave it empty? That warning, shown in Fig. 3-14, should be a signal to you to check your range.

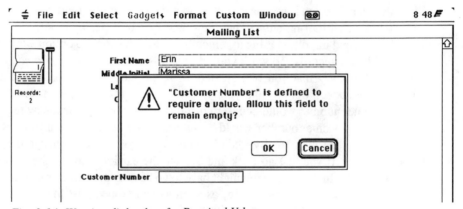

Fig. 3-14. Warning dialog box for Required Value.

This option can be used with text, but it is not suggested that you use it for that purpose. The reason for that is that FileMaker does not actually look at the words or text in the from and to boxes; it merely looks at the letters. Therefore, if you specify the word low in the from box and the word high in the to box, and then enter wig in your field, FileMaker would find that word to be perfectly acceptable because those letters in the word wig are included in the range. A better option when you need to check text in a field is to use Existing value and check the text against a list.

LOOKING AT THE LOOKUPS

The last entry Entry Option is our particular favorite: Look up value from another file. This in itself is what makes FileMaker's semirelational capabilities in that it allows you to cross-reference two different files, or fields, for accuracy in data entry. Lookups can be confusing at first, but once you get used to them, they are really a lot of fun and quite useful.

The Role of Lookups

Often in the business place, you will find yourself creating separate database files for different things, but sometimes the information in the different files overlap. It is time-consuming and frustrating to have to go back and forth between the two files to look up information in one file and then to go back and type the same thing in another file. A good example would be customer numbers. How can you remember what Miss Cobb's customer number is? Is it really practical to have to refer to a printed list or go back and forth between two different files? Of course not, so FileMaker comes to the rescue with *lookup files*!

The first thing you have to remember in working with lookups is that, in order for FileMaker to complete the lookup, the field types in the two areas being cross-referenced *must be the same type*. That means that you cannot have FileMaker look up data in a number field, and then have it copy that data into a text field, for example. The fields can have differing names, but they cannot be of differing types.

The second important thing to remember is that the Lookup option works immediately with new records. To work with old records you must *go back to edit them*. For example, let's say that you had created 16 records before you redefined a field to include the Lookup option, and your lookup was set to insert the customer number. The customer number would be inserted automatically on your next new record, number 17. The customer number would be automatically inserted when you went back to edit records 1 through 16. By "edit," we mean to go back and change the record in some manner. If you just go back and browse the earlier records, the lookup would not take effect. In this case, you might have to go back to the earlier records, delete the name, and retype the name. Then, as soon as you tabbed past the name, your customer number would be inserted with the lookup.

 When you are using the Lookup option with FileMaker, remember that it only looks at *one file* for the information. Therefore, if you want to ensure the accuracy of the file that FileMaker looks at for the information, use the Entry Option of Require a field to contain a unique value in your lookup file. In doing that, you are ensuring the accuracy of the data in your lookup file so that the correct information is inserted in your record.

A Lookup Example

To give you an example of this, let's create a lookup file of customer numbers for your Tour Order model. After we are finished, you will be able to type the customer's last name in the Tour Order, and FileMaker will look for the customer number in the other file and place it in the Tour Order record.

To start select New from the File menu to create a new file. You needn't close your current file, Tour Order, in order to do this. Name your new file WTGT Client List and click New to create the file. When you come to the Field Definition screen, enter the following field names and types:

Field Name	Type
First Name	Text
Last Name	Text
Title	Text
Company	Text
Address	Text
City	Text
State	Text
Zip	Number
Phone	Number
Customer Number	Number

Before you click Exit, select the Customer Number field name by clicking on it and select Entry Options. We want FileMaker to automatically enter a new Customer Number for every record, starting with the number 1000 and, to ensure accuracy, we want to require the field to contain a Value, a Unique value, and a Numeric Value only. In doing that we have FileMaker do a triple check on each Customer Number in this file to make sure that not only does that field contain a number, it is a unique number, and no text is allowed in that field other than a number.

Click Exit, and you will be placed in the Layout mode for your new file. Move your Customer Number field to the top, and resize any fields you see fit. As soon as you have finished, go to the Browse mode, select New Record from the Edit menu, and create three separate records using the information shown in Table 3-2.

After you have finished with these records, close this file and go back to the Tour Order file. (If you did not close it before creating your new file, it should be on your screen after you close the WTGT Client List File.) Before entering any new records in the Tour Order, we need to set up the lookup for the Customer Number field.

Select Define from the Select menu, then pick Customer Number by clicking on it once, and then click the Entry Option button. You will then be in the Entry Option dialog box as shown in Fig. 3-15.

We want the Customer Number field to be required to have a Value and a Unique value, so we select those options as shown. In addition to this, we also want to have FileMaker Look up a value from another file, so select that as well by clicking in the box next to Look Up and then click OK.

As soon as you click OK, FileMaker cycles very quickly through one dialog box, and then another. The one that is immediately placed on your screen is the Mac dialog box which asks you to select the folder, drive, or disk where the file is located that you want to use for your lookup. In this case, we want to select the new file you had created entitled WTGT Client List because that is where the Customer Numbers are stored. Open the WTGT Client List file, as shown in Fig. 3-16, by either double-clicking on the file name, or by clicking once on the name and then clicking Open.

After you have opened your file, the Lookup dialog box appears, as shown in Fig. 3-17, and this is where the Lookup option gets confusing for most people.

Table 3-2. Sample Records.

First record:

Customer Number	(1000 auto-entered by FileMaker)
First Name	Dennis
Last Name	Marshall
Title	Product Manager
Company	Claris
Address	PO Box 58168
City	Santa Clara
State	CA
Zip	95052
Phone	408-987-7000

Second record:

Customer Number	(1001 auto-entered by FileMaker)
First Name	Monty
Last Name	Mountback
Title	President
Company	Mountain Coffee
Address	1234 Java Street
City	Mocha
State	CA
Zip	90000
Phone	415-555-1212

Third record:

Customer Number	(1002 auto-entered by FileMaker)
First Name	Granny
Last Name	Smith
Title	Director
Company	Mackintosh Apples
Address	567 Delicious Drive
City	Rome
State	WA
Zip	98000
Phone	206-555-1212

It is not exactly clear as to what FileMaker is asking for at this point. There are four different areas and three of them are asking you to select a field. To help clarify things a bit, we are going to take some liberties with this dialog box and write a dialog that is a little more helpful:

- **What it says:** Copy into: Customer Number
  What it means: This means that you want FileMaker to put into the Customer

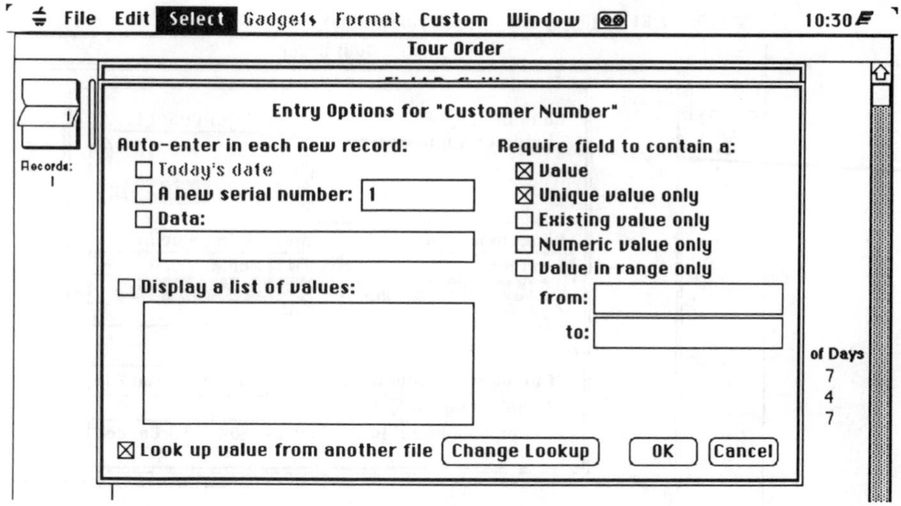

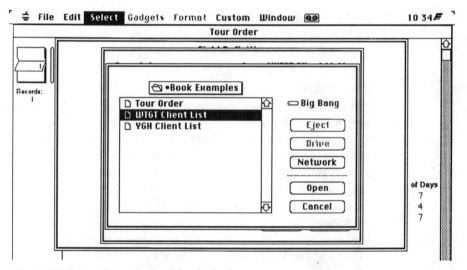

Fig. 3-15. Entry Option dialog box with lookup selected.

Fig. 3-16. Locate file to be used for the lookup.

Number field, in the file Tour Order, something from the next box: from "WTGT Client List".

- **What it says:** from "WTGT Client List"

  What it means: FileMaker wants you to select one of the fields in the WTGT Client List file that will put the correct information into the Customer Number field in the Tour Order file. In this case, the field you want FileMaker to look at in WTGT Client List is the same name as the field in Tour Order: Customer Number. In other words, you want FileMaker to take the Customer Number

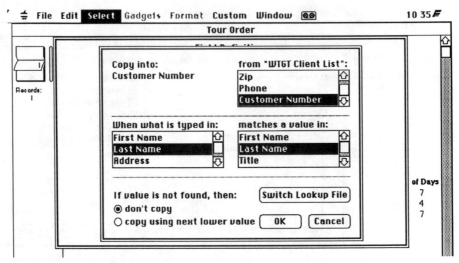

Fig. 3-17. Lookup file dialog box.

that has already been entered in the WTGT Client List and place that number in the blank field called Customer Number in the Tour Order. Select the Customer Number field in this box now by clicking on it once. You might need to scroll down a bit to find it.

- **What it says:** When what is typed in:
  What it means: When do you want FileMaker to place the Customer Number? This box and the next box are playing a match-up game. In order for FileMaker to complete this search, or lookup, there must be at least one field in both files that have the same information. What are those files that you want FileMaker to compare? Because both the Tour Order and the WTGT Client List have the same First Name and the same Last Name of the customer, that would be a logical place to start. Let's select Last Name by clicking on it once. Now what you are telling FileMaker is that, when you type the last name in the Last Name field in the Tour Order file, FileMaker should begin its search in the WTGT Client List file for the same information.

- **What it says:** matches a value in:
  What it means: Where should FileMaker look in the WTGT Client List to find the same information that has been typed into the Last Name field in Tour Order? In other words, what field in WTGT Client List has the same information that is in the Tour Order? We chose the Last Name field because we knew that would be one of the fields in which the two files would have common information. Select the Last Name field by clicking on it once. Now FileMaker knows that the cycle is complete, and the OK button is now active.

To switch the dialog around a little, FileMaker tries to complete the lookup in this manner: When you type in data in the _____ (field), FileMaker should look in the

_____ (field) for the same data. If FileMaker finds a match it should then take the information from _____ (field) and place it in the _____ (field). For those of us who could never get the hang of math word problems, this one can be a real zinger!

When FileMaker looks into a lookup file for a match, case sensitivity and punctuation are ignored. Text in a number field is also ignored.

Click OK now to exit the Lookup dialog box. You will then have to quit through the Entry Options dialog box and then the Field Definition dialog box before you are back to your current file, Tour Order.

To test the Lookup command we have just created, let's go to the Browse mode and create a new record. Because your date is now auto-entered, your next tab stop will be the Salesperson field. Select one of the names from the list tab again and you will be placed in the First Name field. Enter Dennis in this field, and then Marshall in the Last Name field. In your Lookup command, you told FileMaker to look for the Customer Number when the Last Name was entered. As soon as you tap the Tab key after entering the last name, FileMaker has indeed gone through the lookup by looking in the WTGT Client List records for the same last name as Marshall. Once it found that last name in the WTGT Client List, it took the Customer Number from the WTGT Client List, and placed the same number in the Tour Order Client List field.

Because other data in the WTGT Client List file on Marshall could be used in the Tour Order, you can also set up more lookups to place the entire address in the appropriate fields. Without going through the entire exercise again, here are the correct lookups to have FileMaker put the address in the Tour Order record as soon as you type the last name (the fields to be selected are indicated by italics):

Address Field
Copy into: Address
from "WTGT Client List": *Address*
when what is typed in: *Last Name*
matches a value in: *Last Name*

City Field
Copy into: City
from "WTGT Client List": *City*
when what is typed in: *Last Name*
matches a value in: *Last Name*

State Field
Copy into: State
from "WTGT Client List": *State*
when what is typed in: *Last Name*
matches a value in: *Last Name*

Zip Field
Copy into: Zip
from "WTGT Client List": *Zip*
when what is typed in: *Last Name*
matches a value in: *Last Name*

Phone Field
Copy into: Phone
from "WTGT Client List": *Phone*
when what is typed in: *Last Name*
matches a value in: *Last Name*

Further Examples

This example was actually a relatively simple lookup for FileMaker to handle. There are many, many uses for this feature. You could, for example, create another file for your Tour Description. Then, instead of having to type in the tour description into that field, you could have FileMaker look at the Tour Number and insert the correct Tour Description.

 You cannot have FileMaker look for information in a *repeating field*. The field where the information is placed can be a repeating field, such as in the case of Tour Description, but the records that FileMaker goes to look for the information cannot.

A lookup could also be created for a real estate office to look at the address and then look up the correct picture of the house at that address and place that picture in the current layout. You can have lookups for form letters, product pictures, or even Social Security numbers. You can use a lookup on any type of field except a summary field or a calculation field. That means that you can use date, text, number, and picture fields for lookups.

Lookups don't have to be restricted to looking up information contained in another file. You can use a lookup in the same file where you have a record with duplicating fields such as a Bill to name and address and a Ship to name and address. It can be set up so that if the name in Ship to matches the name in Bill to, then the address in Ship to will be automatically filled in.

Lookup Tips

One thing that might be a bit confusing to some is that FileMaker can only look in one place at one time in order to complete a lookup. If FileMaker cannot find the data it needs in the field or fields you have specified, it stops there. There is no warning that no match is found, it just doesn't "fill in the gaps" so to speak. For example, if you type a last name in your Tour Order record that is not included in the WTGT Client List, FileMaker will not fill out the customer number and address fields. You would either have to enter that information into the WTGT Client List, or manually fill out those fields in the Tour Order.

The main reason for some of this confusion is the button entitled Switch Lookup File on the Lookup dialog box. If you look back at Fig. 3-17, you'll see that button next to the phrase If a value is not found, then:. You might think that it is saying, "If a value is not found, then switch lookup file," but it is not. You use the Switch Lookup button only when you actually want to change the file where FileMaker is conducting its lookups. If you change the name of the file that FileMaker is using in its lookups, you would then use the Switch Lookup to choose that new file name.

To make lookups easier, make sure that the lookup file is located in the same folder as the current file. If FileMaker cannot find the file it is looking for, it will ask for the location of the file when it conducts its lookup. Which brings us to the next item on the list. What does that phrase If a value is not found do? That is one more option on the lookup tray for FileMaker to consider in conducting its lookups.

Usually, if FileMaker cannot find the data it's looking for, you have FileMaker give up and not do anything. That is indicated by the default radio button, don't copy. If FileMaker can't find the information, then don't copy anything into the field. The section option copy using next lower value is used when you are working with a lookup file that contains a range of values. That can be anything from A to BBB for a credit rating perhaps, or salary range in a personnel report. What FileMaker does in that case is, if the figure you type in does not exactly match the figure in the lookup file, then FileMaker should insert the next lowest value that *is* in the lookup file. For example, you want FileMaker to insert the correct credit rating for Company XYZ. You type in the figure $35,000,000, but there is no such number in the lookup file. The lookup file does have the figures $40,000,000 and $30,000,000, however. Because FileMaker cannot find the figure $35,000,000, it will look at the next lower value, which is $30,000,000, in order to complete its lookup. In this instance, FileMaker considers the next lower value to be the next lower number, the next earlier date, or the next letter that is alphabetically before the one you entered.

CONCLUSION

You can see that FileMaker gives you great control over the appearance of your data as well as the ability to control data entry. With the ability to look up information in other files, you can make light work of otherwise onerous cross referencing. Chapter 6 has more examples of lookups. In the next chapter, we examine the many options you have when it comes to laying out your FileMaker forms.

4
The Look of Layouts

IN THE PREVIOUS CHAPTERS, we have discussed how fields control the data within FileMaker and how the data within those fields is presented both on your screen and in printed form. Both the fields and the data are controlled by the Layout command. Because today's business environment stresses high standards of visual quality in presentations and reports, it is important that you "lay out" your facts and figures graphically and effectively. FileMaker gives you the flexibility to control both your data, and the look of your data.

THE POWER OF THE LAYOUT

Let's say you have a very simple database with six fields: name, address, city, state, zip, and phone number. With just those fields, you could create many different layouts as shown in Fig. 4-1.

You have a phone list that is alphabetized by last name, one that is grouped by zip, one for the people named Dinkelhoffer, and so on. The layout does nothing to change the data in these different formats. It does, however, control how your data is viewed on the screen or printed. The manner in which you present your data on the computer screen or printed on paper creates a visual impact. If the layout is attractive as well as legible, it gives the reader a positive attitude about your data.

FileMaker vs. the Others

Some database programs limit the presentation of your data to a specific number of formats, and multiple layouts are difficult to handle. Some databases require you, in

Alphabetical Client Phone List

First Name	Last Name	Company Name	Phone
Charlie	Brown	Peanuts	702-555-1212
Dudley	Dinklehoffer	D & D Drums	305-555-1212
Dressa	Dinklehoffer	D & D Drums	305-555-1212
Clarissa	Dinklehoffer	D & D Drums	305-555-1212
Clem	Dinklehoffer	D & D Kettles	305-555-1212

Client Address List by Zip

Company	Address	City	State	Zip
Sleep Sound	789 Market	New York	NY	01000
Reculver Inc	1 Beech Tree	London	CT	01800
Eagle	300 Ura Court	Orlando	FL	32700
Rocky Road	12 Shady Lane	Minneapolis	MN	50000
D & D Drums	123 Beatit St	Percussion	IL	54000
D & D Drums	123 Beatit St	Percussion	IL	54000
D & D Drums	123 Beatit St	Percussion	IL	54000
D & D Kettles	123 Beatit St	Percussion	IL	54000
Good Apple	789 Blossom	Treesweet	WA	80000

Dinklehoffers

Last Name	First	Company	State	Phone	Customer #
Dinklehoffer	Bubba	D & D Drums	IL	904-555-1212	1007
Dinklehoffer	Sharon	D & D Drums	IL	904-555-1212	1008
Dinklehoffer	Horatio	D & D Drums	IL	904-555-1212	1009
Dinklehoffer	Clem	D & D Kettles	IL	305-555-1212	1010

Fig. 4-1. Three layouts within the same database.

effect, to recreate the same database over and over to allow for different layouts. File-Maker places no such limitations on you. You can create as many layouts per database as you have storage space on your disk.

Creating new layouts in FileMaker is so easy, that if you have one person in your office who likes the sales report "this way" and another who likes reports "that way," you can create customized layouts for those two people. Both people will get the same data but in different views. It's much like walking on the left side of the street as opposed to the right side. You still see the same street and the same buildings, but you are viewing the surroundings from different perspectives.

Although we don't actually recommend that you create different layouts for different people just because they like things that way, we can accept that the real business world is often full of duplication and contradictions. You are the best judge as to what type of layouts you will need.

The Layout Tools

FileMaker assists you in creating layouts by providing you with several tools and commands that are unique to the Layout mode. You'll notice that when you are in the Layout mode, the Gadgets menu becomes active.

In FileMaker Pro, the Gadgets menu is replaced by the Layout menu.

The T-square found on the Gadgets menu gives you the control of exact measurements on the page when placement of your fields and objects is critical.

In addition to the T-square, you'll be using the Toolbox quite a bit. The Toolbox is only available in the Layout mode. The purpose of the Toolbox is to change the function of your pointer to allow for the insertion of text, and the drawing of boxes and such, to give you more flexibility in arranging the "look" of your layout. You can also choose lines and patterns from the Format menu to add to your layout.

Again, as we've said before, don't rush yourself. In most cases, you'll find that the more thought that is put into your layout prior to its creation (that is, to rough it out on paper), the easier it will be in creating it on-screen. Allow yourself the time to be creative, and the time to experiment. For layout techniques unique to FileMaker Pro, see Chapter 11.

BITS AND PIECES

When you first create a new database file (after you have created all of your fields), FileMaker automatically provides you with the Standard layout so that you can get right to work. Because the Standard layout places all of your fields in a continuous column from top to bottom, you can begin data entry without having to spend extra time in preparing a layout. Many people find that the Standard layout works perfectly for data entry as the Standard layout includes all the fields that you have created in the order that you created them. All of the fields in a Standard layout are also labeled for your ease and convenience.

Before we go into any in-depth discussions on the different types of layouts, however, it is important to know about all the different "bits and pieces" that are used in the construction of a layout. Although some of this material might seem a bit basic because it has been covered in part in the preceding chapters, we encourage you to peruse this area.

Please remember that the following information refers to the screens and commands as shown in the Layout mode only. The Browse mode is only used in this chapter to illustrate the changes made while in the Layout mode. Figure 4-2 shows you some of the items included by default in the Standard layout.

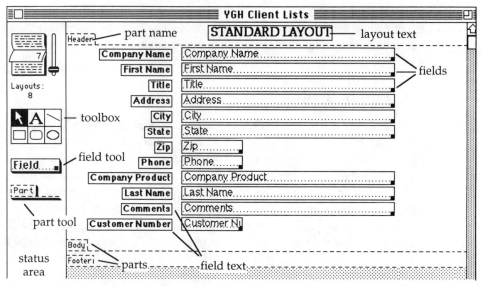

Fig. 4-2. Notation of Standard layout items.

Fields

Fields are the basic building blocks of any database. Without the fields, there is no database. In the Layout mode, the fields are represented on your layout by a solid-line box which has the name of the field inside it (as opposed to the label name you may have given the field). Certain field formatting commands are unique to the Layout mode.

Although you can format the font, font size, and font style while in the Browse mode, you can only format the appearance of dates and numbers, and their alignment, and so on while in Layout mode. Fields can also be resized and moved around the layout at will only while in the Layout mode.

It would do you good to remember that fields are *transparent*. That is, if you place a field on an area of the layout that you have shaded with a fill pattern, when you go back to the Browse mode, that fill pattern will *show through* the field and possibly obliterate the information within that field. This is not necessarily evident on the screen while you are in the Layout mode because the field is *not transparent* in that view. It takes a some trial and error with FileMaker before you get comfortable with this apparent oddity. In Fig. 4-3, you can see an example of how a fill pattern has obscured the information within some fields. (There is more on fill patterns later in this chapter.)

There are no real restrictions as to the placement of your fields on a layout. The placement of fields is usually within the Body part, but fields can be placed in other parts of the layout to affect the display of the data that the fields contain. This is especially true of summary fields. In Fig. 4-4, you can see an example of a layout with multiple parts.

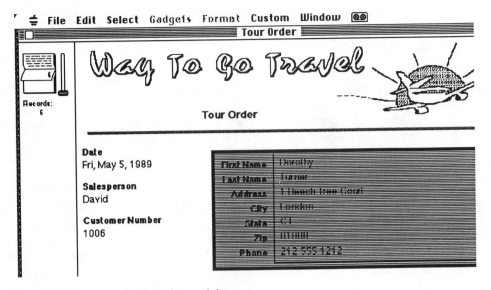

Fig. 4-3. Fill pattern that has obscured data.

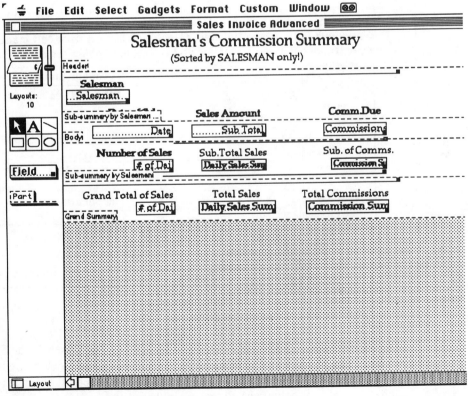

Fig. 4-4. A typical layout with multiple parts.

The most important thing to remember is that you place your fields in a logical order on the layout. If you need further information on what fields do, please refer back to Chapter 3.

Layout Text

Layout text can be added to any part of the layout and is considered a *graphic object* by FileMaker. Layout text differs from text in a field (your data) in that the layout text is not indexed. Therefore, layout text cannot be included in any Sort or Find commands. For example, if you have named a field in the field definitions as First Name, but your layout text has been used to label that field as Name, as shown in Fig. 4-5, you must use the proper field name: First Name, in any Sort or Find commands.

The main usage of layout text is to label fields, or areas of the layout, or to add instructions and explanations to a layout. In Fig. 4-5, you can see a data entry screen where layout text has been used to offer the operator certain instructions. This is very useful in an office where many people are sharing the same computer. It also lessens the training time required to get a newly hired employee up to speed.

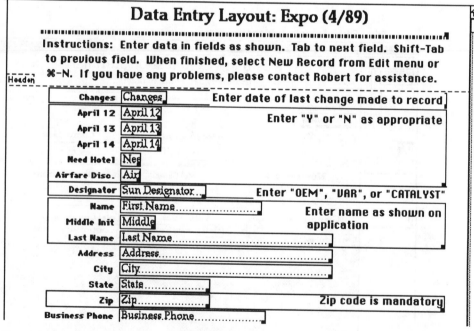

Fig. 4-5. Layout text used as instruction/explanation.

In some layouts, layout text is automatically added by FileMaker. In the Standard layout, the layout text is added to label the fields (the field labels and the field names will be the same, unless you change them). In the Columnar report, layout text is also added by FileMaker as column headings, but no layout text is added by FileMaker for the Label layout or a Blank layout.

Layout text can be added to any layout by using the text tool in the Toolbox (the letter A). Clicking your pointer on the text tool changes your pointer to an I-beam. The I-beam is then used as an insertion point. Any text that is typed in one continuous line on a layout is considered *one object* by FileMaker. If you tap the Return key while typing text on a layout, FileMaker will consider the text on the next line as a separate item. In Fig. 4-6, you can see how layout text on multiple lines is treated as multiple items.

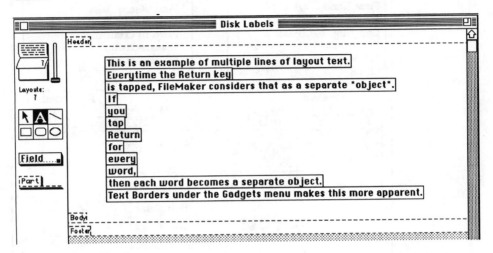

Fig. 4-6. Multiple lines of layout text.

Layout text can be formatted, by using the commands under the Format menu, with any font, font size, or style that you have installed in your System. When you select the text tool, your text will reflect the font, font size, and style that has been selected in the Format menu.

 If you have a number of different fonts and styles on your layout and you want to add some layout text in one of those formats, you can do so without having to go to the Format menu first. First, select the text already on your layout that has the type of font or style that you want before clicking the text tool. When the text tool has been selected, the text you had selected will no longer be highlighted. But, when you begin typing, your font and style will be the same as the text you selected on the other area of the layout.

If you need to change or edit any text on the layout, the text tool must be selected first. If you use the pointer instead of the I-beam to select the text, you have not enabled the text tool and will only be able to move the text, delete it, or change the font attributes. Conversely, you do not need to choose the text tool to change the font style, font size, or style. That can be done with the pointer and, actually, it's a good way to experiment with fonts to get an idea of which font attributes work best for what you are trying to do.

From an artistic sense, the best graphic artists will tell you that it is not a good idea to mix too many different font styles on one page. As interesting to the eye it might be, it is usually not as legible as it could be. And, if you are working on data

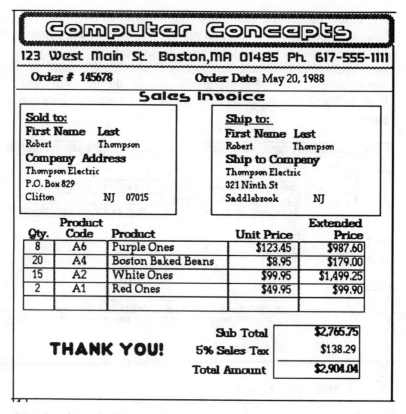

Fig. 4-7. A layout with a good combination of fonts.

entry, the combination can actually be a distraction and an irritation. In Fig. 4-7, you can see a good example of a layout that incorporates both stylistic fonts for interest and bookface fonts for legibility.

On the other hand, Fig. 4-8 is a layout we found in a corporate office that looks as if the designer tried to use every font style available in his System (the name has been changed to protect the guilty).

You can also copy and paste layout text from one layout to another. Bear in mind that cutting items from a layout can permanently affect that layout.

Suppose that a particular piece of layout text was difficult for you to create, and you want to place that same text on another layout. Because you can have more than one file open at a time in FileMaker, simply open the file that has the text you wish to copy and then make sure you are in the Layout mode. With the pointer select the layout text that you want to copy and then choose Copy from the Edit menu. Now you either close that file or switch to the one into which you want to paste the copied text. Choose Paste from the Edit menu. What you will get is the exact same piece of layout text from the other layout, which will be placed about dead center in the current layout. You can then move this text to the appropriate area.

Once you have used the copy-and-paste method to add layout text, it is still considered layout text (rather than a picture or graphic). You can change its placement and

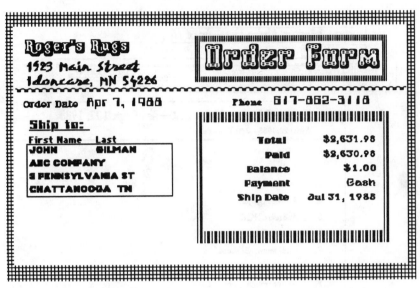

Fig. 4-8. Going for baroque with fonts.

attributes just as you would with any other layout text. Note that the layout text that you cut/copy from another layout will be pasted onto your layout with the same attributes as it had on the other layout (the same font and size, and so on). You cannot cut/copy layout text and select a different font, for example, from the Format menu before pasting. All changes will have to be done after the pasting. You can only cut and paste layout text from Layout mode to the Layout mode. You cannot cut or copy layout text from the Browse mode.

If you need to delete or clear text in a layout, you may use either the text tool or the pointer to select the text and then use the commands in the Edit menu. Alternatively you can select the text and tap the Delete key. If you use the pointer to select text, you can only select an entire line of layout text at a time and then can use your Delete key, or you can choose Cut or Clear from the Edit menu.

If you need to edit the text in some manner, you must use the text tool. With the text tool, you can double click to select one word; click and drag to select an entire line or section, or you can click inside the text to get an insertion point.

Special Symbols

You can type special symbols on a layout with the text tool to date stamp or time stamp your layout automatically, add page numbers, or count your records. These symbols are:

Page number	##	(two number signs)
Date stamp	//	(two slashes)
Time stamp	::	(two colons)
Record counter	@@	(two "at" symbols)

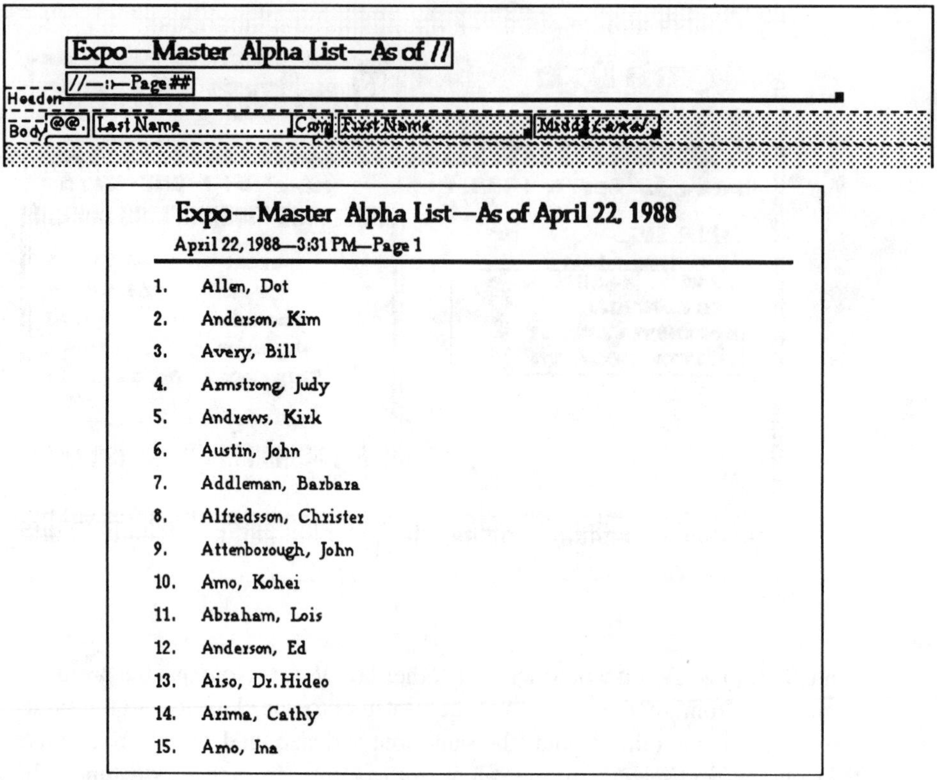

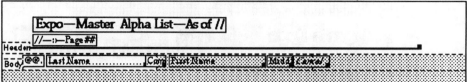

Fig. 4-9. Special symbols on the layout and results in Browse mode.

In Fig. 4-9, you can see these symbols in the Layout mode at the top and the resulting change in the Browse mode.

These symbols do not have the same effect if typed in a field in the Browse mode.

The page number symbol may be formatted with Format number in the Format menu and the date stamp symbol can be formatted with Format date. Remember, though, if you format your date to appear like Sunday, June 4, 1989, there must be enough space on the layout for this date to appear. If you have chosen the long version of the date format, the actual date may run over your fields or other objects on the layout. All of these symbols can be formatted by font, font size, and style as well.

GRAPHIC TOOLS AND PICTURES

With the drawing tools provided by FileMaker in the Toolbox, you can add lines, boxes, circles, ovals, and round-edged boxes to your layout. You can also add various effects with fill patterns and can change the width and pattern of the lines, boxes, and so on. When you select the drawing tools from the Toolbox, the pointer becomes a cross (+). The object is then drawn with a click and drag across the area required.

The Line Tool

The line tool is symbolized in the Toolbox by the slanted line. When selected, the pointer changes into a cross, and you draw your line by clicking on the starting point and dragging to the end point and then releasing. When drawing a straight vertical or horizontal line, make sure the line is straight before releasing, as it will appear jagged on your screen if it is not exactly lined up (hold down Option while drawing). The resulting line will have a handle at one end. The handle is usually on the right side of the line if you have drawn it from left to right, and vice versa. This is not a hard and fast rule, however, and sometimes the handle is on the opposite side.

You can change the handle from one side to another by grabbing it and dragging the line to the other side. Of course, you can always delete that line and draw a new one as well.

If you are drawing a line on an angle, the line might appear broken or jagged on your screen, but it will print as a solid line. If you have drawn a line that is not exactly as long as you'd like, too short, or not even, you do not need to delete the line and start over. You can click on the arrow tool and then move the line into position by using its handle. You can make it longer or shorter, or change the angle of the slant. You can also move the line as is to a new position by clicking on it with the arrow tool and moving it to the correct placement. If you need to align your line with a box or other object, the line will appear to merge with the edge of the object it is being aligned to.

Please remember that the line tool is very different from the Underline selection of the Style command in the Format menu. You can only select Underline for use within a field. That is, if you want the data within a field to appear as underlined, you would format that particular field to Underline. All the data within that field would then appear underlined, no matter how long the data. The line tool, however, can be used within a field, but its length will remain static. Therefore, any data past the length of the line would not appear to be underlined. A more realistic usage of the lines would be for borders to add interest and to separate different sections of the layout as shown in Fig. 4-10.

With the Format menu, you can change the width of your lines. You have a choice of eight line widths, including None and Hairline. You can also choose the width of your line before you draw it, or afterwards.

You might be hard put to find a use for the None width. This is generally used when you are working with filled shapes such as rectangles and do not want an edge around the filling. When you are just drawing lines, there is probably just one use for the None width. If you are experimenting with a design and want to see what it would look like if a particular line was not there, you can assign the width None and the line will seem to disappear. Select a width other than None and the line returns to view. This is an alternative to Cut followed by Undo.

When you use the Hairline width setting for a line there does not seem to be any difference *on the screen* between the narrowest line in the menu and Hairline, but there is a difference when you print the design. The Hairline width prints about half the width of the next narrowest line in the menu.

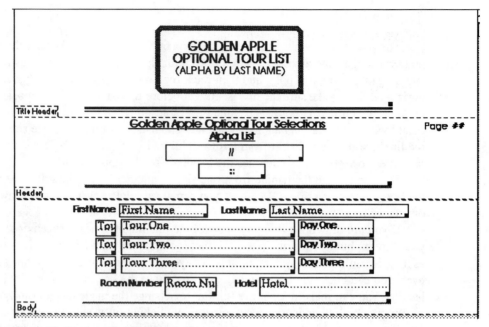

Fig. 4-10. Lines used as borders and separations.

In addition to being able to adjust the widths of your lines, you are also able to select line patterns. There are 24 patterns to choose from, including None and White. The None pattern is actually the absence of any pattern, and is therefore invisible. This option is used when working with filled objects such as rectangles, and you want the line around the object to have a different pattern from the filling.

The White pattern (indicated by the blank box in the Pattern menu, with no words within it) is indeed a white pattern. Not all of the patterns show up on your screen or print very well, particularly when using the narrower line width. For the best view of these patterns, you must use the wider lines as shown in Fig. 4-11.

When you draw a line and have chosen either the None pattern or the White pattern, the only indication of the line you see on the screen (when the line is not selected), is the handle. You cannot always tell by looking at the line whether or not it is None or White, but you can select it and then go to the Line Pattern menu. The pattern that has been chosen for that particular line will be check-marked in the menu. Also, if a line with a White pattern crosses a solid object, you will see the White obscuring the underlying object.

Indeed, the white line comes in very handy when you need to draw lines that will show up against another pattern. In Fig. 4-12, a box was drawn using the box drawing tool; the box was filled with a fill pattern (different from a line pattern), and then white lines of varying widths were drawn across it to create the illusion shown. The neatest thing about using the White line pattern is that you don't have to worry about exact placement in relationship to the edges of the box. Because the paper is white, any excess white lines drawn on the layout will not show up when printed! You can get

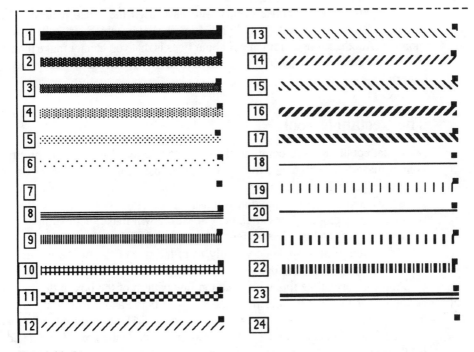

Fig. 4-11. Line patterns.

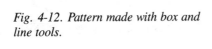

Fig. 4-12. Pattern made with box and line tools.

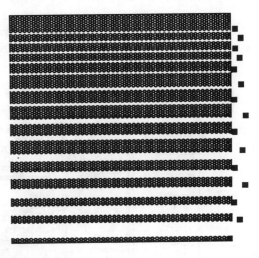

the same result by drawing boxes of varying sizes and changing the fill pattern in those boxes, but aligning them can be a real chore.

Given all this, it is good to remember that lines are *not* transparent in the same way that the fields are. In other words, if you put a very thick line of any pattern into (as opposed to under) a field box, that pattern takes priority over the data within the field. When you change to the Browse mode, the data will be obliterated by the thick line in the field. This applies even if you have used the White pattern. There is a method in which you can "highlight" certain fields which we will discuss in a moment. Another thing to remember about lines is that you cannot make them connect up to make a true box. Your drawing might look like a box, but it will not accept a fill pattern.

The Rectangle Tool

What could be more common than a rectangle tool for any Mac program? The pointer maybe? The rectangle tool is, of course, used for drawing boxes on your layout. When you select the rectangle tool, the pointer becomes a cross (+). You use the same click and drag technique that you use for drawing lines, only you don't have to worry about getting the lines straight. FileMaker will make them straight, no matter what the size of the box. The rectangle tool is used to draw boxes around a group of fields that you want to separate visually from the rest of the fields, to enclose a picture, or to add interest and designs to your layout.

You can format the line width and the line pattern of the box in the same manner as you do for the line; by selecting Line Width or Line Pattern from the Format menu. You can also fill the box with a pattern by selecting Fill Pattern from the Format menu. You can add a fill pattern either before or after you draw the box. If you decide to add a fill pattern after the box has been drawn, select the box with the arrow and then choose Fill Pattern from the Format menu, and you're all set. Choose None as the Line Pattern to create a rectangle of shading without drawn edges. Choose None as the Fill Pattern to create a rectangle that is transparent.

An example of a layout (in the Browse mode) that has made good use of boxes and fill patterns to create interest in the layout is shown in Fig. 4-13.

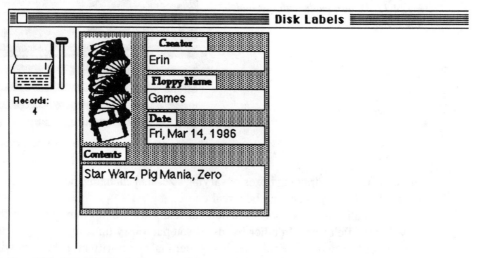

Fig. 4-13. Label design in Browse mode.

In this example, the layout is used for labeling floppy disks. Notice that the fields that contain the data are not obscured by the fill patterns. The method in which this was accomplished was to lay one pattern on top of another and to utilize a pattern which would allow the data in the fields to show through. In this case, the background pattern was created first, and then the boxes for the fields were created with the White fill pattern and then laid on top of the background pattern. The field boxes were then laid in the white boxes so that the data in the fields was *on top* of the White pattern.

The design in Fig. 4-13 is shown in Layout mode in Fig. 4-14, which is shown larger so you can see the borders of the boxes and fields.

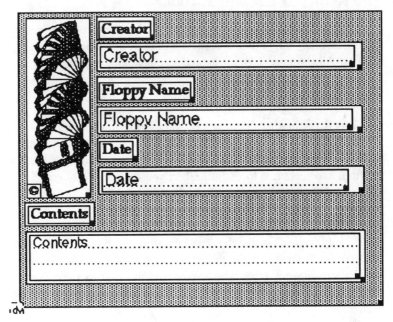

Fig. 4-14. Label design in Layout mode.

We purposefully made the boxes larger than the actual field box for ease in finding the graphics box. You can place the graphics box exactly on top of the field box, but that creates problems. If you place a box exactly on top of the field box, the lines merge and so does the handle. In other words, you won't be able to tell the field box and the graphics box apart.

The only way out of this dilemma is to select an area and drag the object away from the other. There's no telling which will come away first—the field box or the graphics box—but the two will separate. So, it's best to give yourself some leeway by making your graphics box slightly larger than the field box. Because the field box won't be seen in print, it doesn't matter that the graphics box is larger, anyway.

Putting together a layout like Fig. 4-14 can get quite time consuming and, at times, frustrating. But the results are usually worth the trouble. This particular layout has nine boxes. There is one box around each bit of layout text, one box around each field box, and the largest box which is the size of the label. We created the largest box first, with the fill pattern. The layout text was created next, outside the large box, with the Gadgets option of Text Borders to help in the alignment of the boxes around the layout text. The fields were also brought in outside of the large box. The White fill pattern was selected before we created the boxes used to surround the layout text and the fields. Once all those boxes were created, they were laid on the large box, utilizing the T-square Gadget, with the Invisible Grid off. As we mentioned, it takes some time in lining up all these parts, but in the end you have quite an attractive layout.

The Rounded Rectangle Tool

The rounded rectangle tool works exactly as the regular rectangle tool, with the only difference being that the corners will be rounded instead of at right angles to one another. All the same formatting and size changing aspects apply.

The Oval Tool

This is yet another drawing tool you can use to add interest to your layouts, creating oval and circle shapes. This tool behaves a bit differently than you might expect, however. When you select the oval tool, the pointer becomes a cross as it does with the line tool and rectangle tool. But, when you draw the oval (or circle), a box appears with an oval inside of it. Now of what use is that? You would expect there just to be an oval, wouldn't you? The box is a bit misleading because you would expect the box to appear when you go back to the Browse mode. However, when you go to the Browse mode, only the oval is visible. The box around the oval is only visible in the Layout mode and will not appear in the Browse mode or in print. Because FileMaker is not really a drawing program, the box around the oval in the Layout mode serves as a handle for resizing rather than the multiple handles you might see on an oval in a drawing program.

The line width, line pattern, and fill pattern can be used with the oval tool as they are used with the rectangle tool. You can lay ovals within ovals, ovals within boxes, and so on. Figure 4-15 is a rough example of some of the effects you can get by mixing the various drawing tools, patterns, and line widths.

Pictures and Other Graphics

In addition to being able to draw certain objects on the layout, you can also add pictures, or graphics, to the layout through the use of Cut, Copy, and Paste. Any object that is added to the layout through cutting and pasting from another application, is considered a graphic object by FileMaker. The most common graphic objects you will see on a layout (or that you will add to a layout) are a company logo, fancy borders, and drawn figures.

As far as the drawing of pictures goes, the drawing capabilities of FileMaker are quite limited, so elaborate drawings are better made in a draw/paint program such as MacPaint, MacDraw, Canvas, or even a desk accessory like DeskPaint. Scanned

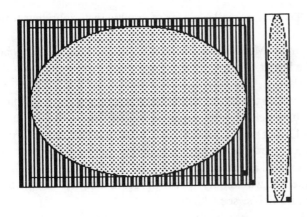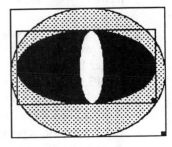

Various designs in Layout mode

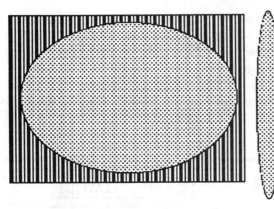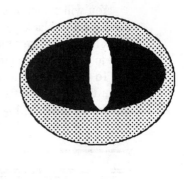

The result in Browse mode

Fig. 4-15. Mixing them up.

images will also work on the layout. The original format of the picture can be TIFF, PICT, or even EPS.

Note that when FileMaker imports pictures for a layout, the format is not retained, and changes cannot be made to the pictures while in FileMaker. If you wish to change a picture, you must make those changes in the appropriate drawing program, and then use Cut and Paste once again to place it on your layout.

To bring in a picture from another application, you must start with that application. Select the picture and then cut or copy it. Open the Scrapbook, and paste the picture in the Scrapbook. Close the application; open your FileMaker file, and go to the layout (you cannot paste a picture in the Browse mode, unless you are pasting to a picture field). Then paste the picture on the layout. The picture will be placed approximately in the center of the layout. You can then resize it with the handles if necessary, and move it to the proper location.

Note that your ability to cut and paste pictures might be limited by the amount of memory your Mac has. Try to use smaller pieces of graphic material rather than large images.

If you are working under MultiFinder, there is no need to use the Scrapbook to place your pictures on the layout. First, Cut, or Copy your picture, switch to your File-Maker layout, and then Paste.

Pictures that are placed on the layout will be seen in every record. Graphics that are to be placed in a picture field should be placed in that field while in the Browse mode (as opposed to the Layout mode), and can only be seen in that record. For example, if you paste a picture of a tree on the layout, then that tree would be seen in every record. But, if you have created a picture field, and you paste the picture of the tree in record number 7, then the tree would only appear in record number 7 and none of the others. For more on picture fields, see Chapter 10.

The Field Tool

You will sometimes find that achieving a complex layout design is best done by starting with a blank layout and adding fields later. You might find that removing some fields helps you work more easily with the graphic tools. The field tool can then be used to place fields on the layout.

To use the field tool, grab it with the arrow tool and drag it to the area of the layout that you want the field to appear. When you release the mouse, a dialog box appears as shown in Fig. 4-16.

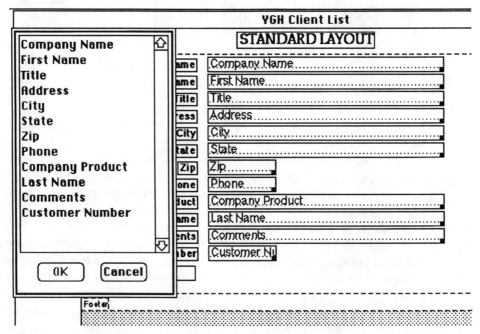

Fig. 4-16. The Field Tool dialog box.

This dialog box gives you a list of all the fields that have been created, and you are to then choose one of these fields from that list. As soon as you choose the appropriate field, that field name will appear in a field box on your layout. You are then able to move it about or change its attributes as you would normally.

When you bring in a field with the field tool, only the field names are shown; not the field types or definitions. If you are unsure of the name of the field you want to place on the layout, check it in the Field Definition screen by choosing Define from the Select menu.

The Part Tool

The part tool places the various parts available on the layout. The tool is used in much the same way as the field tool: by dragging the tool to the layout and then releasing. The dialog boxes for the part tool vary, depending on where in the layout the part is placed, and what other parts already exist. The parts and their dialog boxes are discussed in more detail later in this chapter.

USING GADGETS

As mentioned previously, the Gadgets menu becomes active only when in the Layout mode. As the drawing capabilities of FileMaker are quite limited, the gadgets assist you in aligning objects on the layout page.

The T-Square

You might expect to find this tool in the status area, but it is a Gadgets menu item. However, when you select the T-square tool, its icon appears in the lower left corner of the status area in the form of two arrows, along with a measurement guide in inches, and a magnet, as shown in Fig. 4-17.

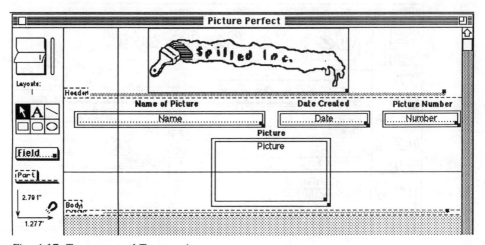

Fig. 4-17. T-squares and T-square icon.

In addition to the icon, the T-square itself also appears on the layout itself in the form of a giant cross that intersects dead center in the middle of your screen.

Actually you have two T-squares: one horizontal and one vertical. Each one can be moved independently of the other by placing the arrow on any part of it *outside of an object*, and dragging the line to the location you want. You have to be very certain that you have a hold of one of the T-square lines outside of an object before you move it, or you will move that object or something else on the layout page instead.

Sometimes, when your layout is full of fields and other objects, the T-squares can get lost in the jungles of lines. If you get caught in such a fix just remember that the T-squares intersect in the dead center of your screen and extend past the right edge and the bottom edge of the page. If you cannot locate your T-squares in the middle of the screen, or don't want to move the fields located there, scroll to the right side or the bottom of your layout, and you'll quickly locate your T-square line. You can then grab and drag your T-square to the needed location on your layout.

The T-square is used to measure the horizontal and vertical axes of the layout and is extremely useful for placing fields, text, pictures, and so on in an exact position on the layout. For example, if you are creating a layout that will fill in the blanks on a preprinted form such as a loan application, and the name field is placed 3″ down from the top and 1.25″ from the left, you can move your T-squares to those same positions and place your field in the correct space. The spacing is indicated in the status area and is correct to $1/72$″.

When the magnet in the status area is turned on (the magnet is black and has little lines radiating from it), the T-squares "suck" the field or object right to them. It really is a funny thing to watch! To toggle the magnet on or off, just click on the magnet with the pointer. When it is "off," the magnet will appear white and will not have the "magnetic field" radiating from the bottom of it. Figure 4-18 gives an example of a field being attracted to the T-square, and the exact measurements of the location of the top of the object and the right side of the object.

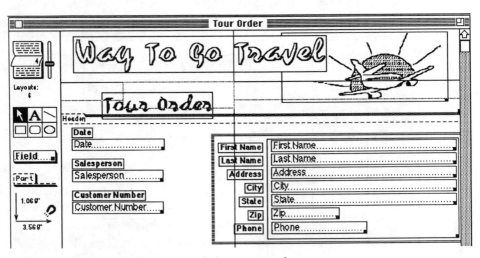

Fig. 4-18. T-square with magnet on and object attracted.

The Invisible Grid

A kissing cousin of the T-square is the Invisible Grid. Because many Mac drawing programs have grids of some sort for alignment, FileMaker has an invisible one which divides the screen into sections $1/12''$ wide when the grid is "on." When the grid is on and you move an object, that object will line up with the grid. When the grid is on, the T-squares will move in $1/12''$ increments only. When you are moving objects around, the grid acts in much the same way as the T-square does, by pulling objects to the closest grid intersection. Because the default program in FileMaker is with the grid on, objects frequently "jump" from one intersection to the other when you are trying to position the object on the layout.

When the grid is "off," there still is an invisible grid of sorts, but its measurements are divided into $1/72''$ and the "jumping" of objects from one intersection to the next is not as visible. With the grid off, the T-squares then move at increments of $1/72''$ instead of $1/12''$. Objects can be aligned much more accurately with the grid off. You can temporarily turn the grid off when you are moving an object by holding down the Command ($\mathcal{H}$) key while you drag the object. When you use Command−drag, it does not affect the placement of other objects on the layout.

No icon or other indicator on the screen tells you whether or not the grid is on. There is also no way that we have found to change the default of the grid to off, rather than on. If you find that you are having a hard time placing an object in a certain position, check in the Gadgets menu to see if the grid is on because that might be the cause of your problems.

 When you are looking at a layout with the status area on the screen, remember that the layout screen is not shown in its entirety and the center of the layout in this view is not the center of the page. If you want to place objects in the center of the page, turn the status area off and widen your screen view by either clicking on the layout icon in the lower left, or by using Command−Shift−S to toggle the area off.

Text Borders

The last little layout helper is the Text Borders option from the Gadgets menu. When you select Text Borders, FileMaker places little boxes around any text found on the layout, and it is used to help you in lining up text. In FileMaker, when you are trying to align fields next to one another, you know you are "right on" when the edges of the two field boxes seemingly merge. The same holds true for the Text Borders. When you align your text with the Text Borders option, the surrounding boxes of any other object will "merge."

Without the Text Borders, it is difficult to know whether or not your placement of some text is in actual alignment with other text or fields, especially when you are aligning text across columns. When you use Text Border in addition with the T-squares, your positioning will be exact.

Although Text Borders option does put boxes around the text in a layout, those boxes are not a graphic and will not be seen in the Browse mode. Text Borders are used as an alignment tool only, and are not the same as using the rectangle tool to draw boxes around text. They are very handy to use when you are trying to align bits of layout text that have been cut and pasted from other areas.

 If you want to draw boxes around the text in exactly the same size as the text borders, the two edges of your rectangle-drawing cross (+) will merge with the text borders when your placement is exact. Then drag your rectangle tool to the opposite corner until the two edges of the cross merge with the opposite corner, and your box is then the same size as the text borders. You can later turn off the Text Borders option, and your graphic boxes will remain around your layout text.

THE READY-TO-WEAR LAYOUTS

For some people, designing layouts is not very high on the list of priorities when it comes to working with a database. For this reason, FileMaker includes three preset layouts for you to use immediately. This is extremely useful when the boss is pacing the room and indicating impatience for your report. If the boss is waiting for a report with columns, no problem, FileMaker has that all set for you. And, if the boss is itching for those mailing labels so you can make the five o'clock mail, again the preset label layout is there for you to use with a minimum amount of setup.

One thing to remember about layouts is, that even though a particular layout will not necessarily show all of the fields that have been defined, those fields are still in your database. Therefore, if you have a label layout with only the name, address, city, and zip, you can still sort those labels by a field that is not showing in your layout. You could sort those labels by the field Region, if you had defined a field as such, or you can sort the labels by the number of days overdue on account.

The Standard Layout

As we've mentioned previously, the original layout that FileMaker gives you is the Standard layout. This is the only layout that gives you *all* of your fields in the order that they were created. So, if you have been making many changes and adding layouts to your database, the easiest way to get a layout with all the fields on it is to create another Standard layout. Once you do that, FileMaker takes all the fields that were created in the beginning, plus all the newly defined fields, and places them on the layout in a straight line, from top to bottom of the screen. FileMaker will add the new fields to a new layout, but it will not automatically add them to an existing layout.

A Standard layout is defined as one including an empty Header part, a Body part with all the defined fields in it, and an empty Footer part. You could begin by naming this layout as the Standard Layout or Data Entry Screen as shown in Fig. 4-19.

You could, at this point paste your company's logo or letterhead in the Header. For the Footer, you might want to place the page number by typing the characters ## (two number symbols) in the Footer. If you do place the symbols for the page number in the Footer, remember that you can also format the number with the Format Number command. The same holds true for the date symbols, // (two forward slashes).

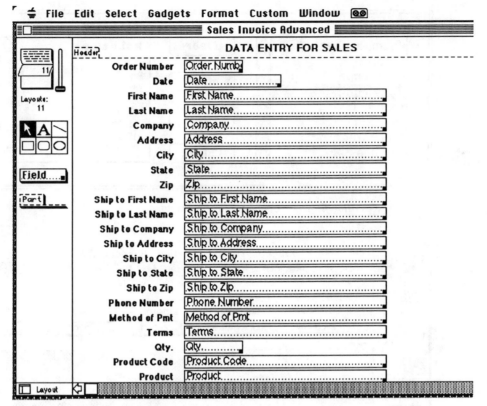

Fig. 4-19. The Standard layout.

The Columnar Report Layout

Sometimes all you need is a very simple layout like a phone list, a bad check list, or a list of items on sale. In FileMaker, this is very easy to do as FileMaker has a preset layout called Columnar report which lays out the fields you want in straight columns. When you tell FileMaker to create a Columnar report layout, the program asks you which fields you wish to have displayed on this layout, as shown in Fig. 4-20.

FileMaker then places the field labels (underlined) in the Header part, from right to left, in the order you had selected them. It also places the fields under the corresponding field label in the Body part. There is also a Footer part left blank for your use, if you care to use it. Your layout then resembles Fig. 4-21.

When your report is then printed or previewed, you will see the fields of each record placed in a tabular type report. You might have to change some of the field sizes as FileMaker makes all the fields approximately the same size on this layout.

Although there is no "maximum" number of fields you can have FileMaker move onto the Columnar report layout, you do have to take into account the size of the paper you are dealing with. You don't want to have more fields than will fit across the top of the page. If you do happen to pick more fields than can be placed on one line across

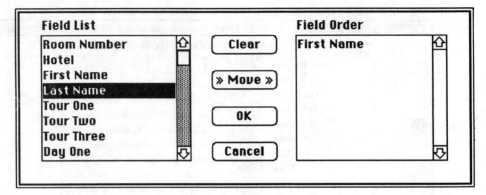

Fig. 4-20. Choosing fields for Columnar Report layout.

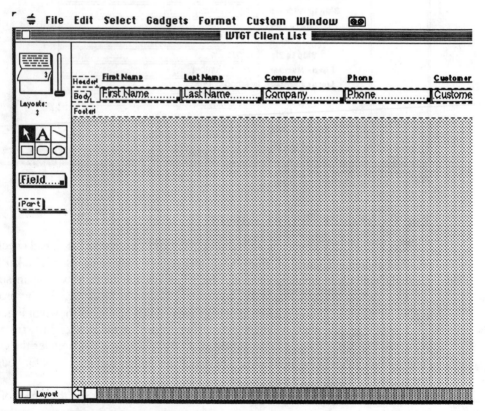

Fig. 4-21. Typical Columnar Report layout.

the top of the page, FileMaker won't tell you that you're in danger of adding too many fields. No, but what it will do is to continue placing those fields across the page, from right to left, in as many rows as it takes to accommodate all of your fields. In Fig. 4-22, you can see what happens when you put too many fields in your layout.

File Edit Select Gadgets Format Custom Window
WTGT Client List
Layouts:
4
First Name
Last Name
Title
Company
Address
Header
City
State
Zip
Phone
CustomerNumber
First Name
Last Name
Title
Company
Address
Body
City
State
Zip
Phone
Customer Numbe
Footer

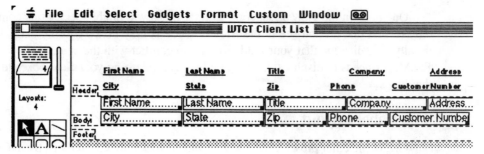

Fig. 4-22. Too many fields on Columnar Report layout.

Of course, all these fields could be resized and placed differently, but that defeats the ease and usefulness for which the Columnar report was designed.

View as List

One other slightly different action taken by FileMaker when it creates a columnar report is that it changes the view in the Browse mode. If you create a columnar report, and then take a look at the Gadgets menu, you'll find that the command View as list is check-marked. Up to this point, you have been looking at only one record at a time in the Browse command. Once View as list is selected, however, your screen in the Browse mode will let you see more than one record at a time as shown in Fig. 4-23.

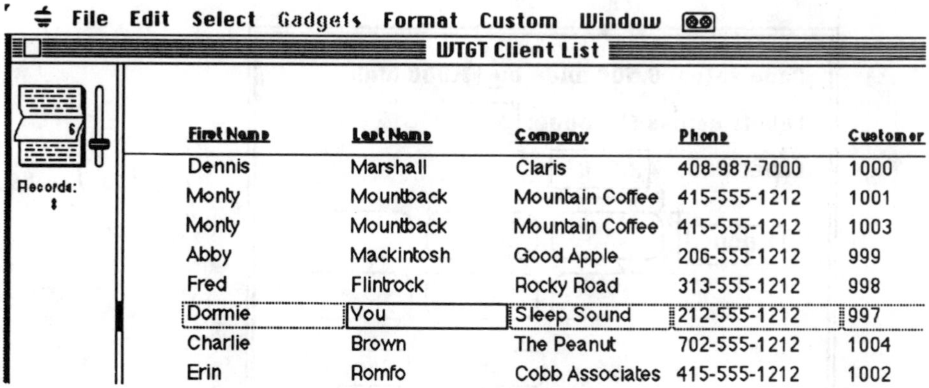

File Edit Select Gadgets Format Custom Window
WTGT Client List
Records:
8
First Name
Last Name
Company
Phone
Customer
Dennis Marshall Claris 408-987-7000 1000
Monty Mountback Mountain Coffee 415-555-1212 1001
Monty Mountback Mountain Coffee 415-555-1212 1003
Abby Mackintosh Good Apple 206-555-1212 999
Fred Flintrock Rocky Road 313-555-1212 998
Dormie You Sleep Sound 212-555-1212 997
Charlie Brown The Peanut 702-555-1212 1004
Erin Romfo Cobb Associates 415-555-1212 1002

Fig. 4-23. View As List in the Browse mode.

Whenever the View as list command is chosen, FileMaker will display as many records as can fit on a screen in the Browse mode. To indicate which record is the current, or active record, FileMaker adds a small column between the status area and the records screen, and in that column is a black line which appears next to the current record. That black line is the same size as the Body part of the layout; the larger the Body part, the larger the black line, and the fewer records are shown on one screen.

One note on the View as list command: at times you might specify this command only to find that all you see in the Browse mode is gray boxes with no data. This is usually an indication that your field sizes are in conflict with the amount of space that FileMaker needs to display this data in a list. Try enlarging your field boxes to see if that helps.

The Label Layout

One of the other preset layouts in FileMaker, which we covered briefly in Chapter 1, is the label layout. This is really a quite handy layout as it has many more uses than as simply a way of creating mailing labels. You can use this layout to create floppy disk labels, video cassette labels, name badges, message slips, and return address labels, for example. The label layout is good for any kind of repeating size that you want to print across and down a page.

Before you create a Label layout, you should first go to the Chooser in the Apple menu to make sure that you have the correct printer chosen. After you have done that, make sure that you check the Page Setup in the File menu. The dialog boxes you get with the Label layout are slightly different for the ImageWriter, for example, than they are for a laser printer. With an ImageWriter, you can use custom-size paper, whereas with a laser printer, everything has to be scaled to fit within an 8.5" × 11" format.

You create a label layout as you do with any other new layout, by choosing New Layout from the Edit menu, or by using Command–N. You are first asked for the size of the labels and the number across, as shown in Fig. 4-24.

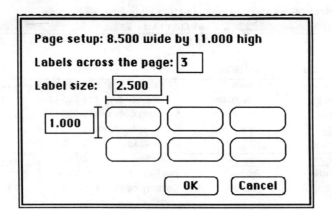

Fig. 4-24. *Label Size dialog box.*

You can specify any number across as will fit, but if your sizes and the number across don't jive with the page size, FileMaker figures that out and gives you the warning as shown in Fig. 4-25. You can either accept the labels as is, or go back and change the size.

As easy as creating labels might be with FileMaker, no label setup that we have found ever works perfectly on the first try, or even the third. The FileMaker labels are no exception. For one reason or another, things just never seem to line up exactly to begin with and there is a bit of fiddling around to do before you are ready for printing.

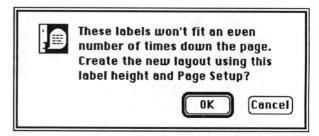

Fig. 4-25. Label size warnings.

Note that there is a blank Header part that is included in the Label layout. This part is crucial to your label sheet setup if your label pages have a blank strip at the top of the page as a page "starter" of sorts. The Header is usually just a bit smaller than the length of your label. If your label is one inch long, the Header is slightly less than an inch, and if your label is three inches long, the Header is just slightly less than three inches long. The length of the Header strip on most label pages we've used is about half an inch so you must change the size of the Header in order for your labels to fit properly on the page. Simply drag the Header up until you have the right length. If your labels start printing too far down from the top, it is usually because your Header is too large, rather than because your labels are incorrectly sized.

Notice also that one label area is white, and the rest of the labels to be printed across are grayed-out, and there is a horizontal dotted line to the right of the white layout area. If you move across your layout to the right margin, you will see positions of the other labels also have a dotted line at their margins (if you have more than one label across the page, that is). The dotted line to the right of the white layout area is movable. You can drag it right and left to adjust the width of your labels. This is the only way you can adjust the width of a Label layout without starting over from scratch. When you move this margin, the margins of the other labels across the page adjust themselves to match the white layout area.

For instance, suppose you had defined your labels as being 3 " across and then discover they are actually 4 " across. Simply drag the margin to the right until you have the right size, and the margin of next label over (in the gray area) will reflect the change exactly. There is no way to change the number of labels across without starting over, however. You cannot change from two across to three across without first creating a new Label layout.

One thing to remember about the Label layout is that FileMaker assumes that all the labels will be on the left margin of the page, therefore it prints from the left margin to the right. FileMaker has no command that will center the label in the middle of the layout page. You can move the label margin to the right page margin and then center your label in the middle of the page to get around this, though. This is important for feeding nonstandard size labels into a laser printer. Because the laser printers have a manual feed which centers nonstandard pages across the carriage, your layout must be in the center of the layout page or you will be printing on the roller instead of your labels.

After you have chosen the size of the labels correctly, you are asked to choose which fields you want placed in the labels. In the Columnar report layout, FileMaker lets you insert as many fields as you wanted without taking into account the size of the paper. With the Label layout, however, FileMaker will only let you move as many fields as FileMaker thinks can fit. If you try to choose more fields than FileMaker thinks will fit, you'll get a warning dialog as shown in Fig. 4-26.

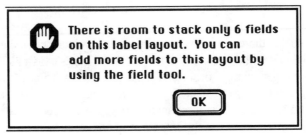

Fig. 4-26. Label warning dialog box, too many fields.

In our example, FileMaker would only allow six fields, but with larger labels, more fields are allowed. Once the layout is set, you can rearrange and resize the fields to suit your needs. Also, you can bring in more fields, if needed, with the field tool.

When placing fields on the label layout, the fields do not necessarily need to be placed entirely within the white layout area. At times, you might have to place a number of fields on one line, and they will not all fit without running into the gray area of the next label. This usually happens when you have City, State, and Zip fields all on one line. If you choose the Gadgets option of Slide objects, the data within those fields will slide to the left when printing and will then appear on the label as you wish. Figure 4-27 shows an example of this, with the result shown as it would print.

Remember that the top of those fields have to be in exact alignment in order for Slide object to work, and you can check the alignment with the T-square. Also, use Preview from the Edit menu to check to see that all of your data fits before you print.

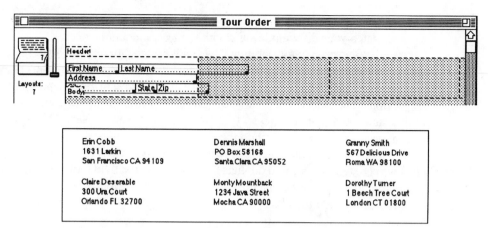

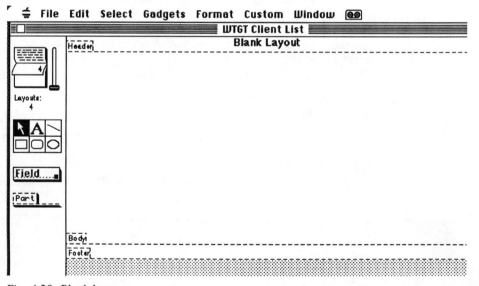

Fig. 4-27. Label layout with fields extending to gray area.

The Blank Layout

Need we say more? The Blank layout is exactly what it sounds like. With this option FileMaker gives you a layout with a Header, a Body that is approximately $3^1/2\,''$ long, and a Footer as shown in Fig. 4-28.

Fig. 4-28. Blank layout.

No fields are associated with this layout; it is left completely blank to allow you to use any fields and graphics you want. To place fields onto this layout, you bring them in with the field tool. You can also Cut and Paste fields from one layout to your blank layout to save you the step of using the field tool. This is especially useful when you are attempting to duplicate some areas of other layouts. Cut and Paste allows you to mix and match your different layouts with the least amount of fuss.

Use the Blank layout for defining new fields. As mentioned previously, when you define new fields, FileMaker places those new fields on the bottom of the current layout. The new fields are also in the default format of Geneva or Helvetica, regardless of the previously formatted fields on your layout. To avoid having to constantly change the format attributes of new fields, first create a new layout as Blank. Then, when you have to create new fields, switch to the Blank layout, define your fields, then return to the layout you were working on. In your current layout, click on a field on that layout with the type style you want to duplicate, and then use the field tool to bring in the new fields. You not only will be placing the new fields where you want them, but you also save yourself the additional step of changing typestyles.

THE LAYOUT PAGE

The page that you see on your screen is controlled not only by the layout you are using, but also is controlled by the type of monitor you have, the printer you have chosen, and the way you have defined your page with the Page Setup command in the File menu. In Fig. 4-29, you can see the Page Setup dialog box for a LaserWriter.

The largest paper size you can use with FileMaker is 36″ by 36″, but this does not mean that all printers can actually handle paper that size. For more information on printers and paper sizes, please refer to Chapter 8.

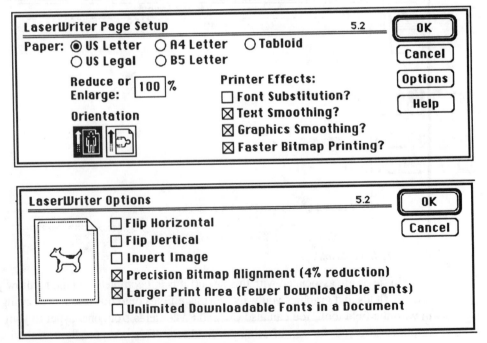

Fig. 4-29. Page setup dialog box for a LaserWriter.

If you want to use a custom paper size with an ImageWriter for your layout, first make sure you have selected the ImageWriter in the Chooser. Then set up your paper sizes by choosing Paper sizes from the File menu. After you have chosen your paper size, then select Page Setup from the File menu *before* creating your layout. In doing this, you ensure that the right and bottom page edges are that of your custom paper size.

FileMaker lets you know where the boundaries of your page are on your layout through the use of lines that cannot be moved manually. The left edge of the layout screen (next to the status area) represents the left edge of the paper, and if you scroll your screen to the right, you will see a solid line which indicates the right edge of the paper as shown in Fig. 4-30.

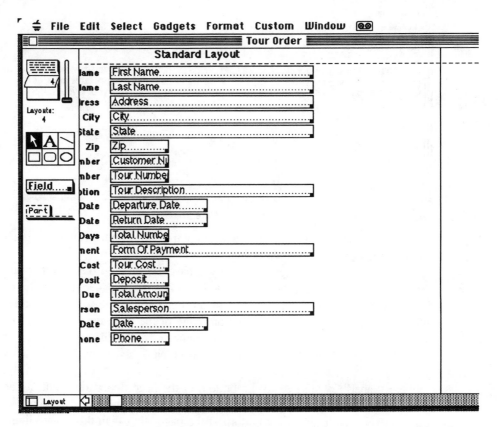

Fig. 4-30. The right edge of the layout page.

But, because most printers can't actually print to the edge of the paper, it's good practice to not place any item on your layout at the very edge of your screen. If you are unsure of the unprintable area controlled by your printer, use Preview from the File menu (Command – U), and you will be able to see whether or not your data will print, as shown in Fig. 4-31.

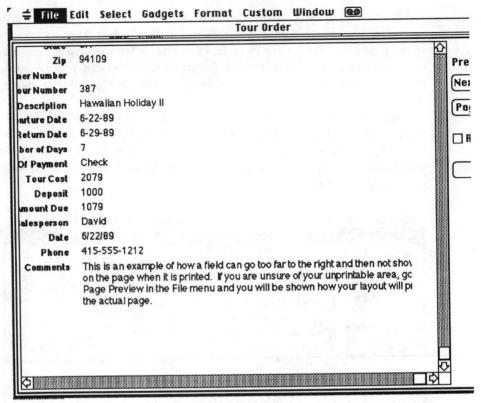

Fig. 4-31. Preview used to view the unprintable area.

The bottom edge of your page is also controlled by your printer and this is indicated by the dotted line shown in Fig. 4-32.

This dotted line *only* appears once you have moved the Body or other part down the page past the page end. The page end is defined by the paper size you have chosen in the Page Setup command of the File menu. Because many layouts are smaller than a full page, you might not see the bottom edge of the page on the screen. The gray shaded area below the Body part is not an indicator of the edge of the page. The gray shaded area is only the bottom boundary of the particular layout with which you are working.

No "label" is attached to the bottom-of-the-page dotted line, and it cannot be moved as the Body part (or other parts) can be moved. There is also no other indication that you have reached the bottom of the page other than this dotted line. Therefore, it is safe to say that if you do not see a dotted line at the bottom of your layout (a dotted line with no label), then you can safely print that layout on one page.

 One quick way to find the bottom of your layout page is to use your T-square. For example, if you know that your page length is 11", then choose the T-square option from the Gadgets menu and then drag the horizontal bar downward. As you move the T-square, the measurement will appear in the icon in the status area. Once the icon reads 11", you know that you have reached the bottom of that layout page.

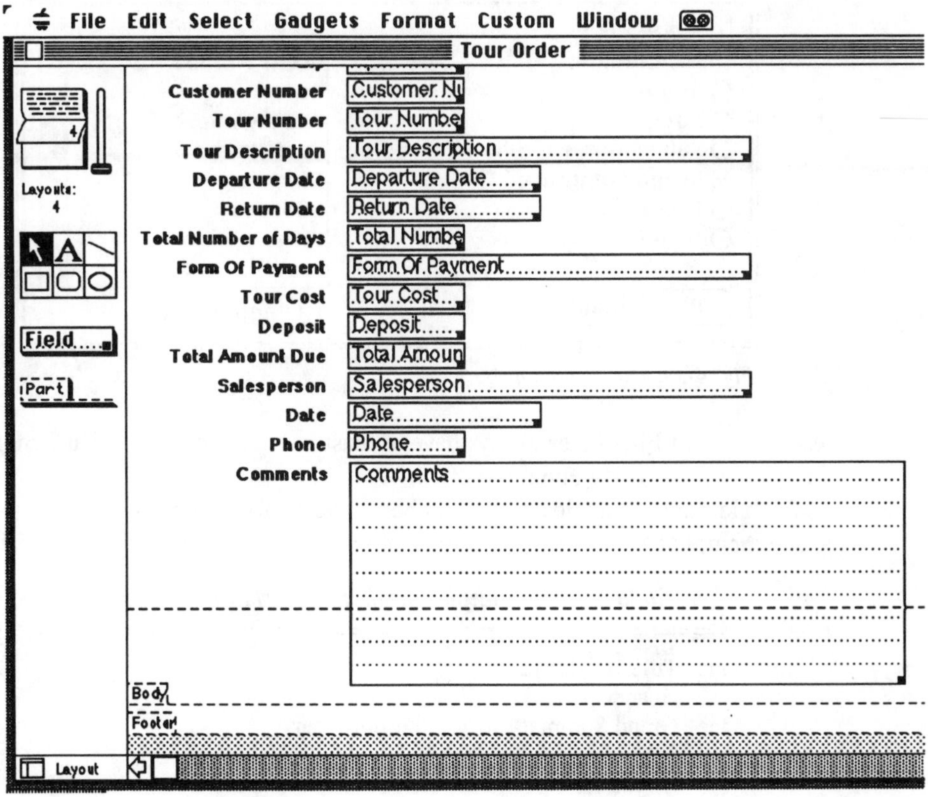

Fig. 4-32. Bottom edge of page.

PARTS

You've seen the references to the various parts on the layout before, but we have not gone into details as to their role. We've been holding off on these explanations until we could devote more space to them because many people find them quite confusing. A simple explanation is that the parts separate the layout page into separate sections; each section (part) tells FileMaker how much space to devote to a certain part of the page, and how to display the information that is contained within the part.

The parts are added to the layout by using the part tool in the status area. When you drag the part tool over to the layout, you get the box as shown in Fig. 4-33.

The type of part that is allowed in that particular area of your layout will appear in black print, and the other choices will be grayed out. If the type you want is grayed-out, you're trying to put that part type on the wrong area of the layout. Simply click the button for the type of part you want and then select OK.

Each part is identified by a horizontal dotted line which has its own *type*, or label, attached to the line it represents. The size of the part is changed by dragging the part line up or down the layout page. There is no minimum size to each part, but you must have a minimum of at least one part on a layout for the layout to work properly. As the

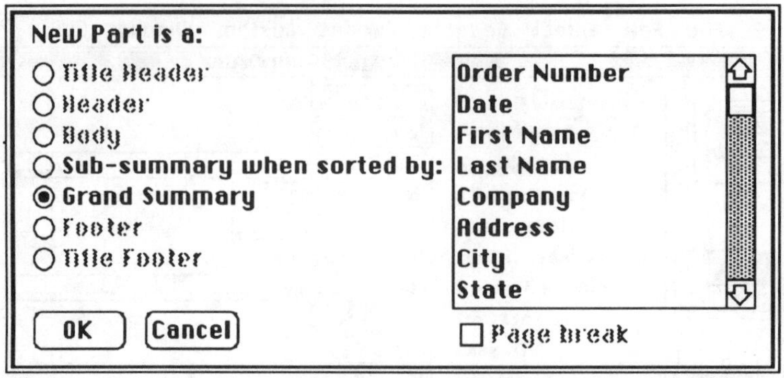

Fig. 4-33. Part tool choices.

preset layouts in FileMaker always have at least one part included, that is not something you have to worry about too often.

Each layout can handle a finite number of parts. You can always remove parts and replace them, but the maximum number of parts per layout is as shown in Table 4-1.

Table 4-1. Maximum Number of Parts Per Layout.

One   Title Header part
One   Header part
One   Grand Summary *within* the Body part
One   Sub-summary *for each field* within the Body part
         (If you have 15 fields, then 15 Sub-summaries can be made)
One   Body part
One   Sub-summary for each field *below* the Body part
One   Grand Summary *below* the Body part
One   Footer part
One   Title Footer part

When you change the size of a particular part, the movement of that part's line can affect the data or graphics on the layout page. If there are any objects above the part, such as fields, layout text, and so on, you will not be able to move that part above those fields or text. If you have any objects below a part when you move the part down, the objects below will remain below that part. In other words, you cannot drag a part over or under objects and fields. For example, let's say that there is a field that you have placed in the Header, and you would rather have that particular field in the Body. You cannot move the Body part up and over that field to include it; you must physically move that field into the Body.

You delete parts by dragging the part upwards to meet the part above it. For example, choosing Standard layout always supplies you with a Footer part. If you do not want a footer on your layout page, you simply drag the Footer part line up to meet the Body part line and then the Footer part is deleted. You have to remember, however, that the area above the part you want to delete *must be empty*. If the part you want to delete still has fields or other objects above it, you won't be able to move the part line above those objects. If, for example, you had placed a page numbers symbol in your Footer part, and then decided that you no longer wanted the Footer part, you would have to delete the page numbers symbol before FileMaker would allow you to remove the Footer. If the part you want to remove is at the top of the page (a Header, for example), move the part line up to the title bar at the top of your screen. If you move the part *past* the title bar, you have cancelled the move and the part will remain where it was prior to the attempted move.

Each part has its own way of displaying the information or graphics placed within it. Once you understand how each part differs from another, you'll know whether you need to choose a Title Header or a Header; a Sub-summary or a Grand Summary part. When you first start working with a new file, FileMaker places you in the default layout, Standard layout. There are three parts of the Standard layout, and because they are the most basic and the easiest to understand, we'll begin with them, and their closest relatives, first.

Header Part

The Header is much like the header in any word processing program. Whatever you place in the Header appears at the top of the page on every page being browsed or printed. The Header is a good place to put your company logo if you are printing sales invoices, for example. The Header is also a good place to put column headings, because you would want those headings to appear on every page to give your reader a continuous reference as to what is in that column. If you place a field in the Header, FileMaker takes the data in that field from the first record on every page to place in the Header. This works in much the same way that the headings are made in a telephone book. If you have an alphabetical list, for example, and have placed the Last Name field in the Header part, then the first occurrence of a Last Name would appear at the top of each page. If the first Last Name on page 2 is Brown, then Brown would appear in the Header.

You can put the special text symbols in the Header to print on every page. If you are doing a commission report for sales people, you might want to put the date symbol (two slashes //) in the Header so that the current date is printed on the commission report. If you put a field containing a salesperson's name in a Header, that name will appear at the top of all pages.

 If you place a field, text, or object on the layout in such a way that it is bisected in whole or part by a part line, FileMaker will place that field, text, or object in the Part *above*. For example, if the picture of your company logo is large, the entire logo need not be *entirely* within the Header for it to be included in the Header. However, you would have to place the logo there by using Cut and Paste. You could not have the logo in place and then move the part above the bottom of the picture.

The Header also controls the top margin of your page. If you enlarge the Header by pulling the part line down, the top margin of the page increases as well. You don't really need to have a Header for every layout you create. To get rid of an unwanted

Header, first make sure there is nothing located in the Header, and then drag the Header part up to the title bar.

Title Header Part

This part is very similar to the regular Header, and it is really only different in one way: the Title Header is only good for one page, the first page that is printed. You could have a Title Header that is nothing but a cover page. Or, if you don't want the company logo on every page, put it in the Title Header and create a regular Header for all the other pages.

Body Part

Everybody needs a body, and the Body part roughly relates to the body of a letter as that is where the most important stuff is contained. If you remove the Body from your layout, you won't be able to see any of your records. That's not bad if you did that intentionally, like to view summary information only. But, if it wasn't intentional, it could certainly give you a scare!

The size of the Body also controls how many records will print on a page. When you print, FileMaker looks at the size of the Body, adds the sizes of any other parts to be included, and then prints as many Bodies as will fit on one page. The remaining Bodies go to the next page, and so on. If you only want one record to print per page, just make sure that you've pulled your Body part down to the bottom edge of the paper. That dotted line that represents the bottom edge won't be there when you go to look for it. You have to continue pulling the part down until it suddenly appears.

If you are creating a layout for summary information only, you probably won't really need a Body. But, for most layouts, your Body will probably be the largest part on your layout.

Footer Part

The Footer is the Header's brother, in that the Footer can imitate anything that the Header can do. If you want the page number to appear at the bottom of every page, type in the symbol ## in the Footer. If you have a border that you like to use at the bottom of your page, put that in the Footer, too. If you put a field in the Footer, File-Maker will take the data in that field from last record in every page to print in the Footer.

The Footer controls the bottom margin of the page in the same way that the Header controls the top margin. If you want a larger bottom margin, enlarge your Footer. If you don't want a Footer at all, for example when you are printing labels, make sure there is nothing in the Footer and then drag it up to meet the part above it.

Title Footer Part

Again, this is the brother of the Title Header. Everything you place in a Title Footer will only appear on the first printed page and not on any of the others.

Sub-Summary Part

The Sub-summary is really one of the great controllers of information in any layout in that it gives you information about a *select group of records*. Some ways that a Sub-summary might be used would be: to get the list of food items that sold on certain days of the week; a weekly commission report for each individual salesperson; or a summary of all of your billings that are more than 90 days overdue. The Sub-summary lists the totals for *each group of records that you have sorted by*.

The Sub-summary's best friend is the Sort command in the Select menu. Sub-summary parts never do anything without first looking to their friend, Sort, to see what information sort is telling them to summarize. Sounds like George and Gracie, doesn't it? When you drag the part tool over to the layout in selecting a Sub-summary, you also have to give FileMaker instructions as to what field will be sorted in order to give the correct information. In Fig. 4-34, you can see what the choices would look like.

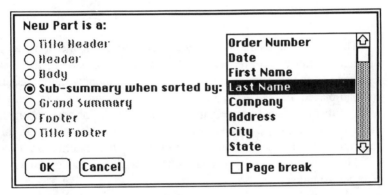

Fig. 4-34. Sub-summary sort choices.

Notice also that the Page break box is activated. What this means is that, if you wish, FileMaker will create a new page after each Sub-summary. For example, if you are creating a Sub-summary for each Salesperson, and you have eight salespersons, FileMaker will give you a one page report for each salesperson, rather than fitting as many Sub-summaries on one page as possible.

As shown in the previous figure, you first have to choose which field will be sorted. Your Sub-summary will only give you the correct data when you sort your records. If you do not sort your records by the correct field, your Sub-summary will either give you the wrong data or no data at all.

Sub-summary parts can only be sorted by text fields, number fields, date fields, or calculation fields. You cannot sort a Sub-summary part by a summary field.

Once you have chosen the sort field for your Sub-summary and click OK, FileMaker places a new dotted line on your layout that says Sub-Summary by XXX, with the XXX being the sort field you selected. If you had chosen a Page break after this Sub-summary, there would also be a small page break symbol (§); the dotted part line is also darker. But, you are not finished yet! You have only just created the part. You still have to place the appropriate field(s) within that part. Usually it is the same field that you have used to sort by, but you might also include other fields as well.

The Sub-summary part really acts a bit like a Header part in that whatever is placed in the Sub-summary part will be displayed before the records. For example, in Fig. 4-35, the Sub-summary by Salesperson was created and the Salesperson field has been placed in that part.

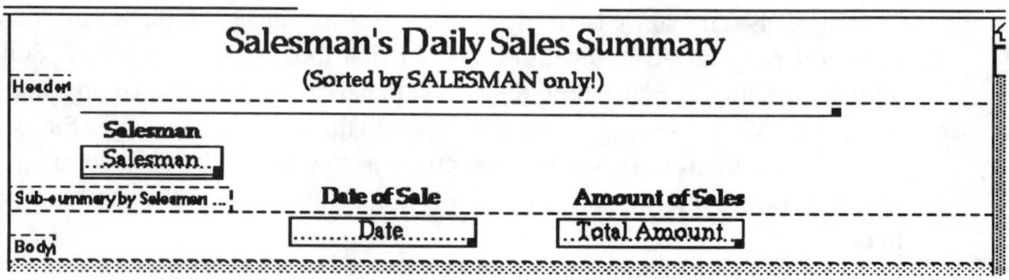

Fig. 4-35. A simple Sub-summary layout.

The actual records that you want to see are placed in the Body rather than the Sub-summary because you are really only sorting, or grouping, the Salesperson fields together so that you have, in effect, a header beginning with the Salesperson name. If you had placed the Total Amount field in the Sub-summary part, only the first occurrence of that field would appear in the Browse mode, or when printed. Note also that the layout text for the Date and Amount of Sales was also placed in the Sub-summary part rather than the Body. Figure 4-36 gives you the resulting print out of this layout.

The Sub-summary also reacts to different placements on the layout. If you want your Sub-summary to appear as a sort of "heading," like a salesperson's name for example, then you would place that Sub-summary part above the Body part. If you want your Sub-summary to appear after your records, like a subtotal of commissions for example, then you would place the Sub-summary part after the Body part. Both Figs. 4-37 and 4-38 are good examples of what we mean.

In Fig. 4-37, there are two Sub-summary parts. The first one is placed above the Body part, with the Salesman field placed in the Sub-summary part. The Body part contains the records that we want to appear. In this case, it would be each day's sales. The second Sub-summary part is placed below the Body part and the appropriate fields that we want to summarize are placed in the Sub-summary part. When you use Preview to see what will actually be printed, we see the Sub-summary for Salesman, Curly, then his actual sales, and then the Sub-summary of all sales for Curly.

Grand Summary Part

The Grand Summary part is very similar to the Sub-summary part in that it separates the fields you specify and gives you a report on these fields on a separate area of the layout. When you use a Sub-summary, however, you are looking for summaries on

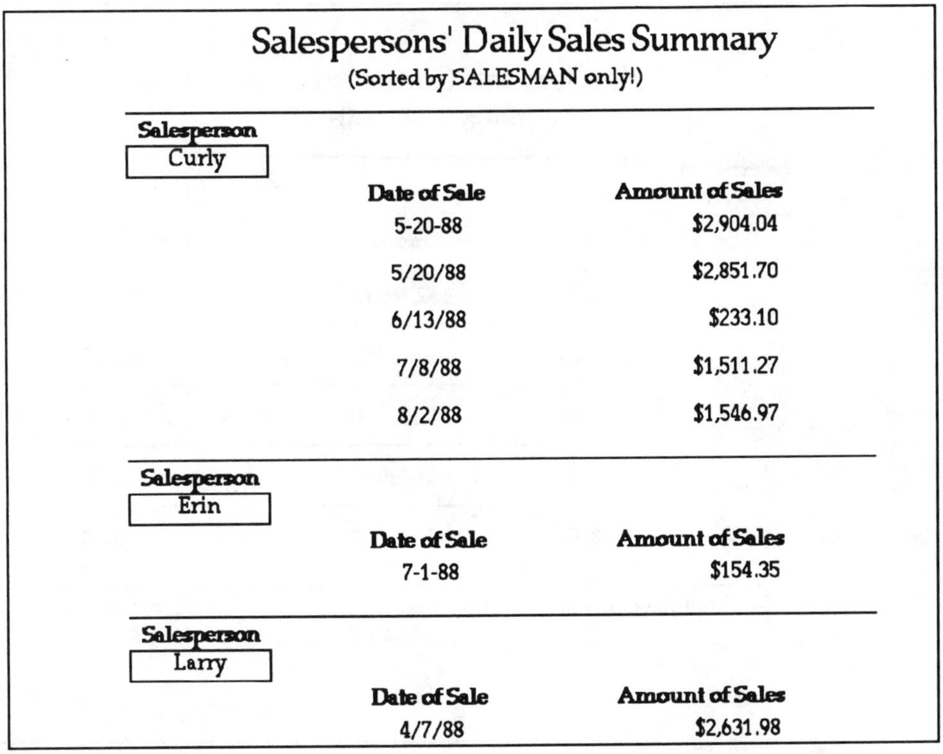

Salespersons' Daily Sales Summary
(Sorted by SALESMAN only!)

Salesperson

Curly

Date of Sale	Amount of Sales
5-20-88	$2,904.04
5/20/88	$2,851.70
6/13/88	$233.10
7/8/88	$1,511.27
8/2/88	$1,546.97

Salesperson

Erin

Date of Sale	Amount of Sales
7-1-88	$154.35

Salesperson

Larry

Date of Sale	Amount of Sales
4/7/88	$2,631.98

Fig. 4-36. The Sub-summary printout.

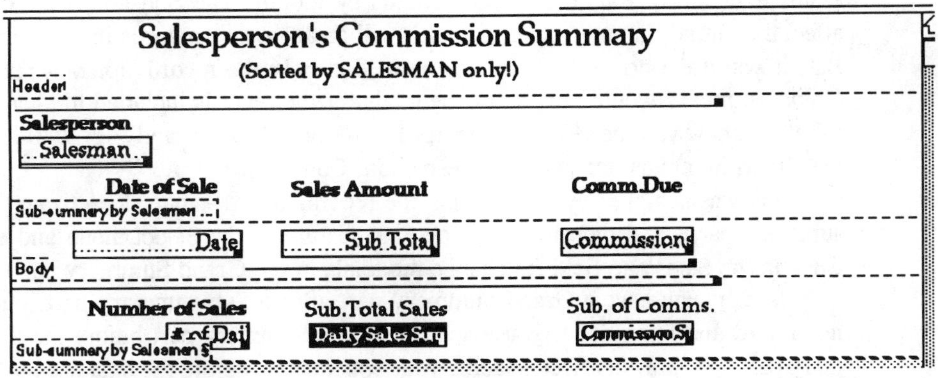

Salesperson's Commission Summary
(Sorted by SALESMAN only!)

Header

Salesperson

..Salesman..

Date of Sale	Sales Amount	Comm.Due

Sub-summary by Salesman ...

...............Date	........Sub Total	Commissions

Body

Number of Sales	Sub.Total Sales	Sub. of Comms.
# of Dai	Daily Sales Sum	Commission S

Sub-summary by Salesmen S

Fig. 4-37. Layout with two Sub-summary parts.

just *some* of the records in a file. When you use a Grand Summary, it acts like its name implies; it summarizes the fields you specify from *all* the records you are browsing in a file. As with the Sub-summary, you can place a Grand Summary part before or after the Body part to act as a kind of header or footer.

As your Sub-summary is affected by the way the records are *sorted*, the Grand Summary can be affected if you use the Find feature to show only certain records. For

Salesperson's Commission Summary
(Sorted by SALESMAN only!)

Salesperson
> Curly

Date of Sale	Sales Amount	Comm.Due
5/20/88	$2,765.75	$55.32
5/20/88	$2,715.90	$54.32
6/13/88	$222.00	$4.44
7/8/88	$1,439.30	$0.00
8/2/88	$1,473.30	$0.00

Number of Sales	Sub.Total Sales	Sub. of Comms.
5	$8,616.25	$114.07

Fig. 4-38. Printout of layout with two Sub-summary parts.

example, let's say you sorted your records by month. The Sort command does not affect the Grand Summary, per se, but it will arrange your records in a certain order. But, if you use Find in the Select menu to find only the records for May, then your Grand Summary would only show the totals for the records included in May. In Fig. 4-39, we show you the Grand Summary for *all* the salesmen, and Fig. 4-40 gives you the Grand Summary for just the salesperson, Curly.

This was achieved by first Sorting the records by Salesman (to activate the Sub-summary part), and then by using the Find feature in the Select menu and entering Curly in the Salesman field (to change the totals in the Grand Summary part).

Usually, you have a Grand Summary part after a Sub-summary part, but this is not a hard and fast rule. If you place the Grand Summary part before the Sub-summary part, you are, in effect, placing your conclusions before the data used to achieve that result.

GRAPHICALLY SPEAKING

To illustrate some of the different ways the various layouts, tools, and commands can be utilized, we'll go back to our example from the Tour Orders database from Way To Go Travel. As we had mentioned in the last chapter, the owner of WTGT wanted to

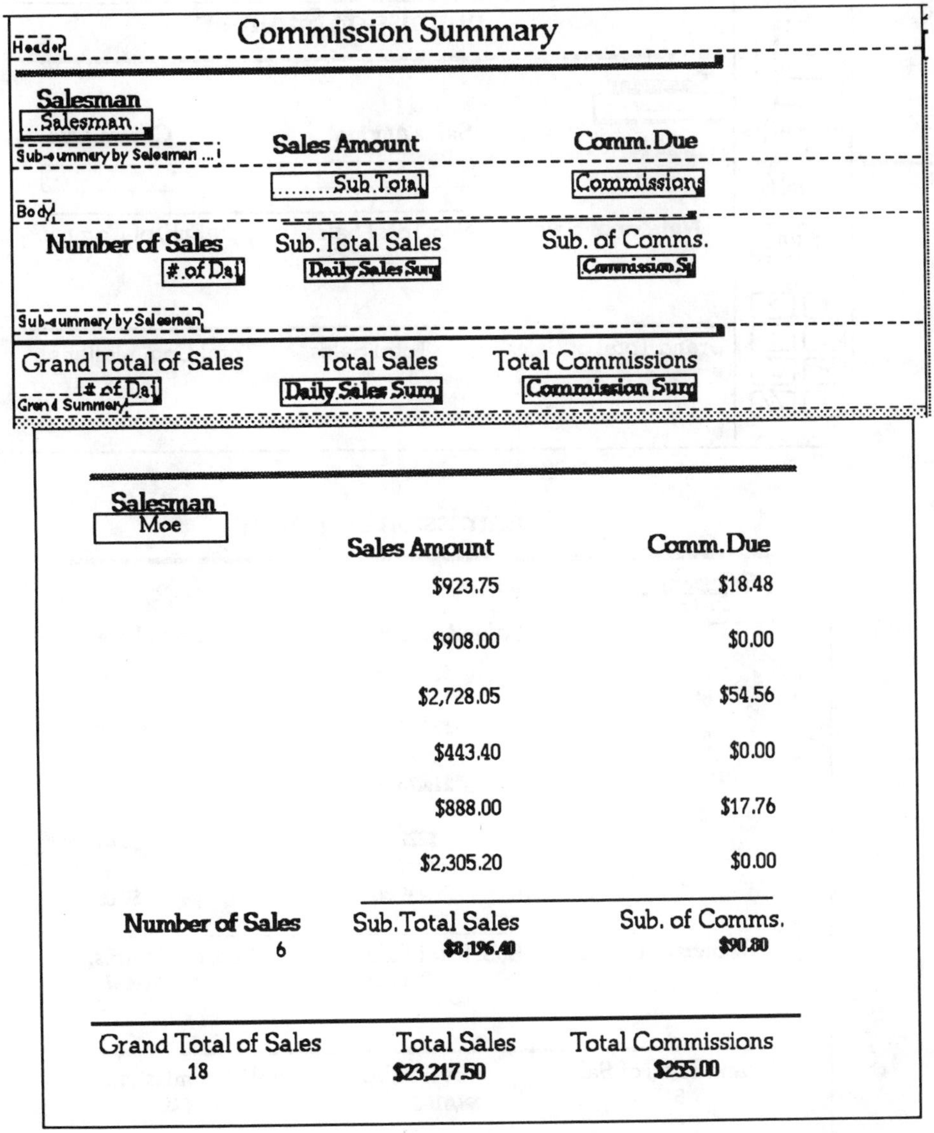

Commission Summary

Header

Salesman
..Salesman..

Sub-summary by Salesman ...

Sales Amount   **Comm. Due**

........Sub.Total]   [Commissions]

Body

Number of Sales   Sub. Total Sales   Sub. of Comms.
[#.of Da]   [Daily Sales Sum]   [Commission S]

Sub-summary by Salesman

Grand Total of Sales   Total Sales   Total Commissions
[# of Da]   [Daily Sales Sum] [Commission Sum]
Grand Summary

Salesman
Moe

	Sales Amount	Comm. Due
	$923.75	$18.48
	$908.00	$0.00
	$2,728.05	$54.56
	$443.40	$0.00
	$888.00	$17.76
	$2,305.20	$0.00
Number of Sales	Sub. Total Sales	Sub. of Comms.
6	$8,196.40	$90.80
Grand Total of Sales	Total Sales	Total Commissions
18	$23,217.50	$255.00

Fig. 4-39. Grand Summary for all salespersons.

be able to prepare various reports from the same file. In addition to having the Tour Order, she wanted to be able to give her clients written confirmation of their trip and to have the ability to generate invoices when necessary. Before we get to those examples, we're going to "dress up" her Tour Order layout with the addition of her logo and other graphics.

In the first Tour Order example, we had moved some of the fields around in order to make data entry more logical. Mrs. Avion, the owner of WTGT, had seen a picture of a plane flying into the sun in a travel magazine that she wanted to use as her logo.

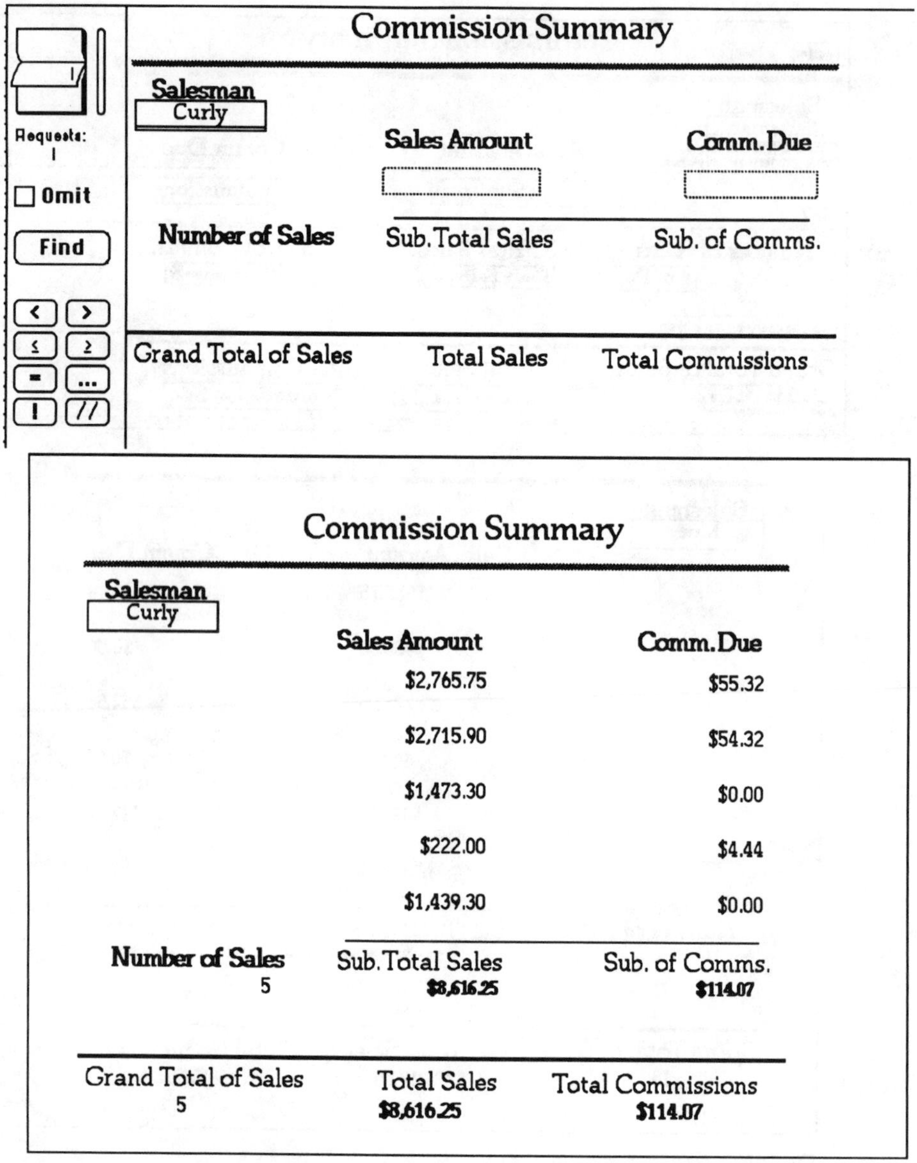

Commission Summary

Requests:
I

☐ Omit

[Find]

[<] [>]
[≤] [≥]
[−] [...]
[I] [//]

Salesman
Curly

	Sales Amount	Comm. Due
	[............]	[............]
Number of Sales	Sub. Total Sales	Sub. of Comms.

Grand Total of Sales	Total Sales	Total Commissions

Commission Summary

Salesman
Curly

	Sales Amount	Comm. Due
	$2,765.75	$55.32
	$2,715.90	$54.32
	$1,473.30	$0.00
	$222.00	$4.44
	$1,439.30	$0.00
Number of Sales	Sub. Total Sales	Sub. of Comms.
5	$8,616.25	$114.07

Grand Total of Sales	Total Sales	Total Commissions
5	$8,616.25	$114.07

Fig. 4-40. Grand Summary for Curly.

She had two choices in duplicating this picture: the first being to scan the picture into her Mac and saving it as a PICT file, and the other choice was to duplicate the image in a draw/paint program such as MacDraw, MacPaint, Canvas, and so on. She could also use a Desk Accessory program like DeskPaint in which to draw her picture. The actual format of the picture doesn't much matter as long as the picture can be cut or copied from the program and transferred by way of the Scrapbook or Clipboard. (Ready-made clip art disks are also a good source of graphics materials.)

In Mrs. Avion's case, she chose to draw the logo herself in a draw program. After she had finished the drawing, she used Copy from the draw program's Edit menu, opened the Scrapbook, and then used Paste to place it in the Scrapbook. She then quit the draw program and opened her FileMaker file, Tour Orders. With the file opened, she changed to the Layout mode because she could not paste a picture into a record in the Browse mode (unless she had a picture field in that record). In the Layout mode, she opened her Scrapbook once again, used Copy on her picture, and then chose Paste from the Edit menu to place the picture of the plane on her layout as shown in Fig. 4-41.

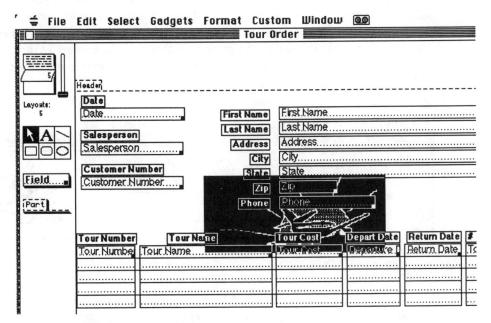

Fig. 4-41. A picture pasted on the layout.

Notice that the Paste command places the picture in the center of the layout. There is no way to indicate ahead of time where you want the picture to be pasted in FileMaker (that is, unless it is to be placed in a picture field), so FileMaker places the picture on the layout, even if it lands in the middle of other objects. FileMaker also pastes the picture *in its original size*. That is, the size it was when it was cut or copied.

Once a picture has been pasted on a layout, you are then free to move the picture to where you want it, and it can be resized by using the picture's handle which is located in the lower right-hand corner of the picture. When you resize a picture, however, it might easily be pulled out of proportion. In order to keep it in proportion you have to keep in mind the shape of the box that it was originally pasted in. That is, if the picture appeared in a square box when pasted, it will be out of proportion if you change the box into a rectangle.

Mrs. Avion resized the picture as she wished. Because she wanted the picture to appear at the top of every record she prints, she chose to put the picture in the Header part. (Any picture or object that is at least partially in the Header will appear in the Header in every record.) But, if Mrs. Avion wanted the picture to appear just on the first page of a multi-page report, she would create a Title Header with the part tool. But as this was not the case, she resized the Header by dragging the Header part's line down a few inches, and then placed her picture in it.

In addition to the picture, Mrs. Avion wanted the company name to appear in the Header. So after choosing her font, font size, and style, she used the text tool to type the company name in the Header. She also added the name of the report Tour Order with the text tool, using a different font and size. Finally, she added a shaded line at the bottom of the Header by choosing Line Width and Line Pattern from the Format menu and then using the line tool to draw it. In that way, she created a visual separation between the Header and the Body as no line otherwise exists in the Browse mode or when printed. This is illustrated in Figs. 4-42 and 4-43.

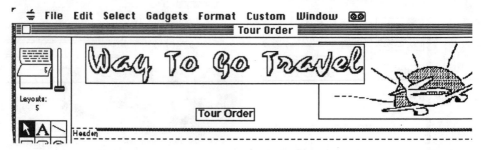

Fig. 4-42. Graphic objects added to the Header in Layout mode.

Fig. 4-43. The Header in the Browse mode.

FURTHER LAYOUT USES

Up to this point, you've been shown some of the possibilities for layout. However, even more can be done with them. Some of the more imaginative ways in which layouts are used are given in the following sections.

Form Letters

Form letters can be made with as many variables as you have fields. These variables are filled in by the values from your records. Figures 4-44 and 4-45 give you an example of a form letter in the layout mode, and its printed result.

You can use Find, Sort, and scripts to automate the printing of these letters. (Find and Sort are covered in Chapter 7, and scripts are covered in Chapter 8.)

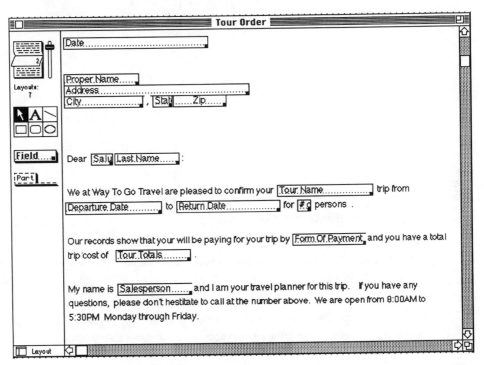

Fig. 4-44. Layout for form letter.

Fill-In Preprinted Forms

Preprinted forms such as loan applications, financial statements, and insurance papers are a terror to fill out on a typewriter with all the various spacings and tab stops to consider. However, you can set up such forms for direct entry by FileMaker.

The easiest way to set up a layout for a preprinted form is to scan an image of a blank form, place it on the layout, and then place the appropriate fields in the allotted spaces. After all the fields are placed, you can then clear the graphic image of the form, and you have a layout ready for print. If necessary, you can duplicate that layout and add layout text as instruction for a data entry screen. If you don't have access to a scanner, you must measure each blank space on the form accurately, and then place the appropriate fields on the layout with the assistance of the T-squares. In Fig. 4-46, we show you an example of a standard form that was painstakingly recreated in File-Maker.

Way To Go Travel

1617 Way To Go Place
New York, NY 01200
212-555-1212

Trip Confirmation

Thursday, April 6, 1989

Claire Deserable
300 Ura Court
Orlando , FL   32700

Dear Ms Deserable :

We at Way To Go Travel are pleased to confirm your Parisian Nights trip from
Sat, Jul 1, 1989 to Sat, Jul 8, 1989 for 4 persons .

Our records show that your will be paying for your trip by Visa and you have a total
trip cost of $5,999.00 .

My name is Christopher and I am your travel planner for this trip. If you have any questions,
please don't hestitate to call at the number above. We are open from 8:00AM to 5:30PM
Monday through Friday.

We thank you for booking with Way To Go Travel and hope you have a pleasant trip!

Sincerely,

Fig. 4-45. Printed form letter.

Christopher

Catalogs, Books, and Manuals

If you think about it, many publications are a collection of single page records,
with coordinated headers and footers, and a body section that varies from page to
page. Catalogs and books that devote a single page to each item often follow a set format that works well as a FileMaker layout. You can see a simple example of this in
Fig. 4-47.

FNMA

Federal National Mortgage Association

REQUEST FOR VERIFICATION OF EMPLOYMENT

Instructions: LENDER Complete items 1 thru 7. Have applicant complete item 8. Forward directly to employer named in item 1.

EMPLOYER Please complete either Part II or III as applicable. Sign and return to lender named in item 2.

PART–I REQUEST

1. TO (Name and address of employer) Ford Motors Sales 222 Becker Lane Ormond Beach, FL 32077	2. FROM (Name and address of lender)

3. SIGNATURE OF LENDER	4. TITLE Sales Director	5. DATE 10/19/89	6. LENDER'S NAME (Optional) Security First Federal

I have applied for a mortgage loan and stated that I am now or was formerly employed by you. My signature below authorizes verification of this information.

7. NAME AND ADDRESS OF APPLICANT (INCLUDE EMPLOYEE OR BADGE NUMBER) Dottie Raspberry 12 Nollwood Est. Dr. Ormond Beach, FL 32076	8. SIGNATURE OF APPLICANT

PART II– VERIFICATION OF PRESENT EMPLOYMENT

EMPLOYMENT DATA	PAY DATA		

9. APPLICANT'S DATE OF EMPLOYMENT	12A. CURRENT BASE PAY (Enter Amount and Check Period) ☐ ANNUAL ☐ HOURLY ☐ MONTHLY ☐ OTHER ☐ WEEKLY $_____		12C. FOR MILITARY PERSONNEL ONLY

10. PRESENT POSITION		PAY GRADE

TYPE	MONTHLY AMOUNT

12B. EARNINGS			BASE PAY	

11. PROBABILITY OF CON'T. EMPLOYMENT	TYPE	YEAR TO DATE	PAST YEAR	RATIONS	
	BASE PAY	$	$	FLIGHT OR HAZARD	
13. IF OVERTIME OR BONUS IS APPLICABLE, IS ITS CONTINUANCE LIKELY?	OVERTIME	$	$	CLOTHING	
	COMMISSIONS	$	$	QUARTERS	
				PRO PAY	
OVERTIME ☐ YES ☐ NO BONUS ☐ YES ☐ NO	BONUS	$	$	OVER SEAS OR COMBAT	

14. REMARKS (If paid hourly, please indicate average hours worked each week during current and past year)

PART III– VERIFICATION OF PREVIOUS EMPLOYMENT

15. DATE OF EMPLOYMENT	16. SALARY/WAGE AT TERMINATION PER (Year) (Month) (Week) BASE_____ OVERTIME_____ COMMISSIONS_____ BONUS_____

17. REASON FOR LEAVING	18. POSITION HELD

19. SIGNATURE OF EMPLOYER	20. TITLE	21. DATE

The confidentiality of the information you have furnished will be preserved except where disclosure of this information is required by applicable law. The form is to be transmitted directly to the lender and is not to be transmitted through the applicant or any other party.

FNMA form 1005

Fig. 4-46. Standardized form.

The categories of information are the fields. The tremendous range of formatting options in FileMaker provide the ability to print this information as a ready-made book. For more on FileMaker applications of this type and other examples of unconventional layouts, see Chapter 10.

Power Tools   Construction

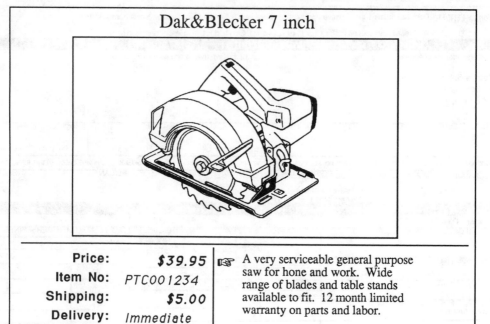

Dak&Blecker 7 inch

Price:	*$39.95*
Item No:	*PTC001234*
Shipping:	*$5.00*
Delivery:	*Immediate*

☞ A very serviceable general purpose saw for hone and work. Wide range of blades and table stands available to fit. 12 month limited warranty on parts and labor.

Tomz Toolz   Page 1

Fig. 4-47. Catalog or reference book layout.

DUPLICATING EFFORTS

Now that Mrs. Avion has finished with her Tour Order layout, she decided that she wanted to create a similar layout. One option was to create a Blank layout, and then use Copy and Paste to move the graphics and such over to the new layout. A much easier way to accomplish this is to simply use Duplicate Layout (Command–D) from the Edit menu. In doing that she creates another layout, exactly the same as the original, but it has a different layout number in the book icon. For instance, if the layout she wanted to duplicate was number 3 and there was a total of 7 layouts in all, when she chose Duplicate Layout, it would be exactly like layout number 3, but its number would be layout number 8. The Duplicate Layout is always placed last, after all the other layouts.

Once she has duplicated the layout, she is by no means bound by it. She is free to change it any manner that she wants. If she chooses to get rid of some of the fields in the duplicated layout, she can do so by simply using Cut or Clear from the Edit menu once she has chosen the fields to get rid of. In doing that, she is not really "deleting" those fields from the layout; more appropriately, she is *clearing* them from this layout.

WINDOW WONDER

Strictly speaking, although the Window command in the main menu does not have much to do with the Layout mode, we've included it here because it might give you reason to reconsider any layout you are designing. As with many Mac programs, you have the ability to open more than one FileMaker file at one time. In fact, you have a maximum of 16 files open at any one time (providing your system has enough RAM to accommodate such a request). Windows, or files, can be opened and resized so that more than one can be viewed at a time. So, if you have a number of files that will be related in various ways, you might want to design your layout so that the maximum amount of data can be seen in a smaller window.

When you have more than one window open, the current file is indicated by the active title bar. You can change the active file by simply clicking on the appropriate file, or by making use of the Window command in the main menu. Note that when you select the Window command, all open files are shown in the menu and the current, or active, file is check-marked as shown in Fig. 4-48. If you open the Window command, you can also select one of the files in the menu and activate it in that manner.

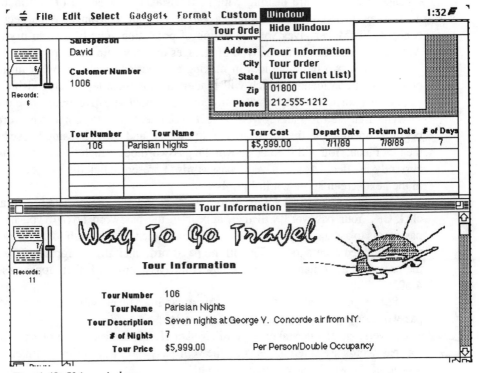

Fig. 4-48. Using windows.

Also shown in Fig. 4-48 is a file listed in parentheses (WTGT Client List). This is a *hidden window*. A hidden window file is not displayed on your screen but it is still open. You can hide a window manually by activating it and then choosing Hide Window from the Window menu. In that case, that file will then appear in the Window menu in parentheses.

There are two main uses for a hidden window. You can hide a window when you are working on a network and want to give others access to a file that you are not currently using or do not currently need. The other usage is for lookups. If you have a file that employs the use of lookups in the field definitions, FileMaker automatically opens the lookup file when you open the main file, and then places the lookup file in a hidden window. If you wish to use a file that is in a hidden window, you can bring it to the desktop by simply selecting the file name in the Window menu. That file name will no longer appear in parentheses in the Window menu and will be the active file on your desktop.

 The use of hidden windows does not apply to Desk Accessories. To remove a DA from the desktop, you have to close it manually.

CONFIDENTIAL LAYOUTS

Given the nature of most business information, it is very possible that a high percentage of data you are dealing with in FileMaker is sensitive or confidential. As we've seen, FileMaker data is quite easy to access and re-arrange. When security is a concern, FileMaker gives you the option of protecting your files from prying eyes. Also, FileMaker can limit the type of changes that any authorized person can make.

You have two basic choices in making a layout confidential: You can make the entire layout confidential which will render the complete layout unreadable, or you can make a portion of the layout confidential in which sensitive areas are blotted out.

The first step in making your layouts confidential is to assign passwords. You begin by opening the file that you wish to protect, and then choosing Password from the Edit menu. You will then be shown the password box which lists all the passwords currently in effect. As you have no passwords at present, click the New button and fill in the next screen as shown in Fig. 4-49.

Type in the password you want to use, then click the appropriate boxes, and then click OK. Your password will then appear in the password box. If you have more passwords to assign, do this before exiting this screen. If you wish for some personnel to have limited access to the file with no password, click the appropriate boxes, leave the password area blank, and click OK. Your passwords will then appear as in Fig. 4-50.

Before you are allowed to leave this area, FileMaker will ask you to type your password once more to verify that it is correct.

 In versions of FileMaker after FileMaker II 1.1, there is an improvement in the way passwords are entered. As you type your password in, a series of bullets appears instead of the word that you will be using.

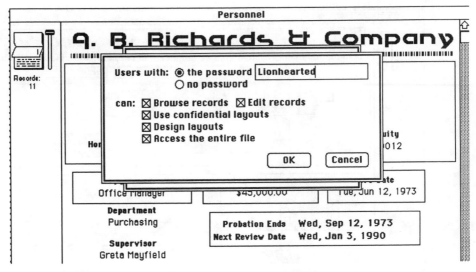

Fig. 4-49. Assigning a password.

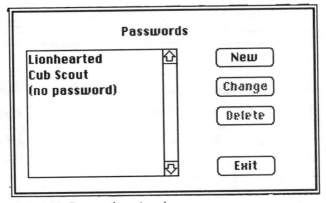

Fig. 4-50. Passwords assigned.

Now that you have your passwords assigned, you must go to the Layout mode of the file you are interested in protecting. The simplest way of making a layout confidential is to blank it out in its entirety. Simply choose the layout you want to blank out, then choose Confidential from the Gadgets menu. That's all there is to it. When you then open this file at another time with your password, all the information is available to you. But, if someone with a limited access password or no password tries to access the file, what they see is shown in Fig. 4-51.

When a layout is made confidential in this manner, a person without the proper password would be able to see the layout, but he could not change the layout or be able to access the Password command in the File menu as it would be inactivated. If there are other layouts in the file that are not confidential, he would be able to switch to those and use them however.

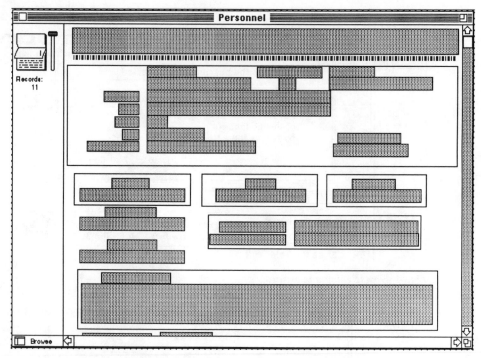

Fig. 4-51. Layout made entirely confidential.

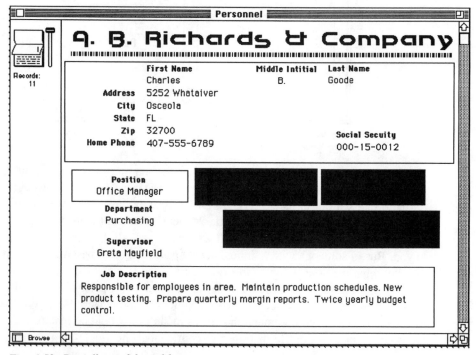

Fig. 4-52. Partially confidential layout.

Sometimes though, you won't want to make an entire file confidential. You might only want sensitive information such as salary levels or a supervisor's review made confidential. You don't have to use the Confidential command to be able to achieve this limited protection. All you have to do (after assigning the proper passwords and access) is to either *remove* the sensitive fields from the layout by using Clear or Cut from the Edit menu, or you can put a graphics box around those fields with a Fill Pattern of Black. In Fig. 4-52, we've shown you a layout that has the sensitive areas blacked out.

In either case, the person with limited access would be able to see the information that he is privy to, but would not be able to change the layout in any way. Remember that the Confidential command is not used in this case, but the proper access must match the assigned password(s).

CONCLUSION

As you can see, FileMaker's Layout feature is a major part of the program, allowing you creative and administrative control over many aspects of the program's appearance and performance. There are many examples of different layouts in the rest of the book. There is more about confidentiality and security in Chapter 9. In the next chapter, we look at the parts in greater depth, examining their role in summarizing data in your database. In Chapter 11, you can see the additional layout features of File-Maker Pro.

5
Part and Partner

IN THE PREVIOUS CHAPTER ON LAYOUTS, we discussed parts just enough to give you a basic understanding of what they are. We did this because parts play an important role in setting up a layout. In our work with FileMaker, we have found that parts are probably the most misunderstood area of the program. It is quite one thing to know what the Parts are called and where they go on the layout, and it is another to be able to use them effectively. Therefore, this chapter expands on the concept of parts and their applications. We begin with an overview of the definitions and uses and then go on to some helpful examples to assist you in planning your reports.

THE TITLE HEADER

The Title Header is best thought of as the "introduction" header. This part is placed at the top of the layout page, above a Header or Body part, and it controls the top margin of the *first page* of a multi-page report. The Title Header only appears once on any report. It's much like using your company's letterhead for page one of a letter and then continuing with plain sheets for each page after the first.

The most effective use of a Title Header is to either introduce yourself or your company, or to introduce the report or data that follows. You can make the Title Header any length. It can be used to create a cover page for a proposal, for example, by dragging the Title Header part down to the bottom of the length of your page. The two figures shown give you two possible uses. In Fig. 5-1 is a small Title Header that is used to give you information about the data that follows.

The header appears at the top of the first page of the report and not on any other page. In Fig. 5-2, you can see the Title Header used as a cover page.

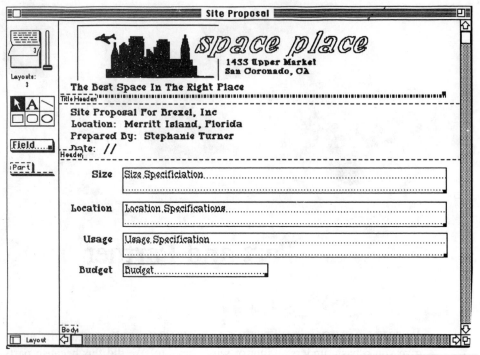

Fig. 5-1. Introductory title header.

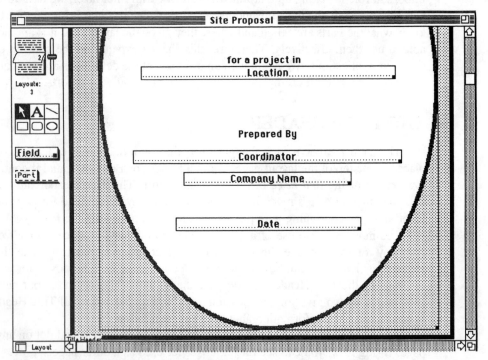

Fig. 5-2. Title header used as a cover page.

In this figure, the names and dates are fields that can change according to which-ever record you are using. A Title Header can only be placed on one area of the layout page and that is *above* all other parts on a layout page. Only one Title Header can be placed on any layout.

THE HEADER

The Header is much like the Title Header with the exception that it appears on *every page* of a multi-page report. The Header controls the top margin of every page and can be adjusted by dragging the Header part up or down the layout page. If you have a Title Header in addition to a Header on your layout page, you must remember to calculate the top margin of the first page by adding the two part sizes together. Then, on each remaining page, the Header remains the same.

A Header part is most often used to give information about the data that follows on the page. You can use a Header to place text above columns, as shown in Fig. 5-3.

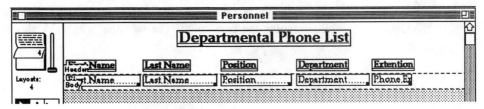

Fig. 5-3. Header used to label columns.

Date and time stamps are very useful in a Header part. If a field is placed in a Header, only the first occurrence of the data in that field appears in the Header. For example, suppose you are preparing a list of post offices sorted by city and state. The listing for some states would run to several pages. If you place the State field in the Header, the current state is repeated on each page of that state's listing, a heading method like you have in a telephone book or in a dictionary.

When you are preparing a label layout, it is most important to consider the size of your Header. Some of the commercially available sheets of printer-ready labels have a small strip across the top of the page. If you find that your labels are printing too low, then decrease the size of your Header by dragging it upwards. If your labels are print-ing too close to the top, then drag your Header lower. Because printing labels is a less than exact science, it is probably best to test print labels on plain paper first, before using expensive label stock.

Remember that only one regular Header can be placed on a layout page. The Header is placed above all other parts except for the Title header.

THE BODY

The Body part is the equivalent of the body of a letter. The Body is where all the information to be presented, the fields, is most often placed on a layout page. The size of the Body is completely flexible and can be made as large or as small as needed by dragging the Body part up or down the layout page. No page break command is associated with the Body. If you need your body to be the full length of your paper size, you must drag the Body part down to the corresponding length. For example, if you are preparing data to print on a 3″ × 5″ postcard, your Body part must be placed 3″ from the top of the layout page. You can use the T-square gadget to assist you in placing your part accurately.

Any type of field can be placed in the Body, anywhere in the Body. The display remains static on all records, and using Find or Sort will not corrupt your data. Graphic images in PICT, TIFF, EPS, and other formats, can be placed in the Body, and they will appear in every record that you have. For more information on arranging and placing data efficiently in a Body, please refer to Chapter 4.

 Sometimes, when you drag one part up to meet another part in an attempt to delete the lower part, the parts become "stuck together." The result is a much thicker part line, almost as if it were bolded. If this happens and you try to add that part again, FileMaker does not give you that option in the dialog box, or it tells you that there is already one of those parts on the layout. To get the parts "unstuck," try holding down the Option key while dragging the part down. The part that was stuck should come away.

THE SUB-SUMMARY

A Sub-summary part is used to extract certain information, such as a subtotal or a section title in your database and place that information all together. Sub-summaries are a category of parts quite different than the other parts: You can have as many Sub-summaries as you have fields. If you have 32 fields in your database, you could conceivably have 32 Sub-summaries on your layout page. That might be a bit overdone, but it is possible. (We go into the exceptions in a minute.)

The reason you can have so many Sub-summaries is that a Sub-summary part is associated with a particular field. If you have a Name field and an Address field, you can have a Sub-summary for Name and another Sub-summary for Address. Just placing a Sub-summary part on the layout doesn't create a proper section title or subtotal. You still have to place the field(s) that you want summarized within that part, and then you have to Sort the records in order to extract that information.

A Summary Example

Let's start with a very basic example, using a Sub-summary part to create a section title. Suppose you have an international name and address database of clients and you want to summarize all the clients by country. You have thirteen countries in your database and want to create a report in which each country starts on a new page. You could just sort your database by Country, but that would only give you a continuous list, rather than a summarized list.

You begin by going to the Layout mode. You can elect to either use an existing layout, or to create a new one. In either case, on this layout you would bring in the part tool to create the Sub-summary part. We use Country as the catalyst for this Sub-summary, as that is the field that the records will have in common by which we want to sort. Drag the part tool to the place between the Header part and the Body part, with no fields in that area. (You could place the part *under* a field that is on the layout, but you might have to move that field later if it is not appropriate.) Your screen might look like Fig. 5-4.

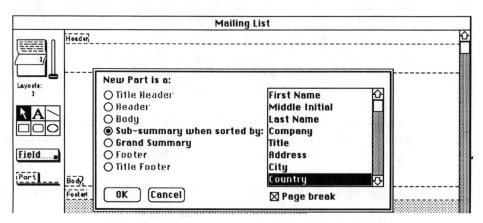

Fig. 5-4. Sub-summaries part dialog box.

Notice that you are only given two options for the types of parts you can place in this area of the layout: Sub-summary or Grand Summary. When you click the radio button for Sub-summary, the dialog box states that the new part will become a Sub-summary when sorted by. . ., indicating that another choice is to be made. As you are going to be sorting by Country, you select the field from the box on the right that lists the fields available. The OK button does not become active until you have selected the field to be used for the sort. Also notice that when you chose Sub-summary, the small box labeled Page Break becomes active. If you want FileMaker to create a new page every time it reaches a different Country, as we do in this case, click in this box. If you do not choose Page Break at this point, FileMaker will place all of the records, in order, in a continuous row.

If you create a Sub-summary part without the page break and then decide that you have made a mistake, the only way to change the part is to delete it first and start over again. Also note that you cannot delete a part that has any fields or graphics in that area, so you must remove all those items before you can drag the part line upwards to join the part line above it. These restrictions are listed in FileMaker Pro.

Once you click OK, you are then returned to the layout that you were working on, and the Sub-summary part will have its own line with the title attached Sub-summary by Country . . . §. The double "S" which looks a little like the sign for a hurricane on a weather map, is the symbol for your page break.

If you have set up a Sub-summary part that acts as a header to a columnar report, and you have chosen Down First from the Column Setup command in the Gadgets menu, do not specify Page Break in your Sub-summary part. If you do choose Page Break, FileMaker will start a new column and not a new page.

The next step is to decide what fields you want to place in this part. The logical assumption would be to place all the fields that are to appear in this report in this part. That might be logical, but it's not FileMaker. The Body part is the part that is used to display the data that is being summarized. The field or fields that you need to place in the Sub-summary part is usually the field or fields that the records will all have in common. In this case, it would be the Country field. In placing the Country field in the Sub-summary part, the part acts like a Header in that respect. The first occurrence of each Country appears in the Sub-summary part, before the records (which are located in the Body) that are within that group. If you were to place the First Name field, for example, in the Sub-summary part, only the first occurrence of the First Name would appear above the records being summarized.

In this case, we place the Country field in the Sub-summary and then the data to be summarized (First Name, Last Name, Title, Company, and so on), is placed in the Body part. The layout now appears as shown in Fig. 5-5.

Fig. 5-5. Layout with Sub-summary part.

To create this particular layout, we have chosen Slide Objects from the Gadget menu so that the names of people will appear on the report without any gaps. We have also chosen to have objects slide up to fill in any gaps above. To make the Sub-summary work, we need to sort the database by Country. If you do not sort, only records appear, and the Sub-summary part will not show the Country field. Choose Sort from the Select menu, move Country over to the Sort Order box, and then perform the sort. When this is completed, you will not be able to see the results in the Browse mode. The only two ways you can view the results is by either choosing Preview from the File menu, or by actually printing a report. We've chosen a preview of page 4 for Fig. 5-6 to show you what the report now looks like.

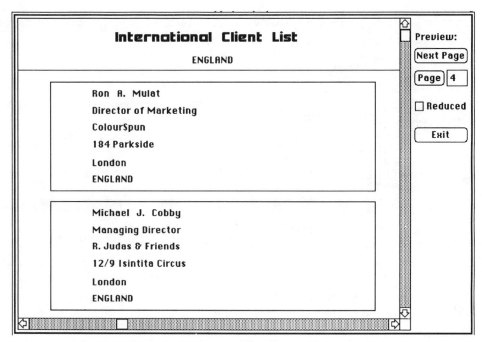

Fig. 5-6. Preview of Sub-summary report.

Several useful variations are possible on this simple Sub-summary. If you want just a list of client names, titles, and companies by country, you could omit the last three fields of the Sub-summary in Fig. 5-5. In some situations, you might want more than one Sub-summary part on a layout. An example of this is described in the next section.

A Calculated Sub-Summary Example

A good illustration of more than one Sub-summary part on a layout would be a Salesperson's Commission Report where you want the Salesperson's name to appear at the top of the report as a header for the commission amounts that would appear below the name in the Body part. But, you also want to summarize further by giving a count of all sales, total sales, and total commission amounts. One of the main differences between this Sub-summary and the previous example is that calculations are used to give us results, rather than showing each and every record entered with that Salesperson's name.

To begin, we put a Sub-summary part below the Header and above the Body and have it sorted by Salesperson. In this Sub-summary part, we place the Salesperson field, as shown in Fig. 5-7, so that the salesperson's name appears at the top of each segment of the report.

We do not choose Page Break at this point because there is more information to follow before we start a new page. We can also type in some layout text to label our

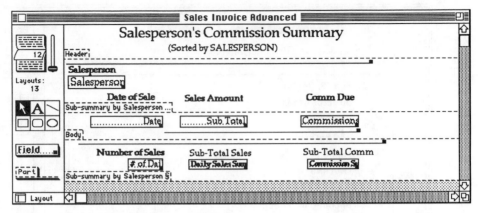

Fig. 5-7. Completed Sub-summary example.

columns of data. In this case, we included the Date of Sale, Sales Amount, and Commission Due. Note that these are just layout text and are not the actual fields.

In the Body, we place the fields that we want printed as part of our report. We have decided not to include every particular about the sales in question; instead we place the Date field to show the date of the sale, the Sub Total field which is a calculation field, and the Commissions field which is also a calculation field. The Sub Total field and the Commissions field are dependent on other fields for their data, so they cannot be changed without first changing the fields that are the source of their data.

After or below the Body of the layout, we place another Sub-summary part that will be sorted on the same field as the first Sub-summary part: Salesperson. FileMaker only allows two Sub-summary parts sorted on the same field if these parts are separated by a Body part. If you tried to place that part directly under the first Sub-summary by Salesperson, FileMaker would tell you that particular Sub-summary has already been chosen. At this point, we want to make a page break so that we will have a one-page report per salesperson. Within this second Sub-summary part, place one calculation field # of Daily Sales, which counts the number of dates in the records to give us a total number of sales made. In addition to this field, we might like to use a couple of Summary fields to give us subtotals of sales and commissions by salesperson.

Summary Fields in Sub-Summary Parts

Many beginning FileMaker users tend to confuse Summary fields with Sub-summary parts. The Summary fields in this example are used to summarize or add up the totals in the Sub Total and Commissions fields. Summary fields are, in effect, calculation fields, but FileMaker sees them slightly differently than calculation fields, which is why they are defined separately in the Define command in the Select menu, shown in Fig. 5-8.

A Summary field does not have to be placed in a Sub-summary part, but it does work better in a Sub-summary part. If you had placed a Summary field in the Body of

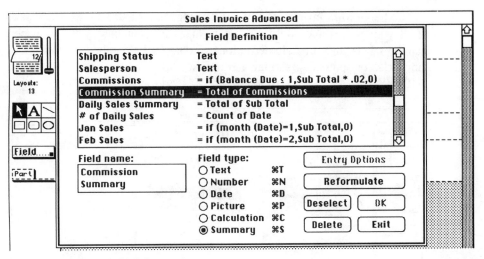

Fig. 5-8. Summary field definition.

this particular layout, the totals of all records would appear in each record, which rather defeats its special abilities. (See Chapter 6 for more information on calculations and summaries.) A Summary field is also one of two fields out of which you cannot make a Sub-summary part. (The other is a Picture field.) If you were to try to create a Sub-summary by Commission Summary, for example, you would receive the warning shown in Fig. 5-9, which tells you that you must choose either a text field, number, date, or calculation field to create this part.

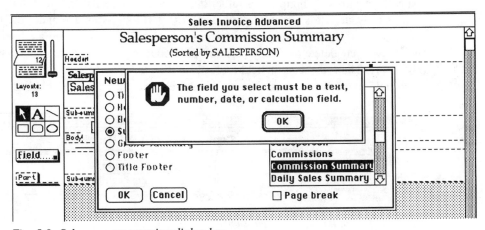

Fig. 5-9. Sub-summary warning dialog box.

A very simple use of a Sub-summary part with a Summary field in it would be a count of zip codes. When you are doing a bulk mailing, post offices ask that you give a count of each zip code in your mailing in order to qualify for special postage rates. Usually, it is a manual task to bundle and count your envelopes, but with a special layout it is very easy to give the post office an accurate count of your mailing.

To begin with, imagine you have a mailing list database that you use for data entry of all your names and addresses. From that same database you also generate your mailing labels. In your field definitions you have a field called Zip Count or Count of Zip Codes or something similar and define it as a Summary field as shown in Fig. 5-10.

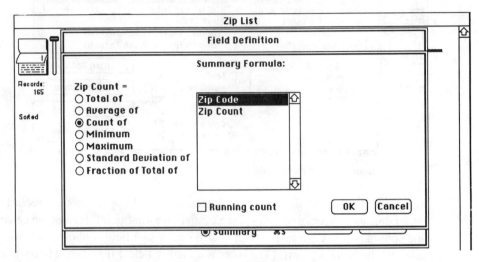

Fig. 5-10. Define count of Zip Codes summary field.

In this particular instance you do not want a "running count" of the zip codes or you will get a total of all zip codes rather than sub-section totals. In layout mode, specify a new layout that is a blank layout. Drag the part tool to a place under the Header part and specify a Sub-summary when sorted by Zip Code. Once you are back to the layout, you may delete the Body part and the Footer part as they are unnecessary for this report. Then, using your field tool, place the Zip Code field and the Count of Zip Code field in the Sub-summary part. Your screen should now resemble Fig. 5-11.

Fig. 5-11. Layout for Zip Code Sub-summary.

Once that is completed, you need only to sort by Zip Code and then print the results. Because the placement of the Zip Code field in the Sub-summary part acts a bit like a Header, you will see only the first occurrence of that particular code and the corresponding count of the total number of zips of that same number. Your report will resemble Fig. 5-12, and is ready for you to give it to the post office.

Zip Code Count For Bulk Mailings

Zip Code	Zip Code Count
48228	13

Zip Code	Zip Code Count
50001	4

Zip Code	Zip Code Count
50420	6

Zip Code	Zip Code Count
50601	6

Zip Code	Zip Code Count
50830	11

Zip Code	Zip Code Count
51001	3

Zip Code	Zip Code Count
52201	9

Fig. 5-12. Printed Zip Code Sub-summary.

If you had placed only the Count of Zip Code field in the Sub-summary part and the Zip Code field in the Body part, you would see a total number of zip codes at the top, followed by the actual zip in that count, as shown in Fig. 5-13, which is all a bit redundant because you don't need to see the same zip printed over and over again.

Further Sub-Summary Uses

For a Sub-summary report that is a bit more complex, we are going to return to a file that we used in a previous chapter. The owner of Way To Go Travel wanted File-Maker to extract certain information to give her a sales report for each salesperson. Since she wanted a report on each salesperson instead of all the salespersons, the Sub-summary part is the appropriate tool to use.

Before the agency owner, Mrs. Avion, prepared the report by putting the Sub-summary part in the layout, she needed to decide how she wanted the report to look when it is printed. She decided that she would like to have the salesperson's name at the top of the report. Underneath that she wanted each client's record, complete with the client's name, the respective tour bookings, and the amount of the booking. At the end of the report she wanted the total of all the bookings made by that salesperson, the total number of travellers, and the total amount of all the tour costs.

Mrs. Avion had also wanted FileMaker to summarize the number of sales, the

Zip Code Count For Bulk Mailings

Zip Code	Zip Code Count
	13
48228	
48228	
48228	
48228	
48228	
48228	
48228	
48228	
48228	
48228	
48228	
48228	
48228	

Fig. 5-13. Result of placing Zip Code in the body part.

number of passengers, and the total of those sales by each salesperson. To accomplish this, the Sub-summary will still be sorted by the Salesperson field, because Salesperson is still the key field. If Mrs. Avion had wanted to obtain the sales for each month, rather than for each salesperson, then the Sub-summary part would be defined to work when sorted by the Date field. In order for her to get the summary for the total number of tours, the total number of passengers, and the total of all that salesperson's sales, she needs to create another Sub-summary part for these totals. Refer to Fig. 5-14 to see how the layout was completed.

The result of this layout is that the salesperson's name appears at the top of each report; all client data attributed to that salesperson appears below the name, and, after the last client record, the total number of tours booked and the total amount of all tours appears as it would appear in a Footer.

Note that the two fields in the second Sub-summary part are Summary fields. The Total Count is simply a count of the Tour Number field and the Total Tour Amount is the total of the Extended Cost field. Normally you could define the Total Tour Amount field as a calculation field, but because we are using repeating fields in this layout, a calculation field would not work. This is due to the fact that the calculation would return the wrong figure because the calculation would only look at the first figure in each of the repeated fields and add them together. If you have more than one entry, as we do here, then your figures would be incorrect.

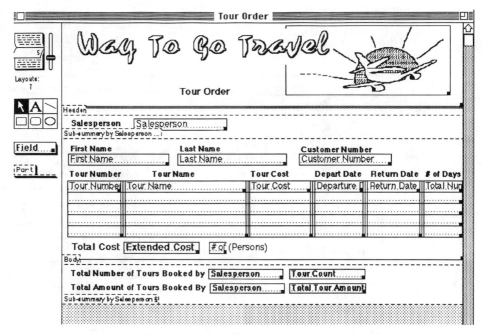

Fig. 5-14. Layout with two Sub-summary parts.

To make another change to the same report, say Mrs. Avion also wanted to sort the client files by the booking date of each file. She could opt to put that in the Body part, along with the other information, but to make it a little more legible, she decided to add another Sub-summary, this time sorted by Date. In Fig. 5-15, we see that the new Sub-summary part has been added below the first Sub-summary part and in that she has placed the Date field and the Total Amount Due field. Her layout is now complete.

In order to properly generate this report, she must make sure that she sorts by Salesperson and Date. The printed result is shown in Fig. 5-16.

 The View as List command in the Gadgets menu is not compatible with Sub-summaries. If you have spent a lot of time assembling your Sub-summaries and then go to Browse and cannot see the results of your Sub-summary, very often the problem is that you have the View as List command checked. Once you turn that option off, you should see your Sub-summary.

A GRAND SUMMARY

Grand Summaries seem to be easier to figure out than Sub-summaries. Perhaps they are a bit more logical than the Sub-summaries. The purpose of a Grand Summary part is to give you the summary information of all the records, as opposed to just some of them. There is no particular sort order to worry about with a Grand Summary. However, you might want either calculation fields or summary fields in the Grand

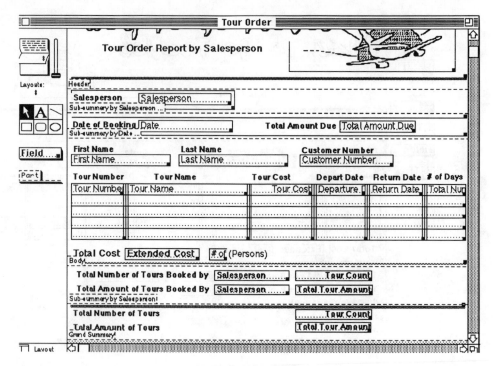

Fig. 5-15. Layout with multiple parts.

Summary because, just as with Sub-summaries, creating this part does not in itself create a calculation.

A Grand Summary Example

To continue the scenario illustrated in Fig. 5-14, we added a Grand Summary part beneath the last Sub-summary part, and placed it in the same fields, namely, the Tour Count field and the Total Tour Amount field. You can see this in Fig. 5-17, which shows the location of the Grand Summary part.

Placed in this location, the Grand Summary appears after all the other records and Sub-summaries. This means that after the last salesperson's Sub-summary appears, the grand totals for the Tour Count and the Total Tour Amount fields will appear in the Grand Summary.

Note that in Fig. 5-17, the Grand Summary does not have a page break command or symbol. When the Grand Summary is placed at the bottom of the layout, it always appears as the last thing on the report. As you can see from Fig. 5-18, the page break command does not appear when you are placing a Grand Summary.

The page break command does not appear even when you are placing a Grand Summary at the top of the layout; it is simply not an option with this part. If a Grand Summary is placed at the top of the layout, the summarized information appears before all other information. Likewise, when it is placed at the bottom, it appears last.

Way To Go Travel

Tour Order Report by Salesperson

Salesperson	Christopher

Date of Booking Tue, Jan 3, 1989   **Total Amount Due** $976.00

First Name	Last Name		Customer Number
Monty	Mountback		1001

Tour Number	Tour Name	Tour Cost	Depart Date	Return Date	# of Days
104	Tia Juana Mama	$339.00	1/19/89	1/23/89	4
103	Sea and Ski	$549.00			4

Total Cost $1,776.00   2 (Persons)

Date of Booking Tue, Feb 14, 1989   **Total Amount Due** $1,792.00

First Name	Last Name		Customer Number
Erin	Cobb		1003

Tour Number	Tour Name	Tour Cost	Depart Date	Return Date	# of Days
102	Dizzy Whirl Adventure	$309.00	6/2/89	6/6/89	4
105	Queenie's Cruise	$1,137.00	6/6/89	6/15/89	7

Total Cost $2,892.00   2 (Persons)

Date of Booking Tue, Mar 14, 1989   **Total Amount Due** $2,776.00

First Name	Last Name		Customer Number
Dennis	Marshall		1000

Tour Number	Tour Name	Tour Cost	Depart Date	Return Date	# of Days
107	Jolly Olde London Towne	$889.00	4/20/89	4/27/89	7
103	Sea and Ski	$549.00	1/5/89	1/9/89	4

Total Cost $2,876.00   2 (Persons)

Total Number of Tours Booked by Christopher   6

Total Amount of Tours Booked By Christopher $7,544.00

Fig. 5-16. Printed result with multiple parts.

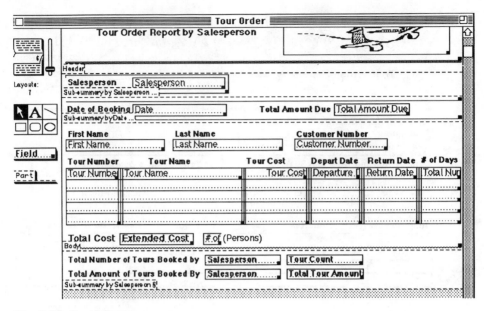

Fig. 5-17. Grand Summary part.

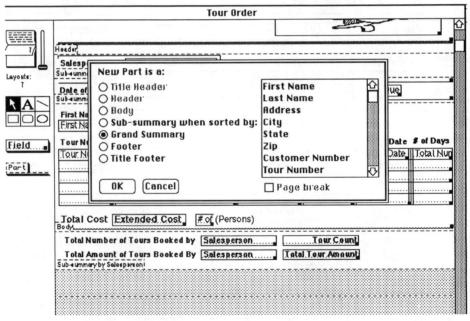

Fig. 5-18. Grand Summary dialog box.

Also note that we have changed the last Sub-summary part in the example in Figs. 5-16 and 5-17. Previously, we had specified a page break after each Sub-summary so that there would be a separate report for each salesperson. We had to move all the fields and text out of the Sub-summary, delete it, and then replace it with another Sub-summary of the same type, but without a page break. If we had left the page break option in the Sub-summary, then not only would each salesperson's report be printed separately, but the Grand Summary would appear on its own page rather than after the last Sub-summary report. You can, however, opt to leave the page break in the Sub-summary if you do want your Grand Summary to appear on a separate page.

Manipulating Grand Summaries

Although the Grand Summary part does not change according to how the records are sorted, the way to manipulate the Grand Summary information is to use the Find feature in the Select menu. Suppose you have an accounts receivable database and want a Grand Summary of all statements issued for a particular month. Using a simple statement layout as our starting point, it was modified by attaching a Grand Summary, as shown in Fig. 5-19.

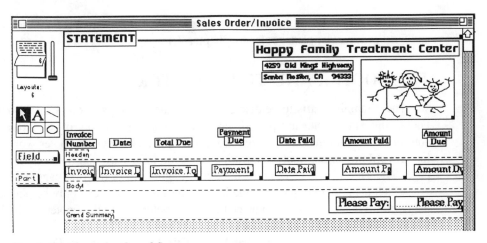

Fig. 5-19. Layout for Grand Summary.

Using that particular layout, we chose Find from the Select menu and specified that we wanted all records dated May 1, 1988, or beyond. This gives the entry ≥ 5-1-88 in the Date field, as shown in Fig. 5-20.

A further criteria, a balance due, was entered in the Amount due field (>0). File-Maker then finds only those records that meet that criteria and holds them separate from the rest. When your find is completed, FileMaker gives you the total number of records in your database, along with the total number found. At that point, you can print your report and the result will be similar to Fig. 5-21 in that only the records that matched what you wanted appear on the report.

The amount in the Grand Summary then reflects the total for the found records, not all records. In addition, you could execute a Sort on your found records to place the records in date order as we have done. The sort in this case does nothing to affect

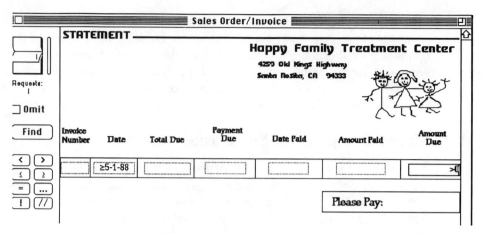

Fig. 5-20. Find statement for Grand Summary.

the totals, it just arranges the records in a logical order. (For more information on Sort and Find commands, please refer to Chapter 7.)

THE FOOTER AND TITLE FOOTER

The remaining parts to be discussed affect the bottom section of the layout. The Footer and Title Footer are placed, rather obviously, at the foot of the layout. They control the bottom margins of printed report pages. The regular Footer works much like a word processing footer, repeating the same information at the bottom of every page. The Title Footer places information at the bottom of the first page only.

When placing these parts on the layout, the Title Footer can only be placed after the regular Footer. If you try to place the Title Footer before the Footer on the layout, you will receive a warning like the one shown in Fig. 5-22.

When assembling a layout that has a Title Header, Header, Footer, and Title Footer, remember to take into consideration the accrued length of your layout as there is no warning in FileMaker to tell you that you have gone over the limit of the page, other than the dotted line that appears when you reach that point.

The best way to get an accurate view of what will appear in printed form is to use the Preview command in the File menu. If you choose a reduced page view in Preview, you can see whether or not your footers appear as planned. Also, if you have a one-page layout and then go to the Preview and see that the Next Page button is active, you know immediately that something is wrong with the layout.

We haven't seen too many exciting uses for the Footer and the Title Footer, which is not to say that there aren't a lot of creative uses. The most common use of a Title Footer is probably to print a message like "Copyright 1990, BFD Corporation," or something similar, on the first page of a report.

STATEMENT

Happy Family Treatment Center
4259 Old Kings Highway
Santa Rosita, CA   94333

Invoice Number	Date	Total Due	Payment Due	Date Paid	Amount Paid	Amount Due
10271	5-5-88	$77.04	06/04/88			$77.04
10272	5-7-88	$32.10	06/06/88			$32.10
10297	5/15/88	$278.20	06/14/88		$0.00	$278.20
10338	5-16-88	$77.04	06/15/88			$77.04
10346	5-19-88	$6.42	06/18/88			$6.42
10355	5-19-88	$423.72	06/18/88			$423.72
10362	5-19-88	$5,127.44	06/18/88			$5,127.44
10379	5-28-88	$147.66	06/27/88			$147.66
10390	5/30/88	$364.34	06/29/88			$364.34
10401	6/1/88	$12,309.22	07/01/88	6/25/88	$1,000.00	$11,309.22

Please Pay:	$17,843.18

Fig. 5-21. Printed Grand Summary report based on Find.

The most common use of a Footer is to place page numbers or time and date information on your printed pages, using special symbols:

:: (two colons)   Print the time (from the Macintosh Control panel).

// (two slashes)   Print today's date (from the Macintosh Control panel). Use the Format Date command in the Format menu to change the appearance of the date.

```
┌────────────────────────────────────────────┐
│  ┌─────────────────────────────────────┐   │
│  │  ✋  A new part cannot be positioned │   │
│  │      here.  Parts must be in the order:│  │
│  │                                      │   │
│  │      Title Header                    │   │
│  │      Header                          │   │
│  │      Grand Summary                   │   │
│  │      Sub-Summaries                   │   │
│  │      Body                            │   │
│  │      Sub-Summaries                   │   │
│  │      Grand Summary                   │   │
│  │      Footer                          │   │
│  │      Title Footer                    │   │
│  │                                      │   │
│  │                     ┌────────────┐   │   │
│  │                     │    OK      │   │   │
│  │                     └────────────┘   │   │
│  └─────────────────────────────────────┘   │
└────────────────────────────────────────────┘
```

Fig. 5-22. Parts placement order.

## (two number signs)	Print the page number. When you choose Print you can specify the number to start with as well as the range of pages to print.
@@ (two "at" signs)	Use in the body of the layout to have FileMaker print the record number.

Remember that the information from these symbols is displayed when you preview or print records, not when you Browse them.

If you have designed a company letterhead to print with FileMaker, and you have a couple different offices or addresses, it might be useful to put the address information in a Title Footer and change it accordingly, without disrupting the rest of your layout.

CONCLUSION

The assembled parts of your layout can greatly affect the data and the appearance of that data. Sometimes changes cannot be easily made (there is a Delete Part command in Pro FileMaker). If you have a layout that works well, but you want to play "what if" with the parts, the best thing to do is to Duplicate that layout rather than change the good one; otherwise, once you make a major change to a layout, your original is gone.

6

Formulating Formulas

FILEMAKER HAS THE ABILITY to perform sophisticated calculations using the information stored in a database. Whether you want running totals, grand totals, tax and interest computations, or simple addition, your needs can be met by FileMaker's calculated fields. So far we have concentrated upon databases that consist mainly of text or number entries, pieces of data that have been typed in by the user rather than generated by FileMaker itself. However, in many situations, FileMaker can formulate new data from your input, using powerful but easy-to-build formulas. Once you grasp the way that FileMaker formulas work, you might well see new applications of the program. In this chapter, we explain how to create formulas and put them to work in typical situations.

FORMULA FIELDS

You can see an example of a simple calculation field called Pay in the database in Fig. 6-1. This field presents data that is not user input. Instead, the entry in this field is generated from the user input in other fields. The user cannot enter anything in Pay field itself.

You perform calculations with FileMaker by defining formula fields, that is, fields with a type setting of Calculation or Summary. (We deal with Summary formulas in a moment.) To create a formula field, you choose Define from the Select menu, type a name for the field, then choose Calculation as the field type. When you select OK, FileMaker takes you to a dialog box like the one in Fig. 6-2, in which you specify the formula to determine the result that you want in the field.

In this case, the field called Pay is being defined as Hours multiplied Rate. Note that the asterisk is used as the multiplication sign.

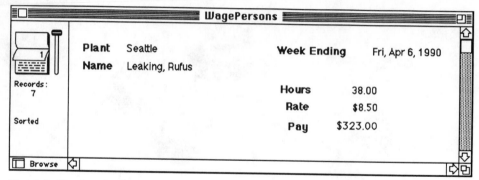

Fig. 6-1. Simple calculation.

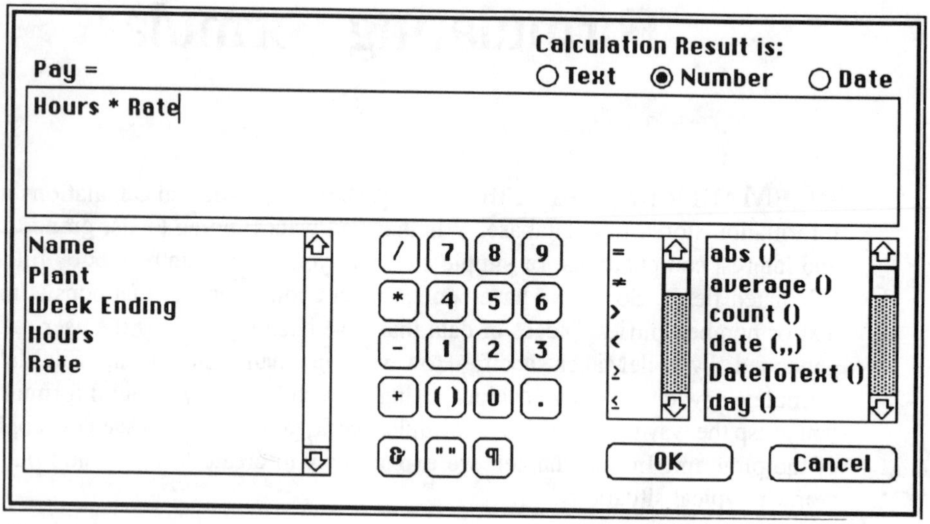

Fig. 6-2. Defining a formula.

Also note that when we describe FileMaker formulas, we normally present them in following format, using field names:

Pay = Hours * Rate

Sometimes we show formulas with field values substituted for field names, in order to demonstrate the operation performed by the formula; for example:

Pay = Hours * Rate
200 = 40 * 5

In this case, 200 would be the resulting value displayed in the formula field Pay, while 40 would be the value in the Hours field and 5 the value in the Rate field.

CREATING FORMULAS

When you define a formula, you first click one of the three check boxes to indicate whether you want the result of the calculation to be text, a number, or a date. In most cases, this is a straightforward decision, and in a lot of cases you will choose Number. For example, if you are multiplying two number fields together, you probably will want the result to be displayed as a number. However, if you are adding days to a date, for example, to determine a completion date, you will want the Date result type. In some cases, you will want a text result; for example, when using an IF statement, as described later in this chapter.

About Operators

Having decided upon the result type, you then create the formula by clicking on or typing field names, numbers, operators, symbols, and functions. The basic math operators are listed in Table 6-1. Other operators, used for logical formulas, are discussed later in the chapter.

Table 6-1. Basic Math Operators.

Name	Symbol	Example
multiply	*	$2 * 3 = 6$
divide	/	$8 / 4 = 2$
plus	+	$2 + 3 = 5$
minus	−	$5 - 3 = 2$
power	^	$5 \wedge 3 = 125$
(also called exponentiation)		

An order of precedence exists among the operators. Multiplication and division occur before addition and subtraction. Exponentiation occurs before regular multiplication. For example, the formula

    Sales Tax = Base Price + Options * Tax Rate

would not give the correct answer because Options would be multiplied by Tax Rate then added to Base Price. To get around this problem, you could create a field called Total Price and define it with the formula:

    Total Price = Base Price + Options

Then you could define the Sales Tax field as follows:

    Sales Tax = Total Price * Tax Rate

You can also use parentheses to alter the normal order of operations. For example, the following formula is correct:

    Sales Tax = (Base Price + Options) * Tax Rate

The calculation within parentheses is carried out before it is acted upon by the operators outside the parentheses. A formula within a formula that results in a value is called an expression. For example, the formula

Height = Volume / (Length * Width)

contains the expression Length * Width. Note that the above formula gives a different result from this one:

Height = Volume / Length * Width

When all of the operators in a formula are equal, the operations are carried out from left to right.

About Formula Editing

You use the standard Macintosh editing techniques to edit your formula. The formula can include any text, number, date, or calculation fields. Special care must be exercised when working with repeating fields, which are discussed later in the chapter. Note that capitalization is fairly arbitrary in FileMaker formulas. Field names and the names of functions, which are described later in this chapter, can be spelled in uppercase, lowercase, or with an initial capital. However, to ensure correct spelling of field names, it is best to select them from the list of names rather than type them out.

One very nice feature of FileMaker is that it automatically updates formulas to reflect changes in field names. For example, if you change the name of the Rate field to Hourly the formula in the Pay field, which was

Hours * Rate

automatically becomes:

Hours * Hourly

There is no need for you to check formulas when you alter a field name.

CALCULATIONS WITHIN RECORDS

The calculations you can do with FileMaker fall into two categories: Calculations within records and calculations between records. Suppose that you have a database of salespersons like the one shown in Fig. 6-3.

You have a field for base salary (Base) and a field for the amount of the annual bonus (Bonus). To show the total compensation for each salesperson, you want a field called Total Earnings that contains the sum of the other two fields. However, instead of doing the addition yourself, you would like FileMaker to do the math for you. This is a case of performing a calculation within records. The field called Total Earnings will appear on each record, and in each case it will show the sum of the Base for that record plus the Bonus for the same record.

Salespersons
Records:
7
Browse
Name Leaking, Rufus
Office Seattle
Hired April 1, 1988
Base $20,000
Bonus $4,565

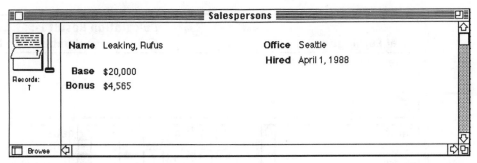

Fig. 6-3. Database of salespersons.

To accomplish this particular calculation, you would define Total Earnings as a calculation field. The first step is to make sure you are clear on calculation you want the field to perform. In this case, you could express the relationship between the fields in a formula:

Total Earnings = Base + Bonus

To create the Total Earnings field pick Define from the Select menu while you are in either the Layout or Browse mode. In Fig. 6-4, you can see the Field Definitions dialog box that appears.

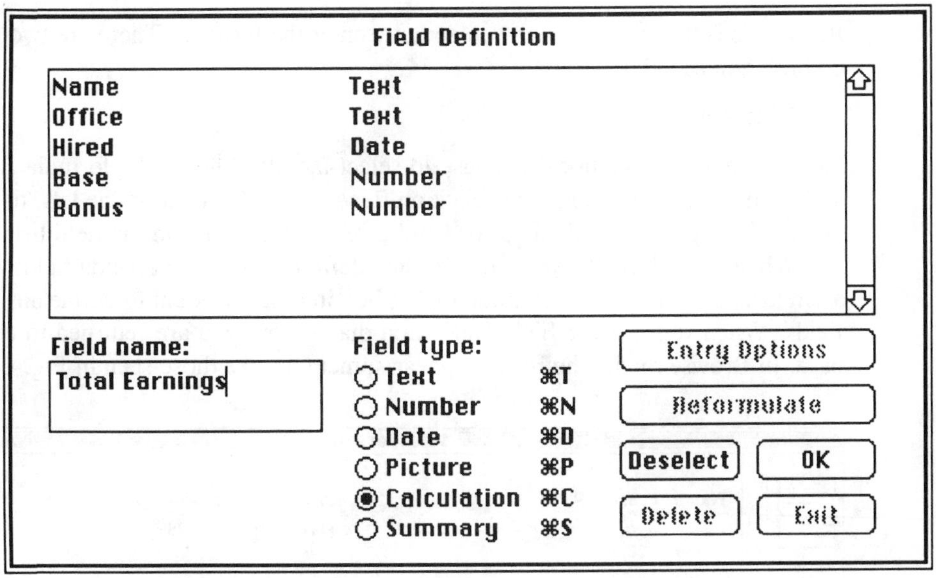

Field Definition
Name Text
Office Text
Hired Date
Base Number
Bonus Number
Field name:
Total Earnings
Field type:
Text ⌘T
Number ⌘N
Date ⌘D
Picture ⌘P
Calculation ⌘C
Summary ⌘S
Entry Options
Reformulate
Deselect
OK
Delete
Exit

Fig. 6-4. The Field Definitions dialog.

The name of the field is being entered, and you can see that Calculation has been chosen as field type. When you select OK after naming a calculation field, FileMaker automatically takes you to the dialog box in Fig. 6-5, which we call the *calculator*.

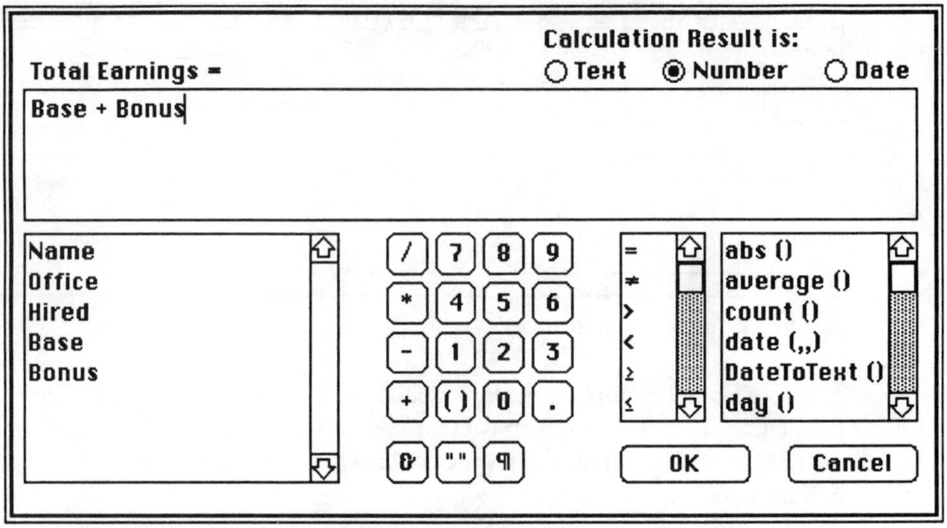

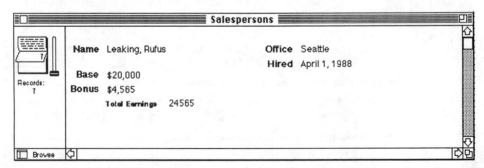

Fig. 6-5. The calculator dialog box.

This is where the formula is defined. You can see that at the top left of the dialog box, FileMaker has entered the first part of the formula:

Total Earnings =

Below this is the area in which you actually enter the formula. There are two ways to do this. You can simply type:

Base + Bonus

Alternatively, you can use the mouse to select the elements of the formula from the various lists below the box. (Just click on Base, in the field list on the left, then click on the plus sign in the calculator pad, followed by the Bonus in the field list.)

When you select OK, you have finished defining the Total Earnings field, and you are returned to the Field Definition dialog box in case you want to define any further fields. When you exit the Field Definition dialog box, you are returned to the database. In Browse mode, the results appear something like those seen in Fig. 6-6.

Fig. 6-6. New field in Browse mode.

Note that the new field does add up the amounts in the Base and Bonus fields. However, the new field could use some formatting. When the font for the field label is improved and the appropriate number format has been applied, the results look something like Fig. 6-7.

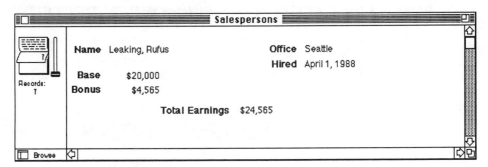

Fig. 6-7. Results of formatting.

Note that the alignment of the numbers in the Base and Bonus fields has also been adjusted. By using the Right option under Format Align in the Layout mode, the numbers are displayed on the right of the fields, lining up correctly. Remember that the default alignment for all fields is Left, and you do not need to change this for a number field unless you have several number fields arranged one below the other that you want to line up.

When you have defined a calculation field, it is placed in all records. Also note that you cannot activate a calculated field. When entering data, you tab straight past calculated fields. This is because the entries in calculated fields are generated by File-Maker, and you cannot override them. However, you can change a calculated field into a noncalculated field by altering the field type to Text, Number, or Date. This replaces the formulas with their results in all of the records in the database. Note that there is no warning when you do this. FileMaker immediately converts the formulas to values when you select the noncalculated field type. You should perform this action with care because it is not possible to use the Undo command to return the values to the formulas.

Converting formulas into their results have some useful applications. For example, suppose you have recorded base pay in a field called Base. You decide to increase the base pay of all employees by ten percent. Define a calculated field called New-Base, so that

NewBase = Base * 1.1

The 1.1 is a number, or *constant*, that does not appear in a field but is supplied to create the correct result—in this case, the new base pay rates. Now you can change NewBase to a Number field, which fixes the values in the field. Next you define Base as a calculated field with the following formula:

Base = NewBase

Then you change Base back to a Number field, which fixes the new values in the field. Finally, you delete the NewBase field. All of this can be done from the Define menu without permanently affecting the layout.

SUMMARY CALCULATIONS BETWEEN RECORDS

You can perform some calculations between records by using *summary* formulas. For example, you can have FileMaker calculate the total of all values in a particular field. In the database in Fig. 6-8, you have the base pay and bonus for the company's salespersons.

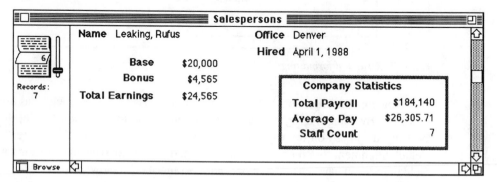

Fig. 6-8. Simple database with formulas.

The field called Total Earnings represents the sum of the Base and Bonus fields, expressed in a formula like this:

Total Earnings = Base + Bonus

If you are managing the company budget, you might want to know the total payments to all salespersons. This is provided by the Total Payroll field, which uses a summary formula. The field is defined as:

Total Payroll = Total of Total Earnings

After typing the field name and choosing Summary as the field type, you define a summary formula by choosing the type of summary and the field that contains the data you want to summarize. In Fig. 6-9, you can see the field Staff Count being defined.

The list of Field Definitions shows the way that the Average Pay field is calculated, as the Average of Total Earnings field. When you select Summary as the field type and click OK, you will see a formula screen like the one in Fig. 6-10.

From the list on the left, you choose the type of summary formula you want. From the list on the right, you pick the field that you want summarized. In this case, Count of has been chosen. You can count the entries in any number, text, or date field. Counting those in the field called Name effectively counts the number of salespersons. At first you might think that this is redundant because the count is probably the same

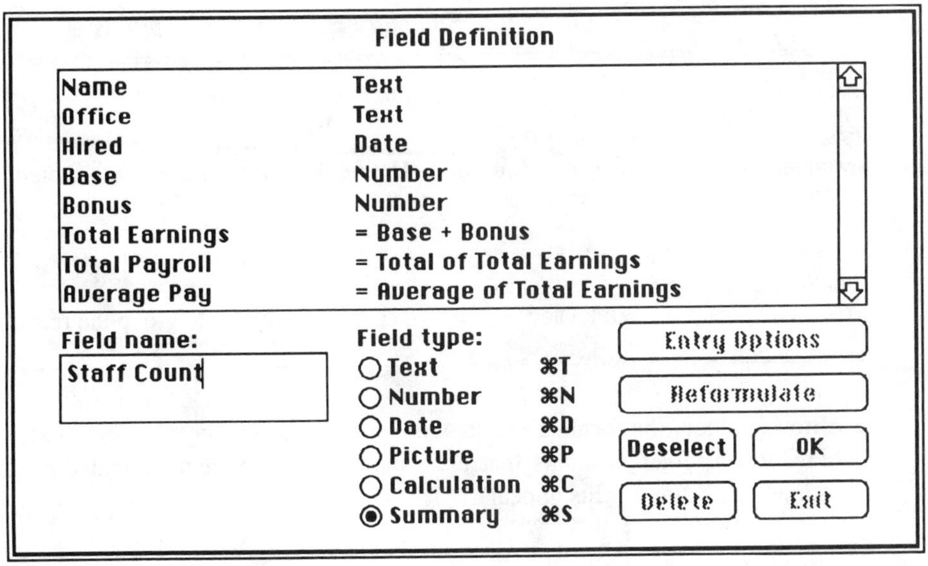

Field Definition

Name	Text
Office	Text
Hired	Date
Base	Number
Bonus	Number
Total Earnings	= Base + Bonus
Total Payroll	= Total of Total Earnings
Average Pay	= Average of Total Earnings

Field name:
Staff Count|

Field type:
○ Text   ⌘T
○ Number   ⌘N
○ Date   ⌘D
○ Picture   ⌘P
○ Calculation ⌘C
◉ Summary   ⌘S

[Entry Options]
[Reformulate]
[Deselect] [OK]
[Delete] [Exit]

Fig. 6-9. Defining a summary field.

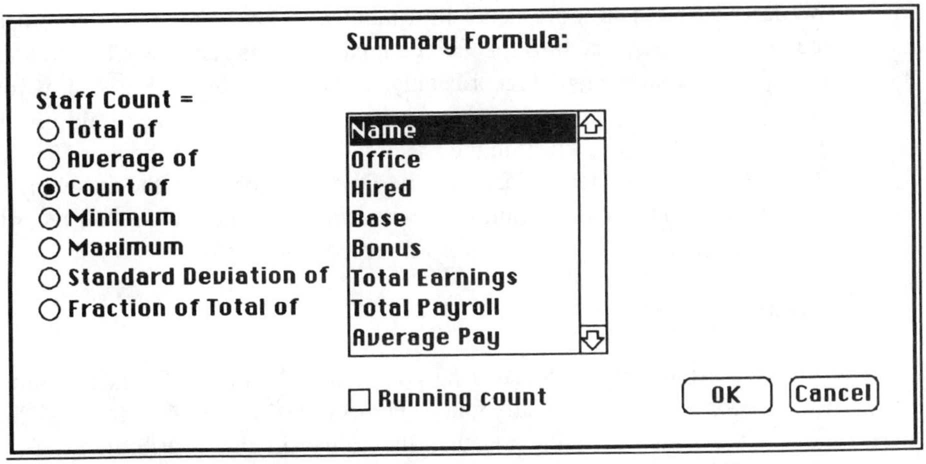

Summary Formula:

Staff Count =
○ Total of
○ Average of
◉ Count of
○ Minimum
○ Maximum
○ Standard Deviation of
○ Fraction of Total of

Name
Office
Hired
Base
Bonus
Total Earnings
Total Payroll
Average Pay

☐ Running count   [OK] [Cancel]

Fig. 6-10. Formulating a summary formula.

as the number of records shown in the Browse mode; however, useful applications for this formula are described later in the section "The Count Of."

Note the check box below the list of field names. In this case, it is called Running count, indicating that you have the option to make the count summary a running one. This option check box changes according to the type of summary formula, as shown in Table 6-2. We return to these options in a moment.

After selecting the summary type, the field name, and checking the option, you can click OK to return to the definition screen. When you pick OK return to the

Table 6-2. Summary Formulas and Options.

Summary	Option	Further Information
Total	Running Total	
Average	Weighted Average	The field by which the average should be weighted.
Count	Running Count	
Minimum		
Maximum		
Standard Deviation		
Fraction of Total	Subtotaled	The field to sort by to group the records for the subtotals.

Browse mode, the formula results will normally be displayed (there is an exception: Fraction of Total formulas that are subtotalled might require that the database be sorted before the results appear).

SUMMARY TYPES

As you can see from Fig. 6-10, FileMaker provides several types of summaries. We describe these in more detail in a moment. However, before we proceed, it is important to understand how the Find command affects summary formulas. Summary formulas work on the found records only. Thus, in the case of Fig. 6-8, if you wanted the total payroll for all salespersons in the Denver office, you would use the Select Find command, enter Denver in the Office field, then execute the Find. The Company Statistics box would then reflect only the Denver records. In the following summary formula definitions and examples, we sometimes use the phrase "all records" when strictly speaking we should say "for all records found."

The Total Of

The Total summary calculates the sum of the values in the field being summarized, for all records that are currently found. For example, in Fig. 6-8, the Total Payroll field is a Total summary, adding together the values in the Total Earnings fields of all records. When you select Total, an option check box appears below the field name list, called Running total. If you check this box, then the field gives you the accumulating sum record by record. For example, in the database of retail stores shown in Fig. 6-11, a field shows the sales achieved so far.

The sales for each store for each week are entered on a separate record. When the database is sorted by the week ending date and all the records for a particular store are found, the cumulative sales figure shows the level of sales achieved by the store at that point in the year. This formula is not particularly revealing when viewed on a single record, but it does enable you to create reports like the one in Fig. 6-12, where the cumulative total is more meaningful.

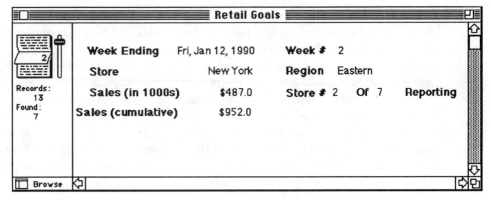

Fig. 6-11. Running total.

Store	New York	Region	Eastern
Week Ending	Fri, Jan 5, 1990	**Week #** 1	
Sales (in 1000s)	$465.0	**Sales (cumulative)**	$465.0
Week Ending	Fri, Jan 12, 1990	**Week #** 2	
Sales (in 1000s)	$487.0	**Sales (cumulative)**	$952.0
Week Ending	Fri, Jan 19, 1990	**Week #** 3	
Sales (in 1000s)	$465.0	**Sales (cumulative)**	$1,417.0
Week Ending	Fri, Jan 26, 1990	**Week #** 4	
Sales (in 1000s)	$345.0	**Sales (cumulative)**	$1,762.0
Week Ending	Fri, Feb 2, 1990	**Week #** 5	
Sales (in 1000s)	$367.0	**Sales (cumulative)**	$2,129.0
Week Ending	Fri, Feb 9, 1990	**Week #** 6	
Sales (in 1000s)	$565.0	**Sales (cumulative)**	$2,694.0
Week Ending	Fri, Feb 16, 1990	**Week #** 7	
Sales (in 1000s)	$385.0	**Sales (cumulative)**	$3,079.0

Fig. 6-12. Cumulative total in a report.

The Average Of

The Average summary gives the arithmetic mean of all the values in the field being summarized. You can see this type of summary used in Fig. 6-8 where the Average Pay field shows the average of the Total Earnings field for all entries in the database. Note that you do not need to have either a Total field or a Count field to perform an average. The average summary formula sums the values in the specified field and divides by the number of values. Blank or text entries in a field do not distort File-Maker's calculation of the average.

When you select Average, an option check box appears below the field name list, called Weight Average. If you check this box, then the field gives you average of values weighted by another field. For example, if you have a database of wage earners show-ing the hours they worked in a week and the wages they were paid for that work, you could create a summary field to show the average wage. However, this would not take into account the fact that each person in the database worked a different number of hours to earn these wages. In Fig. 6-13, you can see a database called WagePersons in which both types of average field are used in the Company Statistics box.

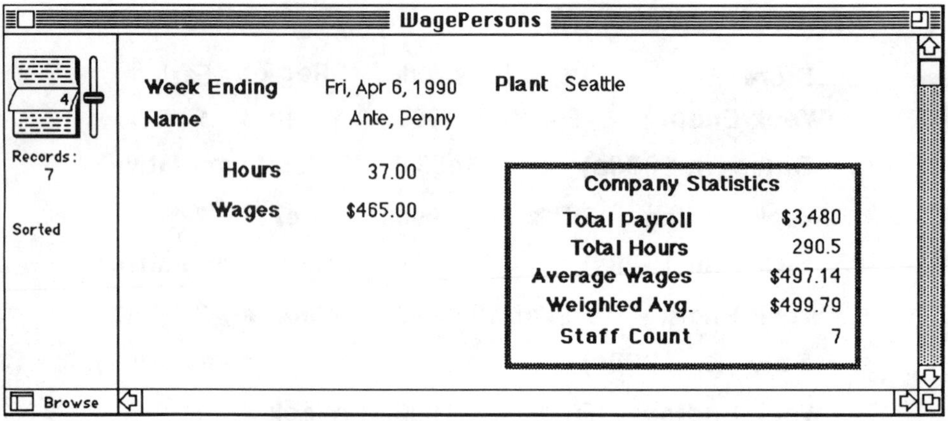

Fig. 6-13. Weighted average example.

The Weighted Avg. field is an average of the Wages field weighted by the Hours field. You can see that the weighted average is greater than the plain average. (You can get the plain average by dividing the figure in Total Payroll by the number in Total Hours.) The weighted average is greater than the plain average because it takes into account the varying hours worked to achieve the earnings. In Fig. 6-14, you can see the formulas for the database in Fig. 6-13.

You can see that the field used for weighing by the Weighted Avg. field is listed in parentheses.

The Count Of

Sometimes you want to know the number of fields that contain a value in the field being summarized. For example, the Staff Count field in Fig. 6-13 shows the number of staff in the database. While you are in Browse mode, a Count formula might be a duplicate of the record counter. However, the record counter does not appear in File-Maker reports, and so counting is very useful for reporting the number of entries in a field or the number of persons in a database. Of course, in some situations, the Count

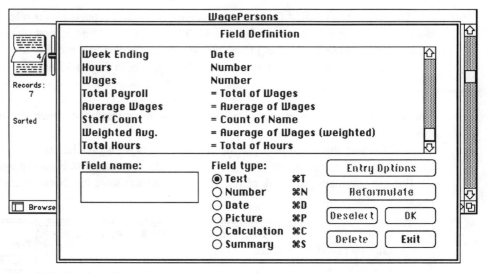

Fig. 6-14. Database formulas.

figure is not the same as the record counter. For example, in a database where you are waiting for entries in some fields, such as a student database awaiting insertion of grades, you might want to count a field to keep track of how many grades have been reported so far. Such a field answers the question, "In how many records has an entry been made in the Grade field?"

When you select Count, an option check box appears below the field name list called Running Count. If you check this box, then the field gives you the accumulating count record by record. This is not the same as counting how many entries are in a field so far. Instead, a Running Count shows what number the current is of the total. Thus the number might change when the database is sorted. In a large database, a Running Count might be helpful in reports to number each record sequentially, as seen in Fig. 6-15.

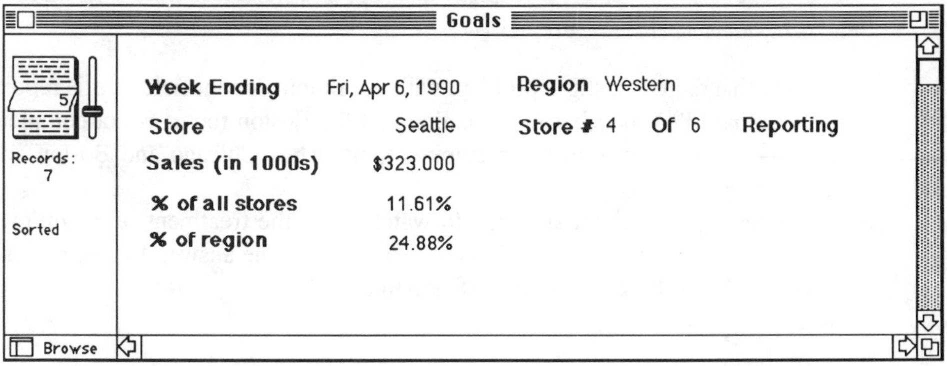

Goals			
Week Ending	Fri, Apr 6, 1990	**Region** Western	
Store	Seattle	**Store #** 4 Of 6	Reporting
Sales (in 1000s)	$323.000		
% of all stores	11.61%		
% of region	24.88%		

Fig. 6-15. A running count example.

The field simply called Of shows how many stores have reported their sales. This is a Count formula applied to the Sales field. The field called Store # shows a running count of the Sales field. By using these two summary fields plus a piece of text on the layout (Reporting), you create the statement that appears in Fig. 6-15 as:

Store # 4 Of 6 Reporting

Note that this is not the same set of numbers as the record counter, which shows that this is record 5 of 7 records.

What causes this discrepancy is the fact that one of the stores has not reported its sales. As you can see from Fig. 6-16 where a report of the database is shown with the File Preview command, the bulk of record for the Boston store has been entered, but the sales figure is missing.

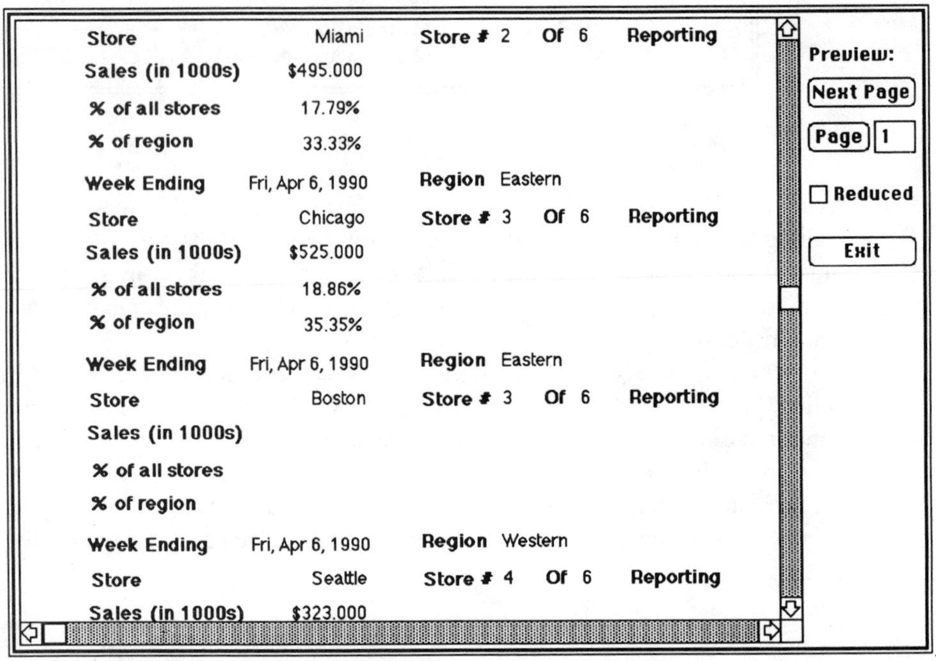

Store	Miami	Store # 2	Of 6	Reporting	Preview:
Sales (in 1000s)	$495.000				Next Page
% of all stores	17.79%				Page 1
% of region	33.33%				
Week Ending	Fri, Apr 6, 1990	Region Eastern			Reduced
Store	Chicago	Store # 3	Of 6	Reporting	
Sales (in 1000s)	$525.000				Exit
% of all stores	18.86%				
% of region	35.35%				
Week Ending	Fri, Apr 6, 1990	Region Eastern			
Store	Boston	Store # 3	Of 6	Reporting	
Sales (in 1000s)					
% of all stores					
% of region					
Week Ending	Fri, Apr 6, 1990	Region Western			
Store	Seattle	Store # 4	Of 6	Reporting	
Sales (in 1000s)	$323.000				

Fig. 6-16. Running count report preview.

Note that there is a slight problem with the running count field in this report. The only way that FileMaker has of indicating that the Boston report is not complete is to repeat the number given to the previous report. Thus Chicago and Boston are both listed as Store 3 of 6 Reporting.

Another special count situation to watch for is the treatment of conditional formula fields. A conditional formula is one that returns the answer 1 or 0, representing Yes or No. Consider the following statements:

Score > 2
Score < 4
Score = 2 * 1.5

The answer to each one is either true or false, depending on the value of Score. If Score is 3, then each one is true. FileMaker allows you to use such formulas and returns 1 for true, 0 for false. You can then format the field to show the response as Yes or No.

Conditional formulas are discussed in detail later in the chapter; for now consider the example in Fig. 6-17. Here you can see a field called Passed, which is defined as follows:

Passed = Score > Pass Level

If the value in Pass Level is 75 and the value in Score is 76, then the result in Passed is 1, shown as Yes in Fig. 6-17 because the field was specially formatted with the Format Number command. Suppose you want to count how many students have passed the exam by placing the result in the Number Passed field. You might be tempted to use the Count summary and apply it to the Passed field. This would be incorrect because a count of the Passed field will return the number of students. Instead, you would use the Total summary on the Passed field. This will add all of the 1 results that represent Yes and give an accurate report of the number of passing students.

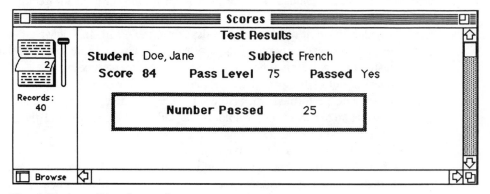

Fig. 6-17. A conditional example.

The Minimum

You might want to know the lowest number or the earliest date in a particular field. This can be accomplished by using a Minimum summary formula. For example, to find the lowest score in the database in Fig. 6-17, you would add a minimum formula as shown in Fig. 6-18.

The Maximum

You might want to know the highest number or the latest date in a particular field. This can be accomplished by using a Maximum summary formula. This is used in Fig. 6-18 to show the highest score.

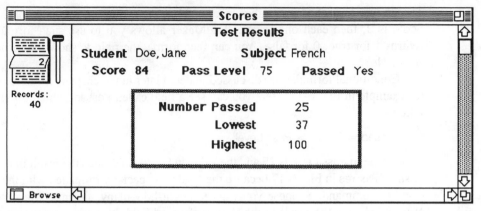

Fig. 6-18. Minimum and Maximum formulas.

The Standard Deviation

For those who are not up on their statistics, the *standard deviation* is a measure of how much a group of values varies or deviates from the mean of the group. This is useful when you want to know if a specific value is particularly high or low; in other words, whether or not it deviates a great deal from the norm. In FileMaker, you can measure standard deviation with a summary formula. For example, suppose that you are an instructor analyzing scores obtained by 40 students taking a test. The test results, marked out of 100, are listed in Table 6-3. While you are interested in how individual students performed, you also want to know if there are any conclusions that can be drawn from the scores as a whole. If you add up all the scores and divide by 40, you can see that the average score was 77.55. You can also see that the scores range from 37 to 100, but this is a very wide range, including the best and worst performances. You would like to know where most students finished. If you organize the test results using the database in Fig. 6-19, the average can be calculated by FileMaker, as can the standard deviation, given in the Std field. This shows that for the 40 results, the standard deviation is 13.37.

Table 6-3. Test Results.

77	68	86	84	95	98	87	71
84	92	96	83	62	83	81	85
91	74	61	52	83	73	85	78
50	81	37	60	85	100	79	81
75	92	80	75	78	71	64	65

Note that the actual result includes many more decimal places but it is normal to round off standard deviation to a level of precision close to that of the data being analyzed. A standard deviation of 13.37 implies that most of the 40 scores will be within

Scores
Test Results
Doe, Jane
Score 84
Average 77.55
Within Range Yes
Std 13.37
How Many? 27
Lower 64.18
Upper 91.32
Records:
40
Browse

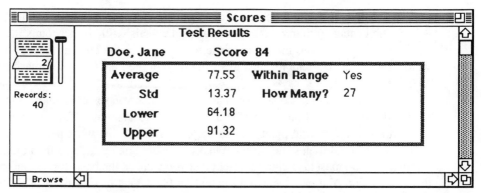

Fig. 6-19. Standard deviation example.

13.37 points of the mean or average, which is 77.55. If you subtract 13.37 from 77.55 you get 64.18. If you add 13.37 to 77.55 you get 91.32. This means that most scores will be between 64.18 and 91.32. This range is referred to as one standard deviation from the mean. A rule of thumb in statistics is that two-thirds of the measurements will be within one standard deviation of the mean. The field called Within Range checks to see if the score on the current record is within this range and returns Yes if it is. The field called How Many? is a Total summary of the Within Range field. This shows that 27 of the scores were within the range, which is 67.5 percent of 40, proving the rule of thumb to be correct in this case. Determination of the Lower, Upper, and Within Range fields are described later in the chapter.

The Fraction of Total

Suppose you want to know what percentage of the total wages each person earns. In Fig. 6-20, you can see that the field Of Total is doing just that, letting you know that Penny Ante's wages were 13.36% of the total wages for all employees.

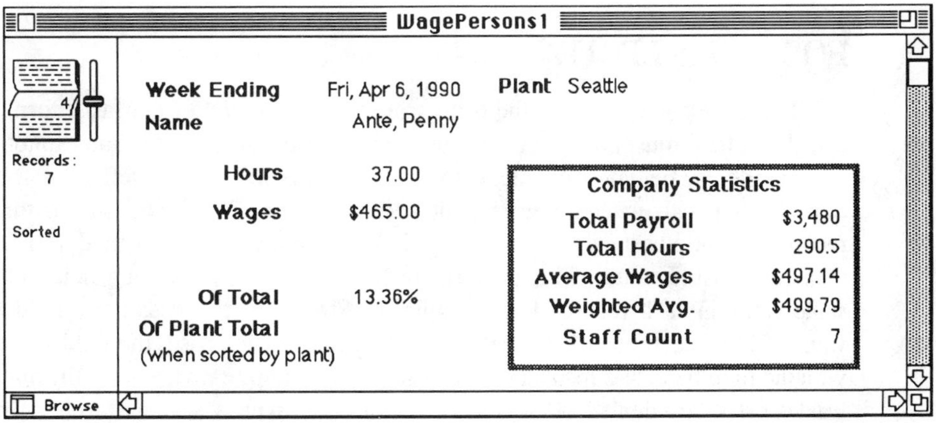

WagePersons1
Week Ending Fri, Apr 6, 1990
Plant Seattle
Name Ante, Penny
Hours 37.00
Wages $465.00
Of Total 13.36%
Of Plant Total
(when sorted by plant)
Company Statistics
Total Payroll $3,480
Total Hours 290.5
Average Wages $497.14
Weighted Avg. $499.79
Staff Count 7
Records:
7
Sorted
Browse

Fig. 6-20. Fraction or percentage of total.

This is done with the Fraction of Total summary formula, with the results formatted as a percentage (otherwise they appear as decimals). FileMaker totals the wages field, then divides it into the value in the wages field of the current record. In other words, the Fraction of Total formula gives the ratio of the field being summarized to its total.

If you use the Subtotalled option that appears when you select Fraction of Total, the field will show the fraction that the field contributes to a subtotal. For example, Penny Ante works at the Seattle plant, so you might want to know what percentage of the Seattle plant's total wages she earns. When you select Subtotalled and then the field to summarize, you must also choose a field that you want as the basis for the subtotal, in this case, Plant. You can see a field called Of Plant Total in Fig. 6-20. This field is defined as a Summary formula, Fraction of Total, Subtotalled by Plant. However, no value is in the field yet. That is because the database must be sorted by the field used as the basis for the subtotal plant before the subtotal appears. In Fig. 6-21, you can see that the database has been sorted and the subtotal figure presented.

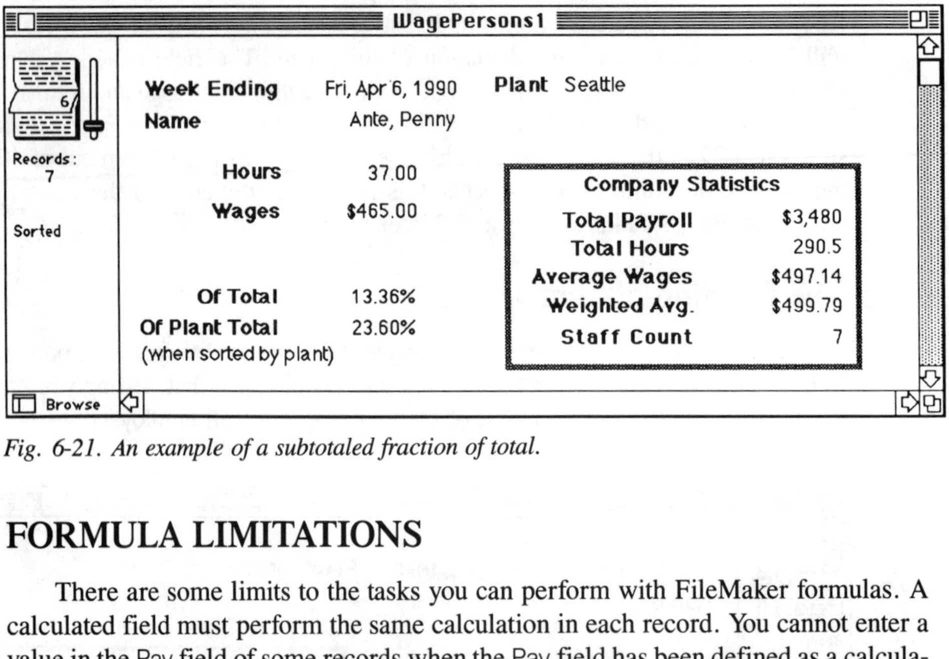

	WagePersons1	
Week Ending	Fri, Apr 6, 1990	**Plant** Seattle
Name	Ante, Penny	

Records: 7

Sorted

| **Hours** | 37.00 |
| **Wages** | $465.00 |

Company Statistics	
Total Payroll	$3,480
Total Hours	290.5
Average Wages	$497.14
Weighted Avg.	$499.79
Staff Count	7

Of Total	13.36%
Of Plant Total	23.60%
(when sorted by plant)	

Browse

Fig. 6-21. An example of a subtotaled fraction of total.

FORMULA LIMITATIONS

There are some limits to the tasks you can perform with FileMaker formulas. A calculated field must perform the same calculation in each record. You cannot enter a value in the Pay field of some records when the Pay field has been defined as a calculation. Indeed, calculated fields cannot accept user input. When you tab through a record, you skip past calculated fields. However, you can create a field as a formula, then convert it to values. This is particularly useful when you want a field to have the same value in each record. For example, in Fig. 6-18, the Pass Level field has the value of 75 in each record. Instead of entering this in each case, the field was defined with the field type Calculation. In response to the prompt Pass Level = , the number 75 was entered. As soon as OK was selected, the field type was altered to Number. The value 75 was thus entered in the Pass Level field of every record. Should the need arise to change the pass level, the field can be redefined as Calculation, the new number entered, and then the field returned to Number type.

There is also a limit to the math you can perform between records. You cannot create formulas that refer to values in adjacent records. For example, you cannot have a field called Price that is the value in the Price field of the previous record plus ten percent. There is no formula to create multiple variations of one record. However, you can use the Duplicate command on the Edit menu and then edit the duplicate record. You can also use the Entry Options to do some automatic entering of data instead of using formulas. The Entry Options, accessed through the Define command, allow entering of today's date, a serial number, or specific data for each new record.

FileMaker's summary formulas are subject to an important limitation: They cannot be used in other formulas. For example, in the database in Fig. 6-18, you might want a field called Spread in order to show the spread of scores obtained in the test. This field would subtract Lowest from Highest, but, because both are summary fields, you cannot create the formula:

Spread = Highest – Lowest

There appears to be no way around this limitation, and you need to bear it in mind as you design formula-based fields.

As another example of this limitation, consider the Lower and Upper fields used in the database in Fig. 6-19. The value in the Lower field is the result from the Average field minus the value in the Std field. The value in the Upper field is the result from the Average field plus the value in the Std field. However, neither the Upper or Lower field can be directly calculated from FileMaker, due to the limitation on the use of summary fields. Instead, the values were entered directly after they were computed with the Macintosh calculator. In some cases, you can use extended fields to get around the problem of calculating with summary fields. If you were to make a single record out of the scores in Fig. 6-18 using an extended Score field with room for 40 entries, then you could use the FileMaker functions described later in this chapter to perform your calculations instead of using summary formulas.

A different limitation related to summary formulas is the fact that browsing layouts created using the View as List option on the Gadget menu, the values in summary fields are not displayed. You can see this in Fig. 6-22.

This is the database seen earlier in Figs. 6-15 and 6-16 where the summary values are visible. That is because Fig. 6-15 shows the Browse mode without the View as List option and Fig. 6-16 shows the File Preview mode. The latter figure shows the same layout as that in Fig. 6-22; the difference is that while FileMaker has no problem printing out summary values from lists, it just doesn't like showing them in Browse mode.

One other limitation that relates to formulas in general is the restriction imposed on field names by the need to avoid ambiguity with what is sometimes referred to as *formula syntax*. The syntax of formulas means the way they are put together. Take this formula:

New Price = Price * 1.01

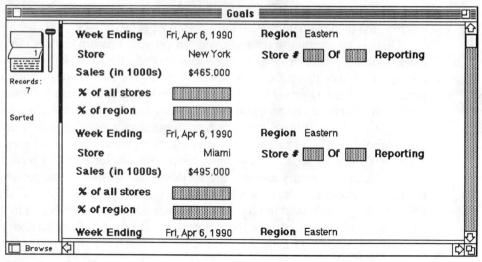

Fig. 6-22. Summary values hidden in list view.

The syntax of this formula is

    Field = Field, Operator, Constant

If you try to create a field called Price/Pound, FileMaker will see that this could be confused with Price field divided by Pound field and respond with the message seen in Fig. 6-23.

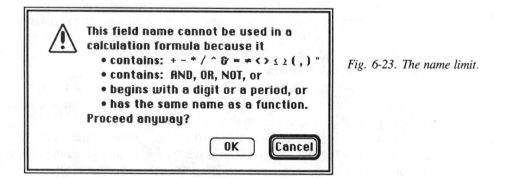

Fig. 6-23. The name limit.

Because the name looks like a formula, FileMaker will not allow the field named Price/Pound to be used in calculations. You can proceed to use the name if this restriction does not interfere with your plans for the Price/Pound field. Otherwise, you can cancel this name and create one without formula operators. In general, it is best to follow the latter course and avoid any possible confusion between the field names and formula statements.

LOGICAL FORMULAS

Sometimes you might want to evaluate the contents of a FileMaker field not as a number, but as a true/false or yes/no response. For example, consider the daycare application form in Fig. 6-24.

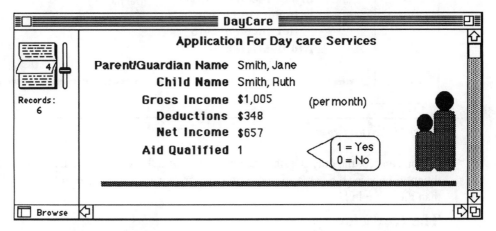

Fig. 6-24. Day care application.

Here the applicant's net income is evaluated to see if the applicant qualifies for financial aid. A response of 1 in the Aid Qualified field indicates that the applicant does qualify for financial aid, as indicated by the explanatory text added to the layout. A response of 1 can be read as meaning *true* or *yes*. A response of 0 would mean *false* or *no*. The formula in the Aid Qualified field is:

Aid Qualified = Net Income < 800

The figure of 800 is the level of income below which aid is available.

This formula is referred to as a *logical formula* or *conditional statement*. The formula evaluates a condition. The only possible result that FileMaker can return is 1 or 0 meaning that yes the condition exists, or no it does not. In the example, the value in the Net Income field is either less than 800 or it is not.

You can see that adding explanatory text to the layout in Fig. 6-24 clarifies the meaning of the formula result to the user. However, a more sophisticated approach would be to use the Yes/No format, which displays Yes if the value in a field is 1, and No if the entry is 0. You can do this in Layout mode, selecting Format Number from the Format menu, then checking the button labelled Format as Yes/No. This format was used in the revised worksheet shown in Fig. 6-25.

You can see other examples of the Yes/No format in the Passed field shown in Fig. 6-18, and the Within Range field in Fig. 6-19. The latter contains two conditions combined by the logical operator AND, described in a moment. The formula is as follows:

Within Range = Score > Lower AND Score < Upper

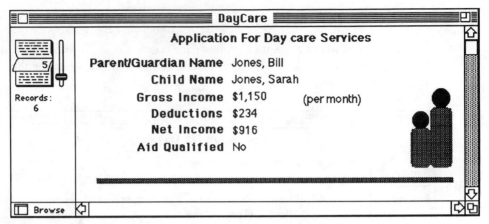

Fig. 6-25. Revised format.

As you can see, the only possible results to this formula are true or false. For the condition to be true, the value in Score must be greater than the value in Lower and less than the value in Upper.

The IF Factor

While the display of a Yes/No answer is a useful application of the logical or conditional formula, the more common use of this type of formula is in IF statements. An IF statement is a specialized formula that uses FileMaker's IF function to make a choice between two possible answers based on a condition you describe. Details on the use of functions are given in this chapter; for now it is enough to note that each has a syntax or format that must be followed. The syntax of the IF statement is as follows:

    IF (Condition, Result If True, Result If False)

The Condition is a conditional statement, like those described in the previous section. The Result If True is a formula, a date, a number, or a piece of text that the IF statement returns if the conditional statement is true. The Result If False is a formula, a date, a number, or a piece of text that the IF statement returns if the conditional statement is false. For example, if you have a field called Score containing test results, you can define a calculated field called Status that returns the text Pass if the score is greater than 75, or Fail if the score is 75 or lower. The formula defining the Status field would look like this:

    Status = (IF Score > 75, "Pass", "Fail")

Note that you need to make sure that the result type for this calculated field is Text, otherwise the answer appears as 0. A more flexible approach might be to enter the passing level (75) in a separate field so that the value can be altered without revising the Status formula. If you use Pass Level as the name for this new field, the following formula would work nicely:

    Status = (IF Score > Pass Level, "Pass", "Fail")

A more sophisticated example might be in a sales invoice database, where quantity discounts are calculated. The Discount field could be defined as follows:

Discount = IF (Quantity ≥ 100, Cost * .1, 0)

FileMaker will return 0 for a discount if the value in the Quantity field is 100 or less. If Quantity is over 100, then the result is ten percent of the value in the Cost field.

You can actually combine more than one IF statement. This is known as *nesting* IF statements. For example, you could define a different level of discount with the following IF statement:

Discount = IF (Quantity > 200, Cost * .15, 0)

To create a discount with two levels you can combine the two IF statements as follows:

Discount = IF (Quantity > 100, Cost * .1, IF (Quantity > 200, Cost * .15, 0))

Note that the second IF statement is introduced as the Result If Fail part of the first IF statement and two closing parentheses are required. You can nest numerous IF statements as long as you do not exceed the character limit of formulas (255). If you find you are developing lengthy multiple IF statements, you might consider using a lookup field instead.

In the childcare example shown in Fig. 6-24, you might want FileMaker to compute the financial aid available if the applicant qualifies for aid. Consider this formula:

Aid Qualified = IF (Net Income < 800, 1000 - Net Income, "Not Qualified")

The calculation performed by FileMaker *if* the Net Income is less than 800 is:

1000 - Net Income

This serves to produce an aid amount that is the difference between 1000 and the applicant's actual net income. If the Net Income is 800 or greater, then the statement Not Qualified is returned, as shown in Fig. 6-26.

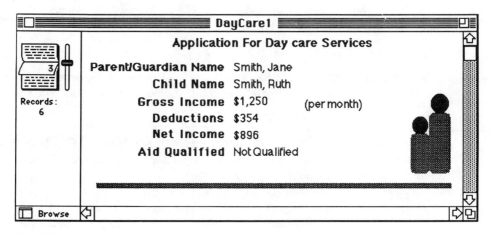

Fig. 6-26. A text response.

Logical Operators

FileMaker provides a comprehensive set of logical operators with which to construct conditional statements. You can see them listed in Table 6-4. You have already seen the > and < operators in use. Note that these mean greater than and less than respectively, and do not include the value that follows them. The statement Pay > 800 would be false if Pay was 800. For the statement to be true at 800, the greater than/equal to symbol is required, as in Pay ≥ 800. The equal (=) and not equal (≠) symbols are useful if you want an exact match rather than a range. The use of AND allows you to combine two or more conditions. For example, to identify Pay values between 800 and 1000, you can use Pay > 800 combined with Pay < 1000 as in:

    Pay > 800 AND Pay < 1000

Note that both statements require that the field be stated.

Table 6-4. Logical Operators.

Name	Symbol	Example	Results (where Age is 21)	
Equal	=	Age = 21	1	Yes
Not equal	≠	Age ≠ 21	0	No
Greater than	>	Age > 18	1	Yes
Less than	<	Age < 30	1	Yes
Less than/equal to	≥	Age ≥ 21	1	Yes
Greater than equal to	≤	Age ≤ 21	1	Yes
And	AND	Age > 18 AND Age < 30	1	Yes
Or	OR	Age > 21 OR Age < 30	1	Yes
Not	NOT	Age = NOT > 30 or < 18	1	Yes

The OR operator creates a wider range of matching values. Suppose you were to substitute OR for AND in the previous example:

    Pay > 800 OR Pay < 1000

You can see that any value for Pay would create a true result. However, if you wanted to exclude Pay values between 800 and 1000, you could use the following:

    Pay < 800 OR Pay > 1000

This would return false if the value in Pay was 800, 801, up to 1000. The NOT operator is another way of excluding values. For example, to return false for all values of Pay except 800, you would use Pay NOT 800.

When using more than one logical operator in a formula, be sure to check the formula results using a range of values. The combined effects of logical operators can be complex and testing can help you avoid unexpected and undesirable results.

FILEMAKER FUNCTIONS

If you are familiar with electronic spreadsheet programs such as MicroSoft Excel or WingZ, you have already got a head start when it comes to performing complex calculations with FileMaker. A system of functions similar to that in spreadsheet programs is used by FileMaker to make powerful calculations easier. These functions operate on values within a record. For example, a bank wants to use FileMaker to track loan applications. A simple form, showing the applicant's name, whether or not the applicant has checking and saving accounts at the bank, together with a rundown of the loan the applicant is applying for, is seen in Fig. 6-27.

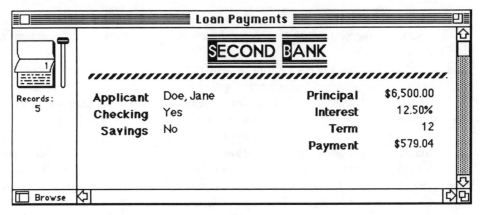

Fig. 6-27. A loan payment calculation.

The three values required to calculate a loan are the amount to be borrowed (the *principal*), plus the length of the loan (the *term*), and the rate of interest being charged. The term is stated as a number of periods, for example, 12 months. The interest is normally stated as a percentage per year, for example, 12.50%. FileMaker, like many other programs, requires that interest be calculated as an amount per period, and so the annual figure needs to be divided by 12 in the formula to give a rate per month. In Fig. 6-28, you can see how the elements of the calculation are brought together by the PMT function.

```
Principal          Number
Interest           Number
Term               Number
Payment            = pmt (Principal,Interest/12,Term)
Applicant          Text
Checking           Text
Savings            Text
```

Fig. 6-28. The payment formula defined.

The PMT function is just one of dozens provided by FileMaker. The format or syntax of most functions is as follows:

FUNCTION(Argument1, Argument2, Argument3)

Some functions only have one argument, but where several are required, they are separated by commas. Parentheses are placed around the arguments. A full list of the functions is provided in the Field Definition dialog box. The function arguments can be names of fields containing data, or constant data that you enter when defining the calculated field. For example, you do not need an interest field to calculate a loan payment. You can enter the interest figure directly, as a constant value, as in:

Payment = (Principal, 12.5/12, Term)

The following sections deal with the functions by grouping them according to their role.

 The way that you enter formulas with functions is open to a considerable amount of latitude as far as capitalization and spaces are concerned. We have chosen to present function names all in capitals to draw attention to them and distinguish them from field names. FileMaker accepts function names entered this way in formulas and does not alter your capitalization in the way that some spreadsheet programs do. Also, File-Maker does not object when you leave spaces between operators and field names, or between commas and arguments within function statements. These spaces are not closed up in the stored version of the formula. However, when you come to use the text functions, you will find that spaces have an important role in some situations and need to be entered with care.

MATHEMATICAL FUNCTIONS

The mathematical functions perform basic math on data, simplifying many operations and improving the accuracy of your work. They include integer, absolute, and modulus calculations.

Using ABS

The ABS function gives you the absolute (non negative value) of a value. The function is applied as follows:

ABS(Value)

Suppose that you want to know how much money could be saved by borrowing money at the rate offered by Bank A rather than that offered by Bank B. You could subtract the B rate from the A rate and use this in your calculations; however, the answer might be negative and you might not want to work with a negative interest rate. By applying the ABS function, as seen in the formula,

Difference = ABS(A Rate − B Rate)

the Difference will always be a positive number.

Using INT

This function gives you the integer component of a value. In other words, it lops off any fractions or decimal places. This is a useful way of simplifying numbers when a fraction would not be valid. For example, to determine how many full truck loads there are when transporting 35 cases of wine with a truck that carries 16 cases at a time, the answer should be a whole number. You would use a formula like this:

```
Full Loads  =  INT(Total Cases/Cases Per Truck)
     2      =  INT(35/16)
```

You can see the function at work in a similar example in the database Fig. 6-29. Note that you do not need to enter the INT function in capitals for it to work correctly.

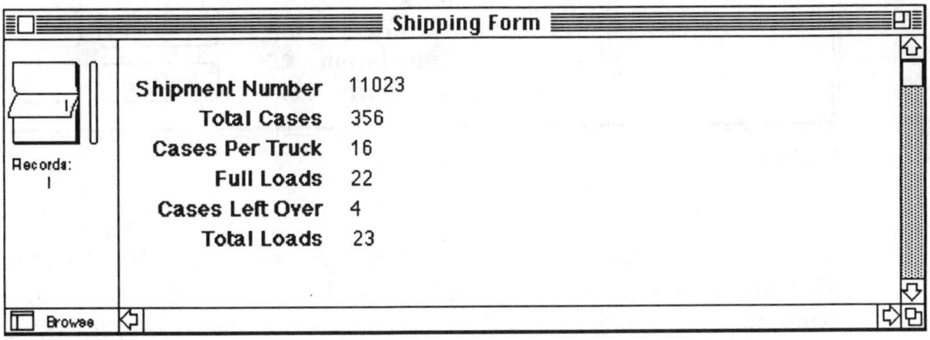

Fig. 6-29. The INT function at work.

Using MOD

The MOD function gives you the remainder of X divided by Y. The two values are combined within parentheses and separated by a comma, *not* the division symbol. A typical use would be to see how many cases of wine are left over after the truck has been filled with full loads. The following formula does the trick:

```
Cases Left Over  =  MOD(Total Cases,Cases Per Truck)
       4         =  MOD(356,16)
```

You can see the MOD function at work in the database in Fig. 6-29. In Fig. 6-30, you can see the way that the fields for this database are defined.

Using ROUND

While the INT function cuts off decimal places, the ROUND function performs standard mathematical rounding. You might wonder why you would need this function since FileMaker correctly rounds numbers for display purposes when you use the Format Number command in the Layout mode. The answer lies in the fact that format rounding is *for display purposes only*. Even when you round a number like 2.35 to 0

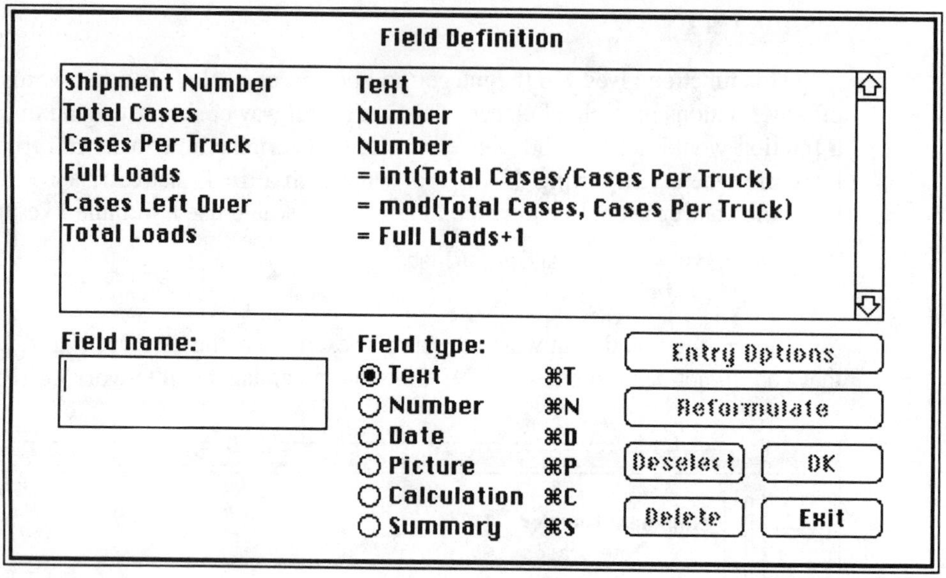

Fig. 6-30. The MOD and INT functions defined.

decimal places using formatting, FileMaker remembers the .35. Calculated fields often contain numbers that have many decimal places, and the Format command is used to tidy their appearance. This is fine unless the formatted value is used in another calculation where the accumulation of decimal portions produces an incorrect or anomalous result.

The Round function is placed around a formula whenever you want the formula to return an answer to a limited number of decimal places. For example, you would use Round when calculating sales tax at six percent, as in:

    Tax = ROUND(Price * .06,2)

The number of decimal places that the ROUND function uses is specified as the second argument in the function statement, in this case 2.

To see where rounding becomes quite a problem, consider the example in Fig. 6-31 where each of three departments is supposed to get one third of the Total Grant, which is 10,000 in this case.

The result of dividing 10,000 by 3 is 3333.3333 recurring. In Fig. 6-32, you can see the field definitions and formulas that produced this database.

With unformatted fields, the results look messy and so the designer of the database formats each dollar field to two decimal places. The effect can be seen in Fig. 6-33.

The problem of format rounding is now apparent as the formatted value in the Total field, which is defined:

    Total = Sciences + Arts + Sport

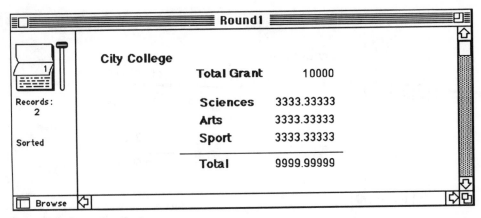

Fig. 6-31. Grant distribution.

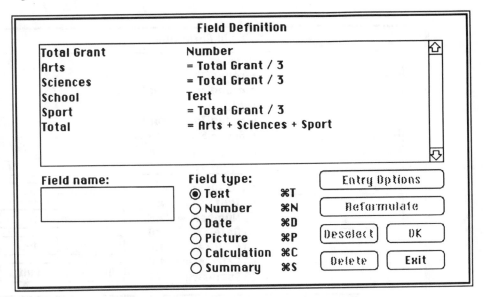

Fig. 6-32. Underlying formulas.

The total does not equal the three numbers above it. This is because 9999.9999 recurring looks like 10000.00 when formatted to two decimal places. This matches the Total Grant, but it does not reflect a sum of the three figures that appear above it.

If you apply the ROUND function to the formulas in the Sciences, Arts, and Sport fields, the answer to each can be rounded to two decimal places. The revised formulas can be seen in Fig. 6-34.

The results seen in the Browse mode look more logical, at least as far as the Total field is concerned. The Total is now an accurate sum of the three figures above it, as you can see from Fig. 6-35.

The problem has not been resolved completely, the Total Grant field does not equal the Total field, but this is not a FileMaker problem, but rather one of accounting; namely who gets the spare penny in a three-way split.

Round1
Records:
2
Sorted
Browse
City College
Total Grant $10,000.00
Sciences $3,333.33
Arts $3,333.33
Sport $3,333.33
Total $10,000.00

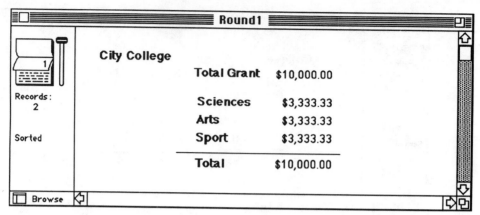

Fig. 6-33. Formatted entries.

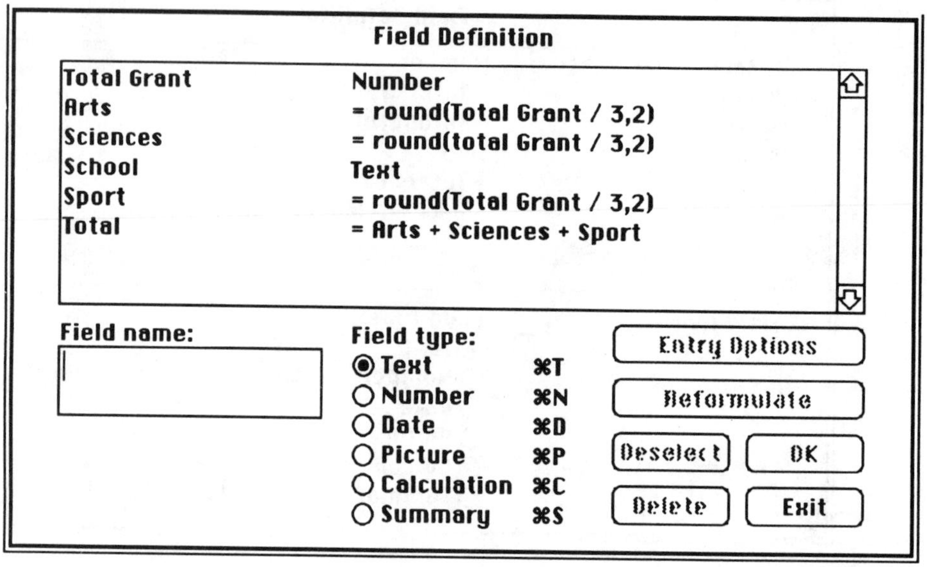

Field Definition
Total Grant Number
Arts = round(Total Grant / 3,2)
Sciences = round(total Grant / 3,2)
School Text
Sport = round(Total Grant / 3,2)
Total = Arts + Sciences + Sport
Field name:
Field type:
Text ⌘T
Number ⌘N
Date ⌘D
Picture ⌘P
Calculation ⌘C
Summary ⌘S
Entry Options
Reformulate
Deselect
OK
Delete
Exit

Fig. 6-34. Revised formulas with rounding.

Using SIGN

In some calculations, you need to know if a value is positive or negative. The SIGN function performs this task, returning 1 if the value is positive, −1 if the value is negative, and 0 if the value is zero. Thus the formula

Profit = SIGN(Revenue − Expense)

returns 1 if Revenue is greater than Expense, −1 if Expense is greater than Revenue, and 0 if both fields contain the same value.

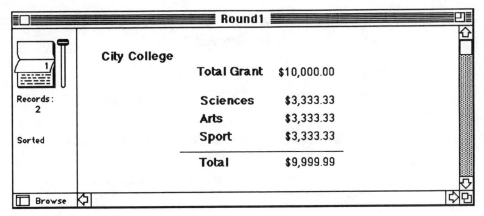

Fig. 6-35. The revised database.

FINANCIAL FUNCTIONS

As you saw from the loan payment example in Fig. 6-27, FileMaker has the ability to carry out useful financial calculations. In addition to loan payments, you can calculate present and future values.

Using PMT

The format of the PMT function was shown in Fig. 6-28 and can be defined as:

PMT(Principal, Interest, Term)

Where Principal is the amount being borrowed, Interest is the interest rate charge per period, and Term is the number of periods. Always make sure that the interest rate is stated per period. If the payment is not an annual one, then the interest will have to be converted from an annual rate to one that matches the periods (for example, divide annual rate by four to get a rate for quarterly payment calculations).

A useful application of FileMaker's PMT function is to develop a payment table showing the different payments required based on varying the interest, principal, and term. You can see an example of this in Fig. 6-36 where the database from Figs. 6-27 and 6-28 has been rearranged and presented using the View as List option.

You can see the different payments required to finance the same amount at the same interest over five different terms.

To further embellish payment calculations, you can determine the total of payments and the amount of interest that will be paid if the loan is carried to full term. These calculations, which show the dramatic "just interest" for longer term loans, have been added in Fig. 6-37.

The calculations for the two new fields are shown in Fig. 6-38, along with the other fields of the database.

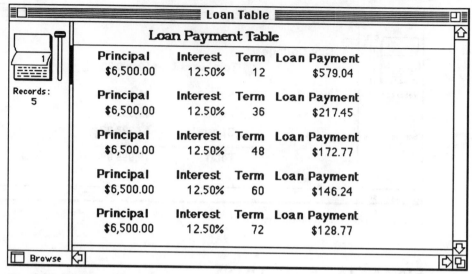

Fig. 6-36. Payment table.

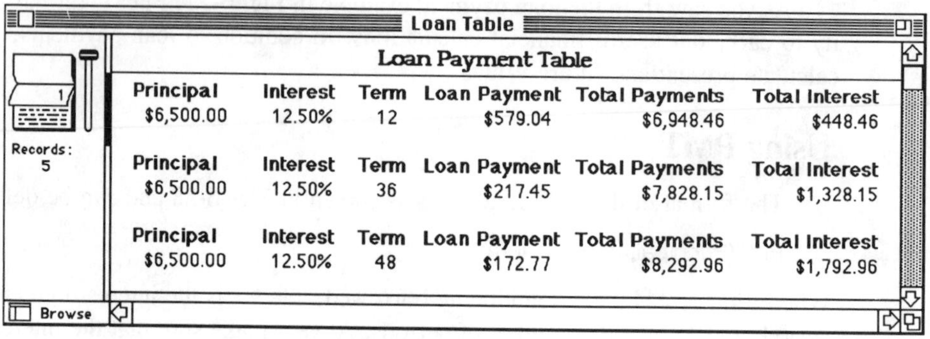

Fig. 6-37. Loan table with payment and interest totals.

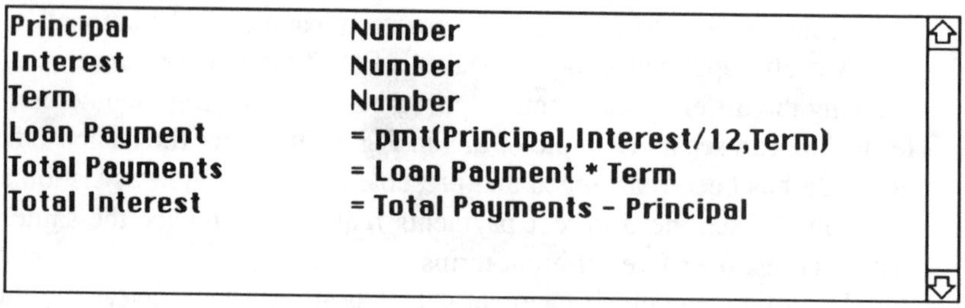

Principal	Number
Interest	Number
Term	Number
Loan Payment	= pmt(Principal,Interest/12,Term)
Total Payments	= Loan Payment * Term
Total Interest	= Total Payments - Principal

Fig. 6-38. Loan field definitions.

Using FV

The future value of money is the amount that you accumulate if you save a regular amount and earn a regular interest for a certain number of periods. FileMaker can calculate this with the FV function. For example, if you save $200 every month for 36 months in an account that earns an annual interest rate of 12.50%, you will accumulate $8,691.70, as seen in Fig. 6-39.

The format of the FV function is:

FV(Payment, Interest, Term)

and the function is defined as the future value of the Payment, at Interest rate per period, for Term number of periods. In the example in Fig. 6-39, the Future Value field is defined as:

Future Value = (Payment, Interest/12, Term)

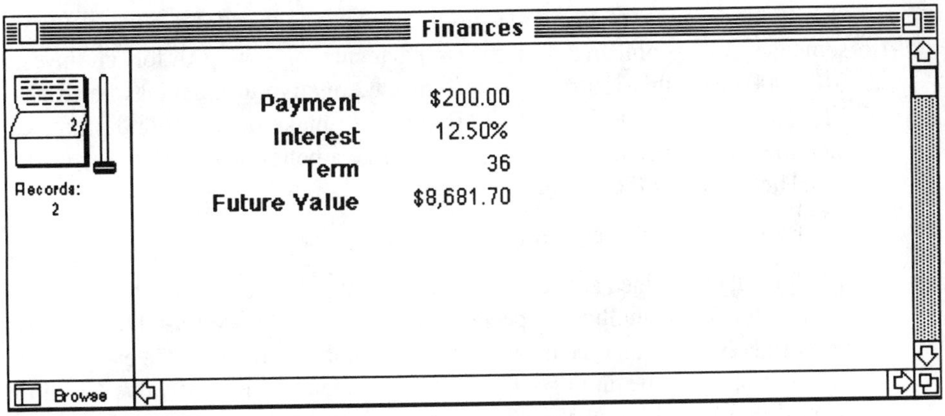

Fig. 6-39. Future value calculation.

Using PV

When you are evaluating an investment, it is useful to know its *present value*. Suppose you are offered a return of $1050 in 12 months if you invest $1000 now. You need some way to tell if this is a good deal. One method is to discount the value of the investment. Because you can get 6.00% annual interest by placing your money in a reliable savings account, you can discount the promised return by 6.00%, using this formula:

1050/(1 + .06) = 989

Since the discounted value of the return ($989) is less than the investment ($1000), the investment is probably not a good one. If the discounted value of the investment is greater than the amount you are planning to invest, then you might want to consider making the investment, although other factors such as comparative risk should also be part of the decision-making process.

In Fig. 6-40, you can see the PV function at work in FileMaker, evaluating a promised return of 5 annual payments of $30,000 each.

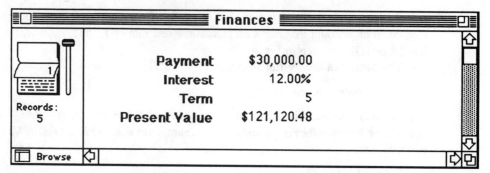

Fig. 6-40. Present value calculation.

A discount rate of 12.50% is used. You can see that the result is $108,143.29. If someone was promising you the 5 payments of $30,000 for an investment of $100,000, then this return looks promising, relative to a savings certificate paying 12.50%. If you had to invest $120,000 now to make the $150,000 promised return, then the savings account at 12.50% looks like a better deal.

The format of the PV function is:

PV(Payment, Interest, Term)

The formula is defined as the present value of the Payment amount, at Interest rate per period, for Term number of periods. Care should be exercised with this function because it assumes that payments and investments are made at the end of each period, rather than at the beginning. If you want to calculate present value based on investment at the beginning of the period, you adjust the formula by adding the first year payment to the result of the formula and subtract 1 from the term, as shown in Fig. 6-41.

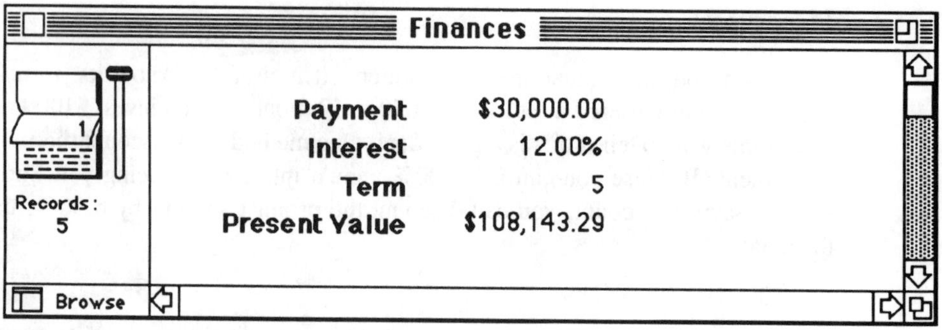

```
                           Finances
        Payment      $30,000.00
        Interest       12.00%
        Term             5
 Records:
   5    Present Value  $108,143.29
   Browse
```

Fig. 6-41. Adjusted present value formula.

You can see the result of altering the assumption in Fig. 6-42, where the present value is considerably higher than in Fig. 6-40.

A similar adjustment can be made to future value calculations performed with FV. To alter the assumption to payment at the beginning rather than the end of the periods

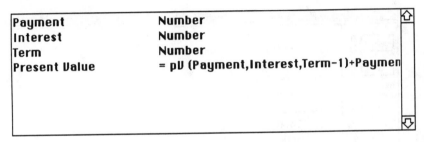

Payment	Number
Interest	Number
Term	Number
Present Value	= pᴜ (Payment,Interest,Term–1)+Paymen

Fig. 6-42. Adjusted present value result.

use the following formula:

FV(Payment,Rate,Term – 1) – Payment

One other financial function NPV is used with repeating fields to discount irregular cash flows. You will find NPV described at the end of the section on repeating field functions.

LOGICAL FUNCTION STATEMENTS

FileMaker has one logical function: IF. The use of the IF function was mentioned earlier under "Logical Formulas." The IF function employs conditional or true/false formulas that need to be understood before using IF. The IF function allows a formula to make a choice between two possible answers, based on a condition you set out. The syntax or format of the IF statement is as follows:

IF (Condition, Result If True, Result If False)

The Condition is a conditional statement, like those described in the previous section. The Result If True is a formula, a date, a number, or a piece of text, that the IF statement returns if the conditional statement is true. The Result If False is a formula, a date, a number, or a piece of text that the IF statement returns if the conditional statement is false.

Remember you can actually combine more than one IF statement. (This is known as nesting IF statements.) For example, in the database shown earlier in Fig. 6-29, you saw a calculation for determining the number of full loads required to truck cases of wine. You also saw how to determine how many cases would be left over. Suppose you want to show whether the cases left over make up a quarter load, half load, or three-quarter load. You can see a suitable field for this in Fig. 6-43.

The formula used to create the Fraction Load field consists of three nested IF statements. You can see the formula being composed in Fig. 6-44.

Note that the results of the formula are strings of text and so they are enclosed in quotes in the formula, and the result type is set to text.

In some situations, multiple IF statements get unmanageable. If you find that the task for which you are using IF is actually selecting a response from a long list, then you might want to use a Lookup field. Consider the sample database in Fig. 6-45, where the field called Customer is actually a Lookup field.

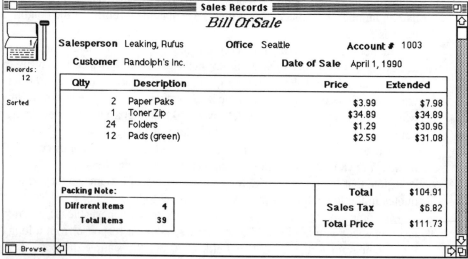

```
┌═════════════════════════ Shipping ═════════════════════════┐
│                                                            │
│  ┌──┐    Shipment Number    11023                          │
│  │  │      Total Cases      356                            │
│  └──┘    Cases Per Truck    16                             │
│ Records:    Full Loads      22                             │
│   I       Cases Left Over   4                              │
│            Total Loads      23                             │
│           Fraction Load     1/4                            │
│                                                            │
├──────────────────────────────────────────────────────────┤
│  Browse                                                    │
└────────────────────────────────────────────────────────────┘
```

Fig. 6-43. Fraction Load field.

```
┌──────────────────────────────────────────────────────────────┐
│                              Calculation Result is:            │
│  Fraction Load =         ● Text   ○ Number   ○ Date           │
│ ┌──────────────────────────────────────────────────────────┐ │
│ │ if(Cases Left Over / Cases Per Truck>.75,"Over 3/4",if(Cases Left Over / │ │
│ │ Cases Per Truck>.5,"3/4",if(Cases Left Over/Cases Per     │ │
│ │ Truck>.25,"1/2","1/4")))                                   │ │
│ └──────────────────────────────────────────────────────────┘ │
│                                                                │
│  Shipment Number       / 7 8 9      =    abs ()                │
│  Total Cases                         ≠    average ()           │
│  Cases Per Truck       * 4 5 6      >    count ()             │
│  Full Loads            - 1 2 3      <    date (,,)            │
│  Cases Left Over                     ≥    DateToText ()        │
│  Fraction Load         + ( ) 0 .    ≤    day ()              │
│  Total Loads           & " " ¶                                │
│                                    [ OK ]   [ Cancel ]         │
└────────────────────────────────────────────────────────────────┘
```

Fig. 6-44. Composing nested IFs.

```
┌═════════════════════════ Sales Records ═════════════════════════┐
│                          Bill Of Sale                           │
│  ┌──┐  Salesperson  Leaking, Rufus    Office  Seattle    Account # 1003 │
│  │  │  Customer  Randolph's Inc.       Date of Sale  April 1, 1990     │
│  └──┘  ┌───────────────────────────────────────────────────────┐ │
│ Records:│ Qtty    Description              Price      Extended  │ │
│   12    │    2    Paper Paks             $3.99        $7.98     │ │
│         │    1    Toner Zip             $34.89       $34.89     │ │
│ Sorted  │   24    Folders               $1.29       $30.96     │ │
│         │   12    Pads (green)          $2.59       $31.08     │ │
│         │                                                       │ │
│         └───────────────────────────────────────────────────────┘ │
│         Packing Note:                     Total       $104.91    │
│         ┌─────────────────────┐          Sales Tax    $6.82     │
│         │ Different Items    4 │          Total Price  $111.73   │
│         │ Total Items      39 │                                 │
│         └─────────────────────┘                                 │
├──────────────────────────────────────────────────────────────────┤
│  Browse                                                          │
└────────────────────────────────────────────────────────────────────┘
```

Fig. 6-45. A bill of sale.

The user enters the customer's account number in the Account # field, and File-Maker looks up the customer's name in a different database and then enters it in the Customer field. If you had a limited number of customers, you could perform this task with nested IF statements. But with a lot of customers, the lookups work better.

To create this lookup, the Customer field is selected in the Field Definition dialog box and the Entry Options button is checked. The Entry Options dialog box appears in Fig. 6-46.

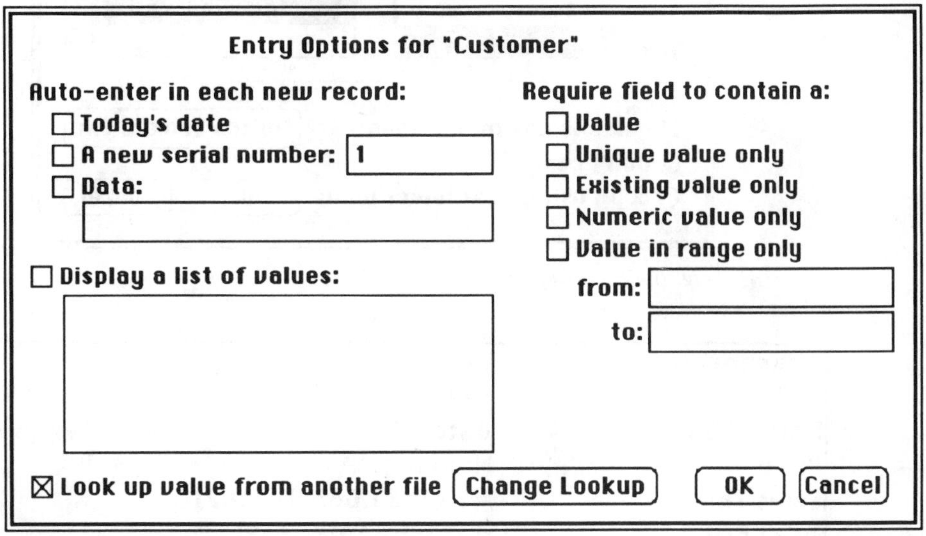

```
              Entry Options for "Customer"

Auto-enter in each new record:        Require field to contain a:
   ☐ Today's date                        ☐ Value
   ☐ A new serial number: [1    ]        ☐ Unique value only
   ☐ Data:                               ☐ Existing value only
      [                        ]         ☐ Numeric value only
                                         ☐ Value in range only
   ☐ Display a list of values:            from: [              ]
      [                        ]            to: [              ]
      [                        ]
      [                        ]
      [                        ]
☒ Look up value from another file ( Change Lookup )   ( OK )  ( Cancel )
```

Fig. 6-46. Entry Options.

You can see that the Look up value. . . option is selected. When the OK button is selected, FileMaker asks for the name of the database that you want to look up values from. A typical Macintosh file list appears. In this case, the file is called CustList. After specifying the file, details of the lookup can be defined using the dialog box that appears in Fig. 6-47.

The selections required for this example have been made. The definition reads: Copy into the Customer field from the Customer Name field of the CustList database, when what is typed in the Account # field of the current database matches a value in the Account Number field of the CustList database. Note that you can tell FileMaker, as in this case, not to copy a value if an exact match is not found.

REPEATING FIELD FUNCTIONS

FileMaker provides repeating fields to list multiple values under one heading, such as Items, Quantity, Price, and so on, used in a bill of sale. You can see an example of this is Fig. 6-45. Four fields repeat in this example: Qtty, Description, Price, and Extended. The last of these is the product of Qtty and Price. You can see the formulas defining these and the other fields in Fig. 6-48.

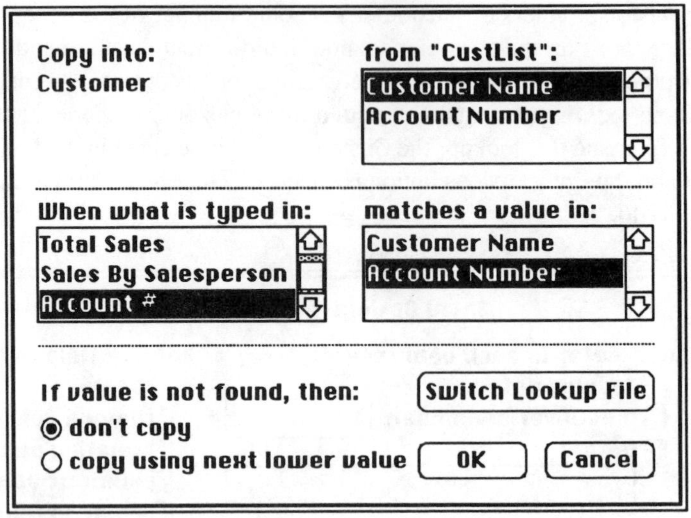
Copy into:
Customer
from "CustList":
Customer Name
Account Number
When what is typed in:
Total Sales
Sales By Salesperson
Account #
matches a value in:
Customer Name
Account Number
If value is not found, then:
Switch Lookup File
don't copy
copy using next lower value
OK
Cancel

Fig. 6-47. Lookup definition.

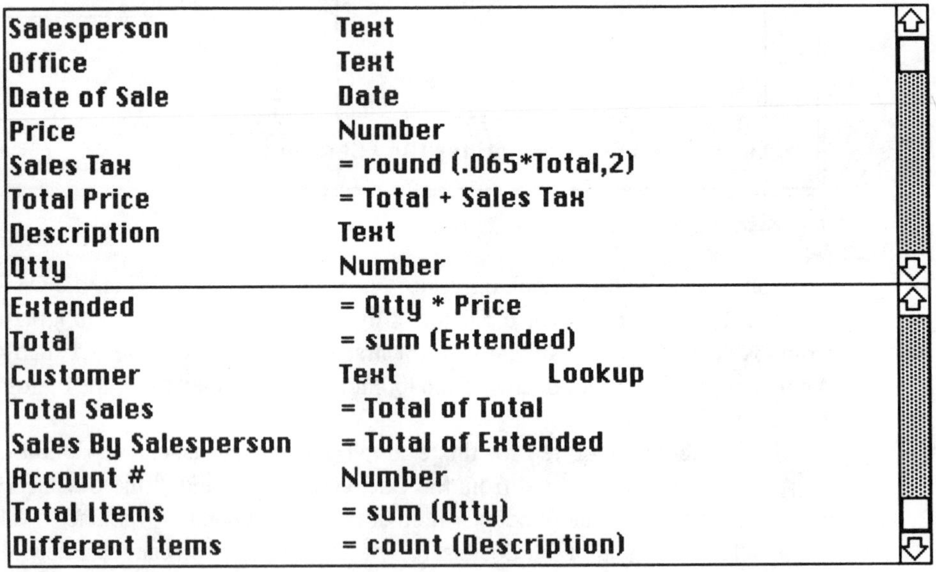
Salesperson Text
Office Text
Date of Sale Date
Price Number
Sales Tax = round (.065*Total,2)
Total Price = Total + Sales Tax
Description Text
Qtty Number
Extended = Qtty * Price
Total = sum (Extended)
Customer Text Lookup
Total Sales = Total of Total
Sales By Salesperson = Total of Extended
Account # Number
Total Items = sum (Qtty)
Different Items = count (Description)

Fig. 6-48. Formulas and fields defined.

Special rules apply to calculations with repeating fields and a special set of functions is provided for them.

Using SUM

To add up the values in a repeating field, you use the SUM function, together with the name of the repeating field being summed, as in the Total field in Fig. 6-45, which is defined thus:

Total = SUM (Extended)

Using COUNT

To count the items in a repeating field, you use the COUNT function as in the field Different Items in **Fig. 6-45,** which tells the packer how many different items the customer is ordering. This field is defined as:

Different Items = COUNT (Description)

Using MAX and MIN

To find the largest or smallest values in a repeating field you use the MAX and MIN functions as in:

Most = MAX (Qtty)

and

Least = MIN (Qtty)

You can see an application of these functions in **Fig. 6-49** where test scores are recorded in a repeating field.

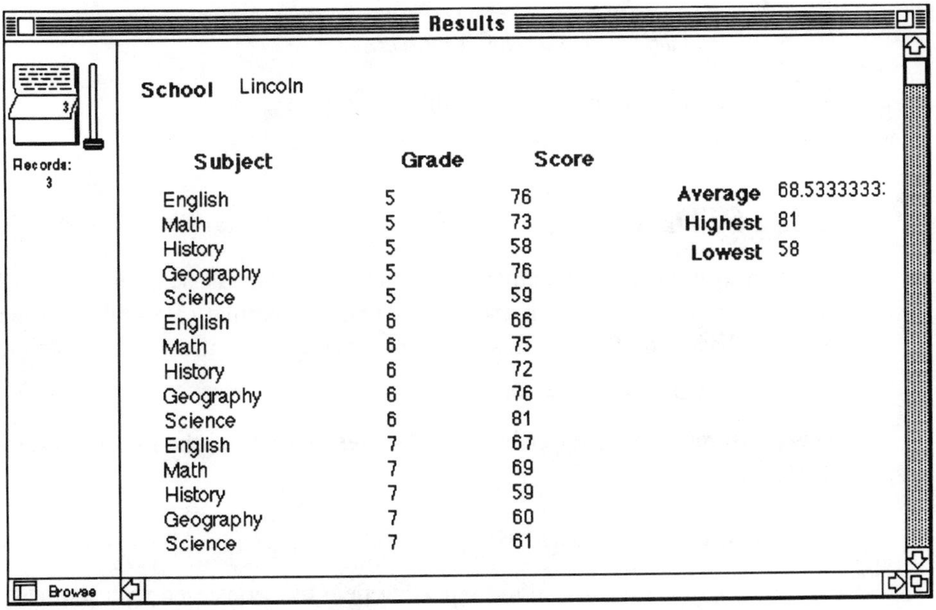

Results					
School Lincoln					
Records: 3	**Subject**	**Grade**	**Score**		
	English	5	76	**Average**	68.5333333:
	Math	5	73	**Highest**	81
	History	5	58	**Lowest**	58
	Geography	5	76		
	Science	5	59		
	English	6	66		
	Math	6	75		
	History	6	72		
	Geography	6	76		
	Science	6	81		
	English	7	67		
	Math	7	69		
	History	7	59		
	Geography	7	60		
	Science	7	61		
Browse					

Fig. 6-49. Repeating field with MIN and MAX.

Using AVERAGE

To find the average or mean of values in a repeating field, you use the AVERAGE function. For example, you might want to know the average of the scores in the record shown in Fig. 6-49. In Fig. 6-50, you can see the definitions for the fields in the example in Fig. 6-49.

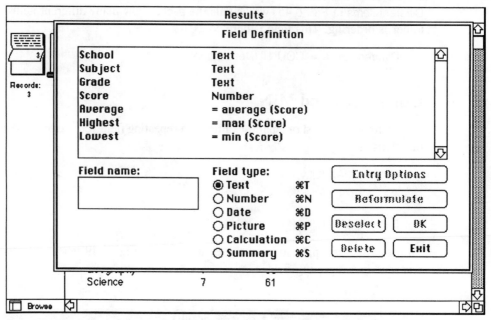

Fig. 6-50. Field definitions showing AVERAGE.

You can see that the AVERAGE field is defined as:

Average = AVERAGE (Score)

Using STDEV

A measurement that you might want to add to the database in Fig. 6-49 is standard deviation, described earlier in the chapter under "Summary Formulas." You measure standard deviation of values in a repeating field by using the STDEV function, as in:

Standard Deviation = STDEV (Scores)

This measures the extent to which most scores differ from the mean or average of all scores.

Summaries and Repeating Fields

It is important not to confuse repeating field functions used with summary formulas. Summary formulas are used to assess all values in particular field of a database, across all records. The repeating functions assess all values in the repeating field of a single record. Thus the structure of the database in Fig. 6-49, used to track scores, is much different from the one seen earlier in Fig. 6-18; there each record was a separate score. In Fig. 6-49, each record is a separate school, and all test results are combined through the use of repeating fields.

Using EXTEND

When you want to do math between multiple values in a repeating field and a single value in a nonrepeating field, this poses a slight logistical problem. You are asking one value in the nonrepeating field of a record to interact with multiple values.

For example, suppose that you wanted to redesign the Bill Of Sale database in Fig. 6-45 to incorporate a price discount to the customer. An annotated view of one approach to design is shown in Fig. 6-51.

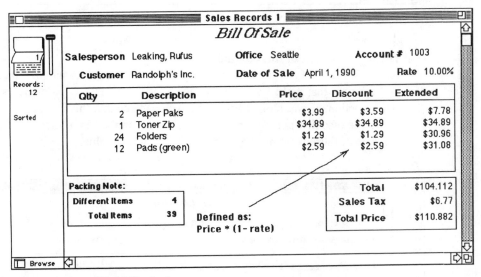

Fig. 6-51. A modified bill of sale.

A field called Rate has been added to take the rate of discount. A new column called Discount has been entered to show the price per item after the discount has been applied. The Discount field is defined as:

Discount = Price * (1 – rate)

You can see the problem that this creates if you examine the results closely. Only the first product gets the discount! This is because there is only one value in Rate, but four in the Price column. To solve this problem, the formula is redefined, using the EXTEND function as follows:

Discount = Price * (1 – EXTEND(Rate))

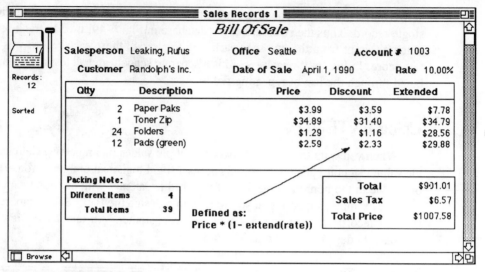

Fig. 6-52. Using the EXTEND function.

You can see the results of this redefinition in Fig. 6-52.

Note that the EXTEND function can only be applied to a field name. Other calculations affecting that field name must take place outside the parentheses of the EXTEND function. If you look at Fig. 6-53, you can see that this is true.

When the discount percentage is simply a value applied in a formula affecting a repeating field, there is no need to apply EXTEND to the value.

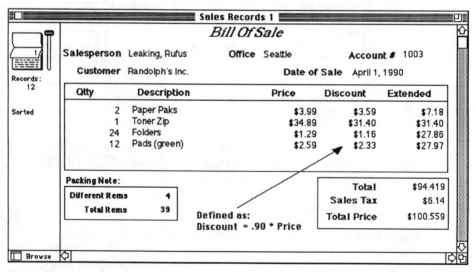

Fig. 6-53. Alternative structure.

Some Repeating Field Dilemmas

In Fig. 6-54, you can see a grant database in which the value of 10,000 in the Total Grant field is divided between three students.

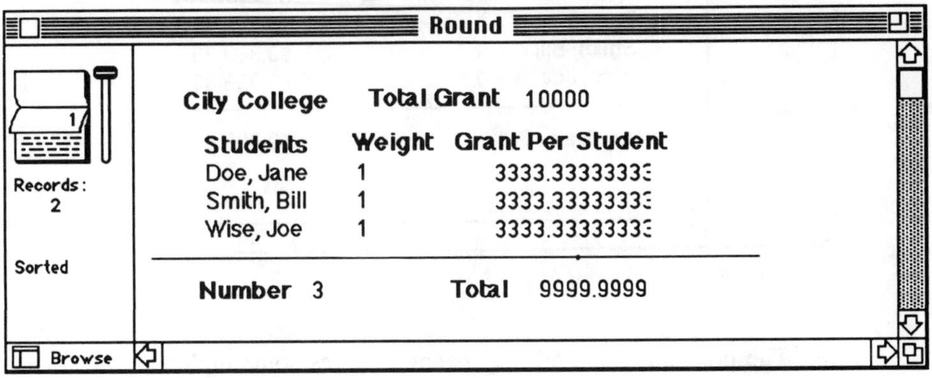

```
▤□▭════════════════════ Round ═══════════════════▱▤
  ┌──────┐ ╷  City College   Total Grant  10000              ⇧
  │    ⊏━━┥ │                                                 ▓
  │   1 │ │  Students    Weight  Grant Per Student            ▓
  │▦▦▦▦▦│ │  Doe, Jane    1          3333.3333333            ▓
 Records: │  Smith, Bill  1          3333.3333333            ▓
    2       Wise, Joe     1          3333.3333333            ▓
                                                             ▓
 Sorted     ────────────────────────────────────────        ▓
            Number  3            Total    9999.9999          ⇩
  ┌──────┐                                                   ▱
  │▭ Browse │◁│                                            ⇨▱⇩
```

Fig. 6-54. A rounding example.

The students are listed by name in the field called Students, which is a repeating field. The repeating field called Weight represents relative claims of the students, which are equal in this case. The repeating field called Grant Per Student shows the amount each student is entitled to receive. The result of dividing 10000 by 3 is 3333.3333 recurring. With unformatted fields this looks messy, and so the designer of the database formats each dollar field to two decimal places. The effect can be seen in the report in Fig. 6-55.

City College	Total Grant	$10,000.00
Students	**Weight**	**Grant Per Student**
Doe, Jane	1	$3,333.33
Smith, Bill	1	$3,333.33
Wise, Joe	1	$3,333.33
Number 3	**Total**	**$10,000.00**

Fig. 6-55. Report with formatted entries.

The problem of format rounding is now apparent as the formatted value in the Total field, which is defined:

Total = SUM (Grant Per Student)

The Total does not equal the three numbers above it. This is because 9999.9999 recurring looks like 10000.00 when formatted to two decimal places. If you apply the round function to the formula in the Grant Per Student field, you get the effect seen in Fig. 6-56, where the Total field adds up correctly.

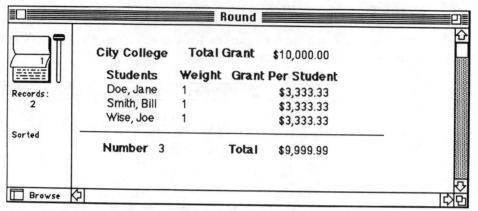

Fig. 6-56. Rounded figures.

The problem of the missing penny requires some diplomatic juggling. Another problem in this database is more perplexing. Without the rounding, the Grant Per Student field is actually defined as:

Grant Per Student = Weight * (EXTEND(Total Grant)/EXTEND(Number))

The Number field is the Count function applied to the Students field. You might wonder why the formula is not simply

EXTEND(Total Grant)/EXTEND(Number)

However, this does not work properly. You only get a result in the first line of the Grant Per Student field. The reason appears to be that nothing refers to the fact that there is a student on each line of the Students field.

At first, we inserted the Weight field just to get the formula to work. As you can see from Figs. 6-54 through 6-56, it does. However, we eventually found a way of eliminating this added field. The following formula works nicely without the Weight field:

(LENGTH(Students > 0) * (EXTEND(Total Grant)/EXTEND(Number))

This is an unusual use of the LENGTH function which measures the length of entries in a text field. The formula

LENGTH(Students > 0)

returns 1 if there is an entry in the Students field for each particular line. There is more about text functions later in this chapter.

Using NPV

When you want to use FileMaker to determine the net present value of a series of variable payments, you can enter the payments in a repeating field. You can see an example of this in Fig. 6-57.

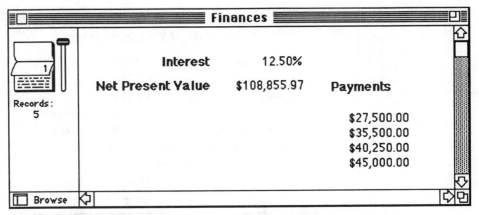

Fig. 6-57. Calculating Net Present Value.

The field called Net Present Value is defined as:

Net Present Value = NPV (Interest, Payments)

where Payments is the repeating field. The four payments represent promised return per period of the investment. The Interest is the discount rate per period, presumably one year. You can see that the net present value of the four payments in Fig. 6-57 is slightly better than that for five regular payments of $30,000 calculated in Fig. 6-40. Both investments offer a return on $100,000 that is better than 12.50% per period.

Unlike the PV function, the NPV function has the ability to work with negative numbers. This means you can enter all of the cash flows of an investment in the payment field, including the initial investment. For example, you could enter the following figures in the Payment field of the database in Fig. 6-57:

```
-150,000
  27,500
  35,500
  40,250
  45,000
```

The result in net present value would be $90.16. A result greater than 0 indicates that an initial investment of $150,000 pays out better than 12.50%.

USING DATE CALCULATION FUNCTIONS

Being able to perform calculations using dates lends great power to a database. FileMaker considers every date as a serial number; this is number of days since the beginning of the Christian Era (C.E. or A.D.) such that December 25, 1990, is day number 726,826. In practical terms, this means that you can do math with dates. You can determine the number of days a payment is past due, the number of days a project has taken, or what the date will be *x* number of days from today. As an example, consider the construction company database in Fig. 6-58.

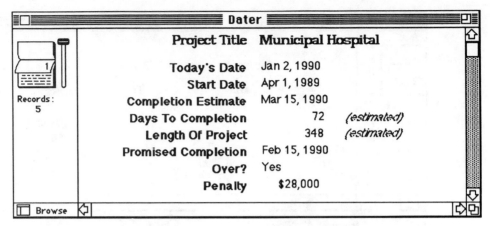

Fig. 6-58. A date math example.

The Days To Completion field is a simple subtraction calculation defined thus:

Days To Completion = Completion Estimate – Today's Date

When you take one date away from another, the answer is a number of days. The Length of Project field is another subtraction formula, defined as:

Length of Project = Completion Estimate – Start Date

Bear in mind that the further into the past you go, the smaller the date serial numbers. Thus you will probably want to subtract older dates from more recent dates to keep the answer positive. Otherwise, you can use the ABS function to make sure that the difference is stated as a positive number. The fields in Fig. 6-58 are defined in Fig. 6-59.

Today's Date	Date	Auto-enter Today
Start Date	Date	
Completion Estimate	Date	
Days To Completion	= Completion Estimate – Today's Date	
Length Of Project	= Completion Estimate – Start Date	
Promised Completion	Date	
Over?	= Completion Estimate > Promised Compl	
Penalty	= 1000 * (Completion Estimate – Promise	

Fig. 6-59. Date math example defined.

Note the Penalty field, which makes use of date math to calculate the amount of the penalty that will have to be paid, based on $1000 per day, if the Completion Date is 28 days past the Promised Date.

What Is Today?

In Fig. 6-59, you might have noted that the Today's Date field is marked Auto-enter Today. This is one of the Entry Options referred to earlier. This option enters the current date, from the Macintosh clock/calendar, in this field of any new record. However, this option acts as a date stamp; it does not mean that the date in this field will reflect the correct date when the file is opened at a later date.

For a reading of the date from the Macintosh clock/calendar that is updated every time the file is opened, you need to use the Today function. This will mean that the field type will be Calculation, and you need to check Date as the result type for the date to appear as a date and not a number. The field would be defined thus:

Today's Date = TODAY

Another way of entering today's date in a FileMaker record is to use the Paste Date command on the Edit menu. Once pasted, the date is not updated automatically as it is with the TODAY function. However, the problem with the TODAY function is that if you select date as the result type for a field containing TODAY, then FileMaker has difficulty adding or subtracting the date created by TODAY to or from regular Date fields. If you use the result type of Number, then the math works correctly, but the date appears only as a serial number. When you need to display today's date and do math with it, the best approach is to create two different fields: One with the result type Date, the other with the result type Number. Use the former for display purposes and the latter for calculations, bearing in mind that a field does not have to be displayed to be used in a calculation.

Dates in Parts

You can enter a date in parts, for example having Day, Month, and Year as separate fields. To assemble a date out of these parts, you can use the DATE function which has the following format:

DATE (Month, Day, Year)

This produces the date resulting from the value in the Month field (from 1 to 12), the value in the Day field (from 1 to 31), and the value in the Year field (given with all four digits).

If you want to know what day of the week a particular date represents, you can use the DAY function. Using the format

DAY (Date)

this function returns the number $(1-31)$ of the day in the date represented by Date, which can be a date field or a calculation or expression with a date result. Bear in mind that the extended date format can give you the day of the week name, such as Monday, Tuesday, and so on, based on Date, not the DAY function.

If you want to know the number of the month in a particular date you can use the MONTH function. Using the format

MONTH (Date)

this function returns the number $(1-12)$ of the month in the date represented by Date, which can be a date field or a calculation or expression with a date result.

If you want to know the number of the year in a particular date, you can use the YEAR function. Using the format

YEAR (Date)

this function returns the number of the year (1 − 3000) in the date represented by Date, which can be a date field or a calculation or expression with a date result.

TEXT MANIPULATION AND FUNCTIONS

You might want to manipulate text data in your FileMaker databases. For example, you might have John entered in one field and Doe in another, and you would like to combine the two in a third field, as Doe, John. You can do this with a form of math between text fields. Numerous FileMaker functions are designed to help you manipulate text.

Suppose someone has entered a whole bunch of customer names all in capital letters, as in JOHN DOE. You want to return the names to normal appearance, known as "initial cap," as in John Doe. You can do this with a text function called PROPER. When describing text functions, we use the term *string* to describe a group of letters. You can call 101 Main Street a string, as well as John Doe or Fred. You can consider a number or a date as a string if it has been entered as text rather than a number or date.

Sometimes the need for text functions and string manipulation arises when you have imported data from another program and the information is not in the form you would like it. We examine importing data from other programs in Chapter 8. In the following sections, the FileMaker text functions are reviewed with some examples of how they are applied.

String Manipulations

You might not have realized that you can perform a type of math with text you have entered into FileMaker. Consider the example seen in Fig. 6-60 where the fields First and Last have been added together to create the Make Check To field.

The formula for the Make Check To field is essentially First Name plus Last Name, but you cannot use the regular plus sign (+) to add text together. Instead you use the ampersand (&):

Make Check To = First Name & Last Name

The ampersand is sometimes called the *concatenation* sign. The two pieces of text combined together are referred to as being *concatenated*.

However, the slight problem with this formula is that the result would be John-Doe. You have to tell FileMaker to put a space between the entries in each of the two fields. To do this, you add a third element to the formula: a single space. This is enclosed in quotes so that FileMaker understands it is a space character and not just a gap between field names. Thus the correct formula is:

Make Check To = First Name &" "& Last Name

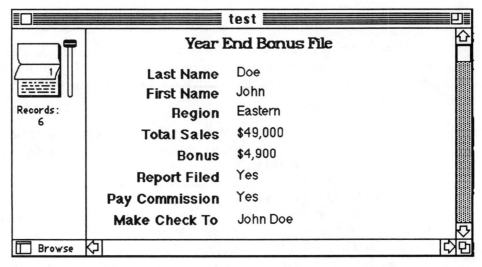

Fig. 6-60. String math example.

Suppose that you wanted to create titles for the people in the database in Fig. 6-60, using the First Name and Last Name fields, together with the Region field. You could use the following:

Title = First Name &" "& Last Name &", Salesperson, "& Region &" Region"

For the record in Fig. 6-60 the result would be:

John Doe, Salesperson, Eastern Region

Note that when you create a calculated field, the result of which is supposed to be text, you need to check the Text result button. Otherwise, you are likely to get a displayed result of 1 or 0 instead of the text you expect.

One other symbol besides the & sign is sometimes used in FileMaker string formulas. The paragraph sign (¶) can be placed in a formula to force a new line, or carriage return, within the result. For example, consider this formula for the field called Opening, using the fields First Name and Amount:

Opening = "Dear "&First Name&":¶Thanks for your recent donation of $"&Amount&"."

This results in the following, when the First Name field contains John and the Amount field contains 100:

Dear John:
Thanks for your recent donation of $100.

The paragraph symbol forces the text to break to a new line after the colon. Note the placement of the dollar sign for the Amount within the text. This is because numbers concatenated into formulas lose their formatting.

The Exact Function

FileMaker allows you to do more that combine text fields and pieces of text. You can size up, alter, and compare text, using functions. The EXACT function is used to test the similarity of two text entries. The function has the format

EXACT (Text1, Text2)

where Text1 and Text2 are text fields, text strings, or formulas that result in text. The function returns 1 if Text1 exactly matches Text2, otherwise the result is 0. (Note that in this function, and the rest of the text function formats, Text1, Text2, and so on are either text fields, the text results of a calculation, or text constants.)

Because the EXACT function on its own returns just 1 or 0, you can format the result as Yes or No by using the Format Number command, to make the results easier to interpret. For example, in Fig. 6-60 the field called Pay Commission actually contains a formula that makes sure the Report Filed field says Yes. If the operator enters anything other than Yes in the Report Filed field, even yes or YES, then the Pay Commission field returns No. The formula used is as follows:

Pay Commission = EXACT(Report Filed,"Yes")

Note that the text constant Yes must be placed in quotes, otherwise FileMaker will think it is a field name.

Suppose you want the result of the formula to be more particular. Instead of using the format to get Yes or No, you use the IF function, as in:

Pay Commission = IF(EXACT(Report Filed,"Yes"),"Yes","Check spelling in Report Filed field")

This type of formula can be used in data entry cross checks.

Note that when you want an IF statement to return text, you must place it in quotes; otherwise FileMaker will think you are using a field name. Also note that the result type for the field will need to be marked as Text for the answers to appear correctly.

Lower, Upper, and Proper

You can alter the capitalization of text with three functions. The LOWER function returns text in all lowercase characters. Thus the formula

Name = LOWER (Customer)

returns fred smith if the Customer field contains Fred Smith or FRED SMITH.

The PROPER function returns text with only the first character of each word in uppercase. Thus the formula

Name = PROPER (Customer)

returns Fred Smith if the Customer field contains Fred SMITH or FRED SMITH.

The UPPER function returns text in all uppercase characters, so that the formula

Name = UPPER (Customer)

returns FRED SMITH if the Customer field contains Fred Smith or fred smith.

Left and Right Functions

The LEFT function reads characters from one text field into another. Suppose you want to obtain the area code from a phone number field that has the numbers in this format: 415-555-1212. The digits you want are the first three on the left. The LEFT function uses the format

LEFT (Text1, N)

and returns the number of characters specified by N, from the text field Text1, counting from the left. For example, the formula

Area Code = LEFT (Phone, 3)

would return the area code 415 from the phone number 415-555-1212.

A companion function is RIGHT, which uses the format

RIGHT (Text1, N)

and returns the number of character specified by N, from the text field TEXT1, counting from the right. For example, the formula

Area Code = RIGHT (Phone, 4)

would return the number 1212 from the phone number 415-555-1212. Bear in mind that the result type must be text for the answer to appear as text. In these examples, it is assumed that the phone number is a text field.

The Middle Function

To extract text that is neither at the left or right end of a string, you need the MIDDLE function. Using the format

MIDDLE (Text1, Position, Number)

this function returns as many characters as specified by the Number argument, from the text field Text1 starting from the character indicated by the Position argument. The Position argument is the number of the character you want to begin with, counting the first character as 1. For example, to extract the three-digit dialing prefix of a telephone number entered as 415-555-1212, you would use:

Prefix = MIDDLE (Phone, 5, 3)

Bear in mind that this formula depends upon the entries in the Phone field being consistent in length and arrangement.

The Position Function

When you want to extract text from a field but the entries are not consistent, then you use the POSITION function:

POSITION (Text1, Text2, Start)

This returns the character position of the string specified as TEXT2 in field TEXT1, starting at the character number represented by Start. If Text2 is not found in Text1, then the formula returns 0.

Note that the result of the POSITION function is the location of the first character of Text2. So if the Text2 argument is the characters Grand in a Model Name field that has the entry Sports Grand Champion, the result is 8, since the location of the first letter of Text2 (G) is 8, counting from the first character. The formula might be stated thus:

POSITION (Model Name, "Grand", 1)

Also note that Text2, like any other text constant in FileMaker formula, must be placed in quotes. The third argument in a POSITION statement, Start, is often 1. If Text2 occurs more than once in Text1, you can tell the function to start looking after a certain character. For example, if all the entries in Model Name began with Grand, as in Grand Sports Grand Champion, then you could set the Start argument to 6 to make sure that the first occurrence was not considered.

As another example, consider customer names that are entered as a single string of text in the Customer field, as in John Doe. You want the names split into First Name and Last Name. You can get the first name with the LEFT function, but you will not know in every case how many characters to count from the left. So you tell FileMaker to count up to the space between the names; this is done by the POSITION function. Thus the formula would be:

First Name = LEFT(Customer, POSITION(Customer," ",1))

Length

When you want to know the length of a piece of text or an entry in a text field, you use the LENGTH function, which has the format

LENGTH (Text)

where Text is a text field *or* piece of text. Thus the formula

LENGTH(Customer)

would return the answer 8 if the entry in the Customer field was John Doe. Alone, the LENGTH function is of little use, but you will find it helpful in combined string formulas and data entry checks. For example, suppose you want to check that all entries in the zip code field meet the new nine-digit format, as in 94109-1021. You could set up a calculated field to flag incorrect entries by using the formula like this

IF(LENGTH(Zip Code) = 10,"Okay","WARNING—Check Zip code Field")

Note that the magic matching number is 10, for the 5 plus 4 numbers plus the 1 character hyphen.

As another example of the application of the LENGTH function, consider the customer names that are entered as a single string of text in the Customer field, as in John Doe. You want the names split into First Name and Last Name. You can get the first name with the LEFT and POSITION functions. You should be able to use the RIGHT function to get the last name, but you need to tell the RIGHT function where to start reading characters. You do this by finding the length of the entry in the Customer field, then subtracting the position number of the space between the names. This gives you the correct number argument for the RIGHT function. The formula would thus be:

Last Name = RIGHT(Customer, LENGTH(Customer) – POSITION(Customer," ",1))

If the entry in Customer is John Doe, then the LENGTH function returns 8 (spaces are counted). The POSITION function returns 5, the location of the first occurrence of a space in John Doe. The difference is 3 (8-5) and the RIGHT function reads 3 characters, Doe.

The Replace Function

You might want to perform a transformation on a text entry: for example, to change all instances of Car to Automobile. One way of doing this is to use the REPLACE function. This function takes four arguments and is arguably the most complex of the FileMaker functions. The format is

REPLACE (Text1, Start, Number, New)

This replaces the specified Number of characters of text in Text1, starting at the character specified in Start, using the replacement text given as New. The exact text that is to be replaced is a string Number characters long, beginning at the Start character. You can see an example of REPLACE in action in Fig. 6-61.

This is a database of product names, possibly used as a lookup file. The company has decided to drop Deluxe in its product names in favor of Super. The REPLACE formula in the New Model Name field uses Model Name as the Text1 argument. The Number argument will be 6 because Deluxe is six characters long. The New argument is "Super" because this is the text to replace the old. The only difficult argument is Start, which cannot be a simple number because Deluxe occurs in various positions within the product names. To create a suitable Start argument, we use the POSITION function to find out whereabouts in the Model Name field the term Deluxe occurs. The formula for New Model Name is thus:

REPLACE (Model Name,POSITION(Model Name,"Deluxe",1),6,"Super")

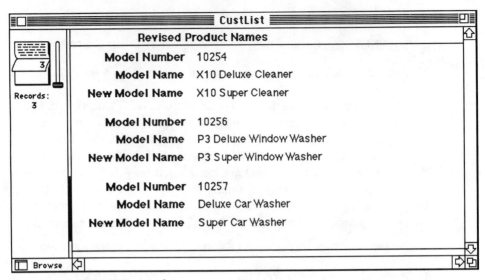

Fig. 6-61. A REPLACE example.

The Trim Function

In some situations, a text entry can acquire extra spaces, that is spaces before or after the main text, known as leading or trailing spaces. The TRIM function removes these, using the format:

TRIM (Text1)

Text1 is usually a text field, often one that is imported from another program. For more on trimming text that is imported, see "Importing Data" in Chapter 8.

CONVERSION CALCULATIONS

By using the appropriate conversion function, you can have FileMaker convert the value in a field to a different value type for use in a calculation formula. You can convert using the following functions:

DATETOTEXT—Converts a date or date field to text.
TEXTTODATE—Converts a piece of text or text field to a date.
NUMTOTEXT—Converts a number or number field to text.
TEXTTONUM—Converts a piece of text or a text field to a number.

For example, suppose you want to use a date from a date field in a string formula. You can see an example of this in the Comment field in Fig. 6-62.

The entry in the Comment field is calculated from information in other fields of the record plus some strings of text. You can see from the formula that creates the comment, displayed in Fig. 6-63, the first date field required in the comment is Start Date.

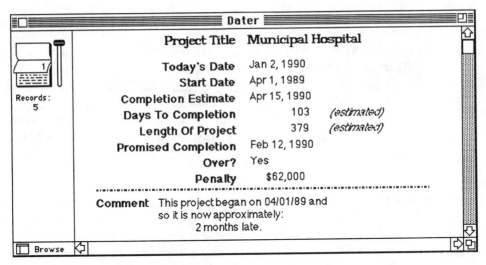

Fig. 6-62. String math for a comment.

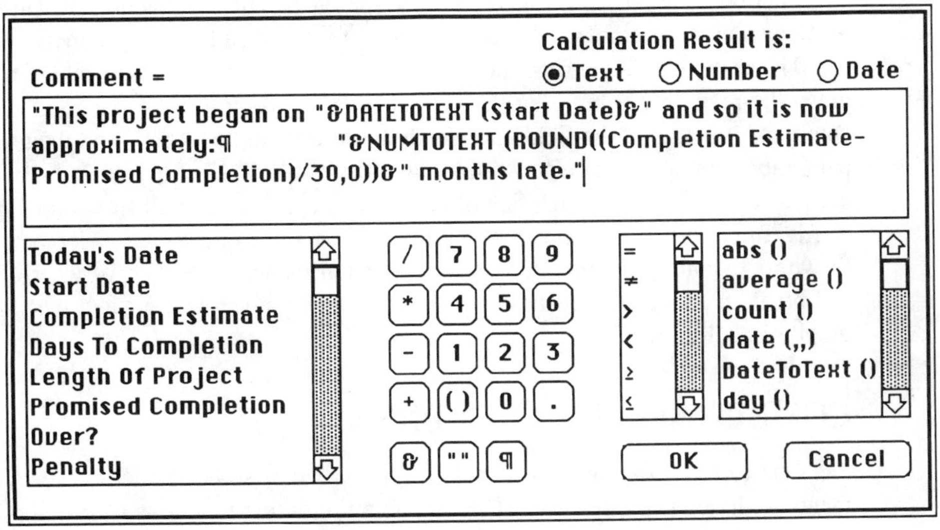

Fig. 6-63. Defining the Comment field.

However, if the Start Date field was used in the formula without the DATETOTEXT function, then the result would be the serial number of the date instead of the date expressed as 04/01/89. Note how the conversion function uses whatever is to be converted as the argument in parentheses. This argument can simply be a field name, or it can be an extended formula, as in the case of the months calculation.

The NUMTOTEXT conversion function is used with the part of the formula that turns the number of days into a number of months. The basis of the formula is:

Completion Estimate-Promised Completion

The result of this is a number of days, which is divided by 30 to produce months. This is rounded to whole months with the ROUND function, and the whole thing is used as the argument for the NUMTOTEXT function, with the result in Fig. 6-62 being 2.

There are some quirks and limitations to bear in mind when dealing with the conversion functions. The TEXTTONUM and TEXTTODATE functions only work if the argument is clearly identifiable as a number or date, and the result type is set correctly. For example, suppose a field called Value contains a piece of text, such as This horse is worth 5000 guineas. You want to get the figure 5000 out of this text. The following formula will work nicely:

Worth = TEXTTONUM (Value)

However, this formula does not work if the Value field contains the following: Worth 5000 plus or minus 10%. The reason that this does not work is that the text string has more than one possible numeric value and is now ambiguous.

The TEXTTODATE function is even more stringent in its requirements. A piece of text to be converted to a date must be clear and unambiguous, and in the 12/25/90 format. Dates in other formats, such as Dec 25, 1990, will not be recognized.

Finally, note that you might not need the NUMTOTEXT function because string formulas that use number fields seem to have no problem handling numeric values.

 The example in Figs. 6-62 and 6-63 is a good one to study when you are trying to grasp the relationship between the size of the Calculation box in the Field Definition command, the size of the field into which the result will be placed, and the use of the paragraph symbol to create new lines within the result. The basic rule is this: FileMaker puts as much text on each line of a multi-line text field as will fit without splitting words; FileMaker puts as much of the formula on a line of the Calculation box as will fit without splitting a number, word, or function name; regardless of where lines of text break in a multi-line text field, an extra line will always be created when a paragraph symbol is used.

COMBINING THE ELEMENTS

One further example should help to pull together some of the text formula elements we have been discussing. One possible use of text functions is to pull pieces of text together to create a unique identification number. In Fig. 6-64, you can see a record printed from a company car inventory database.

Each car is given a unique company I.D. number, which is composed of elements from the Make, Model, Serial Number, Year, and Invoice Date fields. You can see the formula that creates the Company I.D. in Fig. 6-65.

Note that the LEFT, RIGHT, and MIDDLE functions are used, as well as the DATE-TOTEXT function which allows the MIDDLE function to work with the Invoice Date field. The UPPER function is imposed on the rest of the formula in order to make sure that any letters in the resulting I.D. number are capitalized.

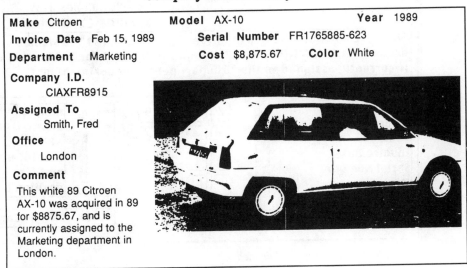

Company Car Inventory   Page 1

Make Citroen	**Model** AX-10	**Year** 1989
Invoice Date Feb 15, 1989	**Serial Number** FR1765885-623	
Department Marketing	**Cost** $8,875.67	**Color** White

Company I.D.
   CIAXFR8915

Assigned To
   Smith, Fred

Office
   London

Comment
This white 89 Citroen
AX-10 was acquired in 89
for $8875.67, and is
currently assigned to the
Marketing department in
London.

Fig. 6-64. Serial number and comment example.

Calculation Result is:
                    ● **Text**   ○ **Number**   ○ **Date**

Company I.D. =

UPPER(LEFT(Make,2)&LEFT(Model,2)&LEFT(Serial Number,
2)&RIGHT(Year,2)&MIDDLE(DATETOTEXT(Invoice Date),4,2))

Make		/	7	8	9		=		abs ()
Model		*	4	5	6		≠		average ()
Year		-	1	2	3		>		count ()
Invoice Date		+	( )	0	.		<		date (,,)
Serial Number		&	" "	¶			≥		DateToText ()
Department							≤		day ()
Company I.D.									
Assigned To							**OK**		**Cancel**

Fig. 6-65. Formulas defined.

In Fig. 6-64, you can also see a Comment field. This is a text formula field that pulls together various facts about the car in a summary statement. The complete formula for doing this is seen in Fig. 6-66.

This formula shows the power of the text functions to assemble long strings of information in a readable way, based on values in a variety of fields.

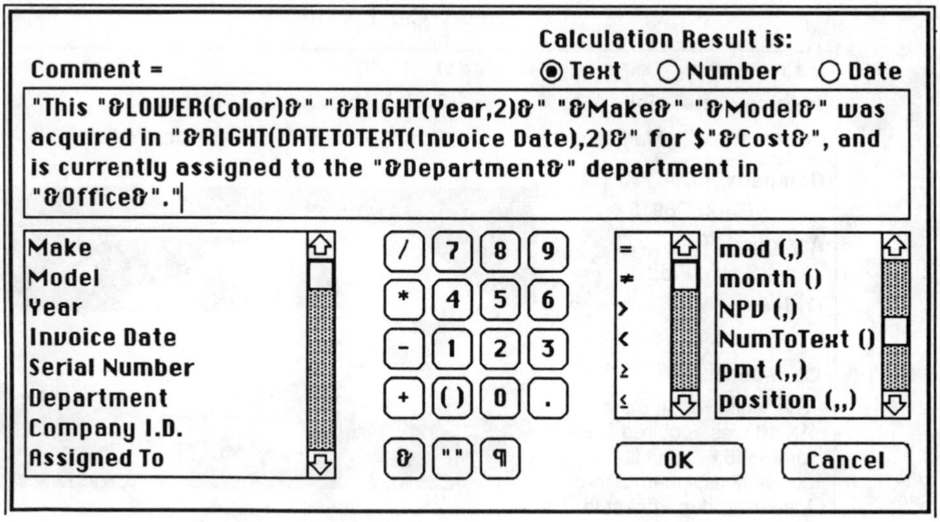

Fig. 6-66. The Comment field defined.

CONCLUSION

FileMaker's various functions supply the program with tremendous power to manipulate figures and text. While many simple databases do not need the power of functions, they are essential to some applications. In any type of database, formulas can be used to enhance the file, with data entry checks and more readable information. In the next chapter, we look at how you search and sort FileMaker databases.

7
We Can Sort It Out

IN THIS CHAPTER, we examine the sorting and searching of information with File-Maker. Organizations use database programs not just because they need to store information, but also because they need to manipulate that information. In FileMaker, one such manipulation involves the use of sort routines to sort the records by a common denominator such as Last Name, Invoice Number, Due Date, and so on. Another kind of manipulation is the use of search routines to locate specific information that is somewhere in the depths of data that has been entered. A database program is of little use in preparing invoices if the records can't be sorted by regions, for example, or if overdue payments cannot be found easily. FileMaker makes both of these operations relatively painless and quick.

THE NEED TO SORT

When your database file is set up and running with FileMaker, the program stores the data you have entered in the order that you have entered it. It doesn't matter to FileMaker that the invoice numbers are out of order, or that you have the Millers before the Browns. You could try sorting your data before entering it into the database, but that would also defeat one of the purposes of the database, not to mention being inefficient.

How the Sort Works

As far as the mechanics of FileMaker are concerned, the order of the records is often of no consequence. In some situations, the order of the records is very important, such as in the case of Sub-summaries. If you have a file set up to give you a running total for a Profit and Loss statement, you would want to have all of your entries in the correct date order in order to give you an accurate balance. That is one of the purposes of the Sort feature in FileMaker; to make such tasks easier for you to accomplish.

When you ask FileMaker to execute a Sort command, the program looks at the index of all the text and numbers that it has accumulated and from that index, arranges the records in the order that you specify. The index is a very useful part of the File-Maker program and is discussed in greater depth in the next chapter.

 FileMaker stores each word separately in the index. Sometimes you might want to store two words as one word. For instance, if you have San Fernando, San Pedro, San Luis Obispo, and San Jose entered, FileMaker looks at all the "Sans" first. By using Option−Space instead of the Spacebar when typing these names, you can tell FileMaker to store them as one word, thus making the Sort faster.

The Sort command for FileMaker is located under the Select menu and can be accessed while you are either in the Layout mode or the Browse mode; it makes no difference. Once you have opened the Sort command, you are presented with a box similar to the one shown in Fig. 7-1. The list of fields on the left are the possible choices for a sort and this list includes only the Text, Number, Date, and Calculation type fields in that file. None of the Picture fields or Summary fields will appear in a Sort command.

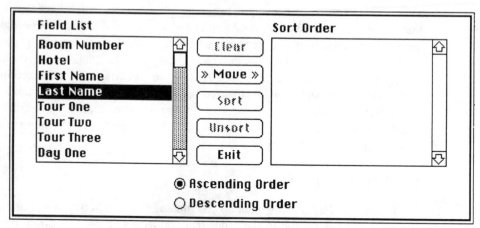

Fig. 7-1. Sort dialog box.

The keyboard shortcut for Sort in FileMaker is Command−S, which is often the Save command in other Mac programs. Because FileMaker automatically saves your work every time there is a lull in keyboard activity, there is no Save command in File-Maker.

Short Sorts

You begin a sort by selecting the field or fields that you want to use as the key to the sort and moving them over to the box on the right of the Sort screen. You can do this by either double-clicking on the field shown in the list to the left, or by selecting and then clicking on Move. Once you have moved a field over to the other box, that field name appears along with a set of "stairs" as shown in Fig. 7-2. This set of stairs corresponds to the order of the Sort.

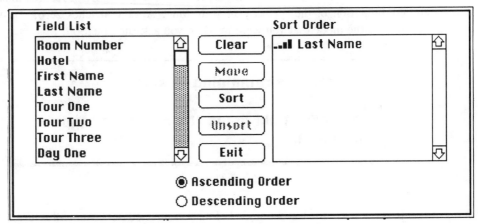

Fig. 7-2. Field selected for Sort.

When you choose Ascending Order (the stairs running up from left to right), File-Maker sorts alphabetical fields from A to Z and numeric fields from 1 to 100, while Descending Order (the stairs running down from left to right) sorts just the opposite way: from Z to A and 100 to 1.

The Sort Order is initially determined by clicking the appropriate radio button in the Sort selection box before moving that field over to the other side. However, the order can be changed after the move, as shown in Fig. 7-3, simply by clicking on the field on the right side and then clicking in the appropriate radio button.

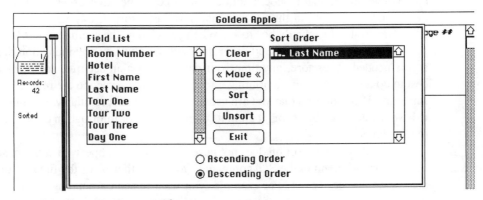

Fig. 7-3. Changing the sort order.

When you have chosen the field that you want your records to be sorted by, all you have to do is either click on the Sort button or tap the Return key. (Usually a button that accepts a Return as an acceptance is surrounded by a set of two rounded rectangles. Although this particular button is not shown this way, a Return does work.)

After you have asked FileMaker to Sort your records, a dialog box appears on your screen like Fig. 7-4. The number of records remaining to sort counts down to zero very quickly. This is somewhat dependent on the number of records to sort and the configuration of the memory in your Mac. After it reaches zero, you will be returned to the mode that you were in when you activated the Sort.

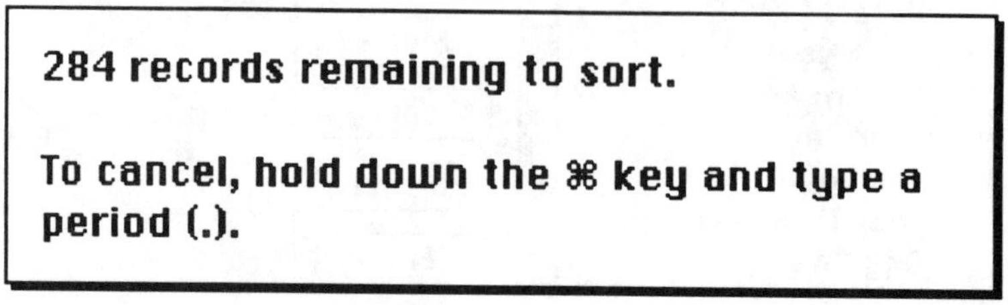

---

284 records remaining to sort.

To cancel, hold down the ⌘ key and type a period (.).

Fig. 7-4. Records remaining to Sort.

If you were in the Layout mode before you selected Sort, you will return the same layout but there will be no indication on the screen that the records have been sorted. You will need to change to the Browse mode to see the results of the Sort. However, if you were in the Browse mode when you started, you will return to the Browse mode. In either case, the only way to tell if your records have been sorted is to go to the Browse mode, and there you will find the word Sorted in the status area, under the book icon.

Once you have completed a Sort, your records will remain sorted in this order indefinitely, with two exceptions. If, after a Sort, you enter new records, the new records will be placed *after* all the sorted records and the word Sorted in the status area will appear in parentheses. This is a subtle warning that the Sort order is only an approximation and that it should not be relied upon. The other exception is if, after a Sort, you change data in the records that have been sorted. Say you notice that the name Brown should actually be Frown. When you change the spelling, FileMaker does not notice any change to the Sort order and will not give you any indication that a re-sort is needed. Therefore, any time your data relies on an accurate sort, it is always best to do a fresh Sort before printing a report or giving someone the results of a Sub-summary. If you do find that you are using a particular sort regularly, you might want to have it automated by setting it up in its own script. (For information on scripts, refer to Chapter 8.)

 The field that you sort on does not necessarily have to appear on your chosen layout to show the result of the Sort command. You can either place the field off the print area or on another layout. For example, you want to send a dunning letter out to all clients whose payments are particularly delinquent. You could have a field called Deadbeats with a Y or N entry and sort on this field to find the accounts to be dunned. If you place that field off to the right of the solid line on your layout, you can look at that field on the screen by scrolling right, but it won't appear on the printed letter to your clients. It won't be noticed by the casual observer of your layout either, as you have to manually move to the right of the layout in order to see this field.

Longer Sorts

You can, of course, choose more than one field in your Sort command. FileMaker will go as deep as you wish into a hierarchy of fields. Say, for example, you want to have your records sorted in the order of Date, Product Ordered, Last Name. File-Maker would give you a sorted group of records in exactly that order, as FileMaker would maintain the integrity of that grouping. Your records would appear in the first priority of date order. For a certain date, all the products ordered on that date would appear in alphabetical order. Lastly, all the customers who ordered the same products would appear in alphabetical order. If you want to sort a list of people in strict alphabetical order, then you would sort on the Last Name field, the First Name, and a Middle Initial field if you had one.

The change of the order of the list of fields in the field hierarchy can be accomplished in one of two ways. You can Move fields out of the box on the right and then replace them from the bottom, or you can Clear all the fields out of the box and start over. For example, in Fig. 7-5, we have the field hierarchy placed like this: Date, Product Ordered, Last Name, First Name.

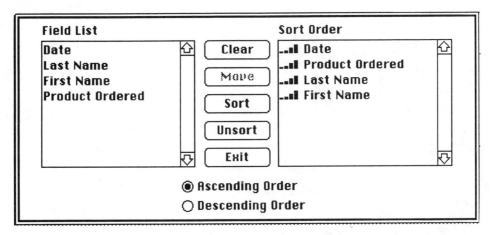

Fig. 7-5. Sort hierarchy.

Now, let's say that you want to have the names sorted first and the products sorted last. You could select the Product Ordered on the right, Move or Clear it, and then Move it back. Any new fields that you add to the hierarchy are always added to the bottom of the list.

If you want to make a lot of changes to the Sort Order list, it is much easier just to click on Clear, which will clear all the fields from the list on the right, and start over again. Once you Clear or Move fields from the left box, they still always appear in the left box in the order that those fields were created in the field definitions. If you make a change to the field sort hierarchy or add extra levels, you must always execute another Sort to make sure that the records are sorted in the correct order.

 While it is true that FileMaker can handle a multilevel sort easily, you might forfeit a certain amount of speed as a result. Each level you add will slow down the processing time on your Mac. If you have a very large database to sort, it might be feasible to split the file into two or more files to avoid excessive sorting.

Permanent Sorts

Once you have sorted records, they will remain sorted until you add new records, instigate a new Sort command, or choose the Unsort command in the Sort command box. If you choose Unsort, the records will revert to their original order, that is, the order in which they were entered. But let's say that you want to permanently change the underlying *unsorted* order in which the records appear. This can be accomplished in a relatively simple three-step process: Sort, Clone, Input. First, sort the records in the order that you want to make permanent. Second, go to the File menu and choose Save a Copy. Once that has been selected, you are provided with three choices in saving this file, as shown in Fig. 7-6. Choose Clone, which means a copy with no records. This duplicates the file exactly as far as layout and field definitions, but this file will have no records.

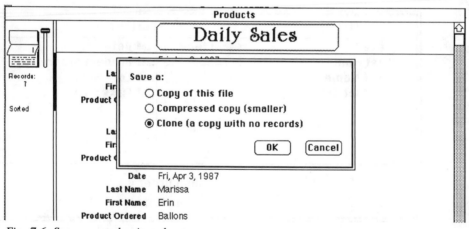

Fig. 7-6. Save a copy that is a clone.

After you ask for a Clone, you will be asked for the name of this clone. The default name is Clone of (File Name), in this case, Clone of Products. We suggest you change the suggested name, for example to Products (Sorted), as that leaves no doubt as to what was done with this file to distinguish it from the original. Now click New, and your cloning is completed. The clone does not appear on the screen, but it is saved in the folder in which you are currently working.

The last step is to take the records from the original file and place them in the new file through the use of the Input From command which is under the File menu. Before you can implement this command, you need to open the new file. Because FileMaker handles the opening of multiple documents quite easily, you do not need to be under the MultiFinder to do this.

With the new cloned file active, select Input From from the File menu, and then select the old file as shown in Fig. 7-7. As soon as you have done that, you are given a mini "report" of what you are trying to accomplish as shown in Fig. 7-8.

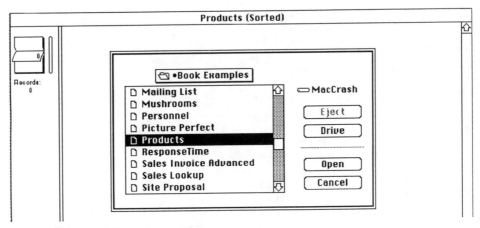

Fig. 7-7. Selecting File for Input From.

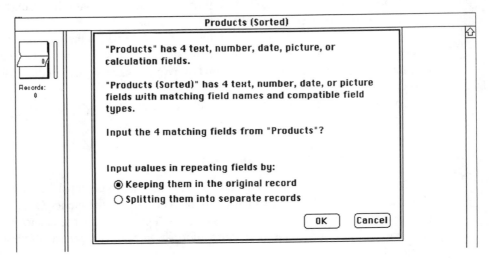

Fig. 7-8. Input From dialog box.

FileMaker will tell you how many fields are in each file and the number of fields that have matching values. This dialog box has a pair of radio buttons. One option is labeled Input values in repeating fields by. You need to select the first option Keep them in the original record. Click on OK to complete the operation. Filemaker will grab the

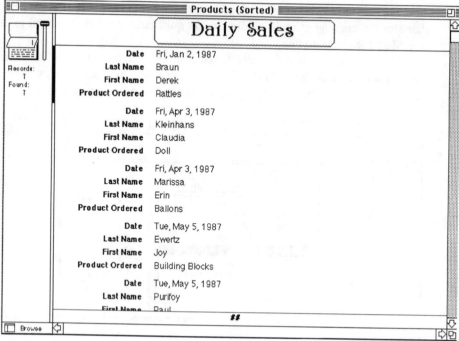

Fig. 7-9. Completed cloned file.

records from the original file and place them in the new file, with the result being a complete set of permanently sorted records in your new file.

In the end your screen should resemble Fig. 7-9, in which the new file is active and the records are in order. Note the Found status in the status area. That tells you how many records in the group were found to have the same values; in this case, it is seven out of seven.

To summarize, the three steps to creating a permanently sorted file are:

1. SORT original file.
2. CLONE a duplicate file.
3. INPUT FROM original file to the clone.

If you are going to undertake this operation, remember all three steps! Also remember which file is the original and which is the permanently sorted clone. Once you are confident that the operation was a success, you will probably want to delete the original file as it is now redundant. (For more information on clones and input/output, see Chapter 8.)

FINDING IT OUT

Sometimes you find yourself happily working along, and someone bursts into your office and breathlessly informs you that he needs to *find* something *now*! Life in the office would be awfully dull without these minor crises, of course. But they get rather tiresome if your only reaction is to rummage through file cabinets and toss papers about and generally create more hysteria. Of what use is data if you can't find it when you need it?

Basic Findings

FileMaker makes short work of finding information without making you jump through hoops trying to prepare tricky And/Or and If/Then statements. The program is designed to find all words and numbers (values) that you specify that are contained in text fields, date fields, number fields, and calculation fields. (Picture fields cannot be "found" because they are not indexed, and summary fields cannot be found because they rely on a group of records for their result, rather than being constant.)

What are some of the ways that the Find command can be used? To begin with, you can use it to find specific information such as all addresses within the state of Florida, or all the Smiths in the database. You can find all the Smiths and all the Browns. You can also find all the Browns, Brownes, or even Brauns with relative ease. You can find all the accounts receivable invoiced in July. You can even find all the sales for the month of January, or all the sales for the year except January. In addition to being able to find specifics, you can also use the Find feature to separate a group of records from the rest. This is particularly helpful when you need to have Subsummaries calculated for a distinct group. Last, but not least, you can use Find to find errors that might have occurred during data entry. You can find empty fields and misspellings that might have gone otherwise unnoticed.

Setting up a Find command in FileMaker is fairly straightforward. When you perform a Find in FileMaker, each value to be searched for is referred to as a *request* and the value entered in the request is referred to as the *criteria*. You access the Find mode by selecting Find from the Select menu, or by using the keyboard shortcut of Command−F. The Find mode screen resembles whichever layout you happened to be using at the time, with the exception that all of the fields are blank, and summary fields (if there are any in that particular layout) are not shown. Also note that there are new symbols in the status area, and the book icon is at zero (0).

In Fig. 7-10, you can see an example of what the Find mode looks like in a mailing list search. In this example, we used one of the report layouts, but if we had been using the label layout at the time of the request, the Find mode would have looked like the label layout instead.

As you can see in Fig. 7-10, the menu selections change when you are in the Find mode, much like they change between the Layout mode and the Browse mode. Three Edit menu items in the Find mode are distinctive to that mode only: New Request, Duplicate Request, and Delete Request (grayed-out until at least one request has been made). Under the Select menu are three Find-related commands: Find itself; Refind, which displays the last Find; Find All, which removes the restriction imposed by Find.

You can enter any criteria in any field at this point. You are not limited to filling in just one field. If you want to find a Smith at a particular address, you can enter those criteria in the name and address fields.

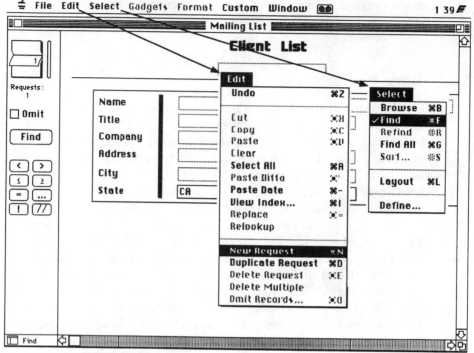

Fig. 7-10. Find mode for mail list file.

General Requests vs. Exact Requests

For a simple request, we have entered the letters CA in the State field of our request, with the result being all records that have all the letters CA in that field. After entering your criteria from the keyboard, either click on the Find button in the status area or tap Return. FileMaker then executes the search and then returns you to the Browse mode of the layout you were working with. This result is shown in Fig. 7-11.

Notice that the book icon has changed to show the total number of records (200) and the number found (147). Simply translated, FileMaker is telling us that, out of a possible 200 records, 147 records were found to match the criteria that we gave.

When entering criteria in the Find mode, you can tab through the fields just as you would in the Browse mode. If you tab to a field that you have defined to Display a List of Values, those values will appear as that field becomes active. You can either use one of these values in your search, or you can override those values by entering your criteria directly in that field.

General requests. The request we made in Fig. 7-10 and accomplished in Fig. 7-11 is referred to as a *general* request. This means that the records which have been found include any word in that field that contains the first two letters CA. Within this group, we could also have records with the words California, Canada, and Caracas. Unless you tell it otherwise, FileMaker looks for records that contain the letters or words you have specified. For example, if you had typed the word Admin in the Title

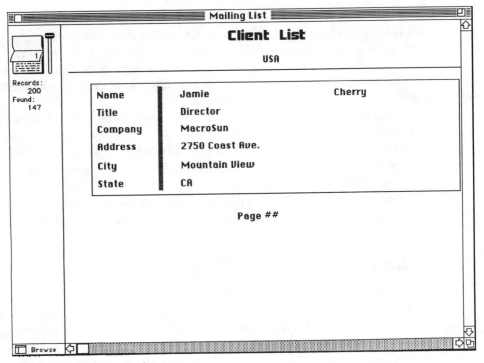

Fig. 7-11. Result of a Find request.

field, some of the possible findings from this request would be Administrative Assistant, Administrator, or even Director of Administration. You would not find Director of Admissions in this group as it does not match the five letters (Admin) given in the request.

Exact requests. In order to *exactly* match the criteria in your request with the found records, you need only to type an equals sign (=) before your criteria. You can accomplish this by using the symbols in the status area. Click once in the field you want FileMaker to search in, and then click once on the equals sign button in the status area. The equals sign will then appear in that field. After the equals sign (no need to enter a space after it) type your criteria. If we wanted only the records with the abbreviation CA in the State field, we would type = CA in the State field.

Bear in mind that an exact request demands consistency during data entry. A request for = CA would exclude Cal and Calif, which might have been used instead of CA. One way to counter such problems is to use a date entry check. For example, a calculated field next to the state field might contain the following formula to warn you that the entry in the State field was too long:

IF(LENGTH(State) = 2," ", "Check abbreviation for State")

This formula returns nothing, represented by the pair of quotes (" "), if the entry in State is two characters long. Otherwise, the warning Check abbreviation for State is displayed.

Fortunately, even an exact formula is not case sensitive. This means that = CA will find CA, Ca, and even ca. If you wanted to find the name Jon Smith, you would type = Jon in the First Name field and = Smith in the Last Name field. You are not limited to criteria in just one field when entering a request. In this instance, you would only receive the records listing Jon Smith and JON SMITH. You would exclude Jonathan Smith or Jon Smithereens, for example.

If you have a name field in which you list the entire name, rather than the first and last name fields, you would enter your criteria as = Jon = Smith in the one field. This would give you the records found with either Jon Smith or Smith, Jon, as FileMaker ignores the actual order of the words in a field. Punctuation is also ignored as is capitalization of letters.

 You can type beyond the boundaries of the field or fields that you use to enter criteria when using Find. In this instance, the boundaries would be temporarily extended for your use.

Failed Finds

If you enter criteria for a Find and FileMaker does not find any records in the database that correspond to your request, you will receive the prompt, No Records Match This Request. This leaves you in the Find mode with the criteria still entered. If you are sure that there are records that match the request, check to see that you have entered the criteria in the correct field and have spelled the request correctly. You might want to return to the Browse mode and check the arrangement of data to ensure that you are making a reasonable Find request.

Forgetting Finds

When you successfully execute a Find, the selected records temporarily constitute the entire database. If you Print or Browse at this point, you will only see the found records. If you execute a Sort, it will only affect the found records. To remove this restriction, you simply select Find All from the Select menu (keyboard shortcut Command−G). This returns access to all of the records. However, it does not mean that you have lost your Find criteria. If you choose Refind from the Select menu (keyboard shortcut Command−R), the last criteria you used will be reinstated.

Repeated Finds

What if you execute a Find, decide that it is wrong, or simply want to try a different Find? Do not choose New Request from the Select menu as this adds a second level to your search (as described in a moment) and does not clear out the current settings. Simply choose Find again. The previous Find settings are always erased when you pick Find mode. Of course, this suggests that you might have problems when you want to reuse a set of criteria (for example, when you Find your California clients, then need to see some records in other states, then want to get back to just the California clients).

Fortunately, you don't always have to start from scratch with a new Find request.

You can use the Refind command instead. Refind is located in the Select menu (with the corresponding keyboard shortcut of Command—R) and is only available if there was a Find command in recent history from which to start. Refind uses the exact same criteria as the last request. This is particularly helpful when you have changed or added records to your file that could change the results of your last Find request. When you activate the Refind, the last Find request is presented to you on screen for you to check for accuracy. You can, of course, alter or change the criteria at this point as well. A simple click on the Find button or a tap of the Return key completes your request.

If you go to the menu to choose Refind and see that it is grayed-out (not active), that means that either no Find request has been made, or that you asked for a Find without entering any criteria the last time the Find mode was invoked. Your only choice in that instance is to reenter your criteria. For example, let's say you asked for all the Model T's sold last year and then decide to find that same data again. But, instead of choosing Refind, you chose Find. Oops! You wanted Refind! So you choose Find All and then go to select Refind. Now Refind isn't active. By asking for Find before Refind, you inadvertently erased all the criteria for the last Find, and you can't get it back once you have asked for a new Find screen.

Finding Tips

Sometimes, especially when fields are not labeled on the layout, it is easy to inadvertently enter Find criteria in the wrong field. If you are not having any luck discovering the reason for a failed Find, try shortening the spelling of the word, or use only the first portion of the value. For example, if you are looking for the word Technician, try entering it as Tech. You might end up with a larger number of found records, but you probably will eventually find the record you are searching for. Usually you'll find an error in that record of either transposed values or misspelling.

Other times, the input of your criteria will affect the result of the search that File-Maker makes. For example, when you are looking for numbers, be sure to enter that number as an *unformatted* number. If you are looking for a percentage in a number or calculation field such as 75%, you must enter that number as .75, or you might find that FileMaker has found all the numbers that begin with the whole number of 75 rather than those requested. The same goes for dates. If you are looking for a particular date, enter in the unformatted form like 7/22/88 or 7-22-88 rather than Fri, July 22, 1988. If you enter the date in any other format though, FileMaker will give you a prompt that asks you to enter the date in the correct form.

In one last instance, what you ask for might be slightly different than what you get. This involves number or calculation fields that contain the values Y or N. If you type a Y in the field for your search, FileMaker will give you all the records that contain either a Y or 1 in that field. Likewise if you type N, you will get all the records that contain the values N or 0.

It must also be noted that when you activate the Find command and FileMaker presents found records on the screen, any Sub-summary fields on the layout will be affected by this request. Although the Sub-summary fields do not appear on the screen during a Find, they do appear again once the Find has been completed. If you have requested FileMaker to find the sales figures for January, for instance, and you have a Sub-summary in that layout that gives you a total of sales for each month, only the total for January will be shown once the records have been found. If you were to print the records at this point, only the found records will be printed. The same holds true for mailing lists. If you want to find all the records for the state of Montana, you can then print your mailing labels directly from the found records once the search has been completed.

In and Out of Find

Now that you have seen how to get into Find and troubleshoot problems, let us go over the question of how to get out of the Find mode. If your Find request is successful, you are automatically returned to the Browse mode of your layout with only the found records being displayed. This does not mean that the other records are gone. This is similar to the Sort command in that the records will remain in this order until you tell FileMaker to do something else. The found records will remain on the screen until you ask FileMaker to Find All, which is under the Select menu. Find All is also available through the keyboard shortcut of Command–G.

Suppose that you've gotten yourself stuck in the Find mode without any found records. Maybe you even asked for the Find mode by mistake. What then? The answer is basically the same. You can go back to the mode you entered from by using Find All, but you can also get out of the Find mode at this point by using the commands for the Browse mode or the Layout mode, which are under the Select menu.

MORE SOPHISTICATED FINDS

Sometimes you need to find records on the basis of more than one set of criteria. This is referred to as an And/Or statement in some database programs, and they can be frightening to less experienced computer operators. One of the gems of the Find operation in FileMaker is that multiple criteria are easy to set up.

This And/Or That

Suppose you need to find all the dolls *and* rattles sold from your toy company inventory so that you can calculate your new orders. If you typed the words Dolls and Rattles in the Product field on one request, you would receive only the records of clients who bought *both* items. But, by asking FileMaker for a New Request under the Edit menu, you can execute a search that will find all records with Dolls or Rattles, or both.

To accomplish a Find based on multiple requests, begin with the layout you want to use and then go to the Find mode. Enter the criteria in the appropriate field and then select New Request from the Edit menu or use the keyboard shortcut of Command–N. You will be given another blank Find screen in which to enter your criteria.

At the same time, the book icon will make note of the number of requests you have made in this particular search.

If you happen to forget what criteria has been entered in each request, you can flip through them with the book icon. When you have finished with all your requests, tap Return or click the Find button. The result will be all the records that have either one set of criteria or the other or both. Please note, however, that these records will not necessarily be in any particular order. You can, however, use the Sort command afterwards to clean the records up for ease of viewing.

 If you need to execute a Find with multiple requests and you have a small layout, choose View As List from the Gadgets menu in the Layout mode before you begin your requests. Then, as you ask for New Requests, each request will appear on your screen and you will be saved the inconvenience of flipping through the requests if you forget what you have entered. An example is shown in Fig. 7-12.

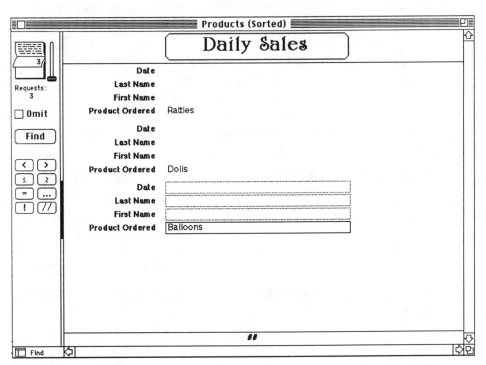

Fig. 7-12. Using View As List for multiple requests.

Acts of Omission

Sometimes it is easier to find what you want by establishing negative criteria; that is, finding records that do not match certain criteria. For example, say you want to find all the clients in your own state *except* those in your own zip code. Or, you might want to find all the sales figures for 1987 except for those in the month of July. Again, this is a very easy request to handle. The only change from a regular request is to make use of the Omit box in the status area. When you enter the criteria and then click in the Omit box so that it contains an X, FileMaker in effect subtracts those records that match the criteria in the Omit request.

In the zip code in the mailing list example, you would enter your zip code in the appropriate field and then click in the Omit box. Then, when you click on the Find button or tap Return, FileMaker would give you all the records except those with your own zip code. You are then ready to print your report, labels, or whatever.

The Omit feature can also be used with multiple requests. You can tell FileMaker to "find this and/or that *except* this." This is very handy when you are working with records that have duplicate values that are not exactly the same in other respects. Suppose you have a mailing list database in which your records contain at least 16 states that have a city named Columbia. You need to find the records with Columbia in the states that begin with the letters C, M, and S, but you don't want the Columbia in South Dakota. You start by entering the first three requests as shown in Fig. 7-13:

(City) Columbia, (State) C
(City) Columbia, (State) M
(City) Columbia, (State) S

In the fourth request, you would specify Columbia again in the City field and SD in the State field and then check Omit in this request by clicking in the Omit box so that an X appears. With your requests now complete, FileMaker will search for all the records that would match your first three requests and leave out any records that were found to contain SD in the State field.

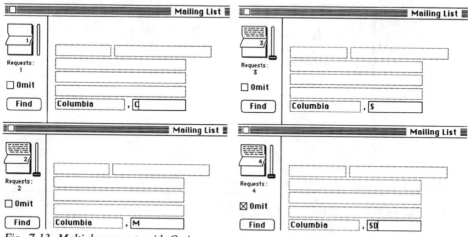

Fig. 7-13. Multiple requests with Omit.

Using the Omit option in the Find mode is completely different from the Omit command in the Edit menu. The Omit command in the Edit menu temporarily removes the current record (or the current record plus any number that you specify) from your view while in the Browse mode. This command is not available when you are in the Find mode or in the Layout mode.

The Trick to Refinding

As is often the case in the real world, things you have found tend to get shuffled aside and then need to be found again. In FileMaker, each time you select Find from the Select menu, all previous requests are erased and you are presented with a nice, new, clean Find screen. That's great, except that you just spent twenty minutes fumbling around with a convoluted Find, and you forgot to print your results. You don't really have to start from scratch with a new Find request. You can use the Refind command instead. Refind is located in the Select menu (with the corresponding keyboard shortcut of Command − R) and is described earlier under "Repeated Finds."

One important note is needed about Refind. If you have changed your layout since last using Find, the criteria remains only for those fields that still remain on the layout. Therefore, if you have just changed the location of the fields, Refind will still work. But, if you have deleted any field or fields that were present in your last request, Refind will either not be active, or will present you with a blank screen. This is to prevent you from using a Find request to find data that can no longer be found on that layout.

What That Thing on the Left Is

In the Find mode, you have seen that the status area contains a number of symbols that can be used in different ways to affect your requests. Those symbols are there for your convenience and efficiency in entering your criteria requests. For example, instead of having to type an equals sign in a field, you can use your mouse to click in the appropriate field, and then click on the equals sign to have it inserted in that field. What follows is a simple guide to assist you with the proper usage of these symbols.

< **(less than).** This symbol is used to find records containing a range that is *less than* your criteria. If you are using text fields as criteria, then using <D would find all the records that are less than D; that is A, B, and C, but not D would be found. If you are using numbers, then <100 would include all the numbers between 1 and 99, but not 100.

> **(greater than).** The greater than symbol is used to find values that are greater than what you have entered in the field. It is the opposite of the less than symbol. For example, if you entered >12-24-68, you would receive all the dates that are after this date, starting with 12-25-68.

≤ **(less than or equal to).** This symbol is similar to the less than symbol with the exception that it is used to *include* the criteria specified as well as the values that are less than the criteria. If you wanted to find the sales figures for January, February, and March, you could specify ≤March to have all three month's figures revealed.

≥ **(greater than or equal to).** Again this is symbol is similar to the greater than symbol, but is used when you want to include the specified criteria in the result of the Find. For example, if you type ≥Clark, you would receive all names in your database that appear beginning with Clark and continuing after Clark.

= **(exact match).** This symbol is used for exact matches only. For example, if you need to find any and all blank records in your file, you would enter just the equals sign and nothing else. You would receive, in turn, all records that have a blank in that field or fields. Likewise, if you need to find all the invoices that totaled exactly $400.00, then you would enter =400 in the appropriate field.

. . . (range). An ellipsis is used to indicate a range in your criteria. For example, you might want to find all the last names that begin with A, B, C, and D. Rather than preparing four requests, you can enter the following in the Last Name field:

A . . . D

In return, FileMaker would give you all the last names that begin with any of these letters, inclusive of the first and last letters. The ellipsis can also be used to find a range of dates in such as:

4/1/88 . . . 4/30/88

It can also be used to find a range of numbers.

! (duplicate). An exclamation mark is used to find duplicate values within a given field. (A duplicate is the same in one record as it is in another.) To use, simply insert the exclamation mark in the field that you wish to search for duplicates and then click Find. The result will be matching values such as the same name, the same number, or the same date. This is quite useful when weeding out duplicates in a database that should contain only unique values, such as invoice numbers.

// (date stamp). The date stamp can be used in any date field in a Find. It automatically enters the current date, according to the Mac's internal clock. When using the date stamp button in the Find mode, the date can only be entered in a field and cannot be placed on the layout.

Using the preceding symbols can result in an increase in speed and efficiency when conducting a search. The more criteria you give FileMaker to compare, the more accurate the match will be in the end. Suppose you have a retail shop and need to get in contact with a particular customer, but you don't remember her name. What you do remember, however, is that she was in sometime between May and July, her last name begins with C, she bought a lot of Yellow Ones (code A5), and she spent over $800.00 on her total purchase. If you were to enter this information as shown in Fig. 7-14, you would have made use of at least three of the status area keys in your Find.

The range was used for the date, the exact match was used for the product code, and the greater than or equal to sign used in the total. The result of this search, as shown in Fig. 7-15, gives two possible choices (and you decide the correct person). Mission accomplished!

MAKING ADJUSTMENTS

Finding the information you need is simply not enough sometimes. The data is still in a raw state and needs to be reconfigured or adjusted in some manner. Basically four options are available to you once you have completed a Find request: Sort, Replace, Delete, and Omit. The number one rule is to always remember to do your Find first, especially when it comes to using a Sort afterwards.

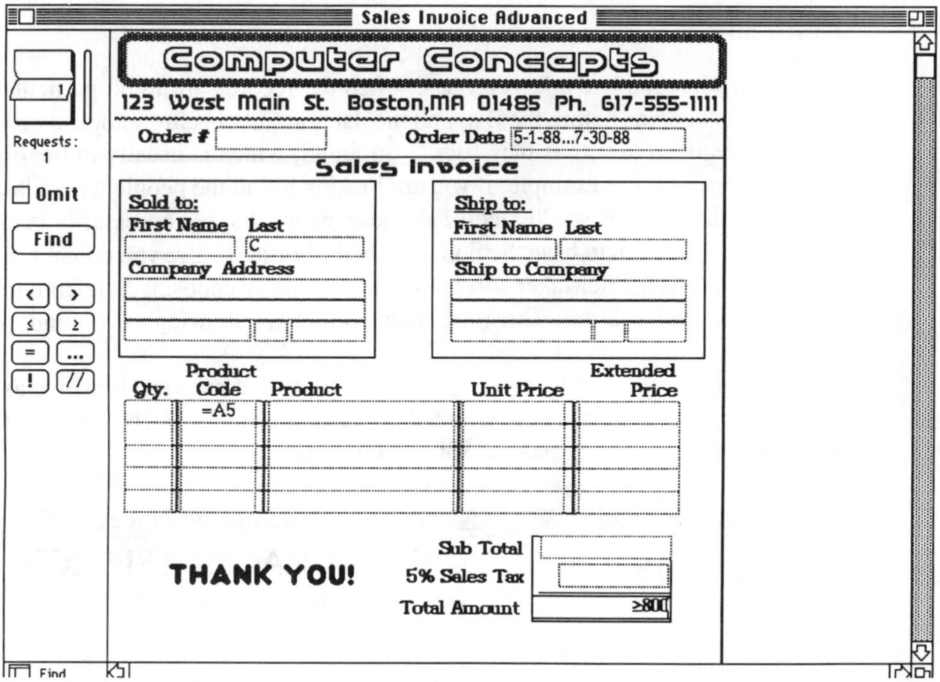

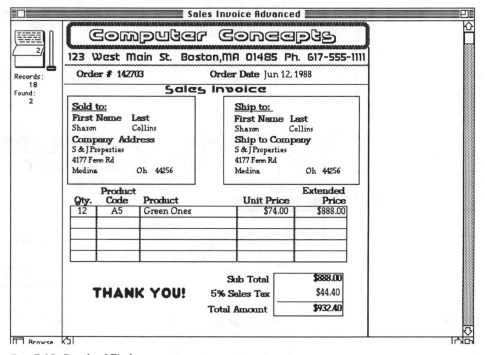

Fig. 7-14. Find Request using status area keys.

Fig. 7-15. Result of Find.

Find/Sort

When you complete a Find request, often the records are in no particular order. The M's might come before the B's, and the dates are not in chronological order. File-Maker gives them to you as they have been found, which is usually in the order that they were entered. For example, if you are looking for all the people whose last names begin with the letter H, you'll receive all those names, but not necessarily in alphabetical order. If you wish to have them in alphabetical order before you commit this list to paper, you can have FileMaker sort the found records by choosing Sort from the Select menu. FileMaker will only sort those records that are showing as "Found" on your screen.

Sometimes you need to find a group of records that are very sensitive as to how they are sorted. Such is the case with Sub-summaries. In Fig. 7-16, we show the Find screen for a layout that employs a Sub-summary section.

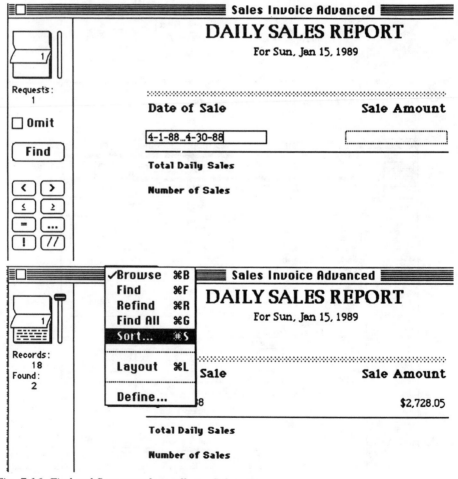

Fig. 7-16. Find and Sort records to affect a Sub-summary.

Notice that the layout text for these fields appear, but the actual fields themselves do not. The information in Sub-summaries cannot be "found" because their information comes from a group of records rather than a single record. The information is not static; it changes according to how the records are grouped. You can affect the Sub-summary, however, by finding only certain records, thus changing the grouping of the records.

With Fig. 7-16, we are attempting to find any and all records for the month of April. Once we have completed the Find, we see that FileMaker has found two records for April but the Sub-summary section is still blank (as shown by the lower part of the figure). Sub-summaries are not activated unless they are sorted, so we still have to execute the sort, according to the field specified in the Sub-summary part. In this instance, the field is the Date field. Once we sort the found records, the Sub-summary is then available, as shown in Fig. 7-17.

DAILY SALES REPORT

For Sun, Jan 15, 1989

Date of Sale	Sale Amount
Apr 5, 1988	$2,728.05
Apr 5, 1988	$443.40
Total Daily Sales	**$3,171.45**
Number of Sales	2

Fig. 7-17. Result of Find/Sort on a Sub-summary.

Grand Summaries are affected in a similar manner by the Find feature. By definition, the Grand Summary is a summary of all records. But, if we exclude all but a select number of records by using Find, you can change the result of the Grand Summary. In the upper portion of Fig. 7-18, we show the Grand Summary for all the records in a database.

In the lower portion of the figure, we show the same Grand Summary, but with a different figure. In the second part, we asked FileMaker to find only the records between 1-1-88 and 6-30-88. The resulting figures reflect the total only for those records found by FileMaker to match our request.

Find/Replace

We once got a call from a frantic client who explained that a temporary office worker had used the wrong coding on over 1000 entries! Did that mean that every one

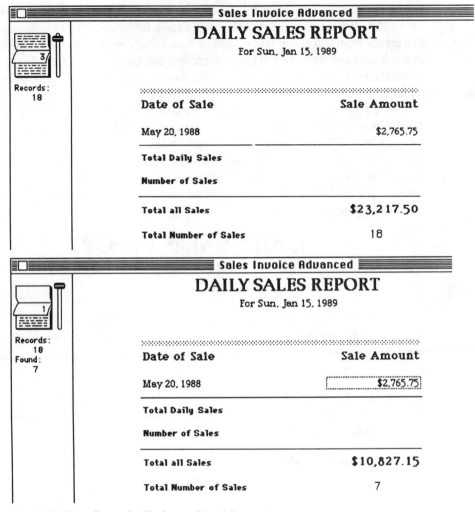

Fig. 7-18. The effects of a Find on a Grand Summary.

of those records had to be changed one at a time? Imagine his relief when we told him that there was a much simpler way to handle this without wasting precious person-hours. This is probably one of the most dramatic cases in which a simple Find and Replace is "just the thing" to help out. All he had to do was to find the records with the wrong code and then replace that code in all of them, all at once.

To give you an example of this in action, we start in Fig. 7-19 by asking for an exact match in the Designator field. We asked for all the records with the letter B in that field because we either know that this is in error, or we have other reasons to change all those records with the code letter B in that field.

When Filemaker has finished looking at all the records, we see that 164 records out of 775 have been found with the letter B in the Designator field. What we want to change every entry B into is BMOC. In the Designator field of this record, we type the

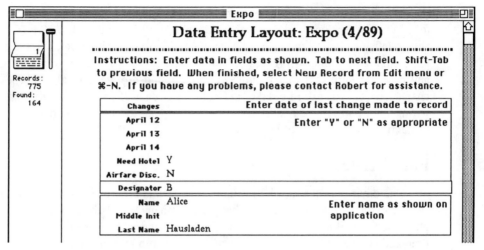

Fig. 7-19. Find the data that needs changing.

letters BMOC, but we do not press Tab to move past that field. Immediately after typing the correct replacement, we choose the Replace command from the Edit menu, or use the keyboard shortcut of Command − = (Command − equal sign). FileMaker then gives us the warning as shown in Fig. 7-20. This warning tells us that it will place the letters BMOC in the Designator field in all 164 records if we click the Replace button.

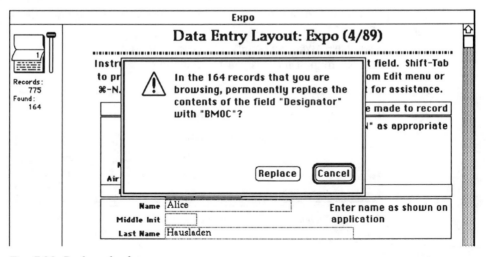

Fig. 7-20. Replace the data.

A few variables might be involved in using a Find in which you will also do a Replace, most of them involving the initial finding of the data that needs to be changed. For example, if you know that the data to be changed is the same in all the records that you will be looking for, then you need only to enter the duplicate symbol

(!) in the field. Even if you have more than one duplicate value, FileMaker will find them all. The drawback to this is that they will not be in any order. Nor will you be able to tell at a glance how many of each there are. You can, however, execute a Sort to put them in order and, by process of elimination, be able to cull out what you need. In any case, be sure that the records you have found are actually all the ones to be changed before you ask FileMaker to Replace any data. If you accidentally replace the wrong information, the results could be disastrous—the Undo key does not reverse this action.

Find/Delete

One other reason you might want to find certain records is to weed out unnecessary or outdated information. Say that your company sells baby products, and you've purchased a mailing list that includes the names and addresses of couples with children and couples without children. You don't want to have the second lot included in most mailings you do since their need for baby-related items is fairly slim. You might want to weed out that group by looking for couples over the age of 50 who are also childless.

After you have had FileMaker find the records you are looking for, then you would choose Delete Multiple from the Edit menu. Notice that this command does not have a keyboard shortcut and is different from the Delete command. The plain Delete command just deletes the current record while the Delete Multiple deletes all of the found records. In any case, FileMaker wouldn't let you make that large of a commitment without some sort of warning, so what you would get then is a warning dialog as shown in Fig. 7-21.

Once you have given the command to delete, there is no turning back, so please be sure that the group of records you're asking to delete is the correct group.

Fig. 7-21. Delete Multiple warning dialog box.

Find/Omit

An additional method of manipulating information with the Find feature is to find certain groups of records with the intention of temporarily omitting them from a screen view or a printed report. There are not very many common reasons for wanting to do this, but it must be noted that this is different from the Omit feature of the Find mode.

Say, for example, that you want to view the commission figures for salesperson Larry, but you only want the figures for the last half of the month. Of course, there are much better ways of handling this request, such as asking for a range or preparing a calculation, but you're in a hurry and you just want a rough estimate. Let's say you have already found the figures for the month you want and the next step is to sort them so that they are in chronological order. You quickly flip through the records to find that record number seven is the cutoff; you want all the data that begins with record number eight. Make sure you go back to record number one and then choose Omit Records from the Edit menu (keyboard shortcut of Command−O). FileMaker then asks you how many records to omit, as shown in Fig. 7-22, beginning with the one showing on the screen.

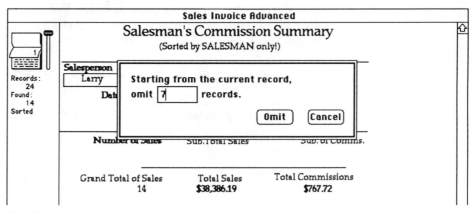

Fig. 7-22. Find, Sort, and Omit.

Simply type in the number of records you wish to omit, in this case seven, and then click Omit or tap Return. As you can see in Fig. 7-23, once FileMaker is finished omitting the records, the total number of records found has changed from the original number with the resulting number being just the ones you want to view or print.

Sales Invoice Advanced

Salesman's Commission Summary
(Sorted by SALESMAN only!)

Records:
24
Found:
7
Sorted

Salesperson
Larry

Date of Sale	Sales Amount	Comm.Due
1/18/88	$2,747.30	$54.95

Number of Sales	Sub.Total Sales	Sub. of Comms.

Grand Total of Sales	Total Sales	Total Commissions
7	$26,718.96	$534.38

Fig. 7-23. Final result of Find/Omit.

As we mentioned, this type of operation is just for quick results. But, to be more efficient and to ensure accuracy, it is much better to use a calculation or to look for a range of dates in your Find.

Applied Finding

The relative simplicity of FileMaker's Find commands, combined with the fact that FileMaker can perform most finds very quickly, opens up some interesting applications of the program. For example, a lot of people need a casual database of notes, ideas, reminders, and so on. The problem with using a normal database management program for such a collection of information is the clash between the rigid structure of a filing program and the casual nature of the information being filed.

As you know, FileMaker is no ordinary database manager. You can very quickly set up a casual database with FileMaker and always be able to find what you enter into it. As an example, consider the writer's database in Fig. 7-24.

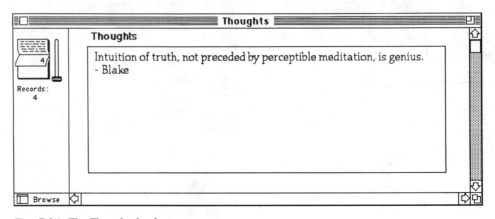

Fig. 7-24. The Thought database.

This single field database is simplicity itself. It has just one field, called Thoughts, and it is a text field. The Layout mode was used to expand the data entry box to about ten lines. As the writer comes across thoughts and ideas, he enters each one in a new record. For simple notes, the standard editing tools of the Mac are all he needs. The entry box performs automatic word wrapping whenever an entry gets too long for the current line.

When it comes time to recall a thought, the writer uses Find and enters the barest minimum of what he is looking for. For example, he remembers that there is an entry concerning wisdom. He enters wis in the field as shown in Fig. 7-25.

Now the user clicks on Find. All records that contain wis are found. This means any record with wisdom, wise, and so on, anywhere in the text of that record. Of course, this includes wishes and other words beginning with wis, but in most cases the user will be able to come up with a piece of text that encompasses the target records without including too many false ones. You can see the result in this case in Fig. 7-26.

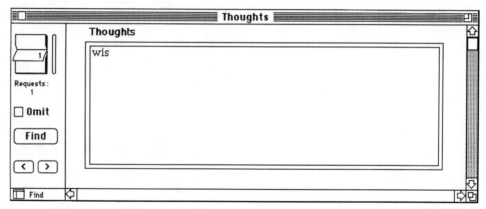

Fig. 7-25. Finding wisdom.

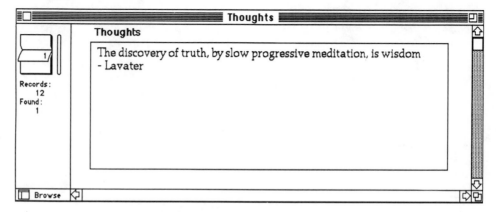

Fig. 7-26. The result of finding wisdom.

CONCLUSION

At this point, you have seen all of the major aspects of working with FileMaker from the design of data entry forms, to editing, browsing, sorting, searching, and printing records. In the next chapter, we look at a variety of more advanced subjects, ways to use the index that FileMaker creates to keep track of your data, plus how to duplicate databases, and how to import and export data to share it with users of programs other than FileMaker.

8

Power Setups

IN THIS CHAPTER, we look at a number of FileMaker's more advanced aspects, such as ways to use the index that FileMaker creates to keep track of your data, how to duplicate databases, and how to import and export data that you want to share with users of different programs besides FileMaker.

USING THE INDEX

If you have used other databases management programs besides FileMaker, you might have wondered why FileMaker has no "indexing" commands. Many database management programs perform a process called indexing in order to speed up the sorting and finding of information. As we mentioned in the last chapter, FileMaker automatically maintains an index of every entry in every field of every record. This helps you avoid the worry of creating an index or going through an indexing process. You can happily use FileMaker without ever bothering about the index. However, FileMaker does give you access to the information in the index, and this can be very useful.

Viewing the Index

Suppose you are helping out a colleague, entering some data into his FileMaker client list. You come to the Title field and wonder whether this means titles like Mr./ Mrs./Ms. or titles like Manager/CEO/President. You could use the bookmark icon to flip through a few records to see what has been entered in this field in other records, and then flip back to the record you are creating. An easier approach is to choose View Index from the Edit menu. This shows you a complete list of all entries in the current field.

A quick look at this screen answers your question: The Title field is for job titles. A closer look actually raises some questions, such as, what exactly is FileMaker listing in the index?

The View Index list contains every *word* entered in the selected field, displayed in "initial cap" format, meaning all lowercase letters except for the first letter, which is capitalized. This means that entries of MANAGER, Manager, and even manager will all appear in the index as Manager. Unfortunately, it also means that USA will appear as Usa. Numeric entries are treated as words, so that 1100, 11, and 1.1 are all words. The index does not record formatting of numbers. Furthermore, the index strips periods from text words, so that Mrs. appears Mrs in the index.

The term "every word" is important because entering Manager of Sales in a field will create three entries in the index: Manager, Of, and Sales (note that of is lowercase in the field entry with initial capital in the index). This aspect of the index might be a problem if you plan to use the index a lot. One way to avoid the problem is to use Option–Space instead of the regular spacebar when typing entries. This creates a *hard space* that connects two words so that they appear as one. Entering Manager_Of _Sales where the underlines represent Option–Space will create only one index entry, Manager of Sales. In fact, using underlines between words will also force File-Maker to treat the entry as one word.

 FileMaker uses several rules when determining what constitutes a "word" for purposes of the index. As far as text is concerned, any character or group of characters followed or preceded by a space is a word, as is any character(s) followed by a period. Even using a hard space will not prevent Dir. Sales from resulting in two words in the index: Sales and Dir, the latter being stripped of the period. Hyphens, commas, and spaces are stripped out of entries in number fields when they are indexed, so that 555-1212 is listed as 5551212.

Pasting from the Index

Besides looking at the index to see what kind of entries have been made in a field, what else can you do with it? One possibility is to use it for data entry. For example, after you determine the type of title required in the Title field in Fig. 8-1, you realize that a lot of your entries in this field will be Administrative Assistant. Instead of typing this over and over, you can paste it direct from the index. When the Title field is active, you press Command–I, the keyboard shortcut for the View Index command. You scroll down the list and click on the title you want. As you highlight an entry in the index, the Paste button becomes active, as shown in Fig. 8-2.

Press Return or click on Paste, and the highlighted entry is pasted into the field. FileMaker does this in full accordance with standard Mac editing practice. If the field already contains typing, the pasted entry is added to that typing. If you select some typing in the field before using the View Index command, the pasted entry replaces the selected text. You might have noticed that the index is limited to displaying the first 20 or so characters of an entry, but the full entry is used when you issue the Paste command.

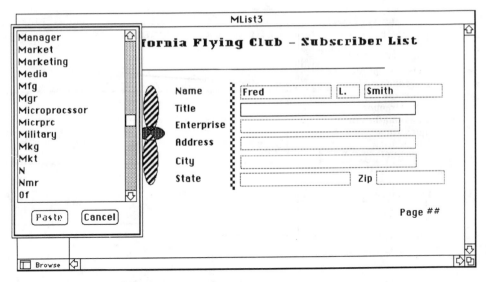

Fig. 8-1. Using View Index.

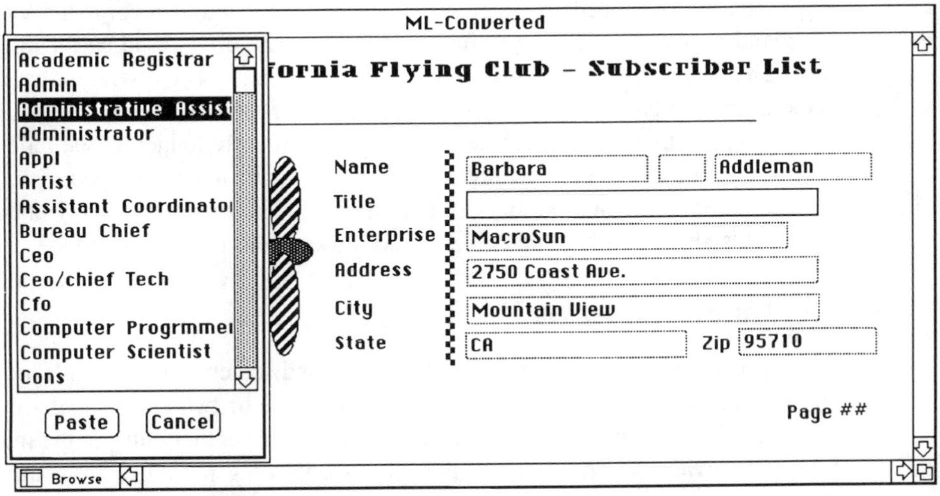

Fig. 8-2. Pasting from the index.

Given the fact that FileMaker indexes individual words as separate items, you might wonder how you can get Administrative Assistant in the index. This was possible because the original entry in the database was made using the Option–Space method mentioned earlier. Later in this chapter, we present a technique for changing spaces in current entries into Option–Spaces.

The ability to paste entries from the index might not seem all that helpful in the above example, but it can be really valuable in two situations. The first case is where the number of possible entries is limited, and this is described in the next section. The

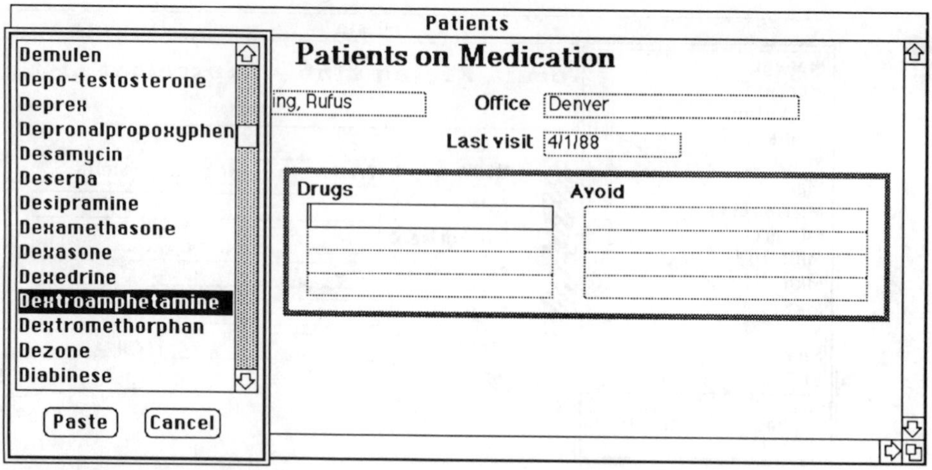

Patients

Patients on Medication

Demulen
Depo-testosterone
Deprex
Depronalpropoxyphen
Desamycin
Deserpa
Desipramine
Dexamethasone
Dexasone
Dexedrine
Dextroamphetamine
Dextromethorphan
Dezone
Diabinese

ing, Rufus   Office Denver
               Last visit 4/1/88

Drugs   Avoid

[Paste] [Cancel]

Fig. 8-3. Drug database index.

other case is where the database requires complex entries that are difficult to spell correctly. Consider the medical database in Fig. 8-3.

When the user needs to enter the name of a drug into a record, the View Index command presents a nicely alphabetized list of all the drugs used so far in the database. The user can then select the appropriate name and paste it without having to go to the trouble of typing it. Typing only needs to be done when a new drug is entered, and as soon as that is done, the new entry is permanently lodged in the index.

 New entries in records are not actually added to the index until you move on from the current record. This prompts FileMaker to update the index. The Find and Sort commands also prompt an updating, as does moving to the Browse mode.

The Index and Error Detection

What if you issue the View Index command and see entries that don't look right? For example, the list of titles in Fig. 8-4 contains one or two entries that are odd.

You might like to know which record contains a particular entry in the index. You can do this with the Find command. If you are viewing the index from the Browse mode, you must put the index away before going to the Find mode. In the Find mode, you select the field you want to investigate, select View Index, and highlight the entry you are concerned about. Select Paste, and the entry will be placed in the field box. You can now select Find, and the entry will be located.

Using View Index in the Find mode is a good method of reviewing a database and correcting errors. For example, you can easily spot the inconsistent phone number in the example in Fig. 8-5. The number should have an area code. By highlighting the entry you want to check on, then selecting Paste, the entry will be placed in the Phone field. You can then select Find and the record will be located, ready for you to edit.

Note that FileMaker has stripped the parentheses, hyphens,and spaces from the phone numbers when showing them in the index. This is because the field type for

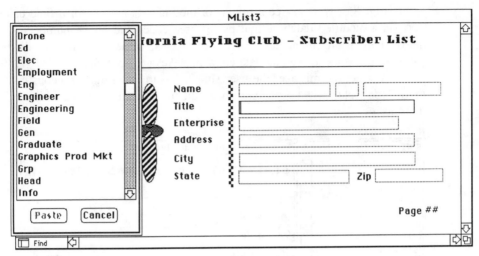

Fig. 8-4. List of odd titles.

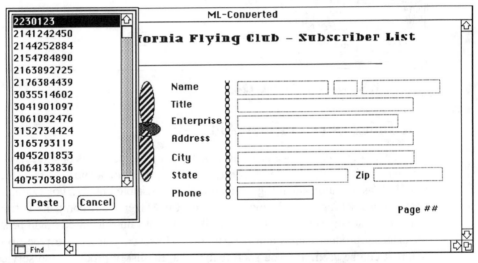

Fig. 8-5. Incomplete phone number.

Phone is number and not text. If the field type was changed to text, then the index would show the phone numbers exactly as they were entered, which is the (415) 555-1212 format. If you use text as the field type, then entering phone numbers with hyphens results in them being treated as whole words. You would not want to paste entries into records from an index list like the one in Fig. 8-5, but FileMaker has no difficulty finding 223-0123 in a number field if you use 2230123 as the search criteria. If you use regular spaces between the parts of a phone number, then a phone number index will show all of the parts separately. If you use Option–Space between numbers, FileMaker will index the numbers as a unit.

In Fig. 8-6, you can see a review of the index of entries for a field called Area Code in a modified database that places area codes and phone number in separate fields. This arrangement has several advantages, some of which we discuss in a moment, but you can see that data entry mistakes are possible.

To correct the mistake, the user simply has to Paste the erroneous entry in the Area Code field, select Find, and then edit the offending record which FileMaker presents.

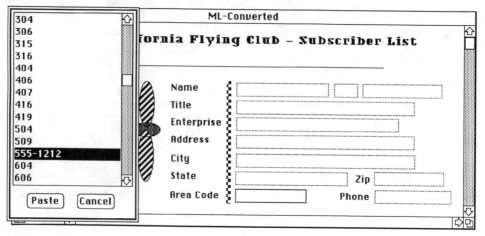

Fig. 8-6. View Index with the Area Code field.

The Index as Data Entry Aid

In previous chapters, we have discussed lookup files and lists of values, set up via the Entry Options with the Define command, as an aid to data entry. In fact, the index can work as an automatically generated table of possible entries. For example, suppose you are setting up an invoice system on FileMaker. Your company is small and sells a modest range of products. You think the list of values featured might be suitable for entering product names and descriptions. However, you have to type up the list before it can be used, and you soon realize that the list of products and services you invoice is actually growing all the time. You have to use the Define command to add new items to the list of values, or type in items that are not listed. However, if you use the View Index command wisely, you can have a custom-made, up-to-the-minute list of values from which to choose, like the one shown in Fig. 8-7.

In this example, the bill of sale is being filled out and the user has come to the Description field. Pressing Command−I, the user pops up the indexed list of previous entries, which contains all of the names of products used so far. The customer is buying a Vecta 2000, which is being pasted from the list. You will notice that the two words in this entry are held together. That is because the user typed Option−Space between them instead of a regular space. Also note that the list contains some descriptive words such as Green. These can be pasted in combination with other entries, as in

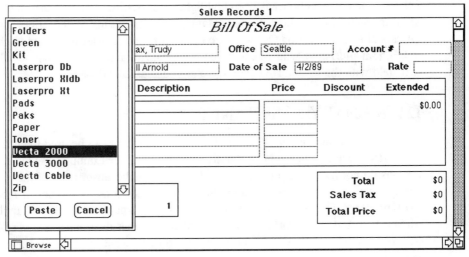

Fig. 8-7. View Index for data entry.

Green Folders. Although the index disappears after the Paste command, FileMaker does not move the data entry edit cursor and so you can quickly repeat the View Index command to paste more than one item into the same field.

This use of the View Index command works best when the field has a limited number of entries. Another limitation is imposed by the way that FileMaker presents entries in the index. Consider the list of states being used in Fig. 8-8.

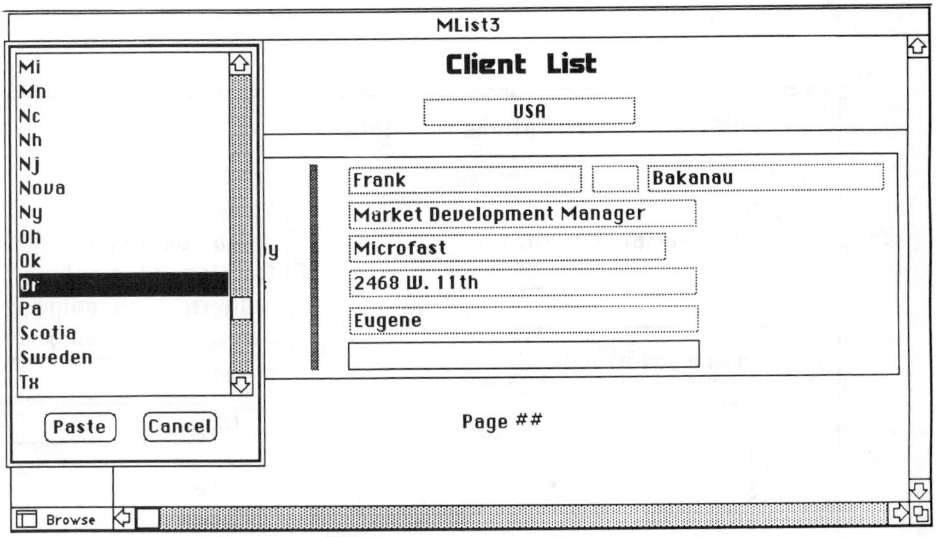

Fig. 8-8. Using View Index for states.

The user has reached the State field of an address. Having forgotten the correct two-letter code for Oregon, the user pressed Command–I to see the list of previous entries. The correct entry has been highlighted for pasting, but note that index shows all of the states in initial cap format. Many people, including mail carriers, prefer an all-capital format. Pasting Or for Oregon is a start, but the user may want to change it to OR. (An alternative would be to have the capitalization done in a separate calculated text field with the formula = UPPER (State) or use an all-caps font.)

DATA ENTRY ASSISTANCE

In this section, we review some of the techniques that can be used to enhance the data entry process. You might have noticed that some of the examples used in our illustrations do not have a lot of records in them. That is because many of the examples were created to demonstrate features that did not need a large number of records to work properly. The fact is that creating new records is hard work. As you apply File-Maker to serious real-world tasks, you will realize that data entry is a very important aspect of database work, a process that you will want to streamline as much as possible.

The List of Values

In the previous section on the View Index command, we suggested that you might want to use it as an alternative to the list of values option provided by the Define command. You will recall that you set up a list of values for a field by invoking the Define command, highlighting the desire field, then selecting Entry Options. In Fig. 8-9, you can see Entry Options being established for the Rate field of the Bill of Sale database shown in Fig. 8-7.

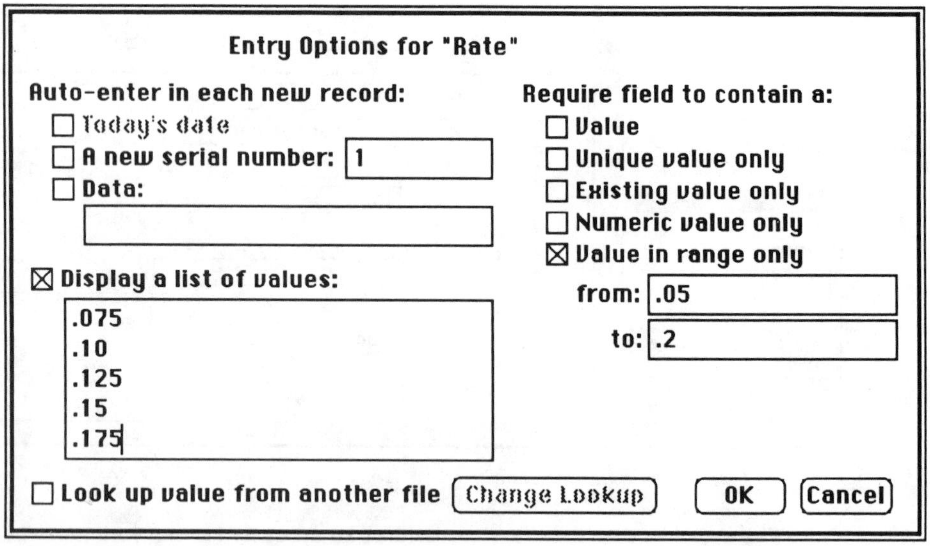

```
┌─────────────────────────────────────────────────────────────┐
│              Entry Options for "Rate"                         │
│                                                               │
│  Auto-enter in each new record:     Require field to contain a:│
│    ☐ Today's date                     ☐ Value                 │
│    ☐ A new serial number: [1     ]    ☐ Unique value only     │
│    ☐ Data:                            ☐ Existing value only   │
│    [                          ]       ☐ Numeric value only    │
│                                       ☒ Value in range only   │
│  ☒ Display a list of values:            from: [.05         ]  │
│    [.075                    ]             to: [.2          ]  │
│    [.10                     ]                                  │
│    [.125                    ]                                  │
│    [.15                     ]                                  │
│    [.175                    ]                                  │
│                                                               │
│  ☐ Look up value from another file [Change Lookup] [ OK ] [Cancel]│
└─────────────────────────────────────────────────────────────┘
```

Fig. 8-9. Setting up Entry Options.

The Rate field carries a discount rate which is applied to the Price field. The rate is from 5 percent to 20 percent, or from .05 to .20. You can see that the Display a list of values option has been selected and a number of rates have been entered. These rates are automatically presented when the user tabs to the Rate field, as you can see from Fig. 8-10.

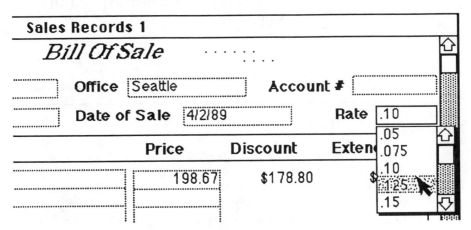

Fig. 8-10. Using the list of values.

The figure of .10 has already been entered in the field but the user wants to give a better discount. The user can scroll down the list and highlight the desired value, clicking on it to enter it in the field in place of what is already there. However, the user is also free to type a value in the field that does not appear in the list.

Entry Limits

In Fig. 8-9, you might have noticed that one of the options in the Require field to contain column had been checked. As proprietor of the store, you decide that nobody should give a discount greater than 20 percent. This means that the Rate field should not contain a value greater than .2. This has been indicated by checking the Value in range only box and entering .2 in the to field. Being a generous proprietor you would like everyone to have at least 5 percent discount, so you enter .05 in the from field, rather than 0.

In action, this feature monitors the entries in the Rate field. Normally the user enters a discount rate from the list of values. Occasionally the user enters a different rate, such as .16, which is not in the list, but is within the proscribed range. Sometimes the user makes a mistake, perhaps entering .6 in the rate field. FileMaker catches this as soon as the user tabs to the next field. The error sound is made and a warning comes up like the one in Fig. 8-11.

Note that the user can select OK to force a value outside of the allowed range, but the default response is Cancel. The proprietor will certainly know that the user deliberately chose a Rate outside the official range.

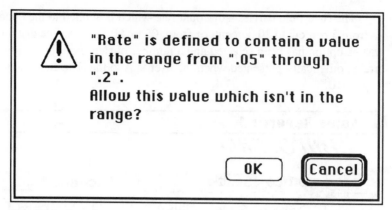

Fig. 8-11. Out of range warning.

The value range works with many types of data. You can limit entries in a Delivery Date field to a plausible range of dates, preventing errors or wild promises. You can make sure that invoice numbers, customer numbers, or item codes are within the range of acceptable values. You can even guard against excessively low or high price entries. This type of check, with the default response to Cancel the out-of-range entry, is a great aid to those performing data entry. Other options under Require field to contain include:

- Value—Forcing the user to make some kind of entry, preventing the field from being skipped.

- Unique value only—Forcing the user to make an entry that is different from those in other records, thus avoiding duplication.

- Existing value only—Forcing the user to stick to values that have already been used, such as existing customer numbers.

- Numeric value only—Forcing the user to enter a number rather than a piece of text, preventing the user confusing fields.

Note that all of these data entry restrictions, except the last one, work with text fields as well as number fields. For example, you could limit entries in a State field from AL to WY, because no two-letter codes for the U.S. states come before AL or after WY in an alphabetical list. However, you cannot use a range of numbers to limit entries in a text field. For example, if you have a Zip Code field you might want to limit entries from 01000 to 99999, but if the field is a text field this will not prevent entries like 100001.

The Lookup File Revisited

The contents of the Price field in Fig. 8-7 are based on the item being sold. In most cases, the price is fixed and so can be looked up from a price list. The price list is entered into a separate file and need consist of only two fields: One for the description, the other for the price. A lookup is then established by going to the Define mode,

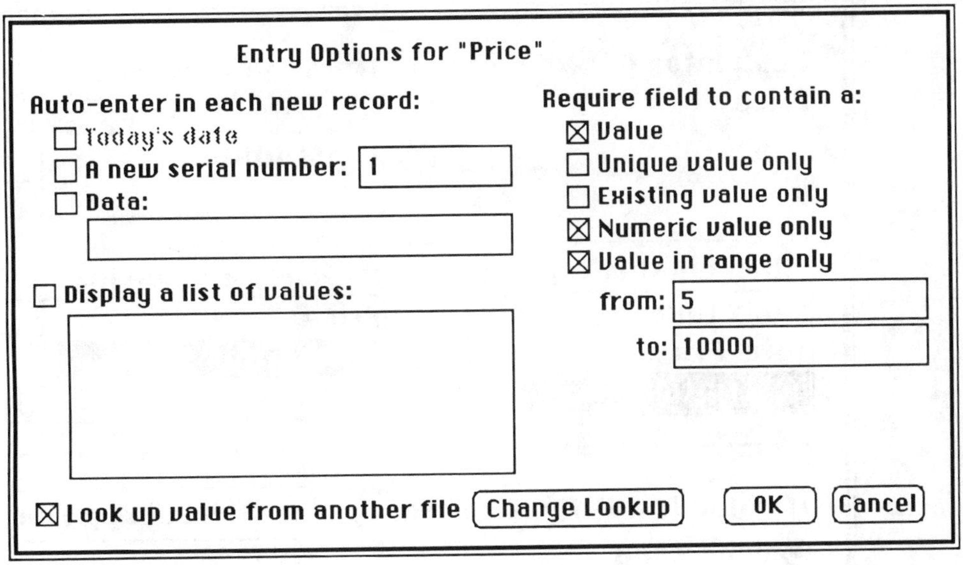

```
┌─────────────────────────────────────────────────────────────────┐
│ ╔═══════════════════════════════════════════════════════════════╗ │
│ ║              Entry Options for "Price"                          ║ │
│ ║                                                                 ║ │
│ ║  Auto-enter in each new record:    Require field to contain a:  ║ │
│ ║    ☐ Today's date                    ☒ Value                    ║ │
│ ║    ☐ A new serial number: [1    ]    ☐ Unique value only        ║ │
│ ║    ☐ Data:                           ☐ Existing value only      ║ │
│ ║      [                      ]         ☒ Numeric value only       ║ │
│ ║                                      ☒ Value in range only       ║ │
│ ║    ☐ Display a list of values:       from: [5          ]         ║ │
│ ║      ┌──────────────────────┐          to: [10000      ]         ║ │
│ ║      │                      │                                    ║ │
│ ║      │                      │                                    ║ │
│ ║      │                      │                                    ║ │
│ ║      └──────────────────────┘                                    ║ │
│ ║  ☒ Look up value from another file (Change Lookup)  ( OK ) (Cancel)║ │
│ ╚═══════════════════════════════════════════════════════════════╝ │
└─────────────────────────────────────────────────────────────────┘
```

Fig. 8-12. Establishing a lookup.

selecting the Price field, and clicking Entry Options. On the Entry Options screen you check Look up value from another file as shown in Fig. 8-12.

You then click OK, and FileMaker will take you to the next stage of selecting the file to lookup from, in this case the file containing the price list. A standard Macintosh file list is used to make the selection. (If you have already established a lookup, you can click Change Lookup to alter the lookup settings.)

After selecting the file, in this case one called SalesPrices, you define the lookup procedure. In this case, you want FileMaker to copy information into the Price field of the current file, from field in the SalesPrices file called Price, when what is typed in the Description field of the current file matches a value in the Description field of the SalesPrices file. In Fig. 8-13, you can see how FileMaker presents this information.

Note that you do not have to call the fields in the two fields by the same name for this to work. FileMaker presents lists of fields in each file that can be scrolled in order to select the right one. FileMaker also gives you a choice between two courses of action if the value that you are looking up is not found in the lookup file. You can either tell FileMaker to forget the lookup (don't copy) or to use the closest alternative (copy using next lower value). Be sure to give some thought to the values you are using before selecting the second option.

When you click OK, you are returned to the Define mode to continue making changes. Once you are back in the Browse mode you can use the lookup feature. In this example, when you make an entry in the Description field and tab to the Price field, the price will already be entered. You can still type in a price that overrides the value provided by the lookup.

The use of lookup files adds a great deal of flexibility in some situations. For example, suppose that you are having a sale and want to change the prices. You can

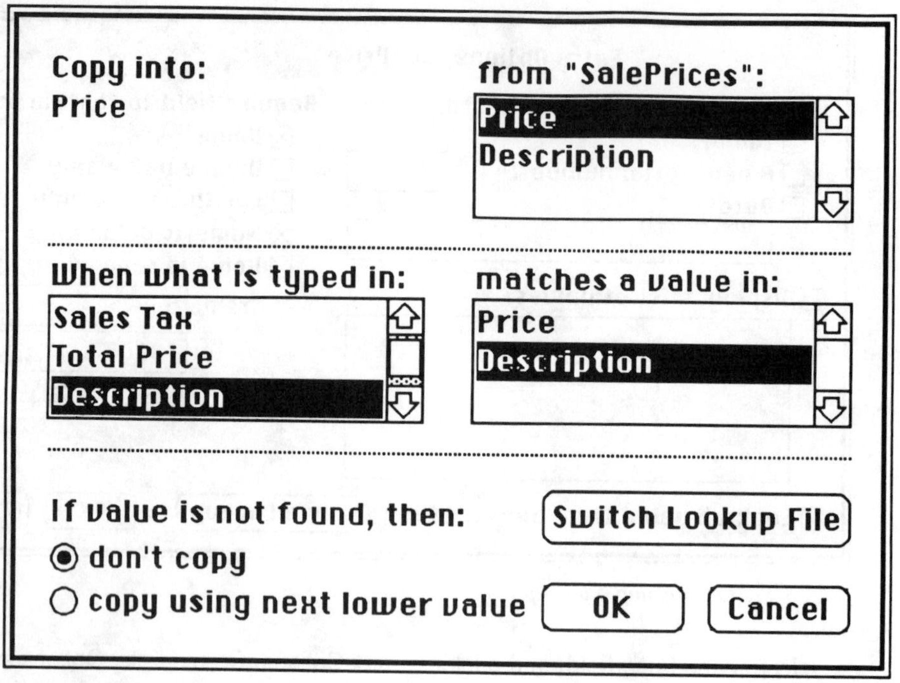

Fig. 8-13. The lookup defined.

edit the prices in the price list file, or create a new file with the new prices. In the latter case, this new file can be selected as the lookup file, using the Define command and selecting Switch Lookup File from the screen in Fig. 8-13.

When you change the lookup arrangement for a field, you need to think about which records you want the new relationship to apply to. By default, the new lookup will work with new records, not the existing records. In the case of sale prices, this might be just what you want, but suppose that you put the sales prices in effect and have some existing bills of sale to which you want the prices applied. To to do this, you would first execute a Find so that the records to be updated were the only found records (the date field might be a good way to do this). Now you select the Description field because this is the one that determines the prices. Next you select Relookup command from the Edit menu. FileMaker will ask if you want to proceed, using the message box seen in Fig. 8-14.

When you select OK, the new prices are entered, based on the values in the Description field. The Relookup command is also useful if you add lookup capability to a field into which you have already entered some values. If you issue the Find All command then Relookup, all of the lookup values based on the selected field will be revised.

A lookup can provide great assistance to a data entry operator. Suppose you have a toll-free number for people to subscribe to your magazine. The operator, with mouse in one hand and phone in the other, begins by taking the caller's name and phone num-

Fig. 8-14. Relookup warning.

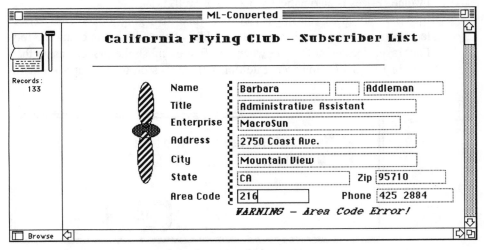

Fig. 8-15. Looking up Area Code to determine State.

ber. The information is entered directly into FileMaker, using a database like the one in Fig. 8-15.

As soon as the area code is entered, a lookup established for the State field enters the state in which that area code is located. As you can see from Fig. 8-16, the lookup file contains two fields: Location and Code. There are about 130 records, one for each area code (this includes Canadian codes as well as codes for the U.S.).

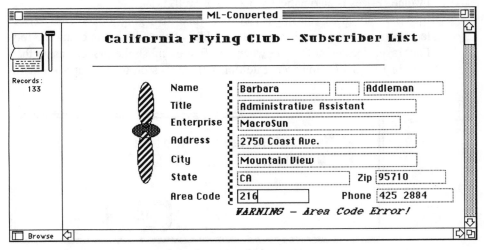

Fig. 8-16. Area Code location file.

The lookup copies from the Location field of the lookup file into the State field of the active file when the entry in the Area Code field of the active file matches an entry in the Area Code field of the lookup file.

This type of lookup has many applications. Apart from cutting down on the typing for the operator, special instructions might depend on the caller's state. The offer might not be valid in some states, or outside the United States. With this lookup, the operator is immediately tipped to the caller's location.

Managing Lookup Fields

When you are using a lookup file, you do not need to issue any commands to open the file. Suppose that the file called Invoice uses the file called Prices. When you open Invoice, Prices is automatically opened as well.

The only hitch you might run into when managing lookup files arises when a lookup file is not located in the same folder as the file that is doing the looking up. FileMaker does point this out when you first establish the lookup, using the warning seen in Fig. 8-17. However, FileMaker then goes on to present a standard file list

Fig. 8-17. Lookup file location warning.

from which to select the lookup file and does not tell you that selecting a file that is not in the current folder will be a problem later.

When you open a file that uses a lookup from another file, FileMaker does not immediately check the current folder for the lookup file. Only when you use the Relookup command, or create a new record and tab past the field on which the lookup is based does FileMaker try to open the lookup file. If it is not found, then you get the same warning seen in Fig. 8-17. When you select OK, FileMaker presents a list of files so that you can point out the correct file, but also provides an opportunity to Cancel the lookup, as seen in Fig. 8-18.

In this situation, canceling the lookup does not undo the lookup connection; it is simply suspended for the current session.

An interesting side effect of using a lookup is that the lookup file is automatically opened when the first lookup is performed. However, you do not see the file in the work area because it is hidden. The fact that it is there can be determined from the

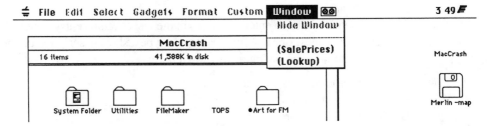

Fig. 8-18. Lookup file not found in current folder.

Window command. This lists the open-but-hidden files in parentheses. You can move directly to one of these fields from the Window command.

A little known fact is that when you close the file that uses the lookup, the lookup file remains open. You can see this in Fig. 8-19, where FileMaker is running under MultiFinder and all the regular FileMaker files are closed. The Window command shows that two lookup files are still open. They can be closed by selecting File Close from the FileMaker menu, once for each file still open.

Fig. 8-19. Lookup files remain open.

 This "quirk" in FileMaker provides a clever means of creating auto-open files. This technique is described in Chapter 10.

Date Entry Checking Formulas

In the last chapter, you saw that conditional formulas and string math provide great possibilities for checking the accuracy of data entry. These can compliment the

Entry Options to provide great assistance to data entry personnel (even if that means you, the database designer). Often you can use an IF statement to compare the contents of a field with the correct range of values.

Take the situation where a field is supposed to contain a code. In Fig. 8-20, you can see a field called Type that is supposed to contain a code that categorizes the companies in the database. The correct code is a single letter, and the possible codes are the letters A through F.

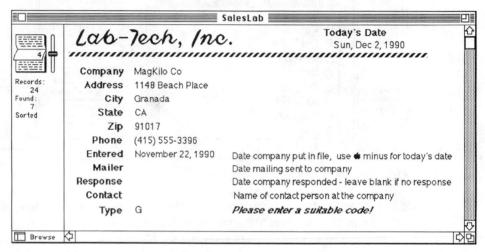

Fig. 8-20. The Type field.

There are several ways of controlling entries in this type of field. The first would be setting the Entry Options to require the field to contain a value. That will make sure the operator does not forget to code the field. You could also use A and F as limiting values in the Range Only entry option.

The next step might be to enter the codes in the List of Values entry option. Instead of just entering the codes, one to a line, you could type a short description on the same line as the code to help the operator, as shown here:

A—Genetic engineering companies
B—Services companies
C—Equipment suppliers

and so on . . .

This would result in both the code and description being entered when the operator selected from the list. You might want to use another field that uses a formula to read the code from the longer entry, as in Code=LEFT (Type,1). A further limitation of value lists is that the data entry list will be no wider than the field, which can pose problems in tight spaces.

A formula to check on single-letter code entries in the Type field might read as follows:

IF (Type<"A" OR Type>"F", "Please enter a suitable code!", "")

This results in the text Please enter a suitable code! if the operator forgets to make an entry or uses a code other than A through F. By placing this calculated field to the right of the Type field that is being checked and dispensing with the field description text, the message can appear as layout text, as it does in Fig. 8-20.

Also note the use of explanatory text in Fig. 8-20. This takes only a moment to type, but it can prevent having to spend time later solving problems arising from incorrect entry of data. (The Apple symbol used in the first note is produced by typing the letter K while holding down the Shift and Option keys.)

In Fig. 8-21, you can see another data entry warning system, which displays the message WARNING—Area Code Error! in a different font to draw the attention of the user. In fact, this message is the contents of a calculated field, displayed without a field identifier. The field is designed so that if a warning is required, the message appears as in Fig. 8-21. Otherwise, that area is blank, and you cannot even tell that a field is there.

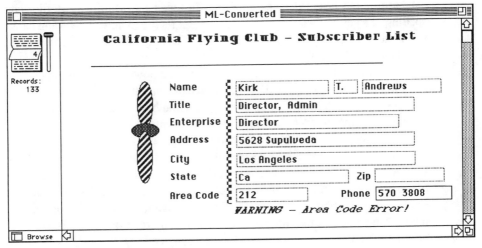

Fig. 8-21. A data entry warning message.

The formula that produces the message is defined in a field called Warning, and uses a further field called Check that does not appear on the layout at all. The Check field contains either the name of a state or nothing at all. FileMaker performs a lookup for the Check field from a file called CodeLocator that contains a list of states and all of the area codes in that state. The Check field lookup is defined so that it copies a state name from the CodeLocator file when the typed area code in the mailing list file matches a value in the field called Code. The lookup is defined so that if a matching value is not found, nothing is copied. This means that when the person using the mailing list types a code into the Area Code field, the Check field returns a state name.

This allows the use of a formula in the field called Warning that compares the entry in the Check field with the entry in the State field. If they do not match, there is an error. The formula is:

Warning = IF (Check=State,"","WARNING—Area Code Error!")

This formula returns nothing if the value in Check matches the value in State and so the space on the layout does not appear occupied. Because the Check field does not even appear on the layout, there is no chance of the lookup entry being overridden by a typed entry.

DUPLICATING FILES

In numerous situations, you might want to duplicate your work with FileMaker. You might want to share a database design with colleagues. You might want to preserve one version of a database design while developing a derivative.

Preserving FileMaker Data and Designs

Whenever you open a FileMaker database, you activate FileMaker's automatic save feature. This feature instantly records every change you make to the data in the database or the layout/design. Suppose you open the Mailing List file, change the spelling of a name, then move on to a different record. There is no going back, no way to abandon the change you made: The action has already been recorded in the file on disk that is called Mailing List.

This feature is great in emergencies such as a power outage, or when you want to exit FileMaker in a hurry. If your Mac is accidentally turned off, you will not lose any changes to your FileMaker databases. Even if you have several FileMaker files open at once, exiting the program is relatively quick, with none of the Save Changes dialog boxes you get with other Mac applications.

Unfortunately, the auto-save feature has its disadvantages as well. If you leave your Mac unattended with a FileMaker database on screen, a curious key-tickling passerby can alter or even ruin days worth of work. If you Find a group of records you want to delete, issue the Delete Multiple command, move on to sort the remaining records and discover that the Find found too many records, it is too late to Undo the damage. The file on disk has already been updated.

The Save A Copy As command on the File menu is your protection against the negative aspects of auto-save. If you perform a Save As prior to editing sessions and prior to deleting, then you have a copy to fall back on if something goes wrong. When you select Save As, you get the dialog box seen in Fig. 8-22.

Note that you have three options here. We deal with the second and third options in a moment. The first option is the one you should select if you want a straightforward copy of the current file. This is the default selection. When you click OK, you are presented with a file save dialog box, into which FileMaker automatically enters a file name. This is composed of the current file name, such as Mailing List, to which the words Copy of have been added. You can see this in Fig. 8-23.

If your reason for creating a copy is to backup your work, then this name might be acceptable. Otherwise, you can type in a name of your choice. You can also choose a different drive or folder. Note that when you complete this command, you are returned to the current file, in this case Mailing List. The copy has been created on disk but is not opened.

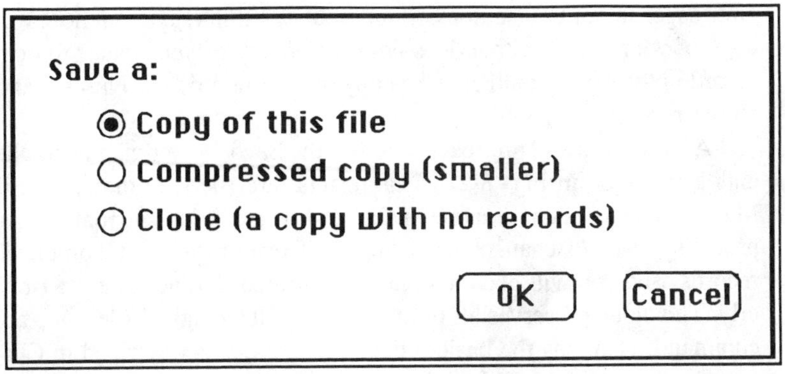

Save a:

⦿ **Copy of this file**
○ **Compressed copy (smaller)**
○ **Clone (a copy with no records)**

[**OK**] [**Cancel**]

Fig. 8-22. The Save As dialog box.

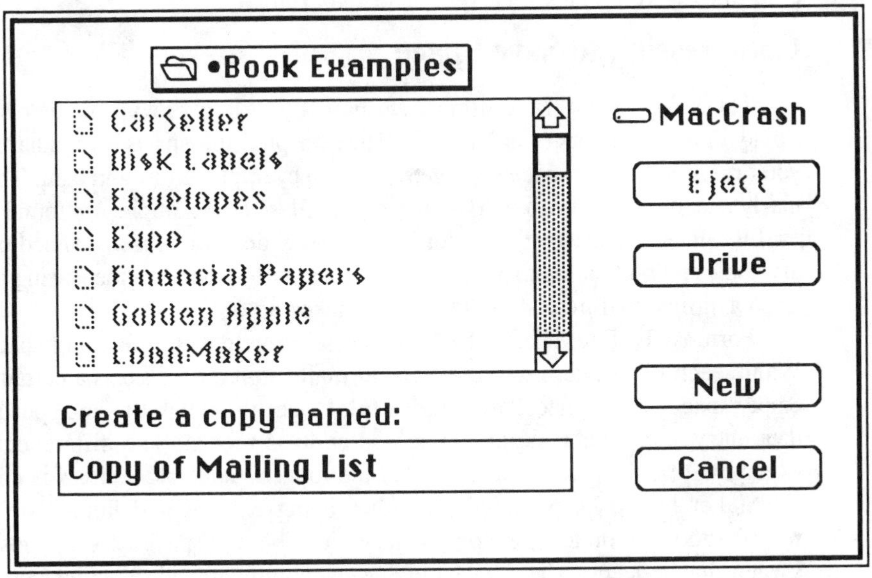

▭ •**Book Examples**

▱ CarSeller
▱ Disk Labels
▱ Envelopes
▱ Expo
▱ Financial Papers
▱ Golden Apple
▱ LoanMaker

▭ **MacCrash**

[**Eject**]

[**Drive**]

[**New**]

[**Cancel**]

Create a copy named:

Copy of Mailing List

Fig. 8-23. The automatic "Copy of" name.

 Bear in mind that you can also copy FileMaker files using the regular Macintosh copy methods. This allows you to copy files without opening them. To perform the copy, drag the file that you want to copy to a different drive.

Clones for the Other Office

Your need for a copy of a FileMaker database might not extend to the actual data; you might just want a copy of the design. For example, you are a junior partner in a law firm and you develop a FileMaker database for tracking time and expense that can be billed to clients. A senior partner sees an increase in your billables, asks the reason, and you show him the database in action. He immediately says, "I want one."

Ever eager to oblige a senior partner, you start thinking about how you can give him a copy of your database that does not contain any of your data. You could Delete each record in turn. You could create a copy of the file, open it, Find All, and Delete Multiple all the records.

A more civilized approach is to use the Save As command and check Clone in the dialog box seen in Fig. 8-22. This results in a file save dialog box into which File-Maker enters the default name of Clone of whatever the current file name is. You will probably want to change the name. The resulting file is completely empty of all records, and you will need to create a new record to activate the Browse mode properly. The clone preserves all of the layouts of the original file. One application of this command, changing the basic order of records, was described in Chapter 7. You can Clone a file and then fill it with records that are input from the original after the Sort command has been used. The records will then be stored in the clone in the exact order they were in the sorted version of the original.

Compressing to Save Space

These days many Mac users have hard disks that provide greater storage than floppy disks by factors of at least 10. However plentiful space is on a hard disk when you first install it, the space soon gets eaten up by applications and data. This is particularly true if you do much work with graphic files. For example, we found that a modest FileMaker database of 12 records, each of which contains a scanned piece of line art, took up 660K of disk space (see the glossary for more on measuring disk space). Even a simple mailing list of 200 records takes up 66K.

Fortunately, FileMaker offers a partial solution to this problem of space shortage. Within each FileMaker record, as it is normally stored on disk, is a certain amount of empty space. This is necessary to give FileMaker the flexibility and speed it needs in data entry. Consider a simple name and address record. The difference in size between the briefest possible address and the longest plausible address is considerable. FileMaker has to be prepared for either being entered and immediately store the record and move on to a new one. This means that the space used by most records is greater than it needs to be. Using the Save As command and selecting Compress a file, you can have FileMaker remove this extra space.

The Compress a file command creates a copy of the current file in which File-Maker stores the same amount of data in a much smaller space. The 660K picture database was reduced to 389K while the 66K mailing list shrank to 42K. In some cases, we have seen file size halved by the compress option.

Compressing a file is exactly like creating a copy. You get two identical files, the original and a copy; the only difference is that the copy takes up less space. When you execute the compress command, you might notice that the compressed copy takes longer to save to disk than a normal copy. However, this delay is a one-time event. If you create a compressed copy and use it instead of the original, you will find that the compressed file is just as quick to open, use, and save as a regular file.

Once a file is compressed, it stays that way with the exception that records added after the compression are not stored in compact form. If you add a bunch of new records, you will want to repeat the compression operation to pack them tight. We found that compression is a good step to take after a database has been created and the bulk of entries made. Later editing and the occasional new record do not increase the size of the file that much, and you get the benefit of the extra disk space to use for something else *if* you remember to remove the original uncompressed file.

INPUT AND OUTPUT

Sometimes you might want to feed values from one FileMaker database into another. For example, two people have been compiling the same type of information, and you want to combine their efforts into a single file. Indeed, you might have encouraged this. Suppose that, as sales manager, you have designed a FileMaker database to store customer profiles. You give a copy of the database to each member of your sales staff and ask them to record information about their customers (each salesperson having their own Mac and their own copy of FileMaker). When they have finished entering the information, they hand you the disk containing their customer database file. Now you want to feed each separate file into a master file for your records. This is a task for the Input command.

The Input Command

The first step in combining the files is to open the receiving file, the one into which you want to feed information (in this case the master customer file). You then select Input from the File menu and are presented with a standard Mac file selection window. When you choose the file that you want to input from, FileMaker compares the fields in the current or master file with the fields in the supporting file that is supplying the input. If the fields do not match, you will get a warning like the one in Fig. 8-24.

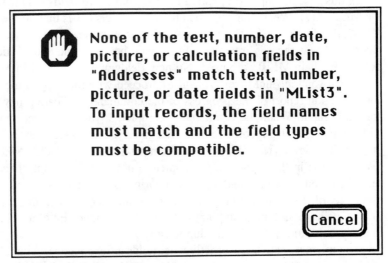

Fig. 8-24. Failed input command.

FileMaker cannot proceed unless some fields match between files. It does not have to be complete matching. For example, your master file might have more fields than exist in the salesperson's supporting file. Alternatively, a salesperson might have added some fields that are not in your master file. As you can see from Fig. 8-25, FileMaker gives you a full report on the matching that exists, before proceeding.

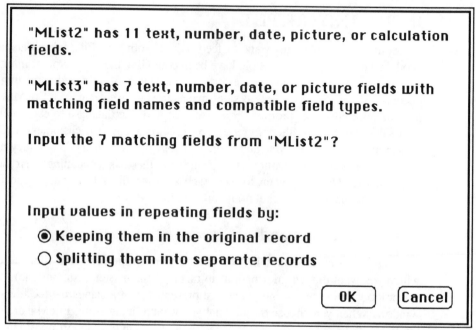

Fig. 8-25. Matching fields report.

In this case the input file, called MList2, has more fields (11) than the receiving file MList 3 (7). What happens when the user selects OK is that all the information in MList2 that fits into MList3 will be copied. For example, if MList2 contains 34 *found* records, 34 new records are created in MList3, but only data in the 7 fields that match existing fields in MList3 are used. No new fields will be created in MList3.

When you tell FileMaker it is OK to proceed with the copy, a message box gives you a running report of the progress of the command, indicating how many records are left to input. When the command is completed, you are placed in the current file with the newly added records found. This gives you a chance to examine them and, if they are the wrong records, remove them with Delete Multiple. Note that only the *found* records in the input file are copied. FileMaker does not check for duplicate records. If you copy a file and input to the original from the copy, you will have two of every record. Remember that you can check for records with duplicate entries in a field by using an exclamation point in the Find command. Enter an exclamation point in every field, and you will find duplicate records.

You might want to know exactly what fields a file contains. After all, not all fields are included in every layout, and the order of fields in the layout is not necessarily the order of the fields in the file structure. To check that structure of a database, you can print a list of field definitions. You can see this option on the File Print menu, as shown in Fig. 8-26.

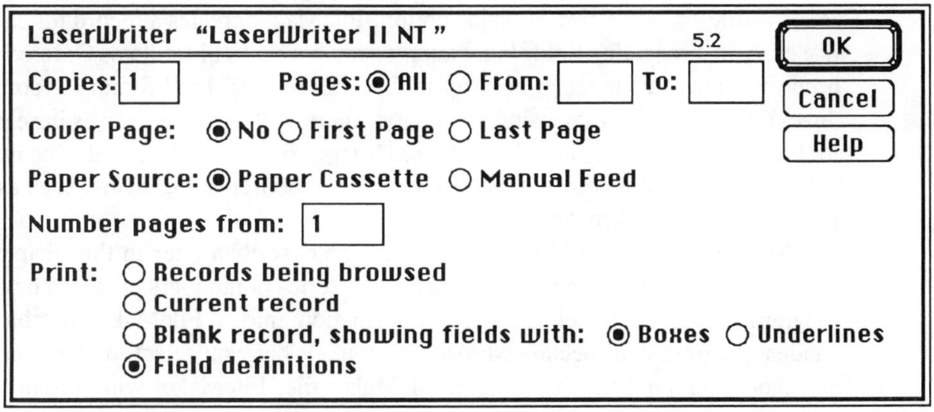

Fig. 8-26. Choosing to print field definitions.

The resulting report is useful to have, and when you are preparing databases for others to use, it can be a valuable part of the documentation. You can see a printed field definition report in Fig. 8-27.

Field Name	Field Type	Formula / Entry Option
First	Text	
Middle	Text	
Last	Text	
Enterprise	Text	
Title	Text	
Address	Text	
City	Text	
Country	Text	
Phone	Number	
State	Text	Value in range from "AL" to "WY"
date	Date	
Zip	Text	Lookup: "Zip Codes" in "Lookup" when "State" matches "States in 2"
Full Title	Calculation (Text)	= left (Title,position (Title," ",1)) & " " & middle (Title,position (Title," ",1) + 1,position (Title," ",position (Title," ",1) + 1)) & " " & right (Title,length (Title) - position (Title," ",position (Title," ",1)+2))
Number	Text	

Fig. 8-27. The field definitions report.

Uses of Input

The Input command has numerous applications. As we have mentioned, the technique described in Chapter 7 uses the Input command to alter the basic sort order of a file. Another useful technique is hinted at by the last option of the screen shown in

Fig. 8-25: splitting repeating fields into separate records. In situations where you set up repeating fields for data, you might decide later that repeating fields were not appropriate. You can split the repeating fields into separate records using this Input option. First you clone the original file, the input to the clone from the original, selecting the splitting repeating fields option. FileMaker creates a record for each separate entry in a repeating field. For example, you have a field for Items Ordered that has been formatted repeating to hold up to five values, and Fred Smith's record shows three items ordered. After using this option, there will be three records instead of one for Fred Smith, with one item in the Items Ordered field in each record. The rest of the data in the original record will be extended to the nonrepeating fields, such as Name, in the two additional records.

Another application of the Input command described later in this chapter is the retroactive addition of record numbers using a series of numbers prepared by different programs, such as Excel. Bringing information into a FileMaker database from another program is a specialized form of input. When you select the Input command and choose an input file that is not a FileMaker file, FileMaker will present you with several options for bringing in data from this file. We prefer to think of the process as importing rather than inputting. The procedure is described in the next section, which also looks at how to export data from FileMaker so that other programs can read it.

IMPORT AND EXPORT

These days, millions of people use a wide variety of personal computers to store information, and they use a lot of different information management programs. All data on personal computers is stored in files, but the arrangement of information within the files varies. Different programs use different arrangements or formats. For example, on the Macintosh you can store pictures in MacPaint format, TIFF format, EPS format, or the Picture format (PICT) that is used by the Clipboard. Some programs can use several formats. For example, Microsoft's spreadsheet Excel can create files in its own format as well as in one called SYLK, which stands for Symbolic Link format, and another referred to as WK1,which is used by Lotus 1-2-3, a spreadsheet program that runs on IBM PCs.

Like any program that wishes to coexist in today's office, FileMaker has the ability to exchange data with other programs by reading from and writing to a variety of formats. Typical applications of this would be to share data with IBM PC users who do not have FileMaker to export data from FileMaker to a graphing program, or to use FileMaker's finding and sorting capabilities on a mailing list that was created by a word processing program.

The Sharing Commands

The Output To command is used to create a file in a format that can be used by other applications. The Input From command, which can be used to copy from one FileMaker file to another, can also be used to copy data from another application into a FileMaker file. These commands can be used to exchange data with a variety of file formats, including Text, BASIC, and SYLK. The range of personal computer programs that can read at least one of these formats is extensive. You can also output File-Maker data to a merge file format that allows you to combine FileMaker data with a form letter created in a word processor such as Microsoft Word. The Input From and Output To commands work together so that you can put FileMaker data with another application, work on it there, and then bring it back into FileMaker. You can use File-Maker's features to manipulate data created by remote systems, across networks, or through modems, and then output the data to a file that can again be used by the original application.

Unlike the regular use of Input (to combine FileMaker's files), the use of Input with files from another application to FileMaker allows you to choose adding new records or updating existing records in the current file. For example, you might use data from a remote sales office that uses Excel to update central records in a File-Maker file.

When you use the Output To command, FileMaker creates a new file, called the *output file*, in the file format you choose. The found records in the current file are copied to the new file in the current sort order. This means that you can use the Find, Omit Records, and Sort commands to specify which records you want output and the order in which they are output. You can also choose all or just some of the fields to output from the current file and can specify the order of fields in the new file. You can output values from text, number, date, and calculation fields. You can also control the formatting of the output for number, date, and calculation fields, either outputting the data unformatted, or using the formats in the current layout.

FileMaker can store the output settings such as the field order and file format to simplify creating the same type of output file on a regular basis. If you regularly export data from the same FileMaker file, you do not have to respecify this information. For example, if you transfer data from your Customer List database into Excel at the end of every month for analysis, you will find that FileMaker retains the export specifications. If you need to change the order, you can add or remove fields in the output order, or you can erase the order and specify a new one. You can also use scripts, described later in this chapter, to automate the export process.

File Formats

Fortunately, among the many programs that run on personal computers, there are some standards when it comes to file formats. FileMaker can create files in a variety of formats, at least one of which should be intelligible to the receiving application. The supported export formats are described in the next few paragraphs.

Text File. Sometimes referred to as tab format, this is a common format that can be used by most word processors and many other applications. You can open a text file from within MacWrite, Microsoft Word, or Excel. This is the same format as the one created in word processing programs when you save a document as *Text Only*. Within the file, the arrangement is this:

- FileMaker field values are separated by tabs.
- Records are separated by Return characters.
- If you have Return characters within a field value, they are output as ASCII vertical tab characters.
- Numbers and dates that are not formatted in FileMaker will be output exactly as you typed them.

You can also request that FileMaker formatting be stripped when records are copied into the text output file. Otherwise, the formatting copied to the new file is the same as that which you can see when you browse or print records in FileMaker using the current layout. A typical text file of name and address information appears like this:

```
Smith   Joe   123 Main        New York   NY   10001
Smith   Tim   101 Lincoln     New York   NY   10011
Smith   Tom   1001 Main St.   New York   NY   10001
```

Between each piece of information on the same line is a tab, between lines is a Return.

BASIC File. Sometimes known as the commas format, or comma separated values (CSV), this format can be read by BASIC programs. A BASIC program is one that is written in the BASIC programming language. Files in this format can be generated from a BASIC program with the PRINT# or PRINT USING# statements. However, a much wider range of programs than just those written in BASIC can read this format. For example, dBASE can read files in this format. The arrangement is this:

- Field values are separated by commas; records are separated by Return characters.
- If you have Return characters in a field value, they are output as spaces.
- All field values are enclosed in quotation marks with the exception of unformatted numbers.
- If your field value contains double quotation marks (" "), then FileMaker outputs them as single quotation marks (').
- If a number field includes text or symbols, only the number is output.

Also note that FileMaker only outputs the first 255 characters of a text field in this format. This is because 255 characters is the maximum field size that can be read by BASIC.

SYLK File. This Microsoft format stores data in rows and columns and is used by spreadsheet applications such as Microsoft Excel. The SYLK format interprets each spreadsheet cell as a piece of text or a number. The arrangement is:

- Each field is output as a column, starting with column 1.
- Each record is one row, starting with row 1.
- If a number field includes text or symbols, only the number is output.

- Dates and formatted numbers are output by FileMaker as text in quotation marks.

- If a number is unformatted, or you choose not to use numeric formatting from the layout, the number is output as a number with no quotation marks.

This format also has a limit on field length; no more than 245 characters can be output for any field.

Merge File. Similar to the text file, this format can be used in creating personalized form letters and other standard documents. For example, Microsoft Word can combine data in a merge file with text in a main document to print form letters or other documents that merge standard text with variable data. The merge file is equivalent to the file Microsoft Word referred to as a *data document*. The arrangement of data is such that:

- Field values are separated by commas.

- Records are separated by Return characters.

- The first record is a header record listing the field names.

- If you have commas in a field value, the entire field is surrounded by quotation marks.

- If you have quotation marks in a field value, the field is surrounded by quotation marks and the quoted word(s) is surrounded by two sets of quotation marks, for example, "the ""Best"" Model".

- If you have Return characters in a field value, they are output as ASCII vertical tab characters (the character that is typed with Shift−Return in Microsoft Word).

Also note that if numbers and dates are not formatted, or you specify that you don't want the formatting to be copied into the output file, the values will be output exactly as you typed them. Otherwise, the same format is used as when you browse or print records in FileMaker using the current layout.

EXPORTING DATA WITH THE OUTPUT COMMAND

Suppose that you want to perform some spreadsheet analysis of the information in the daycare database shown in Fig. 8-28; this is a small database with only a few records in it, which is not a bad way to begin working with the Output command.

The reason for starting small is that, if something goes wrong, you will not have wasted time waiting for a large file to be processed. If you are setting up an Output operation from a large database, you might want to use the Find command to create a small group of found records. Because the Output command only works on found records, you can practice using a small number of records.

The Export Procedure

The first step to exporting data is to select the Output To command from the File menu. FileMaker responds with a file naming dialog box, so that you can name the

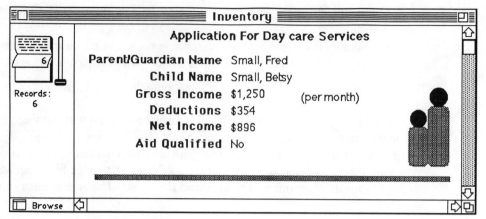

Fig. 8-28. Day care data to be exported.

file you are about to create. We suggest that you use a name that includes a clue as to the format of the file. For example, we used DayCare.SYLK for the SYLK file we created from the DayCare database. This name borrows from the IBM PC-DOS convention of adding an extension to a file name to show the file format.

When you have provided a file name, you are presented with the field selection screen, which is your chance to select exactly which fields you want copied to the output file and what order you want them placed in. These are text, number, and date fields, and calculation fields. Picture and summary fields cannot be output. You can see a completed field selection screen in Fig. 8-29.

Field List		Output Order
Parent/Guardian Nam	« Move All »	Parent/Guardian Nam
Child Name		Child Name
Gross Income	Move	Gross Income
Deductions		Deductions
Net Income	Output	Net Income
Aid Qualified		Aid Qualified
	Exit	

"DayCare.SYLK" will be a:

○ Text file (tabs)
○ BASIC file (commas)
◉ SYLK file
○ Merge file

Output values will be:

○ Unformatted
◉ Formatted using Number and Date formats from layout

Fig. 8-29. Field selection screen.

When you are first presented with this screen the right-hand side, Output Order, is empty. You move fields from the Field List on the left into the Output Order column in the order in which you want the data in the file you are creating. To move fields from the Field List, you select the field then click the Move button. You can also double click on a field name in the Field List to move it. To move all the fields at once in their original order, click the Move All button. When you have made your selections, you click Output.

If you use the Move All command, FileMaker will give you the opportunity to decide between including calculated fields or excluding them, with the latter being the default choice. The message you get is seen in Fig. 8-30.

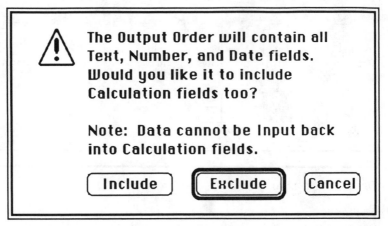

⚠ **The Output Order will contain all Text, Number, and Date fields. Would you like it to include Calculation fields too?**

Note: Data cannot be Input back into Calculation fields.

[**Include**]   [**Exclude**]   [Cancel]

Fig. 8-30. Including or excluding calculated fields.

The decision depends upon what you will be using the data for. If you just need the results of the calculations in the application you are exporting to, then select Include. This tells FileMaker to place the results of the calculations in the output file. For example, suppose you have two number fields called Hours and Rate, and a calculated field called Pay, which is defined as the product of the other two fields. If you select Include, then all three fields can be placed in the output file. The values in the Pay field will be the results of the Hours multiplied by Rate calculation.

If you choose Exclude in this case, the output file will have just Hours and Rate. This is fine if you plan to set up calculations in the other application. You will save time by selecting Exclude. FileMaker warns you that if you select Include and convert data to results, they cannot be returned to the calculated field. This means that if you export the three fields to a SYLK file and later want to return the data to the FileMaker file, the Pay data cannot be accepted back because it is a calculated field in FileMaker and cannot accept direct input.

You click the Output button to have FileMaker go ahead and copy the data to the output file. You can click the Exit button to return to the current FileMaker file without creating the output file. You can stop the process of copying data to the output file; after you have clicked Output, hold down the Command key, and type a period. After the data is copied into the output file, FileMaker returns to the Browse screen in the current file. If you move to the Finder, you will see that the Output file has a blank page icon. This is the case with the DayCare.SYLK file seen in Fig. 8-31.

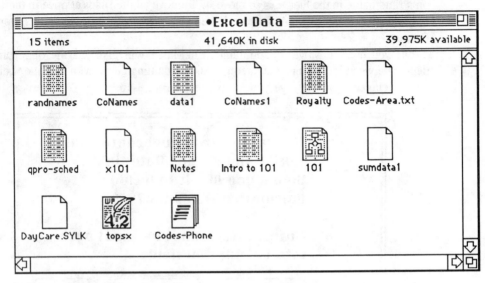

Fig. 8-31. The output file as a blank page icon.

The blank page icon means that the file is not specific to any particular application. In some cases, this means the document cannot be opened by double-clicking. To open the Output file with some applications, you must first launch the application, then use the File Open command. However, the blank page icon does not mean that the file type is not recorded in the file's resource fork. If the application can read the file format you have chosen, you might be able to double-click on the Output file to load it and launch the application. For example, in the case of a SYLK file you can double-click on it to launch Excel and load the file. You can see from Fig. 8-32 that the format of the values in the file were preserved when the SYLK file was created.

	File Edit Formula Format Data Options Macro Window								11 06
A1			Smith, Jane						

DayCare.SYLK

	A	B	C	D	E	F	G	H	I
1	Smith, Jane	Smith, Ruth	$1,250	$354	$896	No			
2	Doe, Joe	Doe, Pam	$1,250	$354	$896	No			
3	West, Jane	West, Ruth	$1,250	$354	$896	No			
4	Smith, Peter	Smith, Tom	$1,005	$348	$657	Yes			
5	Jones, Bill	Jones, Sarah	$1,150	$234	$916	No			
6	Small, Fred	Small, Betsy	$1,250	$354	$896	No			
7									
8									

Fig. 8-32. The output file in Excel.

From FileMaker to the IBM PC

Suppose that you want to export data from FileMaker so that it can be used by an IBM PC user. The two obstacles to this are file format and disk format. You probably know that you cannot just put a Mac floppy disk into an IBM PC. This is because the actual arrangement of data on the disk differs between the Macintosh operating system (OS) and the IBM operating system (DOS). There are several ways of overcoming this, including the use of a network such as TOPS, which is described in the next chapter. You can also use a file transfer program like MacLink from Travelling Software. On newer models of the Mac, you can actually read DOS disks directly in the special Macintosh drive.

When you have arranged the transfer of fields from the Mac to the PC, you still have to consider the question of file formats. Users of Excel on the IBM are fortunate in that it has little problem reading Macintosh Excel files or SYLK files such as those created by FileMaker. One of the most popular spreadsheets on the IBM is 1-2-3 from Lotus. This cannot read SYLK files directly, but can sometimes translate them using the Translate utility (the process is not perfect!). You can read text files into 1-2-3 and convert them to spreadsheet cells using the Parse command. In Fig. 8-33, you can see the DayCare data as a 1-2-3 Release 3 worksheet.

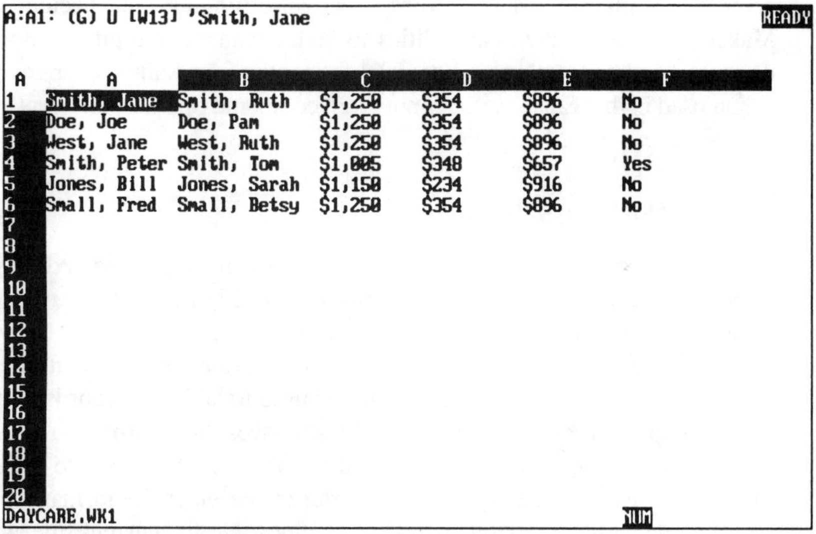

```
A:A1: (G) U [W13] 'Smith, Jane                                        READY

 A         A            B           C        D        E         F
1    Smith, Jane  Smith, Ruth  $1,250    $354     $896     No
2    Doe, Joe     Doe, Pam     $1,250    $354     $896     No
3    West, Jane   West, Ruth   $1,250    $354     $896     No
4    Smith, Peter Smith, Tom   $1,005    $348     $657     Yes
5    Jones, Bill  Jones, Sarah $1,150    $234     $916     No
6    Small, Fred  Small, Betsy $1,250    $354     $896     No
7
8
9
10
11
12
13
14
15
16
17
18
19
20
DAYCARE.WK1                                              NUM
```

Fig. 8-33. The output file in 1-2-3.

This was accomplished by first loading the file into Excel on the Mac, then using Excel to save the file in WK1 format, one that is readily accepted by 1-2-3. The file was then read across a TOPS network by 1-2-3.

Applied Exporting

The exporting of data from FileMaker to other programs has numerous applications. For example, your accounting department might use a spreadsheet to calculate projected budgets, while current expenditures and revenue are tracked in FileMaker. You can export the actual figures to be used as the basis for calculated "what-if" projections.

Another application that might offer several advantages is the creation of a merge file for use in a word processing program. FileMaker can create form letters, but has limited text editing capability. Creating letters is much easier in a word processing program, but few offer the sort and search facilities of FileMaker. By outputting names, addresses and other pertinent data to a word processing program in the form of a merge file, you can combine the best of both worlds. An example of mail merging is given in Chapter 10.

Bear in mind that FileMaker can remember the specifications of an output operation and recall them for repeated use through the script facility described later in this chapter. This means that you can regularly export data in a single step.

IMPORTING DATA

To copy data from another file format into a FileMaker database, you use the Input From command. For example, you might want to take advantage of FileMaker's layout capabilities to present data originally entered in Excel. You might have been compiling a mailing list in a word processing program and decide you need File-Maker's sort and search capabilities to better manage this information. If you have downloaded data from an on-line database, you might want to prepare it for analysis. When used in this capacity, the Input From command operates differently from when it is used to read FileMaker files.

The Import Process

The file that you copy the data from is called the *input file*. When you copy data from a file created with another application into a FileMaker file, you must specify an input order that tells FileMaker what fields are in the input file and the order in which these fields appear. You also specify the file format of the input file, and choose whether the data in the input file should be used to add new records to the FileMaker file or to update existing records. FileMaker saves the information you specify, so if you periodically copy the same field values from another file into a FileMaker file, you do not have to respecify the input order or the input file format.

You can copy text, number, and date values into the current FileMaker file from these file formats: Text, BASIC (CSV), and SYLK. Exporting to these formats was discussed earlier in the section "File Formats." To be intelligible to FileMaker, the input file should conform to the guidelines in the next few paragraphs.

Text. Text is the format in which fields within records are separated by tabs and records are separated by Return characters. A text file has no other structure and so FileMaker cannot pick and choose values when performing the input. When you use a text file to add new records to a FileMaker database, each record in the text file creates one new record in the FileMaker file. Consider the text file in Fig. 8-34 listing of

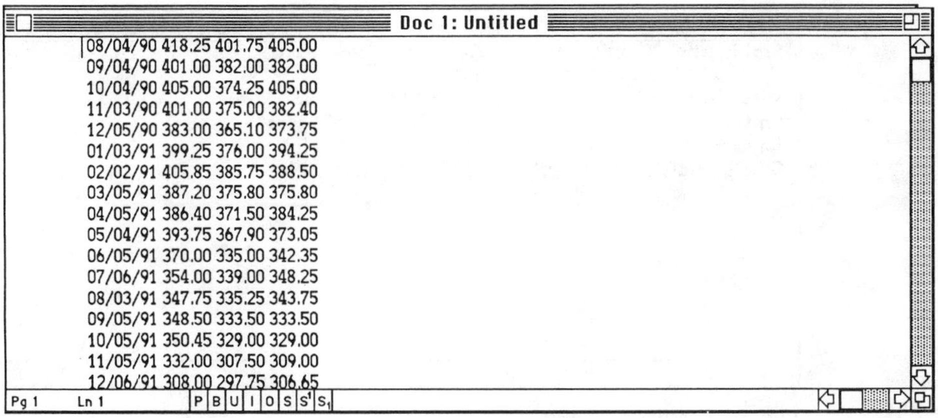

```
≡□≡≡≡≡≡≡≡≡≡≡≡≡≡≡≡≡≡≡ Doc 1: Untitled ≡≡≡≡≡≡≡≡≡≡≡≡≡≡≡
      |08/04/90 418.25 401.75 405.00
       09/04/90 401.00 382.00 382.00
       10/04/90 405.00 374.25 405.00
       11/03/90 401.00 375.00 382.40
       12/05/90 383.00 365.10 373.75
       01/03/91 399.25 376.00 394.25
       02/02/91 405.85 385.75 388.50
       03/05/91 387.20 375.80 375.80
       04/05/91 386.40 371.50 384.25
       05/04/91 393.75 367.90 373.05
       06/05/91 370.00 335.00 342.35
       07/06/91 354.00 339.00 348.25
       08/03/91 347.75 335.25 343.75
       09/05/91 348.50 333.50 333.50
       10/05/91 350.45 329.00 329.00
       11/05/91 332.00 307.50 309.00
       12/06/91 308.00 297.75 306.65
 Pg 1   Ln 1          P B U I O S S¹ S₁
```

Fig. 8-34. A typical text file.

dates and values that are actually gold prices downloaded from an on-line financial information service.

When this file is read by FileMaker, each line will create a new record. If the receiving FileMaker database has four fields, then the data will be input as follows:

Field 1   08/04/90
Field 2   418.25
Field 3   401.75
Field 4   405.00

The values in the text file simply fill fields in each new record according to the Input Order. If there are fewer fields per record in the text file than in the FileMaker file, some fields in the new record are left empty. If there are more fields per record in the text file than in the FileMaker file, some fields in the text file are not used.

The same is true if you use a text file to update records. When the number of fields for a record in the text file does not equal the number of fields in the Input Order, some fields are not updated or some field values in the text file are not used, depending on whether there are too few or too many fields per record in the text file.

BASIC (CSV). In this format, the field values are separated by commas or Return characters. If the field value is in quotation marks, the separator is optional. Field values in quotation marks can contain commas and Return characters. FileMaker uses the same rules for the format of the input file as BASIC uses for the INPUT# statement, except that FileMaker can exceed BASIC's limit of 255 characters for a field value copied into a text field. Some IBM PC spreadsheet programs such as Quattro PRO can import this type of file. You can see the DayCare data in BASIC format in Fig. 8-35.

SYLK. In this spreadsheet-based format, each column contains data for one field; each row contains one record. The important point to bear in mind is that only the cells containing data should be input to FileMaker. This means that if you have a worksheet arranged like the one in Fig. 8-36, you should save a version that has only got cells B4 through E20 in it. Otherwise, the column headings and the blank rows

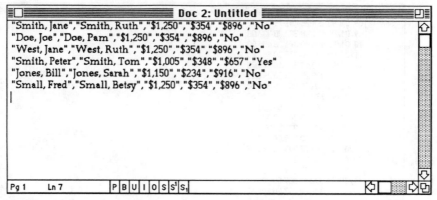

Fig. 8-35. A typical BASIC file.

	A	B	C	D	E	F
1	*Gold Prices – London – Monthly*					
2						
3		**Date**	**High/Ask**	**Low/Bid**	**Close/Avg**	
4		08/04/90	418.25	401.75	405.00	
5		09/04/90	401.00	382.00	382.00	
6		10/04/90	405.00	374.25	405.00	
7		11/03/90	401.00	375.00	382.40	
8		12/05/90	383.00	365.10	373.75	
9		01/03/91	399.25	376.00	394.25	
10		02/02/91	405.85	385.75	388.50	
11		03/05/91	387.20	375.80	375.80	
12		04/05/91	386.40	371.50	384.25	
13		05/04/91	393.75	367.90	373.05	
14		06/05/91	370.00	335.00	342.35	
15		07/06/91	354.00	339.00	348.25	
16		08/03/91	347.75	335.25	343.75	
17		09/05/91	348.50	333.50	333.50	
18		10/05/91	350.45	329.00	329.00	
19		11/05/91	332.00	307.50	309.00	
20		12/06/91	308.00	297.75	306.65	
21						

Fig. 8-36. Excel worksheet that needs trimming.

and columns above the data cells will disrupt the input process, and you will not get complete records.

All you need to do in a case like this is to select the cells containing the actual data, issue the Copy command, then open a new worksheet and Paste the data at cell A1. Then you can save the new file in the SYLK format with the Save As command, and FileMaker should have no problem reading it.

As you might expect, if you use data from an input file to add new records to the current file, FileMaker copies values from the input file into new records at the end of the current file. These new records will be grouped as the records found when the input is complete. This means you can immediately browse the records that have been added. You can check for empty fields, invalid dates, or duplicate values with the Find command.

If you use data from an input file to update current records, FileMaker replaces field values in the records you are browsing in the current FileMaker file with values from the input file. This means you must be sure that the order of the records you are browsing exactly matches the order of information in the input file. FileMaker does not read the incoming data as belonging to a named field. No matching of incoming data to specific fields is performed. All the data is placed in available fields on a "first in/leftover left out" basis. You specify the input order to exactly match the sequence of field values in the input file. The first field value in the input file replaces the contents of the first field in the input order in the current file, the second value replaces the contents of the second field in the input order, and so on. It's wise to make a backup copy of the current FileMaker file before you begin updating records.

The Import Procedure

To import data from a text, BASIC, or SYLK file to a FileMaker file, you first prepare the FileMaker file. This means saving a copy if you are going to use the incoming data to update records. If you are not going to update all of the records, make sure you are browsing only those records that you want updated, and that it is in the same sort order that the information appears in the input file.

If you are inputting to a new FileMaker file, at least one record needs to be created. In Fig. 8-37, you can see a new database that has been prepared to receive a text file of data downloaded from an on-line information service, the same file that is shown in Fig. 8-34.

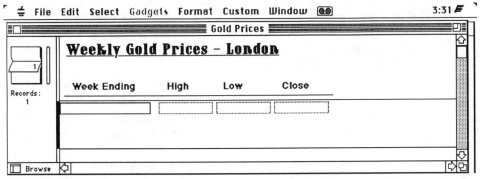

Fig. 8-37. Empty database ready for input.

After you pull down the File menu and select Input From, FileMaker asks you to select the file to use. FileMaker then presents a screen like the one in Fig. 8-38.

This looks a lot like the Input From screen used when combining FileMaker files. The name of the file you have selected is shown below the Field List. You move fields

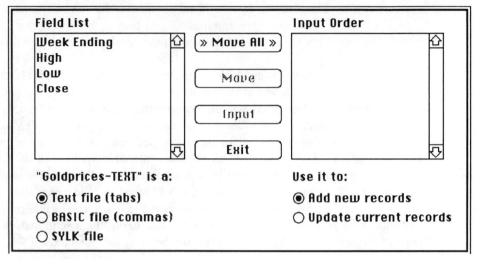

Fig. 8-38. Input From dialog box.

to the Input Order so that they match the order of information in the file you are importing from. In this case, the fields are in the correct order already and so we can click Move All.

Now you choose whether to use the incoming data to add new records or to update current records. Do this by clicking the appropriate button. Now you can click the Input button to begin copying data from the input file to the current FileMaker file. You can also click Exit to abort the process and return to the current file.

Inputting from a large file can take some time. You can use the Command – Period keystroke to abort the process before it is completed, but some of the data from the input file will already have been copied into the current file. If you were adding new records, any records that were added would be the found records in the current file. You could then delete them with the Delete Multiple command. However, if you were updating current records, some of the records will be partially updated and things could be difficult to sort out. You might find it easiest to go back to the backup copy of the current FileMaker file.

After FileMaker has finished copying the information from the input file into the current file, the Browse screen is displayed, as shown in Fig. 8-39, where the gold prices have been input. In this case, we used the data to add new records. You can see that the new records are the found records, the status area showing the number of records added as the number of records found.

Note that there are 61 records total, with 60 found. This means that 60 records were added by the Input From. The other record is the empty one with which the file was started.

If you use the input data to update current records, the status area looks the same as before the Input From command. However, you should check the file to make sure the updated records are as you expect before you get rid of any backup copies of the file.

Fig. 8-39. Completed input.

Applied Importing

Importing data is done for several reasons. You might wonder why the gold prices were placed into FileMaker rather than a spreadsheet like Excel. One explanation can be seen in Fig. 8-40, where FileMaker's flexible reporting capability is clearly in evidence.

This is just one way in which the information can be presented. A fifth field, Average, was added, containing the formula (High + Low) /2. A graphic was copied from

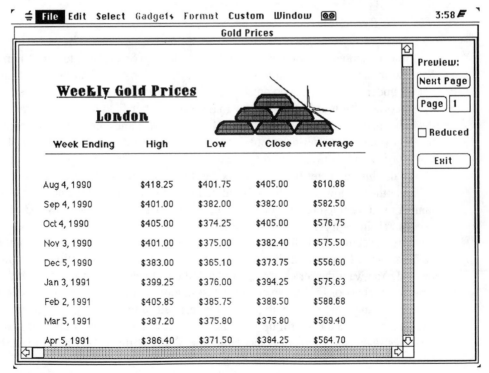

Fig. 8-40. File Preview of enhanced gold prices.

Canvas and pasted into the Header area of the layout. The date field was formatted, as were the price fields. Another interesting application of Input From is to circumvent some of FileMaker's shortcomings.

Suppose that you have entered a large number of records, such as members of a club or subscribers to a magazine. You would like to give each person in the database a serial number. You select Define and create a new field called Number. You can see that this is about to happen in the database shown in Fig. 8-41.

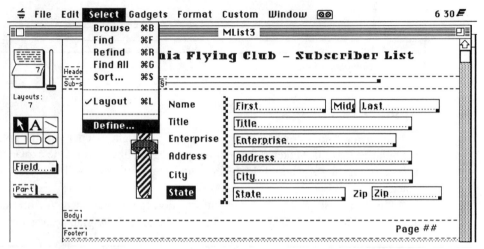

Fig. 8-41. Preparing to add a serial number.

You remember that one of FileMaker's Entry Options relates to serial numbers. You use the Define command to check the Entry Options and find the serial number option under the section Auto-enter in each new record. This option only applied to *new* records. If you do not start out with a serial number field using this Entry Option, it would appear that you are out of luck. To the rescue comes the Input From command that lets you supply a serial number generated by another program. In Fig. 8-42, you can see Excel at work, about to create a series of numbers.

To do this you enter the first number in the series in a cell. Then you select that cell and others below it, selecting a total number of cells equal to the number of serial numbers you want to create. For example, the database in Fig. 8-41 has 133 records, so cells A1 through A133 were selected.

After selecting the cells that will hold the serial numbers, you pick Series from the Data menu. Figure 8-42 shows the dialog box you get. The selections are straight-forward. You want the series arranged in a column, linear in progression, with a step between numbers of 1. You can enter the last number in the series as the Stop Value or leave this empty, and Excel will stop at the last cell in the group you selected. Click OK, and the selected cells fill up with numbers. The next step is to save the file. You use the Save As command and select either the SYLK or the text format. In Fig. 8-43, you can see that the text format is being chosen.

Returning to FileMaker, you open the file to which you want the serial numbers

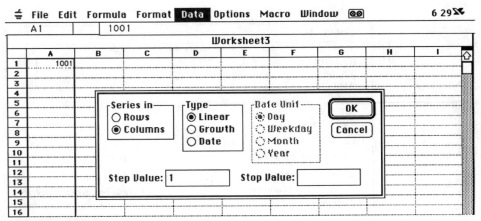

Fig. 8-42. Creating a series with Excel.

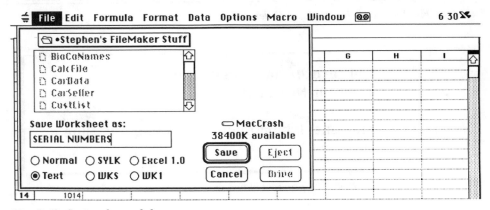

Fig. 8-43. Saving the worksheet.

added. You make sure that the Number field is defined and that all the records are found and sorted in the order you want them numbered (record 1 will get the first serial number, record 2 the second, and so on). Now you select Input From and specify the file containing the serial numbers as the Input file. At the field selection menu, shown in Fig. 8-44, you only have to move the Number field to the Input Order.

Note that the file type has been selected to match the file saved from Excel. Also note that FileMaker has been told to use the serial number file to update the current records, *not* add new records. When the Input button is clicked, the process begins. A record of the progress and a reminder of the "abort command" keystroke appears on the screen, as shown in Fig. 8-45.

When the process is complete, you are returned to the Browse mode and the serial number data will be in the Number field. You can see this from Fig. 8-46, where the Number field is highlighted. Note that this is the last record in the file, record 133, and the serial number is an appropriate 1133.

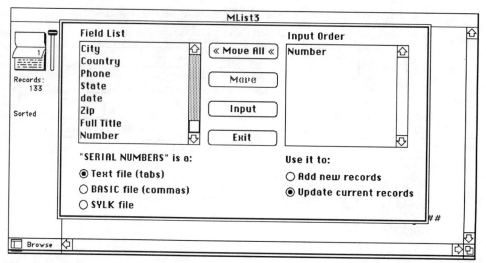

Fig. 8-44. Defining the Input Order.

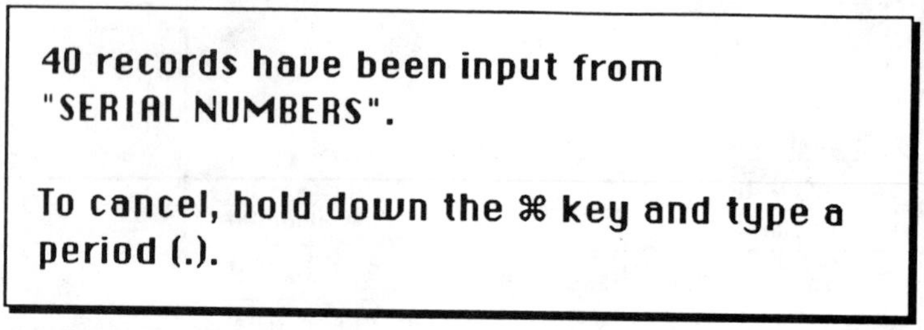

40 records have been input from "SERIAL NUMBERS".

To cancel, hold down the ⌘ key and type a period (.).

Fig. 8-45. The progress indicator.

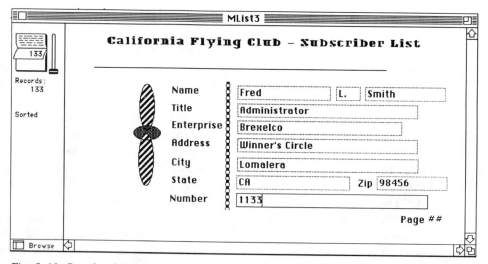

Fig. 8-46. Completed data input.

Now that you have a serial number for each record, you can activate the serial number Entry Option for this field and new records will be numbered. Remember to check the serial number option *and* indicate the correct starting number in the box provided. If you have 133 records numbered from 1001 to 1133, you would enter 1134 in the box.

You could also use the number you have now added in other fields, perhaps combining it with a string formula to include other information to make it more distinctive. You could create a field called Account Number that added part of the name of the person to the number. For example, to combine the initials with the number you could define the field like this, making sure that the result type was Text:

Account Number = NumberLEFT (First,1) &LEFT (Last,2)

Note that the database in Fig. 8-46 has three fields for entering a name: First, Middle Initial, and Last. They are arranged on a single line without the field identifiers, the layout text Name being used instead. For the record in Fig. 8-46, the result of the formula would be 1133FS.

SCRIPTS

When you have developed a FileMaker database and are putting it to use, you might well find that there are certain activities that are performed on a regular basis, certain *routines* that are frequently repeated. Recognizing this fact, and the fact that repetitive work is both boring and error-prone, FileMaker comes with a built-in method of remembering certain activities. FileMaker calls a series of remembered steps a *script*.

In this section, we show you how scripts work and how to set them up. FileMaker allows you to set up numerous scripts for each database file and name them so that they are easy to use. All named scripts can be listed under the Custom item on the main menu, ready to use at any time. Perhaps the easiest way to see a script in action is to use FileMaker's Help system. To do this you select *Help* under the Apple menu. When you do so, FileMaker presents the screen seen in Fig. 8-47.

This screen offers a basic review of commands plus the chance to open the Help file. This is a regular FileMaker file presented in the Browse mode. When you first open this file, it presents record 1 of 69. Each record consists mainly of a title field and a large text field containing information about various aspects of the program. In the case of record 1, shown in Fig. 8-48, the title field displays USING THE HELP FILE, and the large field below it gives information about how to use the Help file.

Below the main text field is layout text describing what to do next. The last of the three bulleted items tells you to use the Custom menu to access other topics. This is being done in Fig. 8-48, where the user has pulled down the Custom menu and is about to select Sorting Records. This menu item, and all of the others below the word Scripts, is actually a script, a series of instructions used to perform a Find. For example, if you choose Arranging Information, you are presented with the screen in Fig. 8-49, which is record 1 of 15 found records.

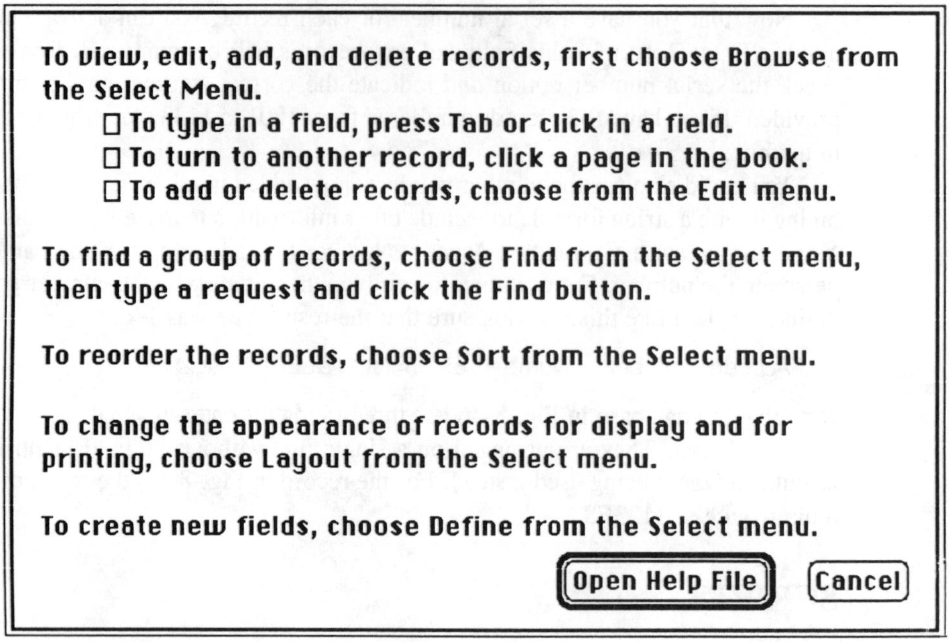

To view, edit, add, and delete records, first choose Browse from the Select Menu.
   □ To type in a field, press Tab or click in a field.
   □ To turn to another record, click a page in the book.
   □ To add or delete records, choose from the Edit menu.

To find a group of records, choose Find from the Select menu, then type a request and click the Find button.

To reorder the records, choose Sort from the Select menu.

To change the appearance of records for display and for printing, choose Layout from the Select menu.

To create new fields, choose Define from the Select menu.

[Open Help File]   [Cancel]

Fig. 8-47. The Help screen.

Fig. 8-48. The first record in the Help file.

You can browse through these 15 records about layouts. If you realize this is not the information you want, you can pull down the Custom menu again and select another item. This will perform a different Find, in this case locating records about Defining Fields. Note that another field on this layout is cleverly hidden at the end of

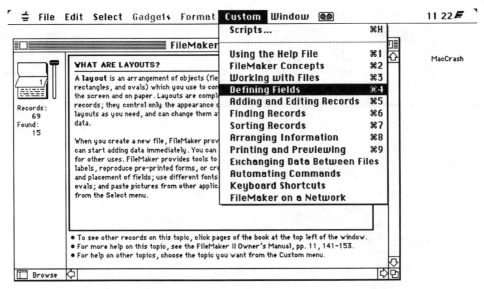

File   Edit   Select   Gadgets   Format   **Custom**   Window   [👓]   11 22 ⚡

Scripts...   ⌘H

≣≣[□]≣≣≣≣≣≣≣≣≣≣≣≣≣≣≣ FileMaker

WHAT ARE LAYOUTS?

A layout is an arrangement of objects (fie   **Using the Help File**   ⌘1   MacCrash
rectangles, and ovals) which you use to con   **FileMaker Concepts**   ⌘2
the screen and on paper. Layouts are compl   **Working with Files**   ⌘3
records; they control only the appearance o   **Defining Fields**   ⌘4
layouts as you need, and can change them a   **Adding and Editing Records** ⌘5
data.   **Finding Records**   ⌘6
                                             Sorting Records   ⌘7
When you create a new file, FileMaker prov   **Arranging Information**   ⌘8
can start adding data immediately. You can   **Printing and Previewing** ⌘9
for other uses. FileMaker provides tools to   **Exchanging Data Between Files**
labels, reproduce pre-printed forms, or cr   **Automating Commands**
and placement of fields; use different fonts   **Keyboard Shortcuts**
ovals; and paste pictures from other applic   **FileMaker on a Network**
from the Select menu.

• To see other records on this topic, click pages of the book at the top left of the window.
• For more help on this topic, see the FileMaker II Owner's Manual, pp. 11, 141-153.
• For help on other topics, choose the topic you want from the Custom menu.

Records:
69
Found:
15

[□] Browse

Fig. 8-49. The effect of selecting Arranging Information.

the second bulleted item below the main field, after the word see. This field refers you to appropriate pages of the manual for more information about the subject of the record.

The FileMaker Help file is a good example of the creative use of FileMaker. It is a useful learning tool that can be left open on the Mac desktop while you are working on other FileMaker files. (If you promise to keep an original copy safely stored away, you can experiment with the Help file, possibly adding your own notes.) When you have learned how scripts operate, you will appreciate how easy it is to create your own Custom menu, like the one used by the Help file.

Creating a Script

The basic theory behind creating scripts is that you perform an action or series of actions, and then select Scripts from the Custom menu to attach a name to those actions. Actions that can be recorded include switching between layouts, inputting and outputting data, finds, sorts, prints, and previews.

To see how scripts are made, suppose that you use a database to keep track of prospective clients for a specialized medical testing lab. Company name, address, and phone number are entered whenever someone locates a new prospect. A layout like the one in Fig. 8-50 is used for data entry, the Entered field being the date that the client was entered into the database.

You can see a series of five named scripts on the Custom menu. The first of these, Print Alpha List has been created to print out a list of the companies in the database in alphabetical order. To create this list, you have to run through most of the commands necessary to perform the task. As you do this, indeed, all the time you work with File-

Fig. 8-50. Data entry layout with Custom menu.

Maker, the program is watching what you do. When you select Scripts from the Custom menu, you can attach a name to your actions. In this case, you begin by using the Layout command to go from the data entry screen in Fig. 8-50 to the list format shown in Fig. 8-51.

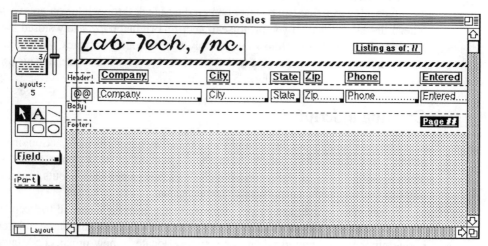

Fig. 8-51. List layout.

You then select Find All to make sure that all companies appear in the list. Next you select Sort and pick Clear to remove the previous settings. You highlight the field name Company and select Move to transfer it to the Sort Order column. You check Ascending and pick Sort. You return to the browse mode to see the results. Finally, you select Page Setup from the File menu and select Letter size paper and any other options you want for the printed report.

At this point, you do not have to print the report. Instead, you choose Scripts from the Custom menu. When no scripts have yet been created for a file, the screen appears as in Fig. 8-52, with a blank list and five buttons, only two of which are active.

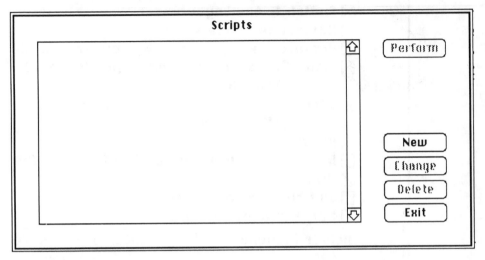

Fig. 8-52. The blank scripts screen.

You can either choose Exit to cancel the command, or you can select New to create a fresh script. Later, when scripts have been created, you can use the Perform button to execute them. The Change button will allow alterations to scripts, and the Delete button will allow you to remove scripts that are no longer needed.

When you select New, you come to a screen that has a lot of options. These can be selected or not to make the script perform just what you want. You can see the default selections in Fig. 8-53, where the standard new script name is entered in the Script Name box.

The first step is to give the script a sensible name, one that describes the role of the script. This name can be up to 30 characters long, so that a descriptive phrase can be used. In this case, the name Print Alpha List was used. The next item to note is the bottom one, Include in menu. This allows you to have the script appear on the Custom menu as well as in the list that appears when you select Scripts from the Custom menu. All scripts appear in the list, but only those with the Include box checked appear on the menu. This box is normally checked, and you will probably want to leave it checked unless you want to keep people away from a particular script. You can always alter the status of the script later by using the Change button, for example, if you later want to remove a script from the menu.

The rest of the options in Fig. 8-53 refer to what actions you want the script to perform. The point to bear in mind is that the Find, Sort, and Layout settings that you used prior to choosing Scripts are the ones that will be remembered in this script. The

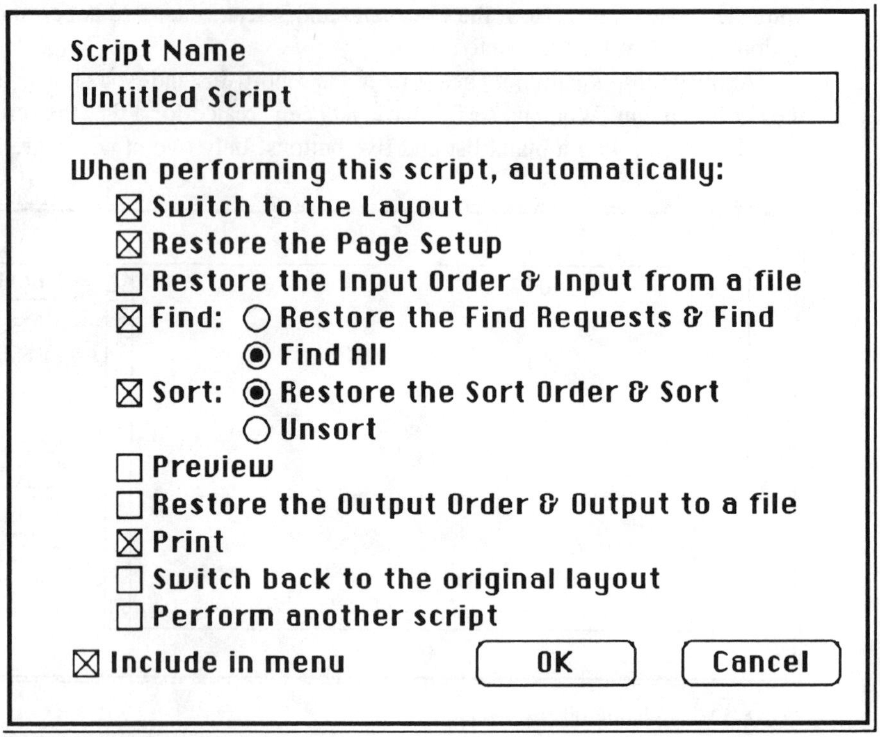

Script Name

| Untitled Script |

When performing this script, automatically:
- ☒ **Switch to the Layout**
- ☒ **Restore the Page Setup**
- ☐ **Restore the Input Order & Input from a file**
- ☒ **Find:** ○ **Restore the Find Requests & Find**
          ⦿ **Find All**
- ☒ **Sort:** ⦿ **Restore the Sort Order & Sort**
          ○ **Unsort**
- ☐ **Preview**
- ☐ **Restore the Output Order & Output to a file**
- ☒ **Print**
- ☐ **Switch back to the original layout**
- ☐ **Perform another script**

☒ **Include in menu**   (**OK**)   (**Cancel**)

Fig. 8-53. The standard script settings.

default selection means that when performing this script, FileMaker will switch from whatever layout you happen to be using to the one now in effect. The Page Layout in effect at the present time will be restored. The Find All command will be issued, and the Sort command will be executed using the sort order currently in effect. FileMaker will then print the results.

This is exactly what you want in the case of the alpha list. The only change you might want to make is to check the Preview box. This tells FileMaker to preview the report before it is printed. When you have made your selections from this screen, you click OK and the script is saved. The script is now part of the file and will be there the next time you choose Custom, or select Scripts from the Custom menu, as shown in Fig. 8-54.

Using a Script

To execute the new script, you can either highlight it in the Custom Scripts list and select Perform, or you can choose the item from the Custom menu. A further alternative, available for the first nine scripts you define in each file, is to use the Command–Number option. As you can see from Figs. 8-49 and 8-50, FileMaker places a number on each script, allowing the script to be performed by pressing Command and the number.

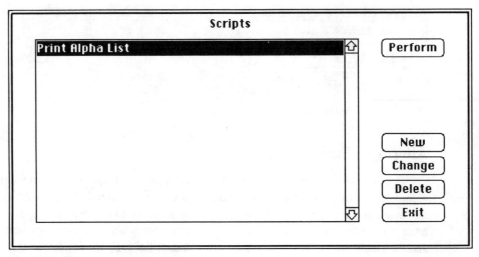

Fig. 8-54. The new script listed.

Suppose that you have just entered a number of new companies in the database, using the layout in Fig. 8-50. You want to print an updated list of companies. You simply type Command − 1, and the whole process is carried out automatically. The only step that requires your involvement is to confirm the printing. In any script involving printing, FileMaker will present the regular File Print dialog box and require you to click OK or press Return to confirm the printing. This is a safety measure to avoid unintentional printing. If you checked the Preview box, the report is previewed and then printed as soon as you exit from the Preview mode.

After the script has been executed, you will be left with the layout chosen by the script, in this example, the list layout. If you want to continue entering data, you might want to return to the data entry layout, find the most recent records, and then sort them according to name. When you do this, you can again use the Script command to store the procedure. In Fig. 8-50, you can see a Script called Enter Data that carries out these steps. Note that this script will have the Preview and Print boxes unchecked.

Suppose that you want to send out information packages to prospective clients. You use the Find command to find all of the recently entered records have not yet been sent any information. Using the Mailer field for the Find, you can enter >01/01/1950 and then check the Omit box. This will find all records that do not have a date greater than January 1, 1950; in other words, all records that have not got a valid date in the Mailer field. After finding the records, you switch to the mailing label layout, shown in Fig. 8-55.

Now you sort the records by the Zip field, and alter the Page Setup ready to print labels. At this point, you select Scripts and check the options. You want Print to be checked. All the other selections should be correct, including Switch to the Layout, Restore the Page Setup, Find with the Restore the Find Requests & Find option, Sort with the Restore the Sort Order & Sort option. Name this script Mailing Labels, and you have automated the process.

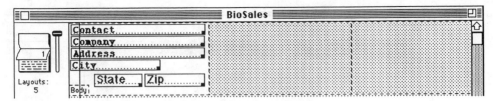

Fig. 8-55. The mailing label layout.

Altering a Script

One wrinkle in creating scripts arises when you want FileMaker to find a group of records based on a field that is not in the layout you want to use. FileMaker will go to the layout associated with the script, but when it comes to perform the Find, it cannot enter the conditions. This would be the case if you switched to the mailing label layout and then attempted to find records based on a date field. Even if you record the script with the Find preceding the change of layout, FileMaker will have a problem executing it. This is because the script is not (strictly speaking) a *macro*, or a literal record of your keystrokes. A script is a programmed shortcut through a series of operations. The layout associated with the script will be put in place before the Find is carried out.

The way around this is to perform the operation in two parts, creating two scripts. The first performs the Find and Sort ready for printing, using a layout that has the Find field in it. The second script switches to the layout to be used for printing and proceeds with the print process. You can then link the two scripts so that only one needs to be invoked for the process to be completed. The first script could be called, in this case, Print Mailing Labels, and the second script would be called something like Actual Label Print. The second script would not need to be listed on the Custom menu. The first script would then be altered to include the option that is called Perform another script. When you check this option and click OK to leave the script definition screen, File-Maker presents a list of scripts from which to choose.

The technique of telling one script to perform another script has considerable potential, but several drawbacks. When you select this option, FileMaker provides a list of existing scripts to choose from, meaning that the second script has to be in place already. Furthermore, once you supply the name of a script, it is permanently attached to that script and cannot be changed. To change the connection, you have to delete the script that invokes the second script and try again. If you want to get rid of a script, just highlight it in the list and click Delete. FileMaker will ask you to confirm this action as there is no way to undo it.

To alter a script you have already made, you select the script in the list and click Change. You are then presented with the script option screen seen in Fig. 8-53 where you can make changes. When you click OK, the altered script does not immediately replace the previous version. You are required to confirm the changes, in the dialog box shown in Fig. 8-56.

This box is a review of the alterations you have made. In this case, no alterations have been made, and so the Keep buttons are checked for all of the pieces of informa-

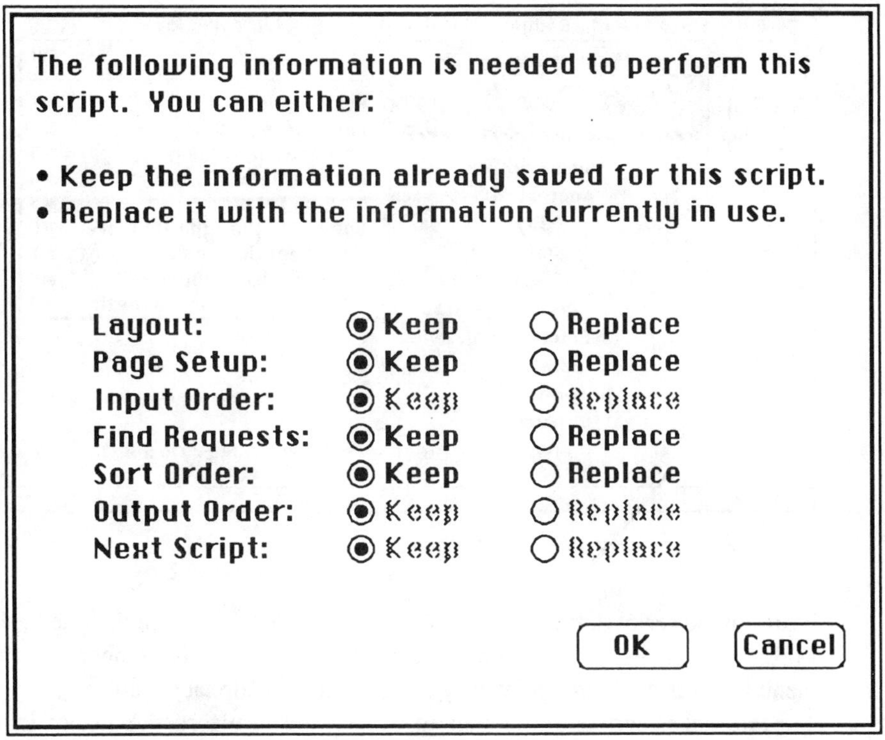

```
The following information is needed to perform this
script. You can either:

• Keep the information already saved for this script.
• Replace it with the information currently in use.


    Layout:          ◉ Keep      ○ Replace
    Page Setup:      ◉ Keep      ○ Replace
    Input Order:     ◉ Keep      ○ Replace
    Find Requests:   ◉ Keep      ○ Replace
    Sort Order:      ◉ Keep      ○ Replace
    Output Order:    ◉ Keep      ○ Replace
    Next Script:     ◉ Keep      ○ Replace


                          ( OK )   [Cancel]
```

Fig. 8-56. The script change confirmation screen.

tion. If you have made changes, they will be reflected in Replace buttons being checked. At this point, you can click OK to confirm the changes or click Cancel to return to the script definition screen.

In some scripts, you might want to use the second-to-last option in the script definition screen: Switch back to the original layout. This will allow you to go from browsing in one layout, printing in another, then returning to the original layout for further browsing.

Script Applications and Macros

You can use scripts for all sorts of activities, including no activity at all! That's right, you can create script that does nothing. Why would you do this? Well, the Custom menu is the one part of the FileMaker menu system that you design. The names of your scripts appear as regular menu items. Furthermore, the width of the Custom menu is flexible, to accommodate long names (FileMaker will show up to 30 characters in the menu; entries longer than that are shortened and signified by an ellipsis.) You could use the script name as a method of supplying information to users, such as product codes. You can see an example of this in Fig. 8-57.

Note that the indentation of the last three items is produced by typing three spaces in front of the text of the item. Remember that to create a text-only script, all choice

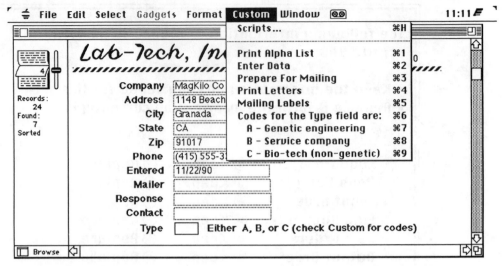

Fig. 8-57. Using script titles for information.

boxes on the script definition screen must be unchecked except the one that tells File-Maker to include the script on the Custom menu. Also remember that the Custom menu lists scripts in the order they are created, not alphabetically.

FileMaker scripts are similar in some ways to macros. A macro is a series of actions that is remembered so that it can be executed with a single command. This is not exactly what scripts are because FileMaker does not carry out the commands in the order you do, instead it takes a shortcut to the results you want. You might want to turn to a third-party program, such as AutoMac III, to provide more conventional macros to use with FileMaker.

AutoMac III allows you to record any activity you carry out with the Mac, from typing the company name to launching applications. You can assign a string of text, like a company name, to a single keystroke. Whenever you need to type the company name you just hit the special keystroke, whether you are using FileMaker, MacWrite, or Excel. You can have macros specifically for one application or universal macros that work with any application. You can even tell AutoMac III to load FileMaker and a FileMaker database as soon as your Mac is turned on. Macros of this kind bring a new level of automation to your work.

To begin exploring macros, you might want to examine the MacroMaker program that comes with the most Macs. This is a simple macro system that does not have all of the features found in AutoMac III, but it will give you an idea of what is possible. In Fig. 8-58, you can see a list of MacroMaker macros pulled down from the cassette tape icon on the Finder menu.

The cassette icon reflects the fact that MacroMaker acts like a tape recorder, recording your actions for later replay. You can see that several macros have been set up for use with the Finder. These macros operate particular applications. For example, the one called Canvas loads the graphics program Canvas. This macro can be

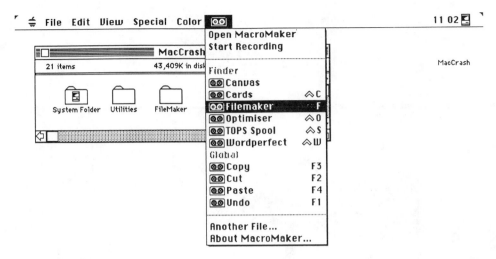

Fig. 8-58. Using MacroMaker.

activated either with Command−C or by selecting the macro from this menu, as is being done with the FileMaker macro that loads FileMaker. The Optimiser macro is used to run the disk optimizing utility from PC tools. This very handy program reviews the storage of files on the hard disk and consolidates fragmented files for better disk operation. The benefits of a macro for this operation are that it can run the application *and* put it away when it is finished, completely automating and simplifying a housekeeping chore that might otherwise go undone.

You can also see that several global macros have been created. These allow the use of the function keys F1 through F4 on the newer keyboards for Copy, Cut, Paste, and Undo operations. While MacroMaker is useful, it has a serious limitation in that it records mouse actions, not program events. This means that the macro to open File-Maker moves the mouse pointer to the FileMaker folder, double-clicks to open it, then double-clicks on the FileMaker application. If you move the FileMaker folder to a different place on the desktop, MacroMaker will not find it and the macro will not work. A program like AutoMac III actually records which menu items you choose in order to overcome this problem.

CONCLUSIONS

This chapter has covered a lot of ground, from the index to import/export and scripts. Hopefully, the rich possibilities of FileMaker are now becoming clearer. Chapter 10 has further examples of how FileMaker has been applied to a wide range of tasks. In Chapter 9 we look at how FileMaker operates on a local area network, permitting you to share information in FileMaker database with other users. We even look at how you can save money expanding your office's computing capacity.

9
Networking FileMaker

IN THIS CHAPTER, we look at how FileMaker handles situations in which several people need access to the same files. By now it should be clear that FileMaker has all the sorting, searching, and reporting power that is required to carry out most of the database management tasks in today's office. As more and more important tasks in the office are assigned to FileMaker, it is inevitable that FileMaker users will need to share information (early warning signs are well-worn tracks between computers and people flitting from Mac to Mac carrying disks). A more efficient means of sharing information is to connect computers together with cables into a *local area network* (LAN). FileMaker supports network operation. Several people can use the same database file at the same time, referred to by FileMaker as multi-user operations. With the right combination of hardware and software, several people can load the same copy of FileMaker from the same computer at the same time, referred to by FileMaker as multi-launch operations.

WHAT A LAN IS

We begin this chapter with a look at how local area networks have developed, how they work, and the terms that are used to describe them. We then review the operation of two popular Macintosh networks, TOPS and AppleShare. This will lead to a full examination of how to use FileMaker on a network.

A local area network is formed when two or more computers in the same area are connected in order to share resources. The resources that are shared can be either hardware, such as mass storage devices (typically hard disks); output devices (typically as printers and plotters); or software, such as data files and programs. A typical

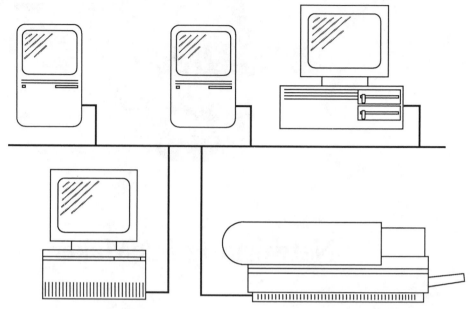

Fig. 9-1. A star type LAN example.

LAN is diagrammed in Fig. 9-1, where the arrangement of machines is essentially a trunk. This is one of several possible network layouts or topologies.

The definition of *same area* is what distinguishes a local area network (LAN) from a wide area network (WAN). Typically, same area means same office, same department, or same building; in other words, any area in which computers can be directly connected without resorting to long distance telephone lines, satellite links, or microwave transmissions. On the other hand, a wide area network is used to connect users at separate sites. The distinction between a WAN and LAN is becoming one of convenience rather than precision as communications technology grows more sophisticated. For example, users on a LAN can connect to remote computers over the phone lines using a network modem.

The physical size of a local area can be extended significantly through the use of *bridges* and *gateways*. A *bridge* is a combination of hardware and software that enables you to connect one LAN to another and communicate across the connection as though it was a complete entity. The LANs being connected can be of the same kind, or they can be two different types of LAN. You can see a bridge diagrammed in Fig. 9-2.

A *gateway* provides a network with a high-speed communication to a large computer. By means of the gateway, which is usually a combination of hardware and software, users on the network can access data and software on the large computer, just as though they were directly linked to it as a terminal. You can see a gateway in the arrangement shown in Fig. 9-3.

Local area networks with bridges and gateways are at the upper end of the scale. In its simplest form, a LAN is just a piece of cable and a set of commands. The cable

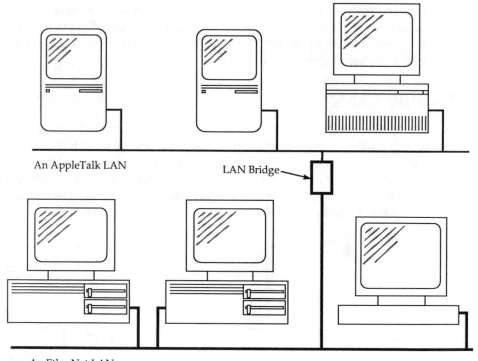

An AppleTalk LAN

LAN Bridge

An EtherNet LAN

Fig. 9-2. A LAN bridge.

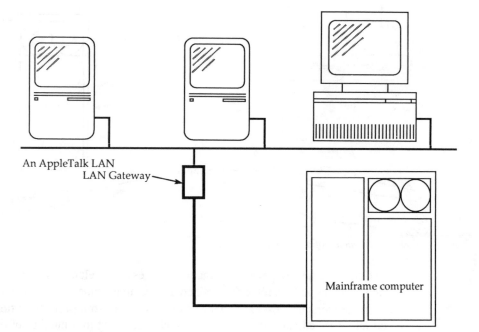

An AppleTalk LAN
LAN Gateway

Mainframe computer

Fig. 9-3. A LAN gateway.

wires the computers together. The commands control the communications between the computers. Commands that control communications are often referred to as *protocols*. Thus software commands that are supposed to work across a network must conform to the appropriate network protocols.

WHY LANS?

To understand the merits of LANs relative to other approaches to computing, we need to look at the background of personal computers. If we define a computer as a data processing device that has facilities for data input, storage, and output as shown in Fig. 9-4, then the first "personal" computers were those developed in the mid 1970s by such companies as MITS, which marketed the Altair, and later Apple, which put out the Apple 1 in 1976.

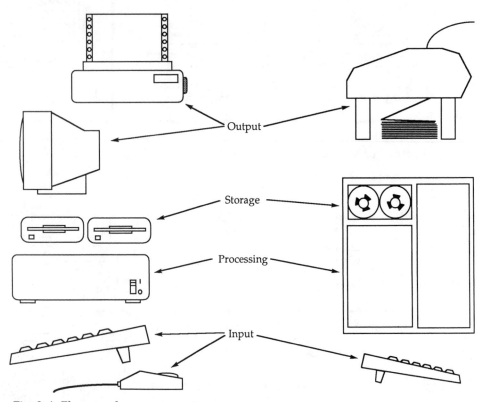

Fig. 9-4. Elements of a computer system.

These computers were personal in that the four essential elements (input, storage, processing, and output) were self-contained in one unit, capable of being grouped together on one person's desktop. This was quite a break from previous systems that were centrally located and provided storage and processing to a number of different users. You can see a diagram of this distinction in Fig. 9-5.

Fig. 9-5. Personal computers versus central systems.

These large "central" computers were referred to as *mainframes* because they consisted of numerous components assembled in a large framework, one that might occupy a whole room specially designed to accommodate it. The mainframe computer, with its centralized storage and multiple users who shared its processing power, was a natural evolution from the early days of computing. The first computers only came into being through the combined efforts of teams of scientists and engineers. In order to make these machines economically feasible, their power was shared. Computing time was parceled out around the clock. Because not everyone who needed computer power could afford the great expense of building one, connections were made from the central computer to remote terminals to allow access.

While the advent of computer power was welcomed by many companies and government institutions, the original centralized, multiple user systems had several disadvantages. They imposed a need for coordination between the different users. Some times this meant scheduling of work for certain times of the day. Often it meant uniform procedures that were centrally imposed. Making changes to improve programs required consensus, followed by lengthy programming efforts to achieve changes that were often outdated before they could be implemented. Individuals eager to apply computer power to their specific tasks found this restrictive.

The Personal Computer Arrives

When the personal computer appeared, it promised to free computer users from central authority and restrictions. Individuals could set their own work timetable and no longer had to wait for a free terminal. As you have seen with FileMaker, users prepared to learn how to run the personal computer can organize their data in ways that make sense to them and make immediate changes to system design and procedures rather than submit changes to lengthy approval and implementation processes.

Although a breakthrough in design, the early models of personal computer were limited in their storage capacity. This seriously hampered their ability to cope with tasks such as database management. In the early 1980s, the advent of hard disks that worked with small computers offered increased storage and opened up new applications. Yet these disks were perceived as expensive. For example, in 1983 you had to pay one and a half times as much for a hard disk drive as you did for the computer itself. At this price point, the idea of sharing a disk between computers made sense.

The Network Idea

In addition to the savings that it offered, the idea of sharing a hard disk appealed to some systems managers because that was the way earlier computers had worked, sharing large storage devices between many users. Thus early attempts to connect personal computers into a network had both economic and philosophical justification. Although connecting computers clearly had a cost involved, it was thought that this would be offset by the sharing of hard drive costs. One of the first personal computer networks was Omninet from Corvus, introduced in 1981. Omninet was designed primarily to provide multiple user access to a central hard disk drive.

The cost of networking could be further offset by the savings from additional printers. In the early 1980s, a good letter-quality printer could cost you more than a computer system. Because nobody is printing all the time, people sought ways to make greater use of printers shared between workers. Thus several personal computers with floppy disks networked together and sharing a common printer and a hard disk were seen as an economic alternative to everybody having their own hard disk and printer.

There were other reasons for wanting to network users together. Almost as soon as individuals found uses for the personal computers, they had need to share the data between several people. Consider a FileMaker database of clients. The person who designed the database might want someone else to type in the existing client list. Without networks, this meant giving up the computer so that the typist could enter the information. Alternatively, the data entry done on another computer and transferred back to the original by means of copying to and from floppy disks. Thus was born the infamous "Sneaker Net" that saw people swapping disks from machine to machine. When the clients have been entered into the database, several people might want to sort the list and print out their own copies: more Sneaker Net as copies of the database proliferated to different computers. The benefits of wiring everybody together quickly become apparent.

A further reason for wiring personal computers together was the need to transfer data between dissimilar machines. Early personal computers for business came from several different companies, each with their own system of managing files. The way data is arranged on a disk is called the *disk format*. The way data is arranged in a file on the disk is called the *file format*. Even today, competing companies use different disk and file formats. As we mentioned in the last chapter, Macintosh disks cannot be read by IBM compatibles (unless you have special software). Early network designers saw the potential of a network to overcome the problem of data stored onto disk by one company's computer not being readable by another company's system. There were also hopes that networks would facilitate access to data stored on large computers. If users of small computers could share a single link to a large computer, it would increase the cost effectiveness of such a link.

The Continuing Need to Share

The circumstances that gave rise to the desire to network personal computers together have changed somewhat since the early mid-1980s. The price of letter-quality printers and hard disks has declined significantly. This means that it is more feasible for everyone to have a hard disk, and some form of printer. However, the economics of sharing devices have not gone away, particularly for Macintosh users. Laser printers that support PostScript remain relatively expensive, and yet they will sit idle for many hours of the day if only used by one person. New peripheral devices for the Mac such as typesetters, CD-ROM drives, and scanners are easier to justify if shared between several users. Furthermore, Macintoshes themselves remain relatively expensive in terms of raw computing power and storage, due in part to the high quality of graphics hardware they use. With the right network hardware and software, you can create a LAN in which the main computing work is performed by cheap IBM-clone hardware that does not require graphics to serve as central storage for a group of Macintoshes. (By 1990 a reliable IBM-clone with a powerful 80386 processor, 2 megabytes of RAM, 80 megabytes of hard disk storage, and monochrome display could be purchased for under $1500.)

Although the relative cost of different pieces of equipment can change, the basic justification for a network—the idea of sharing, remains valid. Networks allow users of single computer system to share with others the three elements storage space, data, and peripherals. In many ways, the need to share is greater now than it was when personal computers first entered the office. The extreme diversity of systems in the early years of personal computers has given way to increasing standardization, but today's offices have to contend with at least two standards: That derived from the IBM PC, and that used by the Apple Macintosh.

We refer to computers based on the Apple Macintosh standard as Macs and use the term PC to refer to any personal computer that runs PC-DOS or MS-DOS: This use of PC is distinct from the term *personal computer*, which refers to any computer used primarily by a single person, and which includes both Macs and PCs.

Several aspects of data sharing have recently increased in importance. One of these is *electronic mail*. This is a means of distributing messages and documents to different users on a network. As the percentage of workers with computers on their desks approaches one hundred, electronic mail becomes increasingly practical as a means of communication and sharing specific data with specific individuals.

Another way in which the sharing of data is becoming more important arises from the snowball effect of computerization: The more people who have computers, the more data there is on computers that needs to be shared. Users now want to connect to mainframes, the large centralized systems that many companies and government institutions still use to accumulate data.

NETWORK ORGANIZATION

When the first networks were designed, the traditional paradigm of the central computer was still very influential. Early systems envisioned one particularly powerful personal computer supporting a number of less powerful machines. The powerful computer, dubbed the file server, would have the expensive hard disk and would be the centralized storage for the network, as seen in Fig. 9-6.

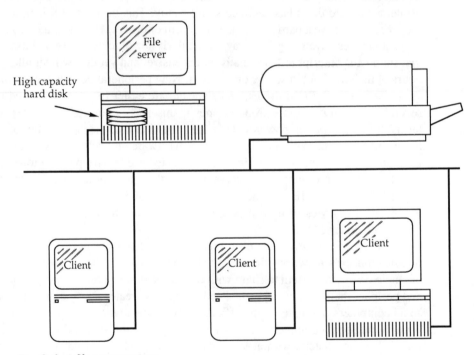

Fig. 9-6. A file server system.

In the early networks, this file server could not be used for anything but serving and was called a dedicated network server or dedicated file server. Omninet and Novell's NetWare follow this pattern. Networks such as Apple's AppleShare, IBM's PC Network, and TOPS from Sun Microsystems can be configured with file servers, but they can also be arranged in ways that dilute the relative importance of the file server.

A personal computer that is attached to a network to use the storage and computing power of a server is called a *client*. As you can see from Fig. 9-7, a typical client computer might consist of a keyboard, monitor, system unit with single floppy disk drive, and network interface.

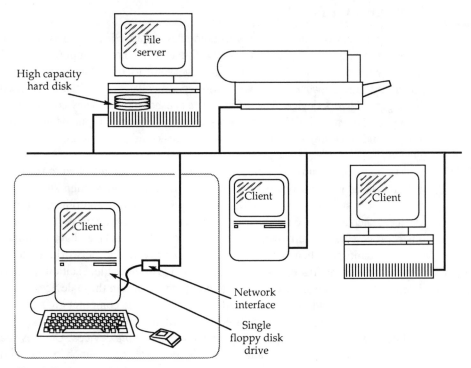

Fig. 9-7. A network client.

This client has limited storage of its own, but it can write data to its own floppy disk. The floppy disk is also used when the computer is turned on. A disk containing the programs that connect the server to the network, or *sign on* is placed in the drive. This is sometimes referred to as a *boot disk* (as pulling the system up by its own boot-straps, not kicking it).

You might wonder what distinguishes a simple client computer or workstation from a computer *terminal*. The usual distinction involves the processing power of the client. A personal computer acting as a client has computing power, which a terminal does not. When performing a task, the client might use both programs and data that are stored on a file server, but the processing of data is done on the client. The client computer's memory holds information as it is entered and juggles data that is copied, cut, and pasted.

There are three models of communication between users of a computer system. The early model is the dumb terminal connected to a powerful central computer. The client/server network model has intelligent terminals, machines that have their own computer power, borrowing storage and other resources from the server, a computer that is usually more powerful than the clients it serves. The third model is peer-to-peer communications, in which each computer has client and server capability. This is sometimes referred to as a *distributed network architecture*.

Stations and Nodes

While the word *station* refers to computers attached to the network, computers are not the only equipment that a network supports. For example, you can attach a LaserWriter printer to the network for everyone to use. The term for each item attached to the network is a *node*. More specifically, a node can be defined as any intelligent network device. The word *device* is used to refer to any component part of a computer system. Thus both monitors and printers are output devices, while keyboards and mice are input devices. A hard disk and a floppy disk are both storage devices.

In network terminology, pieces of equipment that are attached to the network are referred to as network devices. Computers or workstations often share the network with devices such as printers, modems, CD-ROM Disks, and others. Some of these devices, such as LaserWriters, are referred to as *intelligent devices*, because they have microprocessors of their own that control them. Such devices have communications abilities built into them and are attached directly to the network. Other kinds of devices are not intelligent and must be attached to an individual station. Access to non-intelligent devices is controlled by the computer to which these devices are attached.

The devices and disks that are attached to a specific computer are said to be *local*. Your own hard disk, in this terminology, would be your local disk. Disks and devices that belong to another computer are referred to as *remote* devices. Devices such as the LaserWriter that are directly attached to the network, are neither local or remote but are referred to as network devices.

As an example of using these terms, suppose that you are printing a document on a printer that is attached directly to your machine: You are printing it to a local printer, as opposed to a remote printer (attached to someone else's computer), or a network printer, such as a LaserWriter directly attached to the network.

LOCAL AREA NETWORKS FOR THE MAC

Writing about the current state of affairs in LAN technology is a bit like trying to sketch a wave. Every week, new products are announced that alter the overall picture. However, some standards have emerged in the last few years. Although these will doubtless continue to evolve and change, the basic descriptions here will hold true for some time.

General Networks

First we examine the major players in personal computer networking in general. Then we focus on two of those that cater to Mac users, TOPS and Appleshare.

ARCnet. Datapoint's ARCnet was originally developed in the 1970s as a network for *minicomputers*, computers that are between mainframes and personal computers in terms of power and number of users supported. Many vendor companies have licensed the ARCnet technology, and many brand names of ARCnet are now available for personal computers.

Ethernet. One of the most popular network systems is Ethernet, which originated in a joint project of Digital Equipment Corporation (DEC), Intel Corporation, and Xerox Corporation. Most major computer companies offer Ethernet-based networks (although IBM has long been a hold-out in this field). Ethernet was not originally developed as a personal computer network, but in 1983 the 3COM company introduced its EtherSeries network for personal computers. In simplest form, Ethernet is a standard method of connecting computers and, with the right equipment, Macintoshes can be connected to networks that follow this standard.

To connect PCs or Macintoshes to Ethernet cabling requires an Ethernet adapter or interface card and Ethernet driver software. In the case of TOPS running on Ethernet, the driver is referred to as EtherTalk since it is an adaption of the AppleTalk protocols to the Ethernet cabling system (we explain these terms in a moment).

IBM Networks. There are three elements to consider when discussing networks and IBM. The IBM technology referred to as Systems Network Architecture (SNA) is not a network for personal computers, but rather a system for connecting to larger computers, as well as an overall strategy for distributing data. In 1983 IBM announced a wiring system for networks called the *token-ring* standard. However, the IBM PC Network that was released in 1984 used technology from a company called Sytek and did not follow token-ring standards. IBM did agree with Microsoft to incorporate network support in version 3.1 of the IBM PC operating system (called PC-DOS if you buy the IBM brand, MS-DOS if you buy the generic offering from Microsoft). All subsequent versions of DOS have maintained this network support. IBM's first actual token-ring network products were released in 1985, and networks based on this standard are now quite widespread. Both the IBM PC Network and the token ring support a set of protocols called *NETBIOS* and so you will see some network products advertised as NETBIOS compatible. For example, the TOPS network is NETBIOS compatible.

Apple Networks

By building network support into the Macintosh, Apple gave a big boost to the whole idea of networking in the office, preparing for the day when all manner of computer resources will be tied together for greater productivity. Every Macintosh comes with a hardware interface to LocalTalk, a low-cost cabling system. Apple uses LocalTalk to connect LaserWriters to Macintoshes, and the software that drives communications over LocalTalk cabling is built into the Macintosh system software.

AppleTalk. The LocalTalk driver is referred to as *AppleTalk*, more formally, the *AppleTalk Network System* (ANS). AppleTalk's seven-layer architecture is similar to the Open Systems Interconnect (OSI) model established by the International Standards

Organization (ISO). In technical terms, AppleTalk supports peer-to-peer communications between networked devices. In simple terms, this means it is great for connecting equipment that is on equal terms. However, AppleTalk does not allow several computers to pool their resources on a central file server.

AppleShare. AppleShare, introduced in January 1987, is designed to extend the simple networking of Apple computers to other systems and provide file serving for AppleTalk networks. This means that one computer is used to run the network, a network that can include PCs as well as Macintoshes. To put these terms in perspective: AppleShare is a network product that uses LocalTalk cabling and AppleTalk protocols.

AppleShare features a set of tools for assuring the privacy of folders and documents residing on volumes attached to the file server. The person managing or administering an AppleShare network can create groups of users with clearly defined access privileges to folders and the files they contain. This is a very powerful means for protecting sensitive information and for decreasing the number of files available to everyone.

AppleShare PC, also from Apple, is a set of programs that allows PCs to serve as workstations on an AppleShare network. Aside from the software, it requires that the PC also have an AppleTalk interface board installed. AppleShare PC conforms both to Apple's standards for file and record locking and to those standards established by IBM and Microsoft for file and record locking among DOS programs. This allows Macintosh servers to be repositories for DOS programs and data files, even if they are to be used exclusively by, and shared among, PCs.

Although the Local Talk connection is built into Macintoshes, the AppleTalk protocol can run on other media. Technically defined, LocalTalk is shielded twisted pair wiring. AppleTalk will also run on unshielded twisted pair, such as Farallon Computing's PhoneNet, Fiber-Optic LAN from DuPont Connector Systems, and EtherNet coaxial cabling.

The TOPS Network

One of the best-selling local area network systems is TOPS, a product of Sun Microsystems. The designer of TOPS, Nat Goldhaber, had been developing a network system for personal computers for some time before the Macintosh came out, but he was stymied by the fact that most machines lacked a network interface. Goldhaber was attracted to the Mac because Apple had made a network interface part of the basic design.

Seeing that Apple had not provided any network software, Goldhaber founded Centram to fill the gap and called his product the Transcendental Operating System, TOPS. The basic principle of TOPS is that it transcends boundaries between operating systems, providing what is referred to as *inter operability*. This means that computers controlled by different operating systems can deal with each other as though they had the same operating system. This makes for greater ease of use and a smaller learning curve for users. Although any network requires rules and an organizational structure,

TOPS does not require a full-time administrator to control levels of access and sanction each sharing of information.

When TOPS is loaded in your computer, it catches all the commands that you give that are addressed to the operating system, either DOS on the PC or OS on the Macintosh. TOPS examines the command and passes it on to local equipment or to remote systems. For example, if you issue a command on a Mac to open a file that is on a remote PC, TOPS takes the OS command to open a file and translates it to a DOS command that means the same thing. As a user, you see none of this activity; after all, TOPS is a transcendent operating system.

To accomplish its goals of power and ease of use, TOPS employs the decentralized concept of distributed servers. TOPS allows each user to be both server and client, as is described in the next chapter. This provides much greater flexibility and user control and promotes sharing of the responsibility for the network, rather than concentrating it in the hands of an administrator.

TOPS originally ran on Macintoshes, using the LocalTalk ports and cabling of unshielded twisted pair telephone wire, with simple RJ-11 telephone jacks for connection. Instead of driving the LocalTalk ports with AppleTalk, TOPS uses its own LocalTalk driver, called *FlashTalk*, together with TOPS network software, software that is easily ported to work with other operating systems. TOPS developed the LocalTalk driver called FlashTalk to operate much faster than Apple's LocalTalk (for the technical: at 770 Kbps versus 230 Kbps, where 1 Kbps is 1000 bits of information per second).

This higher speed was first implemented on the FlashCard, an interface card for the IBM PC that allowed the PC to run TOPS network software and print to LocalTalk printers such as the Apple LaserWriter. Later came the TOPS Flashbox, a connector for the Macintosh that enabled FlashTalk's higher speeds for Macintoshes on a TOPS network. More recently TOPS has introduced drivers for Ethernet networks so that TOPS users can take advantage of the higher speed of the Ethernet system and still have the ease of use of the TOPS network software.

BASIC APPLESHARE OPERATIONS

Many of the terms and concepts used in networking FileMaker are derived from Apple's own networking products, including AppleShare. In this section, we review some of the basic commands used to run an AppleShare network.

The Server

As mentioned earlier, AppleShare requires that at least one Mac on the network be the dedicated file server. This means you cannot run other programs on the server at the same time as it is being a server, with the notable exception of applications like the LaserShare print spooler and some electronic mail programs. Furthermore, only volumes connected directly to the server can be shared among users.

Other workstations on the network might have hard disks attached to them, but these hard disks cannot be shared directly on the network. However, you can have more than one server on the network, and multiple networks can be joined with a bridge, described earlier. The different networks connected by bridges are called *zones*.

The AppleShare Administrator

When running an AppleShare LAN in a typical office situation, one individual is assigned the task of supervising the running of the network. This person is referred to as the AppleShare administrator. One of the administrator's main tasks is the registering of users and assigning of passwords. Using the AppleShare Admin program, the Administrator registers the names and passwords of all those who will be using the server. Only those who are registered users are allowed to use all the features of an AppleShare server.

To be registered, a user must have a registered user name and password given by the AppleShare administrator. Users who do not have a network name and password are able to log onto the server as guests. This means they can use many of the folders on the volume, but they cannot assign access privileges to the items they create. The folders they create are public, and everyone can make changes to them. Guests can only see or make changes to folders that have the privilege set for everyone.

On an AppleShare network, users are often organized into groups. A *group* usually consists of individuals who work together or regularly share information. Individuals can belong to several groups. With these groups, it is possible for users to limit access to information in folders to just members of a specific group. Only the AppleShare administrator can create groups. Guest users cannot be part of a group.

Access Privileges

To ensure the protection of information on the server disk, AppleShare provides a series of access options. When a registered user creates a folder on an AppleShare server, that folder is automatically set up as a private folder. Only its creator may see or change its contents. However, the user can assign privileges for that folder to others on the network. To understand how these privileges are assigned, look at the three categories of users:

- *Owner*—The owner of the folder is the registered user who created it.
- *Group A*—A group of users that has been created by the administrator.
- *Everyone*—This includes all users who access the server, including both registered users and guests.

Privileges for a folder are typically assigned separately for each of these three entities. The privileges that can be assigned are: See Folder, See Files, and Make Changes.

See Folders. See Folders allows others to see the folders that exist in a folder or volume. If you have this privilege, the folders within that folder are visible when you open a folder. Whether you are able to manipulate those folders depends on the privileges you have for that folder. If this privilege is not assigned to the users, then folders are invisible.

See Files. See Files allows you to see the icons of documents and applications within the folder. Files inside the folder can be copied out of the folder to another, where they can be changed. If you do not have this privilege, then the files within the folder are invisible. If neither See Files nor See Folders is set, then you will not be able to open the folder. With this privilege, you may work with the files in the folders but might not be able to change their contents, depending on the next privilege, Make Changes.

Make Changes. Make Changes allows you to make changes to the folder's contents, including creating, editing, or deleting files. If Make Changes is not available to you, the folder acts as if it were locked, and the applications program treats files as if they had been loaded from a locked disk. Even with the Make Changes privilege available, folders within the folder have their own privileges.

All of these privileges are set at the folder level and can be set separately for all the folders on a volume, or even all the folders within another folder. If the privileges of a particular folder are not specifically set, then privileges for any new folder are limited to the user who created that folder.

Logging on to AppleShare

A Mac connected via AppleTalk to an AppleShare server is called a Macintosh workstation. To use a server volume or folder, the workstation Mac must be connected to that server first. The Chooser desk accessory is used to do this. When working with AppleShare, the Chooser presents an icon in its left-hand window, as shown in Fig. 9-8.

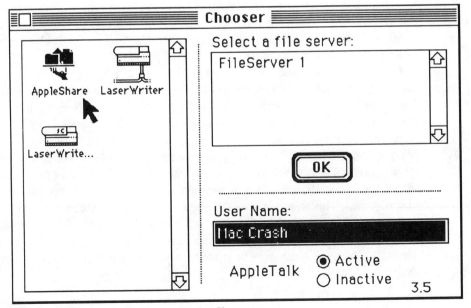

Fig. 9-8. Selecting AppleShare with the Chooser.

This icon represents the AppleShare servers on the network. If you click on the icon, the Chooser's right-hand window will display a list of servers on the network. If additional zones are available, an additional window will appear, showing the various zones. If you select one of those servers and click on the OK button, a new window will appear, asking how you want to connect to the server, as shown in Fig. 9-9.

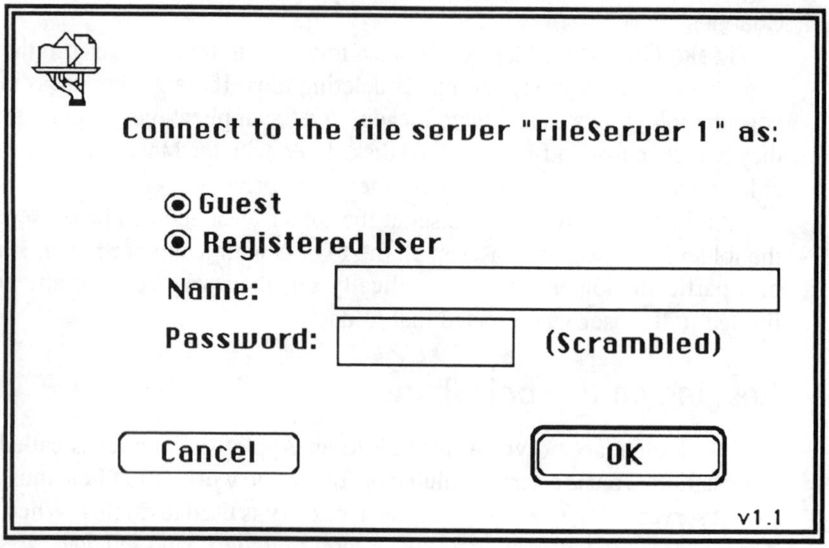

Connect to the file server "FileServer 1" as:

⊙ Guest
⊙ Registered User
Name:
Password: (Scrambled)

Cancel   OK

v1.1

Fig. 9-9. Connecting to the file server.

If you are connecting as a registered user, you must type in your network name and the password. The password appears scrambled to prevent unauthorized access by people who might be looking over your shoulder. Clicking on the OK button brings up the window shown in Fig. 9-10.

 Those who are particularly security conscious will be pleased to know that the password is protected by DES encryption. This is a very hard to untangle method of data scrambling. Even if someone was using electronic eavesdropping to listen in on your network and gain access to passwords they would be unlikely to be able to unencrypt the AppleTalk password.

The window in Fig. 9-10 shows the volumes that the server has made available to the network and asks which volume you want. A box to the right of the volume name allows you to specify volumes that are mounted automatically when the workstation Mac is started. This feature allows the normal use of server volumes with the System, so that you do not need to log onto that volume every time the System is started. At startup, AppleShare will just request your password, then connect to the server automatically. The System can even be made to remember the password and enter it automatically.

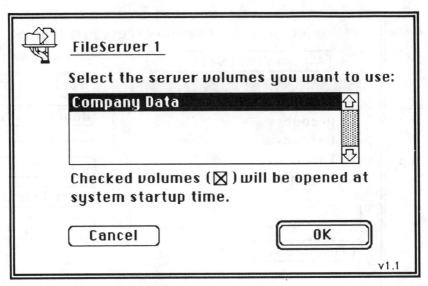

Fig. 9-10. Selecting volumes on the file server.

Working on AppleShare

Once the workstation Mac is connected to the server, the Mac functions as it did before. The server volumes can be accessed using standard Mac methods. It appears to the users and to software as if it were simply another disk connected directly to the Mac. If you no longer want to use a server volume, then you must drag the icon for that volume into the trash. The Finder will release the volume, and the server will be aware that the volume is no longer in use.

To allow users to review and change the access privileges for a folder, Apple Share uses another desk accessory, called Access Privileges, the initial screen of which is shown in Fig. 9-11.

The scrolling window shows all the folders at the current level of the server volume. You can scroll through this list of folders, open other folders, or use the standard Mac techniques for viewing other folders higher up in the folder hierarchy. Double-clicking on a folder opens it. When you have found the folder whose privileges you want to review or change, click on the Folder Info button.

The next window, shown in Fig. 9-12, has three sections. The top panel shows the name of the folder and the volume it is on, along with your user name and your privileges for that folder. The middle section shows who owns the folder, that is, the folder's creator. If you created the folder, then your name will appear here. Checking boxes in the middle section allows those privileges for the item listed at the top of the window. If you want to assign privileges for a different group, type the name of the group in the box above. To work with a different folder, you click the View Another button, and you return to the folder selection menu.

Folders You Create. When you first create a folder, AppleShare automatically makes this a private folder. As the owner, you will be able to see folders, see files, and

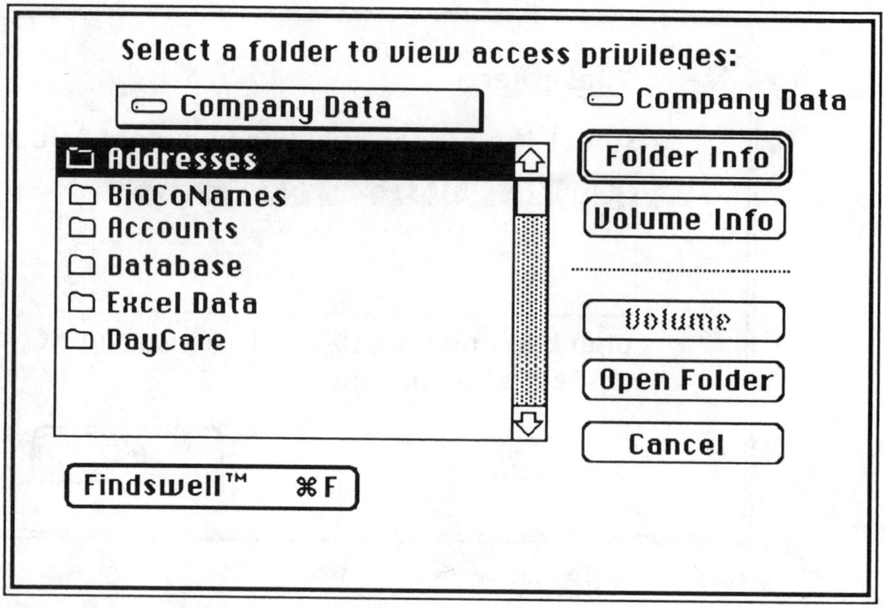

Select a folder to view access privileges:

⊂ Company Data   ⊂ Company Data

🗀 **Addresses** ⇧	(**Folder Info**)
🗀 BioCoNames	(**Volume Info**)
🗀 Accounts	
🗀 Database	
🗀 Excel Data	(Volume)
🗀 DayCare	(**Open Folder**)
⇩	(**Cancel**)

(Findswell™   ⌘ F)

Fig. 9-11. Using the Access Privileges DA.

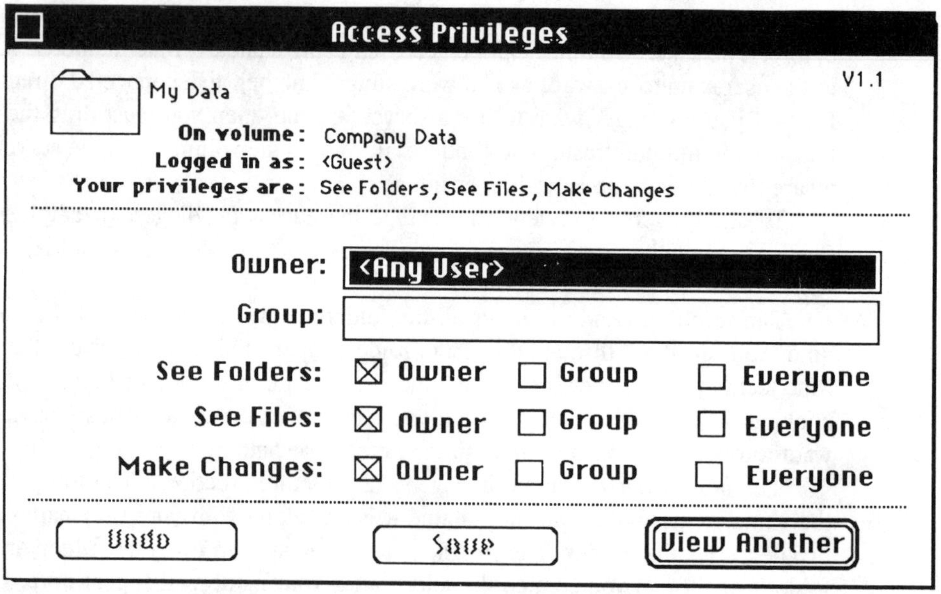

Access Privileges

🗀 My Data   V1.1

On volume : Company Data
Logged in as : <Guest>
Your privileges are : See Folders, See Files, Make Changes

Owner: [<Any User>]

Group: [ ]

See Folders:	☒ Owner	☐ Group	☐ Everyone
See Files:	☒ Owner	☐ Group	☐ Everyone
Make Changes:	☒ Owner	☐ Group	☐ Everyone

(Undo)   (Save)   (**View Another**)

Fig. 9-12. Setting access privileges.

make changes to the items in the folder. No other privileges, for a group or for everyone, are assigned automatically. This is a level of security since AppleShare assumes you are creating private, not public, data. To make that data available to others, you have to take deliberate action. However, if you are logged onto the server as a guest, all the folders you create are automatically public. Everyone has all privileges for these folders, and you are not allowed to change those privileges.

Folders Created by Others. If you are viewing the privileges of a folder created by someone else, this display is quite different, as you can see from Fig. 9-13. The middle panel of the window now shows the name of the owner of the folder and of which group he or she is a member. Because you are not the creator of the folder, you cannot change its access privileges, and those options are not presented.

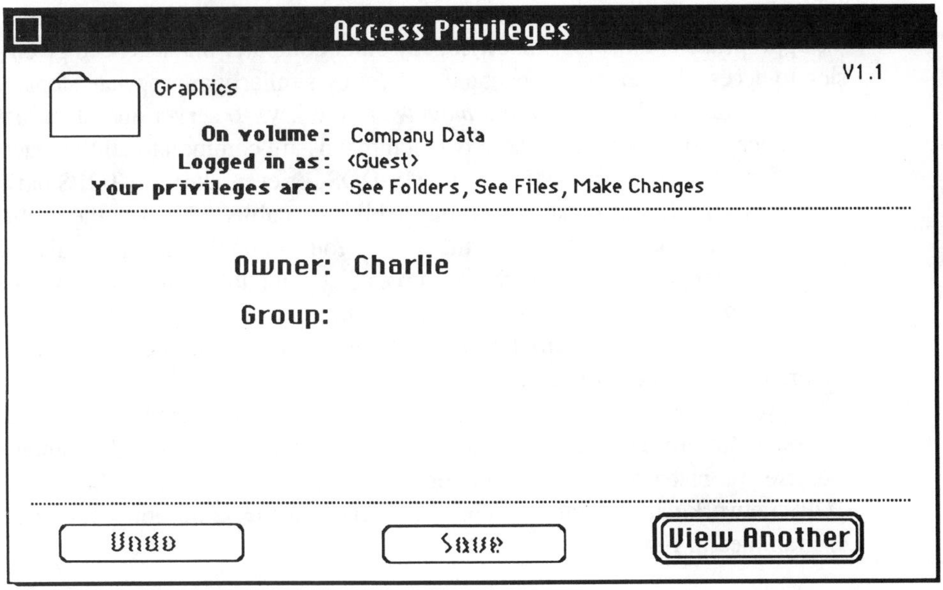

```
┌─────────────────────────────────────────────────────────────────┐
│ ☐                        Access Privileges                        │
│                                                           V1.1    │
│   ┌──────┐  Graphics                                              │
│   │      │        On volume :  Company Data                       │
│   └──────┘    Logged in as :  <Guest>                            │
│          Your privileges are :  See Folders, See Files, Make Changes │
│   ······································································ │
│                                                                   │
│            Owner:  Charlie                                        │
│                                                                   │
│            Group:                                                 │
│                                                                   │
│                                                                   │
│   ······································································ │
│   ┌──────────────┐   ┌──────────────┐   ┌──────────────┐        │
│   │     Undo     │   │     Save     │   │ View Another │        │
│   └──────────────┘   └──────────────┘   └──────────────┘        │
└─────────────────────────────────────────────────────────────────┘
```

Fig. 9-13. Privileges in a folder created by someone else.

BASIC TOPS/MACINTOSH OPERATION

Strictly speaking, TOPS/Macintosh is the software that enables TOPS networking on a Macintosh. Other varieties of TOPS include TOPS/DOS, which runs on IBM PCs. All versions of TOPS can run on the LocalTalk cabling that is built into Macintoshes. To create a TOPS network, you connect two Macs through their LocalTalk ports, load a copy of TOPS/Macintosh into each one, and begin networking.

TOPS Teleconnectors are used to connect LocalTalk ports on Macintoshes, LaserWriters, and FlashCards to the actual network wiring. The TOPS FlashBox can be used to connect LocalTalk ports on Macintoshes to the network while at the same time implementing the higher speed of FlashTalk. Each station that is to communicate via the TOPS network must have its own copy of the TOPS software. If you are connecting an MS/PC-DOS based computer then you must have a copy of TOPS/DOS. If you are connecting a Macintosh, you must have a copy of TOPS/Macintosh. Although TOPS is not copy protected, this does not mean that you can buy one TOPS software package and make one copy for each of the stations on the network. The TOPS licensing agreement requires that you buy a copy of the software for each station. Each software package has a serial number that identifies the station on which the program is installed. If a station with the same number as one that is already on the network attempts to connect to the network, TOPS denies network access.

Access to Files

The two basic states of computers on a TOPS network are servers and clients. On a TOPS network, any computer user can make his or her computer a server by issuing the appropriate commands. Likewise, any other computer that has been given permission to access the server can become a client by similarly appropriate steps.

Two commands, *publish* and *mount*, are the keys to server and client activities. The concepts represented by these two commands are common to all the machines on a TOPS network, whether Macintosh, MS-DOS, or even Unix. In TOPS parlance, to become a server, you make something public, or publish. To become a client, you mount what has been published by the server. You can publish an entire disk or only a selected folder. TOPS refers to the resources that you publish or mount as *volumes*. A volume can be either an entire disk, or just a folder or directory. Note that it is the disks and folders that are published or mounted, and not the files. Volumes are containers in which files are stored.

If you choose to publish a folder or an entire disk and therefore become a server, that does not prevent you from also mounting something published by another user. Nor are you restricted to publishing or mounting only one volume. So a station on a TOPS network can be both a client and a server at the same time. You can see this diagrammed in Fig. 9-14.

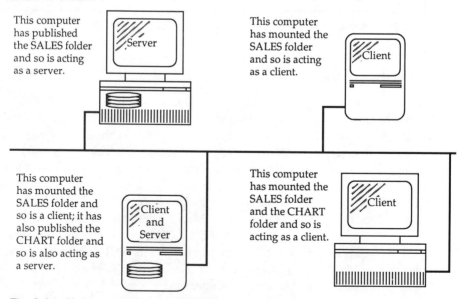

Fig. 9-14. Client and server on a TOPS network.

Some applications might always need a particular volume published. TOPS accommodates this need with automatic publishing features that can publish a specified volume at the time the server boots. Mounting can also be automated; however, timing becomes important when auto-mounting. The server needs to be allowed to start first and finish publishing before the client auto-mounts.

Inter-Brand Networking

Users whose experience is limited to just one kind of machine like the Macintosh, but not MS-DOS, or vice versa, need not be deterred from mounting volumes on the other machines. The user who mounts a volume over the network will see and use the volume as they would any other disk on their own machine. In Fig. 9-15, you can see the TOPS DA after a Mac user has mounted a PC volume called UTILITY (note that MacCrash is the local Mac hard drive, which is shaded out in this screen).

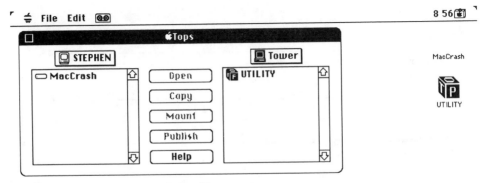

Fig. 9-15. A PC drive mounted on a Mac.

To an MS-DOS user the mounted volumes are available as drive letters, such as a drive E, F, and so on. In Fig. 9-16, you can see a directory listing from a PC, showing some of the contents of a Macintosh system folder.

At first the names appear garbled, but this merely reflects the differences between the DOS and Macintosh file naming conventions (DOS does not allow file names as long as those permitted on the Mac, and all file names are stored in capital letters). This directory listing was produced with the dir/w command. If the regular dir command is used, then the file size and date/time information is shown. TOPS also provides utility programs to help DOS users handle Macintosh files.

To a Mac user, the PC's drive appears as just another icon on the desktop. The icon is in the shape of a cube, as seen in Fig. 9-15. As you can see from Fig. 9-17, DOS files are shown with PC icons, while any Macintosh files stored on the PC appear with their normal Mac icons.

A PC drive mounted by TOPS acts like a regular Macintosh drive even though the server to which the volume belongs is a different kind of machine.

With the publishing and mounting commands, users control what they want to do

```
$ C:\>dir J: /w

Volume in drive J is System Fold
Directory of   J:\

ALDUS_PR        APPLE_FI        APPLESHA        BACKGROU        CANVAS_P
CAPTURE         CLARIS_F        CLIPBOAR        COLOR           CPSDELET
DAJHANDL        DCA-RFT0        FILEMAKE        FINDER          FINDER_S
FINDER(K        FONTS           GENERAL         GENERAL   APD   INTERBAS
KEY_LAYO        KEYBOARD        KOLOR           LASER_PR        LASERWRI
LASERWRI  APD   LASERWR0        MACROMAK        MACROMA0        MACROS
MACWRITE        MACWRIT0        MAIN_DIC        MAP             MENU_CLO 0
MONITORS        MOUSE           MULTIFIN        PAGEMAKE 0_D    PC_ICON
PMUSUSER  OLD   PMUSUSER  TXT   PYRO!-          QD2       LOG   RESUME_E
SCRAPBOO        SOFTTALK        SOUND           SPOOL           START_TO
STARTUP_        SUITCASE        (SYSTEM)        TOPS            TOPS_DA
TOPS_DIR        TOPS_HEL        TOPS_KEY        TOPS_PRE        UNIX_ICO
USER_DIC        VMS_ICON        WORD_SET        WP_100    2_D
       64 File(s)   39665664 bytes free

$ C:\>
```

Fig. 9-16. Mac files as seen on a PC.

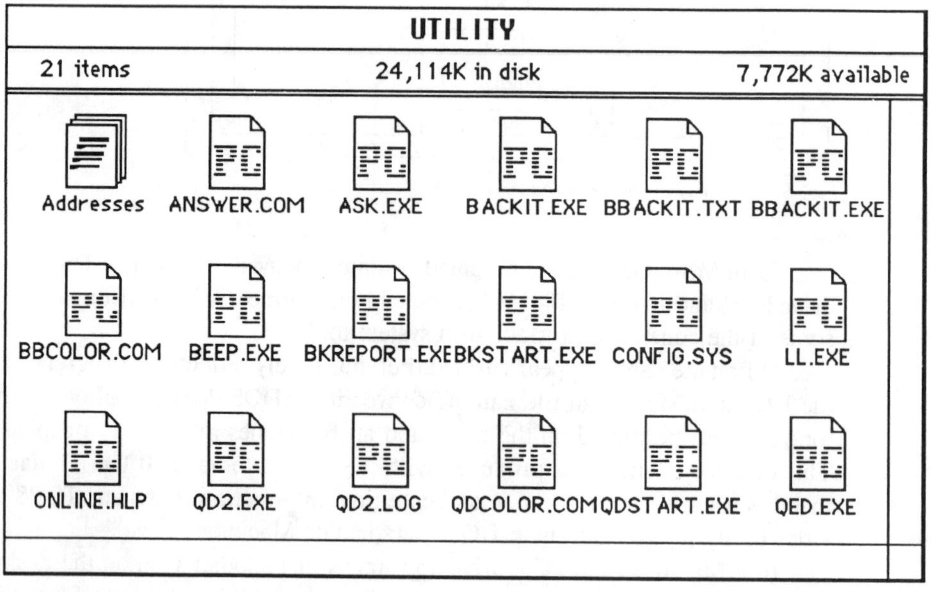

Fig. 9-17. IBM files as seen on a Mac.

on the network. Users possessing information that others need to share publish that information, and those others have access to it. There is no need to copy data to floppy disks to share it, and there is no particular need to store data on a central server.

A Typical Session

Suppose that you want to make some of your FileMaker data files available to another user on a TOPS network. You first make sure that the files are in a folder that contains no files besides those that you want the other user to see. Then you publish the folder, using the TOPS DA. This allows you to issue network commands without leaving an application. The TOPS DA lists the folders on the desktop, as shown in Fig. 9-18.

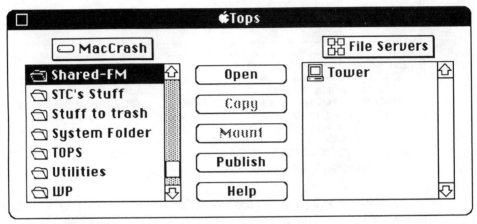

Fig. 9-18. Publishing a volume on the Mac.

When you select a folder in the list, such as Shared-FM, the Publish command is "ungrayed," and you can click on it to publish the volume. After that the folder appears with a special symbol next to it in TOPS DA list. As soon as the folder is published, it is available to other users.

When other users run TOPS DA on their systems, your Mac will appear in the File Servers column on the right. In Fig. 9-18, you can see a PC called Tower that is currently acting as a file server. The name you chose for your network identity when setting up TOPS/Macintosh will appear in the list next to Mac icon. The other users can then click Open to see what volumes you have published. They can then select the Shared-FM folder and click Mount. Your folder Shared-FM will appear as an additional drive on those computers that mount it, and users can open the files there.

In a situation where a PC is being used as a file server on the network, the PC user needs to load TOPS/DOS and publish the necessary parts of the server's hard disk so that others can mount them. Loading TOPS/DOS and publishing one or more volumes involves a series of steps that can be completely automated with what DOS users refer to as batch files. Indeed, if the file server is set up properly, simply turning it on will cause the necessary volumes to be published. In Fig. 9-19, you can see part of the TOPSMENU program that is the TOPS/DOS equivalent of the TOPS DA.

The PC has been called Tower. Users of DOS will recognize that a directory called FM on drive D has been published (D:\FM). The user gave this the simple

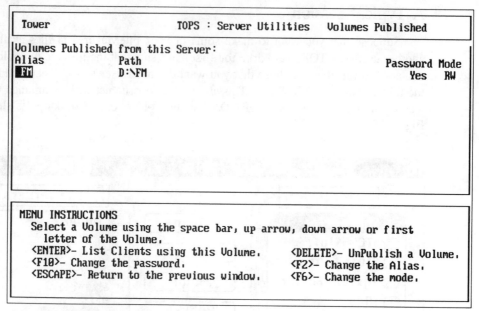

Fig. 9-19. Publishing a volume on the PC.

alias FM and made it password protected. The designation RW means that users who mount this volume can read data from, and write data to, this volume.

Password protection and limited read/write privileges can be set when publishing Mac volumes as well as PC volumes. All you have to do is hold down the Option key when clicking Publish.

Back on the Mac, you can use the TOPS DA to list the available file servers, and Tower will be there. Open Tower and you will find FM, as shown in Fig. 9-20.

Select FM and click Mount, and the volume will be mounted as disk for you to use, *if* you have the password (Fig. 9-21).

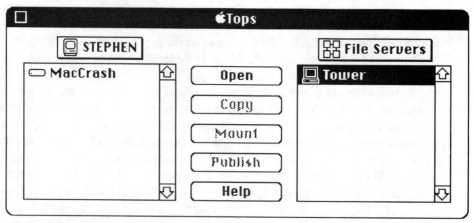

Fig. 9-20. Mounting the PC volume.

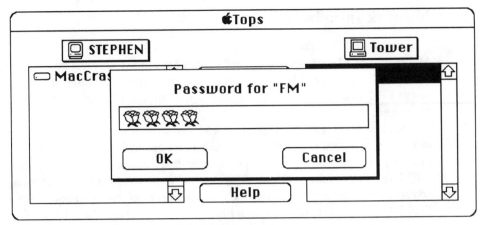

Fig. 9-21. Password protection while mounting a volume.

To unmount a TOPS volume mounted on a Mac, you make sure that all files you opened from that volume are closed, and then you drag the drive/volume icon to the trash, just as you would to eject a floppy disk.

Privacy is ensured by users only publishing what they want others to access. When you mount the volume called FM from the PC called Tower, that in no way allows you to get at files other than those in FM. A further level of privacy is provided by the password. Only holders of the correct password can mount volumes. If you are using TOPS to network FileMaker, these security features add a level of safety above and beyond those available within FileMaker when it is in network mode.

NETWORKING FILEMAKER

You can network with FileMaker and share your FileMaker files if you have Macintosh, FileMaker, and a network. For the network, you can use the simple AppleTalk connection built into your Mac or more sophisticated network systems such as AppleShare, TOPS, or indeed, any other AppleTalk compatible network.

Several users can load the same copy of FileMaker stored on a server. FileMaker refers to this as *multi-launch* operating. Alternatively, each user can load their own copy of FileMaker and just share data files across the network, referred to as *multi-user* operations. Bear in mind that your FileMaker licensing agreement allows only one person at a time to use a single FileMaker package. You must own the same number of copies of FileMaker as the number of people using FileMaker on the network.

The advantage of an AppleShare or TOPS network over a simple AppleTalk network is that any user can host a file residing on a file server or in a folder mounted using TOPS. With just an AppleTalk network, a user can host only those files residing on their own Macintosh. However, because Macintoshes come with AppleTalk built in, setting up an AppleTalk network and using it to share your FileMaker data is probably the quickest way to get into database networking.

Network Installation

To install FileMaker for multi-launch purposes, you only need to install File-Maker on one Macintosh with a hard disk. This Macintosh must be set up as a file server with a program like AppleShare, or as a Macintosh with TOPS installed. To install FileMaker for multi-user purposes, you can install FileMaker on each user's Macintosh.

Shared Hard Disk. To install FileMaker so that several users can launch the same copy, you need to create a FileMaker folder on a networked Mac or a FileMaker directory on a networked PC. Copy the FileMaker application file from the original FileMaker disk to your new folder/directory. If you are copying FileMaker onto a PC, you should use the network commands to copy carry out this operation. Also copy the FileMaker Help file to the new folder because the FileMaker Help file must be in the same folder as the FileMaker application if you want to access it from the Help menu. Be sure to use the most up-to-date version of the AppleTalk System resource. Also make sure that the printing resource for your printer is located in the System folder on the Macintosh from which you are printing.

The computer to which you have copied the FileMaker application will act as the FileMaker server to FileMaker clients. All that the operator of the server has to do in order for clients to launch FileMaker is to make the folder/directory available to the network. If you are using a distributed-server network like FileMaker, then the person operating the server can also launch FileMaker and use it.

Local Hard Disk. If you have installed the FileMaker application on your own hard disk, you might want to leave it there and launch your own copy of the program in the normal manner, using a server just for file storage. This results in faster operation. FileMaker responds more slowly with more people using the same copy at the same time. Later in this chapter tables can help you organize work to minimize network constraints.

Floppy Disk Use. If your computer has no hard disk drive, you can still use File-Maker on a network. First load the network software to connect to the file server. Then you load the FileMaker application. You can either launch your own copy of the application from floppy disk, or you can load a copy of FileMaker stored on the file server. How you organize your disk for this operation will depend on the size of the network software files and the capacity of your floppy disk. You should not install FileMaker for multi-launch purposes without a hard disk as the response time when using the program would be unacceptable.

Basic FileMaker Network Commands

You only need to learn a few new FileMaker commands to begin sharing files on a network. The first step is to open a file that other users want access. The first command to look at is the Exclusive item in the File menu, seen in Fig. 9-22.

In normal, nonnetwork mode this item has a check mark next to it, meaning that only you can use the current file. If you select this item when the check mark is

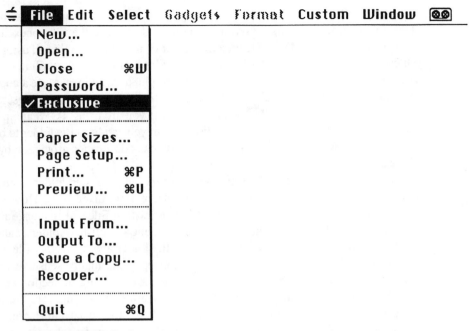

Fig. 9-22. The Exclusive item.

present, you will remove the check mark. This means that multiple users can share the current file.

The first person to open a file is called the *host*. If you are using just an AppleTalk network, a user can host only those files residing on his or her own Macintosh. If you are using a file server, such as AppleShare or TOPS, anyone can host a file residing on the file server or in a folder mounted by TOPS. All subsequent users are *guest* users.

Guests can access nonexclusive files open on other Macintoshes using the Network button in FileMaker's File Open dialog box. Once the file is opened by the guest, the host and the guest can begin sharing the same information residing in the host's file. All the additions, deletions, and modifications made to the file appear in each user's window and are saved to the disk from which the host opened the file.

File Access

The opportunity for multiple users to share the same information offers great potential. One Mac could be used to create invoices with FileMaker, while another could use FileMaker to update an inventory database. However, in some situations, you might want to limit who can open your files and see your information. For example, as a personnel manager working with a file listing salaries, you would want to limit access to the file. When networking FileMaker, you have ample protection for the privacy of data, and multiple levels of access control.

To make a FileMaker file available to multiple users, you must first open the file. This file must be stored on a Macintosh that you are allowed to use, on a file server such as AppleShare to which you have been granted access, or in a folder published by TOPS to which you have the password. You must then make the file nonexclusive.

If you place a FileMaker file on a file server or in a folder published using TOPS, you can set different limits on who can access files and folders depending upon your network system. For example, if you are using AppleShare and you place a copy of the FileMaker application or a FileMaker file on the file server, you can limit users to See Folders, See Files, or Make Changes to a folder. If you are using TOPS and publish a folder containing the FileMaker application or file, you can limit the folder to be Write-Protected, One Writer Only, or Many Writers. You can add further protection by means of a password.

Limiting who can access files on a server or mount published folders using TOPS is the first step towards controlling the sharing of FileMaker files. However, you might also want to limit who can open a file from within FileMaker. For example, if you are using TOPS, you might limit who can mount a published folder containing a highly sensitive file. But if one person mounts the folder and opens that file and does not check the Exclusive command, a guest can open the highly sensitive file from within FileMaker using the Network button, thus avoiding the protection set on the published folder. Using the following FileMaker features, you can avoid "uninvited" guests by limiting who can open a specific FileMaker file, what information can be seen when the file is open, and what actions can be performed on the data in the file.

Passwords and Other Protection

You use the FileMaker Password command to limit who can open and use your file. Passwords are word keys that unlock different levels of access to a file, and you can set the levels, choose the passwords, and decide who to give them to. After you assign password to a file, no matter where a user opens the file, from within File Maker, the Finder, or a folder mounted using TOPS, FileMaker will ask for a password before opening the file. Figure 9-23 shows where the user is opening the file called Addresses.

When creating passwords you assign privileges or *access rights* that allow users to perform actions in the file. Five different access rights are provided when creating a password. You can create any number of passwords with as many levels of access that

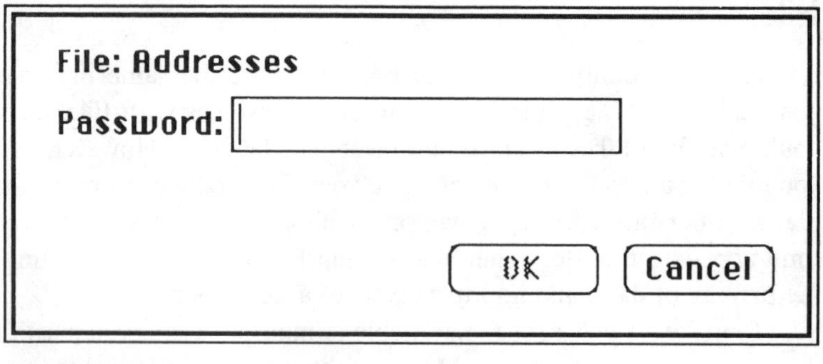

Fig. 9-23. The password request.

you want as long as you have access to the entire file. You can also change and delete passwords.

FileMaker allows you to restrict the information a user can actually see once a file has been opened. This is done by creating confidential layouts, available only to users with the correct password. By creating a password, making a layout confidential, and not giving a user access to confidential layouts, you can limit what information a user can see. For example, if a file contains a confidential layout and your password does not let you view confidential layouts, all objects on the confidential layout appear in gray, as shown in Fig. 9-24.

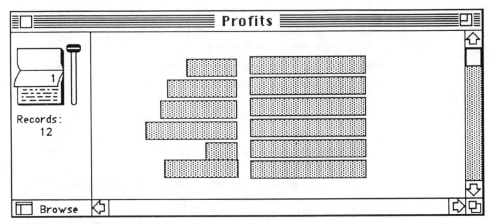

Fig. 9-24. A confidential layout.

Passwords also allow you fairly detailed control over the actions that can be performed. For example, if a password lets a user only browse records, that user cannot print field definitions or add records to the file. The five separate access rights can be combined in many different ways to create a variety of levels of access. You can create one password that is for browsing and editing records while another lets a user browse and edit records, use confidential layouts, and also design layouts.

One other level of control in FileMaker is the ability to assign a set of access rights to *no password*. This means that a user can open a file without typing a password and receive a certain set of access rights to the file. This is useful for making a file available to numerous users while reserving entire access to yourself so that operations such as defining fields can only be performed by you.

Creating a Password

Suppose you have just created a FileMaker database and entered the first few records. You want to share the file with other users on the network. Having first made sure that Exclusive is not checked, you select Password from the File menu. Because there are as yet no passwords for this file, the dialog box that you see at first is rather empty (Fig. 9-25).

Later, this dialog box will list the passwords you have created for the file and you

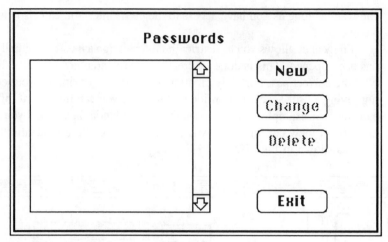

Fig. 9-25. An empty password list.

can select Change to alter a password or Delete to remove one. At this point, however, you want to select New. FileMaker presents the dialog box seen in Fig. 9-26, which is used to type the password and define the access rights associated with it.

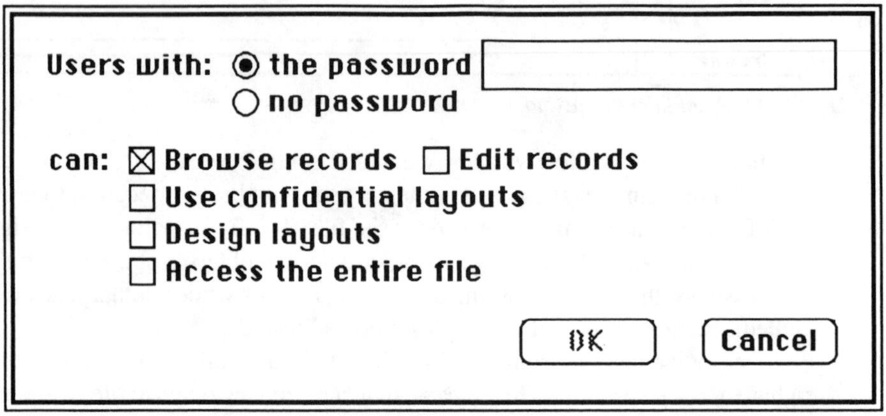

Fig. 9-26. The password definition dialog box.

The password is typed in the box. FileMaker passwords can be up to 31 characters in length, although only about 20 will appear in the password entry box at one time and more than 10 characters is probably redundant. FileMaker passwords are not case sensitive, so using Apple will mean that both APPLE and apple will be accepted. You can use the Option characters, such as Option−3 for the £, and punctuation characters are allowed, as well as numbers. For more on password design, see the later section on "Additional Security."

Note the two radio buttons in Fig. 9-26 called the password and no password. The effects of selecting no password are described in a moment. The five different rights that you can choose from are activated by checking the boxes. The default setting is simply Browse records. The rights are:

- Browse Records—Allows a user to view to records and layouts that are not confidential, to sort records, and to find information. This is the preset or default access right.
- Edit Records—Allows a user to add new records and delete and modify existing records in a file. When you choose Edit Records, FileMaker automatically chooses Browse Records.
- Use Confidential Layouts—Allows a user to view records using layouts checked as Confidential in the Gadgets menu. When you choose Use Confidential Layouts, FileMaker automatically chooses Browse Records for you.
- Design Layouts—Allows a user to create new layouts and modify existing layouts, including any layouts checked as Confidential in the Gadgets menu. When you choose Design Layouts, FileMaker automatically chooses Browse Records and Use Confidential Layouts for you.
- Access the Entire File—Allows users to browse and edit records and create new and modify existing layouts (including any layouts checked as Confidential in the Gadgets menu). When creating passwords, you must create at least one password with access to the entire file. When you choose Access the Entire File, FileMaker automatically chooses all of the other access rights.

You can see a password entered and several rights selected in the dialog box shown in Fig. 9-27. In this case, anyone who knows the password Alpha@630 can browse and edit records, including fields protected by confidential layouts. The holder of this password cannot create new layouts. You might want to create a different password for each user who needs access to your file.

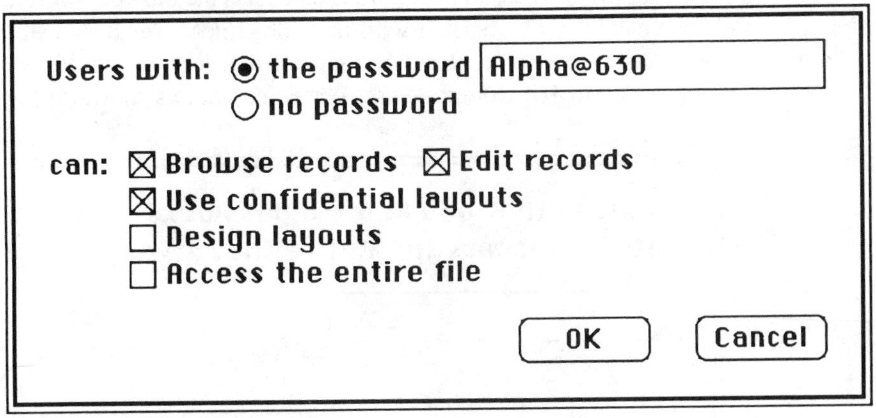

```
Users with:  ● the password  Alpha@630
             ○ no password

can:  ☒ Browse records  ☒ Edit records
      ☒ Use confidential layouts
      ☐ Design layouts
      ☐ Access the entire file

                                 [  OK  ]  [ Cancel ]
```

Fig. 9-27. A completed password entry.

After selecting the rights you want to be associated with the password, you click OK and are returned to the password list. The password you have created will be listed there. You can select Change to alter it, Delete to remove it, or Exit to return to the file.

If you already have access to the entire file, which is the case if you have just created it, you can create as many different passwords as you want. If you like, each one can have a different combination of access rights; however, you must create at least one password that lets you access the entire file. If you return to the list and click Exit, FileMaker checks to see that there is a password with complete access rights. If there is not, the warning seen in Fig. 9-28 is displayed.

In this set of passwords, no user can access the entire file. At least one user must be able to access the entire file.

OK

Fig. 9-28. Password warning.

As you can see in Fig. 9-27, you can also assign a set of access rights to no password. This means that any user can open a file and work with it based on a set of access rights you have chosen without typing any password.

We suppose it goes without saying that it is important to remember your passwords, but we'll say it anyway: *Remember your passwords*! If you forget a password, you could cripple your access to a file or even seal it forever. One password always exists that gives access to the entire file. This is the only password that permits you to change passwords associated with that file. FileMaker does help you in this regard, by requiring you to reenter the password that lets you access the entire file before it allows you to exit from the Password command, as shown in Fig. 9-29.

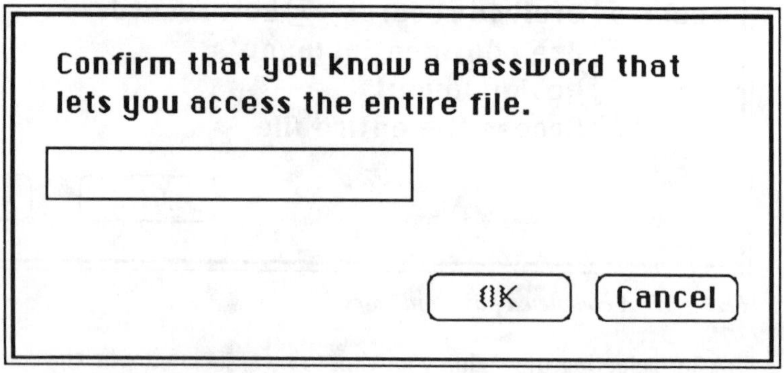

Confirm that you know a password that lets you access the entire file.

OK   Cancel

Fig. 9-29. Master password confirmation.

Note that if you choose no password and assign entire access to the file, File-Maker will allow users to open the file as if you never used the Password command. This is because no password means just that: No word is necessary to receive the assigned access rights. If you choose no password and you assign limited access rights, meaning anything other than entire access, FileMaker will display a special dialog box to anyone opening the file, as shown in Fig. 9-30.

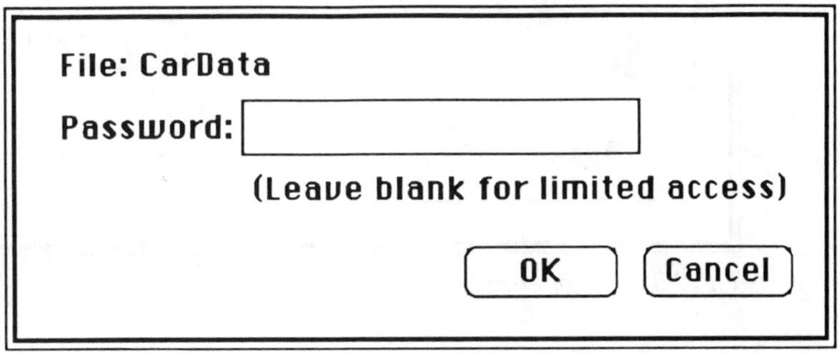

```
┌─────────────────────────────────────────────────┐
│  ┌───────────────────────────────────────────┐  │
│  │                                           │  │
│  │  File: CarData                            │  │
│  │  Password: ┌──────────────────────────┐   │  │
│  │            │                          │   │  │
│  │            └──────────────────────────┘   │  │
│  │       (Leave blank for limited access)    │  │
│  │                                           │  │
│  │              ( OK )   ( Cancel )          │  │
│  │                                           │  │
│  └───────────────────────────────────────────┘  │
└─────────────────────────────────────────────────┘
```

Fig. 9-30. The no password message.

This tells users that by clicking OK without first entering a password they can use the file, but their rights are limited. Unfortunately, FileMaker does not say exactly how limited the rights are. They may just be browsing rights, or they might include editing. At this point the user can proceed or ask for someone for a password that provides more complete access. For example, if you ask someone to update the inventory file and they get this message, they might come back to you and ask for a password that will allow fuller access. Nevertheless, the no password option is useful for making a file freely available to users while reserving to yourself such basic operations as defining fields.

Changing Access Rights

If you can access the entire file, you can change the access rights for any password you want. To do this you first choose Password from the File menu. A list of existing passwords appears, like the one in Fig. 9-31.

Select the password you want to modify and click the Change button. FileMaker displays a dialog box like the one in Fig. 9-32.

Edit the selections to make your changes. You can edit the password to which the access rights are assigned. You can click the check boxes for the various access rights. When you are ready, click the OK button and FileMaker will return you to the password listing dialog box. You can continue using this dialog box or Exit. Before the Exit command is executed, FileMaker checks to make sure that there is at least one password that lets you access the entire file and makes you create one if one does not already exist. If you changed any passwords, FileMaker also asks you to confirm that you know a password that lets you access the entire file.

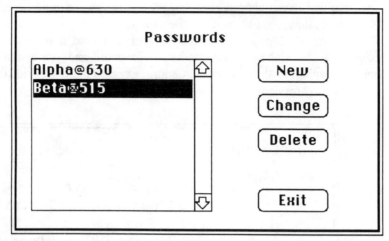

Fig. 9-31. List of existing passwords.

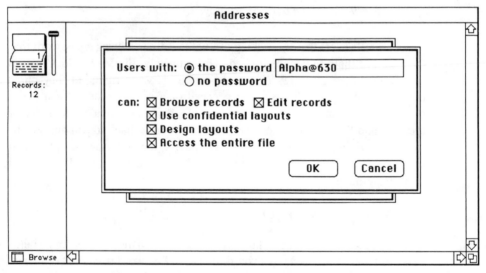

Fig. 9-32. Making changes to a password.

Passwords in Action

If you are creating passwords while others are using the file, the current users are not affected by it. However, FileMaker will ask any subsequent users for a password. If you do not have access to an entire file and you choose the Password command from the File menu, FileMaker displays the dialog box shown in Fig. 9-33. This allows you to change your password but not your access rights.

When a user selects the Open command to use a file that is password protected, FileMaker asks for a password, using a dialog box shown in Fig. 9-34.

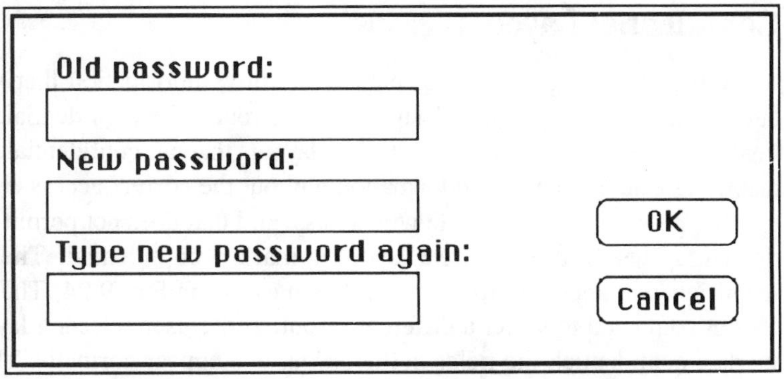

Old password:

New password:

OK

Type new password again:

Cancel

Fig. 9-33. Changing a password.

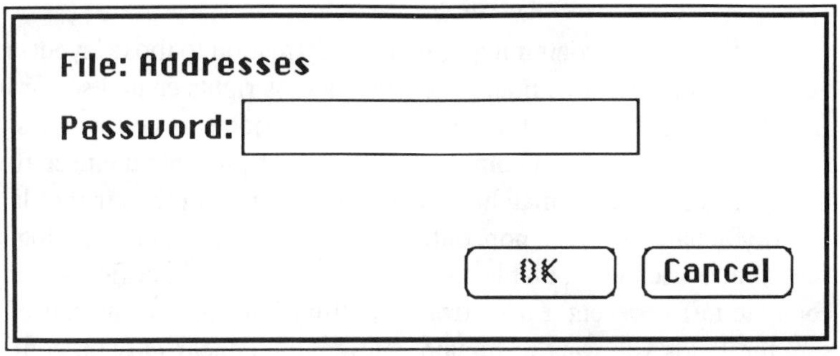

File: Addresses

Password:

OK   Cancel

Fig. 9-34. The password request.

⚠ This password is incorrect.

Try Again   Cancel

Fig. 9-35. The Try Again dialog box.

The user types the password that he or she has been given and clicks OK. If the password is incorrect, FileMaker offers the change to try again or abandon the attempt to access the file, using the dialog box shown in Fig. 9-35.

FileMaker allows you to make repeated attempts to guess the password, which is helpful if you have forgotten it, but a weakness in the security system. Although the error sound is made each time you fail to enter the correct word, you can turn off the sound and sit trying passwords until you guess the right one.

 Passwords are not just for networking. You can use passwords on FileMaker databases at any time. This will prevent someone from using the file while you are away from your desk.

Confidential Layouts

When designing a layout displaying sensitive information that you do not want other users to view, you can designate that layout to be confidential. By limiting the fields containing sensitive information to layouts that are confidential, you are assured that users cannot view that information without the correct access rights.

Suppose a user opens a file with a password that does not permit the use of confidential layouts, and the current layout is marked confidential. The fields and field identifiers will appear grayed out, as shown earlier in Fig. 9-24. The user can use the Layout command to select a different layout. If the user selects a layout that was not marked confidential, the fields in that layout will appear normally. This means that to maintain the confidentiality of a particular field, you would place that field only on confidential layouts. You cannot assign confidentiality to individual fields, only to layouts.

Limiting fields containing sensitive information to those layouts that are confidential assures that users without the correct access rights cannot see or use these fields in any way. If a user without access rights to confidential layouts tries to input information using the Input From command, FileMaker prevents the user from inputting data from files that contain matching fields that are not on the current layout.

If you have created a nonconfidential standard layout containing all of the fields in your file, a user will be able to input data into all of the fields using the Input From command. To prevent a user from inputting information into all of the fields, make sure the fields you want to remain confidential appear *only* on confidential layouts.

You designate a layout to be confidential by choosing the Confidential command from the Gadgets menu when in Layout mode. This is a check-mark command, like Exclusive. Remember that to secure the confidentiality of a layout and the information to be displayed on the Browse screen, you must also create a password limiting access to the confidential layout.

If a user without the proper access rights tries to use a confidential layout, File-Maker displays the objects on the layout screen in gray, including field names, thus preventing the user from deducing what type of information is stored in the file. The ability to add, edit, use, and view information through that layout is not available. In addition, a user without proper access rights cannot print the field definitions to see what the fields are.

FILE SHARING IN ACTION

The factors involved in sharing files include making a file available for multiple users, opening files, knowing where information is saved, sharing files, and quitting FileMaker. Remember that the first user to open a nonexclusive file is the host of that file. All subsequent users of the file are guests. Guests can open files using the Network button on the Open dialog.

The Network Signals

FileMaker uses two special symbols to indicate when network activity is affecting files and FileMaker operations. Additions, deletions, and change made to a file appear in each user's window and are saved to the file on the disk from which the file was opened. As FileMaker processes data across the network to update each user's window, the normal mouse pointer will temporarily acquire a second arrow head to let users know that updating is taking place.

Sort orders, find requests, and page setups are specific to each user. This allows each user to work with just the records they need (for example, all invoices dated within the last 7 days) in the order they need it (for example, in alphabetical order by customer last name). While FileMaker is processing another user's request to sort or find, the mouse pointer becomes a coffee cup. As you might imagine, this means that such requests can take some time to complete.

Files for Multiple Users

For two or more people to share the same file, the Exclusive command in the File menu must not be checked. In every new file you create, FileMaker automatically selects the Exclusive command. When a file is exclusive and a user has access to the entire file, all FileMaker operations are available to the user. The first step in making a file available to multiple users is to toggle the Exclusive command, removing the check mark and making the file nonexclusive.

You can make a nonexclusive file stored on your Mac available to multiple users in one of two ways. First you can keep the file open on your Macintosh. When you host a file like this, guests can open the file by using the Network button on the File Open dialog box. When you click on the Network button, FileMaker displays a list of all nonexclusive files open across the network. When a host and guest are using a file, only the host can make the file exclusive again.

The second approach is to place the file on a file server, such as AppleShare, or in a folder published using TOPS. Multiple users, both hosts and guests, can then open the file directly from the file server or a folder mounted using TOPS.

Files for the Single User

You can limit a file to one user only if you are the host, that is, the first user to open a file. First you toggle the Exclusive command, adding a check mark. If there are any guests using the file at the time, FileMaker lets you know with the message seen in Fig. 9-36.

You can ask those who are using the file to close it by clicking the Ask button. This results in a request being displayed on the screen of each user of the file, like the one seen in Fig. 9-37. As soon as the guests close the file, FileMaker checks the Exclusive command.

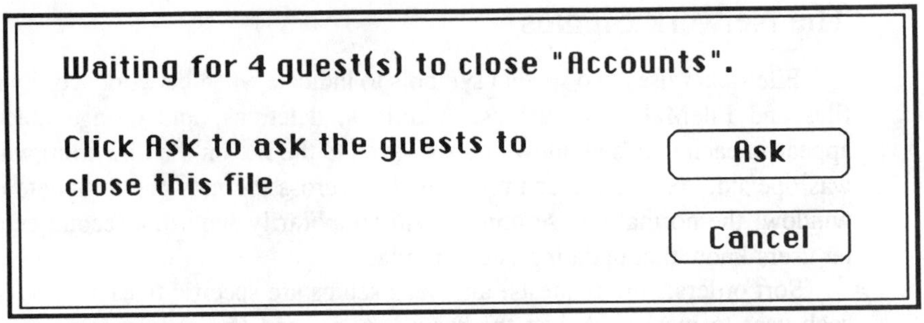

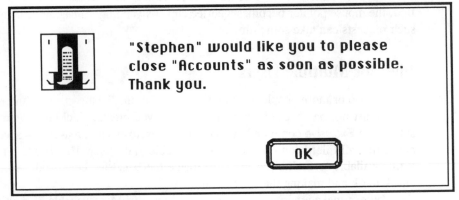

Fig. 9-36. Waiting for a file.

Fig. 9-37. The close file request.

Hosting a File

You open a file as a host as you normally would as a single user by double-click-ing on the file icon, or selecting a file on your own Mac, a file server, or a folder mounted using TOPS, and then using the Finder's or FileMaker's Open command. Bear in mind that AppleShare and TOPS present servers as extra drives on your Mac, so you will need to click the Drive button in the Open dialog box to see the files on the server.

When opening a file as a host, you should bear in mind the responsibilities associ-ated with opening the file first. The host must open any lookup files associated with the hosted file to ensure that the lookup files are available to any guests. When running FileMaker with MultiFinder, a host should only use applications that support back-ground processing and not switch to other applications besides FileMaker for long periods of time.

A few operations are best performed as a single user. These include using the Replace, View as List, Delete Multiple, Sort, Relookup, and Print commands in a file containing a large number of records. For more information, see "Operations Best Performed as a Single User" later in this chapter.

When you open a file as the host, you get the previous host's sorting order, find requests, page setup, and all changes made to the file by both the previous host and guests.

Opening a File as a Guest

A guest is the second or subsequent user to open the file. You use the Network button on the Open dialog to open a nonexclusive file as a guest from within File-Maker. As long as you have an AppleTalk network, you can open a file already open by using the Network button. If you have a file server or TOPS, you can also open a file as a guest as you normally would from the Finder as a single user by double-clicking on the file icon, or selecting a file on your disk, a file server, or a folder mounted using TOPS and then using the Finder's or FileMaker's Open command. Remember that to find a file on a file server such as AppleShare or in a folder mounted using TOPS, you use the Drive button on FileMaker's Open dialog box.

As guests, you might be mindful of the responsibilities associated with being a guest. You are using the file through the consent of the host. If the host asks a guest to close a file, network etiquette says you should comply. You should also close any files that you are not actively using. This improves performance for all users. In addition, a few operations are best performed as a single user. These include using the Replace, View as List, Delete Multiple, Relookup, Sort, and Print commands in a file containing a large number of records. For more information, see "Single User Operations" later in this chapter.

Opening Files with the Network Button

When you choose Open from FileMaker's File menu and click the Network button, FileMaker displays a list of all of the nonexclusive files open across the network, that is, open on other Macs, as shown in Fig. 9-38.

FileMaker also lists the name of the person hosting the file. FileMaker has a clever way of dealing with the possibility that two users might have the same name on a network. A temporary random number is added to the end of one of the duplicate names in this list. In this way, FileMaker recognizes each user by a different name.

When you select one of these files, the Open button becomes active. If you click Open and the file does not open, try opening the file a second time, holding down the Option key while clicking on the file. When you open a file as a guest, FileMaker tells you that you are a guest. As such, you get changes made to the file, but not the host's sort order, find requests, or page setup. For more information on what is saved to a file, see "Simultaneous File Use" later in this chapter.

Networking with MultiFinder

As you know, you can run FileMaker with MultiFinder, and you can network FileMaker under MultiFinder. However, when you are sharing files under Multi-Finder, you should run only applications that support background processing and use

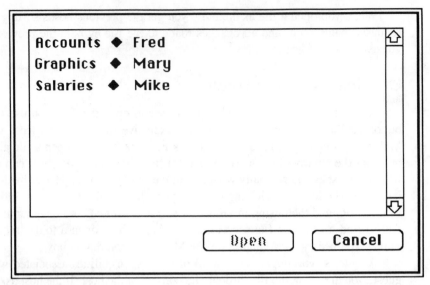

Fig. 9-38. Files open on the network.

these applications only for short periods of time. If you are the host of a file running FileMaker with MultiFinder and you switch to another application for ten minutes, guest use of the file will be impaired for those ten minutes. That is the good news! If you switch from FileMaker to an application that does not support background processing and start an operation that takes longer than two minutes, all users of the shared FileMaker file might be unexpectedly interrupted.

Closing and Saving Shared Files

As you know, FileMaker automatically saves files for you. This is handled through the host when the file is being shared, and only a host or a single user can use the Save a Copy command. For more information on what is saved to the file, see "Simultaneous File Use" later in this chapter.

Whether you are the host or the guest, you close files as you normally do when you are a single user. The only difference when sharing files is that a host cannot close a file unless all the guests close the file. If a host tries to close a file and guests are still using the file, FileMaker displays the dialog box seen in Fig. 9-36. To ask guests to leave the file, click the Ask button. After the host clicks the Ask button, the dialog in Fig. 9-37 appears in each guest's window. Network etiquette says that if a host asks a guest to close a file, the guest should comply. As soon as all the guests close a file, FileMaker closes the host's file.

Guests working under MultiFinder with another application in the foreground will not see the close file message; however, they will hear a beep. At that point, they can switch back to FileMaker and close the file. This feature should be explained to all users on the network who are likely to be running FileMaker under MultiFinder.

When networking FileMaker, you quit the application as you normally would as a single user. A guest can quit FileMaker at anytime, but hosts must wait for any guests to close the file. If a host tries to quit FileMaker, FileMaker checks to see if any guests are using any of the host's files. FileMaker displays the dialog box shown in Fig. 9-36 if there is a guest, and the host must click Ask to alert guests to close the shared file. As soon as the guests close the file, the host's Quit command is completed.

Simultaneous File Use

When host and guest have access to an entire file they can usually perform the same operations, ranging from adding records to creating passwords. However, some exceptions are described in this section and the accompanying tables. When you are sharing files, you are sharing the information contained in the files. You are sharing layouts and data. If one user modifies the data by deleting a record, adding a record, or changing the contents of a field, then the information you are sharing is changed. FileMaker automatically saves these changes to the file and updates each user's window to reflect these changes.

If your shared file contains summary fields and/or summary parts, FileMaker recalculates summaries only when you choose Browse, Preview, or Print. While File-Maker processes data across the network to update each user's window, the pointer has two arrow heads. This list shows the operations that both host and guest can perform and the results of which they share:

Add, delete, and modify records.
Add, delete, and modify layouts.
Create, delete, and change scripts.
Create, delete, and change passwords.
Set paper sizes.
Input from a FileMaker file.

Even though these operations are available to both the host and the guest, it makes sense that only one person can edit one record or layout at a time. In a file of 50 records, only one person can edit record 27. Others can browse record 27, but they cannot edit it until the current user is finished editing it. A person is considered to be finished using a record or layout when they have gone on to another record or layout, switched to a different screen, or pressed the Enter key.

FileMaker lets each user generate their own find requests, sort orders, and page setups. This means that one user can work with a set of ten found records, while another user is adding records, and yet another worker is browsing all the records sorted by name. While you are waiting for FileMaker to process another user's request, the pointer becomes a coffee cup. The following is a list of the operations that are specific to each user:

Sort records.
Find records.
Set page setups.

Hide windows.
Switching layouts.
Using scripts.

Even guests with access to an entire file are limited in certain respects. These are the operations that a guest cannot perform:

Make a file exclusive.
Define fields.
Input data from a text, BASIC, or SYLK file.
Save copies (copy, clone, compressed).
Output data to another file.

Note that if you are a guest creating a label layout, FileMaker automatically sets the page setup to the standard ImageWriter setup. If you are printing to a different printer, you must reset the page setup before you create the label layout. For this reason, you might want to capture the layout and page setup in a script.

Host Operations

Only a host can perform a few operations. When guests are sharing a file in which the host wants to perform one of these operations, the host must ask the guests to close the file. In all cases, except making a file exclusive, after the host has completed performing the intended operation, guest can reopen the file and continue working. The following is a list of the operations only a host can perform:

Make a file exclusive.
Define fields.
Input data from a text, BASIC, or SYLK file.
Save copies (copy, clone, compressed).
Output data to another file.

Single User Operations

Sometimes you might want to perform operations that either affect all of the records in the file, such as replacing field contents, or are affected by all of the records in the file, such as printing a summary report. Performing one of these operations can slow down the performance of the file for the other users. For example, if you want to use the Replace command, you will slow down performance for other users and there's the possibility of some records not getting the replacement value because another user could be editing a record at the same time you are replacing values. Or, if you print a summary of all the records in a file while a guest is deleting a record, your report might not be accurate. The following operations are best performed as a single user:

Delete multiple records.
Replace field contents.

Print records.
Sort a large number of records.
View a large number of records as a list.
Relookup information.
Recover files.

Shared File Saving

All additions, deletions, and modifications made to a file by the host and guests are saved to the file on the disk from which the file was opened. Because a shared file is always saved through the host and the sort orders, find requests, and page setups are not shared, FileMaker saves the host's sort order, find requests, and page setups but not those of guests. A guest does not see the sort order, find requests, or page setups that are saved for the host. If a guest wants to save a sort order, find request, or page setup, it should be captured in a script.

Table 9-1 summarizes the various limits on shared-file operations, showing which operations a host or guest can perform. When the results of an operation are specific to each user, the operation is designated *specific*. When results are shared by all users, the operation is designated *shared*.

Table 9-1. File Sharing Summary.

Operation	Host	Guest	Shared or Specific
Open a file	Yes	Yes	
Close a file	Yes	Yes	
Define fields	Yes	No	
Input non-FileMaker files	Yes	No	
Input FileMaker file	Yes	Yes	Shared
Save copies (copy, clone, or compressed)	Yes	No	
Output data to another file	Yes	No	
Make a file exclusive	Yes	No	
Find records	Yes	Yes	Specific
Sort records	Yes	Yes	Specific
Hide windows	Yes	Yes	Specific
Change page setups	Yes	Yes	Specific
Use scripts	Yes	Yes	Specific
Switch layouts	Yes	Yes	Specific
Browse and edit fields	Yes	Yes	Shared
Design layouts	Yes	Yes	Shared
Create scripts	Yes	Yes	Shared
Passwords	Yes	Yes	Shared
Papersizes	Yes	Yes	Shared

Table 9-2 lists some guidelines for sharing information while working together in a group. Keeping these items in mind will ensure that FileMaker's performance is not unnecessarily degraded so that you will get the best possible processing speed in a networked situation.

Table 9-2. File-Sharing Tips.

---

1. Remember who you are. Hosts should provide the best performance for guests and guests should comply with the requests from the host.
2. Remember your passwords, particularly the ones you create. Lose all the passwords that permit entire file access and you will lose the file forever.
3. Let other users know the passwords you want them to use.
4. Close all files when you are finished with them. Limit the number of files open at one time.
5. Remember that you will increase processing speed by making a file exclusive.
6. Make sure you know the commands that are best performed when you are a single user and arrange to be a single user when you carry them out.
7. When sharing files and running FileMaker with MultiFinder, run only applications that support background processing.

ADDED SECURITY

If the information in your FileMaker files is important enough to share on a network, then it is important enough to be protected. Data security is a matter of growing concern in today's offices. Security can be defined as freedom from risk and danger, and data security means keeping your data free from such risks and dangers as hackers and other interlopers; viruses, worms, and logic bombs; vandals and thieves; competitors and industrial spies; employees, both belligerent and careless; power failures; and fires and other catastrophes.

A Growing Problem

In the early 1980s it became clear that by using a microcomputer, an individual could carry out a wider range of tasks with faster and better results. As this fact sank home in corporations and institutions, the personal computer spread to the point where it is now a universal item of office equipment. These days few people would think about setting up any type of commercial enterprise without a personal computer on-hand. However, because so many tasks have been entrusted to personal computers, the weak points of these machines have become increasingly problematic. To the extent to which personal computers are subject to outside forces, they jeopardize the endeavors of the people who trust them in their work, their recreation, and their self-expression.

In recent years, we have seen a steady increase in the number of questions asked by students in computer classes that directly relate to matters of security. There are several reasons for this. Obviously, the extent to which organizations rely upon personal computers has increased dramatically. The media can now be relied upon to dramatize large-scale breaches of security. However, the main reason for more questions is the growing sophistication among users, who now see the broader implications of questions like "How do I stop other people from retrieving my personnel files?" and "What will I do if my Mac is stolen?" Personal computers have been out there long enough and in sufficient numbers for most users to know of at least one "disaster" in which a lack of security has negative consequences for an organization or individual.

A personal computer store in one of the more exotic parts of California, was approached, back in the mid-1980s, by a customer who was engaged in the world's oldest profession. She had a particular interest in the password protection systems used by the various database management programs she was considering for the tasks of bookkeeping and maintaining a client list. Subsequent raids by vice squads upon computerized houses of ill-repute have shown the client's concerns to be well-founded. An unprotected database of names and addresses from such an establishment has, on more than one occasion, provided a ready-made arrest list. The moral of the story is that, whatever endeavors we engage in, serious consideration of how to preserve and protect the growing quantity of data that we entrust to personal computers is part of the price we must pay for tremendous benefits of personal computers.

These days, more and more organizations are connecting personal computers, both Macs and PCs, on local area networks. Indubitably, this increases the chances that computer operations can be disrupted by forces outside the user's control. While you can take steps to protect your network, the potential threats are probably increasing in number, rather than decreasing. In their rush to utilize the cheap and convenient power of the personal computer, many organizations have left the door open behind them, providing ample opportunities for the interloping, theft, and fraud. Fortunately, it only takes common sense and diligence to close the door. Beyond that you can look at locks, alarms, and the finer points of personal computer security.

You have already seen that FileMaker on a network offers several levels of protection for data. Protection of the network software itself can control who uses the network. The password system within FileMaker controls what holders of passwords can do with files. However, other matters have bearing upon security and should be considered.

What Is at Stake?

Assessing the value of a personal computer system, the tasks it performs and the information it handles in order to carry out those tasks is a complex task. The four main aspects to the value of any personal computer system are the hardware itself, the software used by the hardware to process information, the information that is processed, and the system's ability to continue doing the processing.

Most hardware is easy enough to value. You might know what you or your company paid for it. You can assign a value to hardware using normal business concepts like purchase cost, replacement value, depreciated value, and so on.

The value of software is a trickier issue. You normally buy the right to use software rather than the raw material of disks and manuals. Someone could steal your copy of the FileMaker manual, and even your FileMaker system disk, but, under typical licensing agreements, you would still own the right to use FileMaker. Of course, you will need to prove you really did purchase the program for this right to have any real value.

The value of the information that is handled by a personal computer has several aspects. The following sections attempt to place these in perspective.

The Value to You. Suppose your FileMaker database contains your cost estimates for a major competitive bid. Recreating the file will cost you time and effort. You might also experience a loss in terms of credibility and goodwill within your organization if the missing file means you disrupt the schedule for submitting the bid. This demonstrates the personal value of the information to you. If the lost file results in a lost bid, then the wider value of the data to you and your organization becomes clear.

The Value to Others. Suppose the file that contains the cost estimates disappears from your personal computer system into the hands of your competitors, who use it to win the bid. This is probably the most obvious demonstration of the value of your information to others. Such data as customer lists and marketing plans fall into the same category. Yet direct competitors are not the only people who might covet the information on your personal computer system. If you are in the business of selling information itself, then some people are likely to be thinking about how to get your information for free.

The Negative Value. Information that is not of direct value to you or your competitors might still have negative value. Many of us have at one time or another used a personal computer to prepare a nice-looking resume. If the resume is intended for a prospective employer, discovery of the resume file on your current employer's personal computer can be embarrassing to say the least.

It is interesting for all users of networks to note that negative value was at work in the infamous Willard Scott/Bryant Gumbel affair. An internal memo in which NBC television presenter Bryant Gumbel expressed personal observations about coworkers was made public, and much was made of Gumbel's negative assessment of coworker Willard Scott. In fact, the memo was written by Gumbel at the request by his boss, but this did not lessen NBC's embarrassment. The memo came to light because it was stored on an insecure computer network.

Other examples of information with potential negative value include internal findings about product safety, employee evaluations, environmental test results, and so forth. Indeed, most internal documents that reflect negatively on an organization or individual have potential negative value.

The Value of Immediate Access. Suppose that you come to work in the morning and your Mac does not work the way you expect it to. The FileMaker file that you need is not where you thought you left it. In a situation like this, you learn the value of immediate access. The file might not be permanently lost, but access to it is delayed, wasting time and effort, causing a dent in productivity.

Closely akin to the value of immediate access is the ability of your personal computer system(s) to keep doing the job. As personal computers increase in processing capability, they are assigned increasingly important tasks. Using personal computers for such tasks as order processing, customer reservations, stock management, and data acquisition means that their role is critical. The cost of system disruption, in terms of lost business and goodwill, can be considerable.

Of course, the tasks you perform with your personal computer might not be critical to an organizations profit and loss, but they might still be very important to you. While personal computer security is clearly about letting personal computers get on with what they do, precise statements about the value of personal computer systems are difficult because any respectable list of the different things that personal computers do would be far too long.

You could try a theoretical answer to the question "What do personal computers do?" For example, it is true to say they are used to process information. Yet, as we have seen, the nature of that information is the critical factor. One personal computer might process information about the activities of a simulated airplane as the user attempts to shoot down a simulated enemy. The value of this information to people other than the user is limited. Another personal computer might process information about the activities of a real airplane, information that is of vital importance to the pilot and passengers. What exactly it is that a personal computer does is less important to the discussion than the fact that it plays a valuable role in an ongoing endeavor.

Do You Need Help?

Have you stored valuable information on your personal computer? Are you sure it will be there in the morning? Are you sure it will not appear in the next edition of the *Times* or *The Wall Street Journal*? What will you do if your hard disk crashes right now, or if the office is gutted by fire over night? Are you happy letting the clerk from the temporary agency update your payroll files or finish typing that competitive quote? Could your competitors use the information that is on your personal computer to their advantage? Are you sure they are not at this very moment reaping a windfall from the airwaves in your office?

If you are not comfortable with your responses to the above questions, then you need to do some serious security planning. In the next section, we make some suggestions as to where to start, but we would suggest that you get a copy of the Windcrest book, *Stephen Cobb's Complete Book of PC and LAN Security* for more detailed assistance. However, just buying the book and putting it on the office bookshelf might help our standard of living and might help you feel slightly more comfortable, but reading the book and taking its suggestions to heart will definitely improve your security.

Eight Steps to Safer Computing

The following steps, briefly described, will guide you in assessing what you can do to increase the security of your data network. There is little need to invest in expensive specialized security products if you follow common-sense rules when setting up and running your network.

Backup. The greatest safeguard against data loss is regular backup, the copying of files to ensure that the same data is in two places at the same time. If you keep your FileMaker data files on floppy disks rather than a hard disk you already have a level of security—you can lock up the floppy disk. But you should still copy the data disk regularly to have a backup in case of damage to the original. You can copy FileMaker files from hard disk to floppy, using the Finder or the Save a Copy command (creating compressed files for backup is a good idea). You can install a tape backup unit for your Mac or for the file server on a network. Remember to store the backup media separate from the computer, and update the backup regularly. Complete hard disk backup can be performed with the HD-Backup program that comes with the Mac, or you can use high-speed backup programs such as PC Tools.

Lock Up. Control who can get to your computer to steal it or abuse it. Lock the building at night, lock your office when you are not in it, lock backup away, lock disks away, lock your Mac to the desk using one of the many kits on the market, such as MacSafe. You could install one of the many site access control systems to prevent people wandering where they shouldn't. Badges, card readers, even hand or eye print systems are now available. Keep track of all serial numbers, hardware and software, for faster recovery if the worst happens.

Tighten Up. Control access to your Mac. Use a password system to prevent unauthorized users from booting up your Mac. Control who uses your system when you are not around. An excellent program for this is Pad-Lock, referred to by its author as a "safeguarding utility." Pad-Lock blanks the screen on your Mac while you are away from the desk and requires a password to be unlocked. You install Pad-Lock as a function key. In our Macs it is activated by Shift−Option−O. Suppose you are leaving your Mac unattended. You press the Pad-Lock function key and up pops a dialog box like the one on the left in Fig. 9-39.

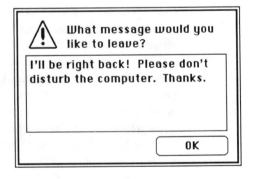

Fig. 9-39. Setting up Pad-Lock.

You type a password and a little padlock icon appears for each character you type. This password will be required when anyone, yourself included, attempts to use the Mac. If you check the Leave a Message box, you get the dialog on the right of Fig.

9-39 in which you can type a message that will be shown to anyone who attempts to use your Mac while you are gone. The fairly polite message in Fig. 9-39 is the default message, but you can type more dire warnings if you like. When you click OK, the screen goes black except for a padlock icon that bounces around to show that machine is still on. After activating Pad-Lock, anyone who clicks the mouse or presses a key will get the message on the left of Fig. 9-40, requesting the password.

Fig. 9-40. Trying to access the Mac.

Entering the wrong password results in a triple error sound, plus the message on the right of Fig. 9-40 which informs the interloper that they have been seen. When the legitimate password is entered, the message shown in Fig. 9-41 is displayed if there has been an attempt to use the Mac. Otherwise, if nobody has touched the machine during your absence, the correct password will simply restore the display as it was before Pad-Lock was activated.

Fig. 9-41. The interloper warning.

This is a simple but effective program, either to keep kids away form work-at-home Macs or to deter nosy coworkers. Expect a rising tide of such products as computer security awareness grows.

Power Up. Without a smooth and steady supply of electricity, your Mac is not

happy. Even fleeting fluctuations in voltage can corrupt data and break network connections. Install surge/spike/noise protectors, from a reputable manufacturer, on
power sockets used by computer equipment. For networks based on a server, install an
uninterruptible power supply (UPS). Power at least the server from the UPS. When
main power fails, the UPS gives an alarm, allowing the network administrator to close
all of the files on the server before the batteries in the UPS give out.

People Power. Happier employees are safer employees. All Mac users beyond the
neophyte stage know enough to wreak havoc if they want to. Successful personal computing is based on trust. Foster a friendly work force, and you are less likely to find
files missing. Use discretion in hiring as well. Do not expect to get data entry done
cheaply by paying low wages to persons of dubious character. If you have to hire temporary workers, use a reputable agency that supplies Mac-literate staff who are
bonded.

Password Power. Do not squander the protection offered by passwords in network and application software. Consistently use passwords, and use good ones. A
good password is at least five characters long, but no longer than ten; mixes characters
and numbers; and is completely unrelated to the file contents.

Do not use your name, your company's name, the last four digits of your phone
number, "open sesame," "password," or any of the other obvious choices. Develop a
system of words that are not too hard to remember, but do not give away the subject
matter they are protecting. Include punctuation characters and numbers. (Using the
nouns on a particular page of a novel in turn is one way to come up with the words.)

Phone Power. Computers can communicate one to another over the phone lines if
they are equipped with modems. If you have no modem connected to your computer
or the network to which the computer is connected, you have nothing to fear from
hackers hunched over home computers dialing up your system and invading it. Even if
you have a modem, it will not provide an open door to intruders unless it is set up to
answer the phone automatically. If you need to have your modem answer the phone,
for example, for another office to call you up and transmit information to you, then use
a call-back system or other means of authentication that verifies that the caller is unauthorized to access your computer.

Spy Power. If you are working with information that is very valuable to outsid-
ers, such as sensitive government data, then be aware of the possibility of eavesdropping. This is electronic interception of signals used by your computer as it produces
screen images, disk files, and printed reports. Fortunately such eavesdropping is difficult to do, and Macs are much harder to listen in on than PCs. But there are counter-
measures you can take. Check for consultants specializing in TEMPEST-type security
for advice on this.

A final word on the question of security—viruses. While these are a matter of
serious concern to all personal computer users, they are relatively easy to protect
against if you can stick to these rules:

- Put no disk into your Mac unless you know exactly what is on the disk, where it
  came from, and who gave it to you.

- Only use fresh, sealed, off-the-shelf software published by a reputable software house and purchased from a reputable supplier.

- Do not use copies of software, particularly ones that have been begged, stolen, or borrowed. Only download software from reputable sources such as CompuServe, and check all downloaded software for virus infections using one of the commercial virus detection programs.

- If you are using a network, make sure that all users of the network abide by these rules. To assist in this, set up a test Mac that is not connected to the network and stores no valuable data. Do a test run of new software on this system and check for virus infections using one of the commercial virus detection programs.

We realize that these rules are easier to write than they are to enforce, but by following them you can virtually guarantee that the next time you have a problem with your Mac(s), you can rule out a virus attack. Sticking to the rules costs very little; the price of a good virus detection program such as Vaccine is minimal. The time it takes to think twice before using disks of doubtful origin is well worth your attention.

CONCLUSION

The possible permutations of hardware and software in a local area network are impossible to number. This chapter could never hope to tell you how to run your network, or exactly how to use the network that is in your office. Indeed, if you are using a network that is administered by a designated individual, you should ask them for instructions on the *modus operandi* they have developed and the rules and regulations that apply. What we hope to have accomplished here is an overview of what networks are, how FileMaker works on a network, and what some of the larger issues surrounding LANs might be. In the next chapter, we look at some of the more unusual examples of FileMaker in action.

10
Special Applications

IN THIS, THE FINAL CHAPTER, we look at some of the more interesting applications of FileMaker, and encourage you to have fun exploring the program's possibilities. Hopefully you have had some fun with FileMaker already, along with the lessons you have learned about how FileMaker works. We have tried to use a wide variety of examples throughout the book to illustrate the various features of the program, and this variety in itself should suggest the versatility of the program.

MERGES AND MAILINGS

A particularly good software match exists between FileMaker and some of the leading word processing programs for the Macintosh, Microsoft Word and MacWrite II. By using FileMaker's Output command, you can create a list of information that is recognizable to these programs and can be used to perform "mail merge" operations.

What Mail Merge Is

A classic example of mail merge is the "standard" letter that has to be sent to a number of different people. You are probably familiar with this sort of correspondence:

> Dear MR COBB! You may have won $100,000! Just imagine, MR COBB, driving down POLK STREET in a new car, or buying a brand new house in the finest part of SAN FRANCISCO! To find out if you have won. . . .

You get this kind of letter from a company that has obtained your name and address, along with thousands of others, and sent essentially the same letter to each person on their list, usually in the hope of selling them something. Few people confuse this kind of mail with a personal or business letter. Apart from the other clues, you can usually tell from the style of printing that this letter was produced by a machine (a machine that does not know the current price of real estate in San Francisco!). However, a lot of business and personal correspondence does follow a similar pattern. The bulk of the text is the same from letter to letter, just a few items, such as the name and address, vary. Within certain limits, which are discussed later, your Mac can address a standard letter to a list of people, and make it look like each letter was individually written.

The Mechanics of Mail Merge

The idea of mail merge is to combine a list of variables, such as names and addresses, with a standard document, typically a letter. The variables are used to customize the letter so that what would otherwise appear to be a standard form letter appears as a personalized piece of correspondence. A typical example of the results of mail merge can be seen in Fig. 10-1.

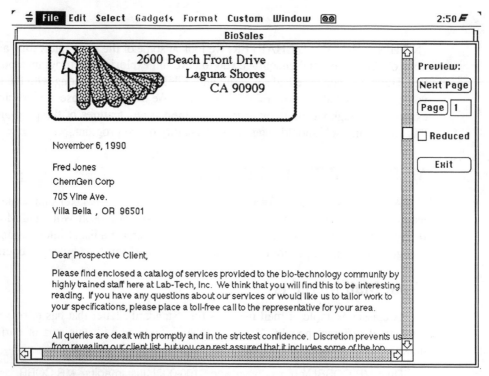

Fig. 10-1. An example of mail merge.

A mail merge operation creates multiple final documents, typically customized letters like this, out of two preliminary documents, often called the *data document* and the *form document*. The data document contains the list of names and addresses or other variables. The form document contains blanks that are filled in with items from the data document.

Given the flexibility of FileMaker's Layout mode, you might think that such a document could be composed within FileMaker. To a certain extent, this is true. The letter seen in Fig. 10-1 was actually created with the FileMaker layout shown in Fig. 10-2, but not without some difficulty.

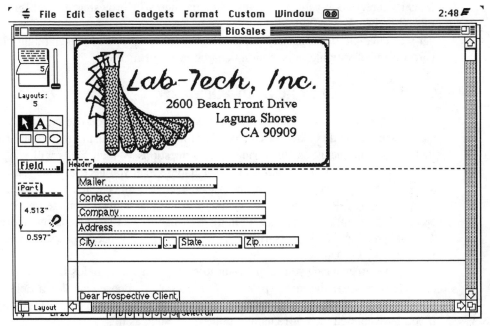

Fig. 10-2. FileMaker form letter layout.

Word processors offer several features that FileMaker does not, the most important of which is probably word wrap. As opposed to rap, a feature of street music, word wrap the word processing feature is the ability to flow text from one line to another. FileMaker does provide word wrap in text fields, wrapping entries that will not fit on one line onto a second line, and so on. However, the bulk of a form letter consists not of text fields, but of layout text. Only the variable information in the letter is provided by fields, the rest is static from letter to letter. This fact has two practical implications. When you insert variable information within a paragraph, that paragraph will not reform if the entry is particularly long or short. Also layout text must be entered and edited one line at a time, which is a pain when you are creating long paragraphs. Even if you attempt to paste text into a FileMaker layout that has been copied from another document, you will find that it can only be pasted one line at a time.

Beyond word wrap, word processors offer other features that FileMaker layout text does not. Formatting such as bold and italic, as well as font changes, can be applied to any part of the text in a word processor. In the Layout Mode, you can only format a field or a piece of layout text. Boldfacing one word in the middle of a line of layout text would mean creating three pieces of text.

Given these limitations, plus the fact that you can create lists of names and addresses for merging within a word processing program such as Microsoft Word, you might wonder why you would use FileMaker in merging at all. The answer is simple: The power of FileMaker to sort and search information. Few word processors possess the ability to perform multi-level sorts on lists of variables, and none offer File-Maker's direct approach to finding individual items or browsing through groups of related items. We are certainly not aware of any word processors that offer FileMaker's calculation and summary capabilities. Furthermore, FileMaker might already contain lists of variable information that you need for merging.

Getting the Data File from FileMaker

To create a data document from a FileMaker database, you use the Output command, which was described in Chapter 8. However, before using the command you should do some planning, answering several questions. Which fields will you need? You might have more information in your database than you need in your final document. For example, suppose you want to send a letter to all customers reminding them of an upcoming sale. You have the necessary names and addresses in the Invoice database, but this database contains a lot more information than just names and addresses. To avoid creating an unnecessarily large data file, you will need to be selective about which fields you output.

On the other hand, you might want to create some new fields in the FileMaker database to assist in the merge process. For example, suppose you have a field called Contact, in which you have entered the name of a contact person at a client company. If you have entered the entire name in one field, such as this:

Contact: Fred Smith

You will not be able to use the Contact field to address a letter to this person as Dear Fred. You might want to split the name into First Name and Last Name. A basic set of formulas for this is shown in Table 10-1. Of course, the benefit of having a single field for a person's name is that you can refer to the name as one variable. So you might want to create a field that combines separate First Name and Last Name fields and use the combined field in your merge.

Also, which records do you need? If you want one final document for every record in the database, then you need to use the Find All command before the Output command. If you want to address a letter to only a few records, then you have two options: You can use the Find command to select just those records you want to merge to, or you can export all of the records to the word processing program and use special commands within the word processor to select which records are used in the merge (typically, these commands are called conditional statements).

Also consider what order you would like the records to be in. Sorting in FileMaker is much easier than sorting in a word processing document, and so you should place the records that are being exported in the order in which you would like the final documents printed. For example, you might sort by zip code in order to bundle mail for lower postage rates. You would use Sort to put them in the desired order *after* selecting the records you want with the Find command.

Text or Merge

When you have decided the above issues, you are ready to use the FileMaker's Output command. When you do so you are provided with a list of field names, as seen in Fig. 10-3.

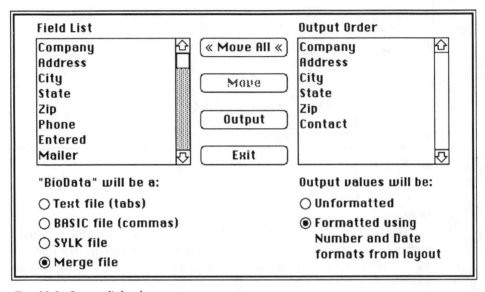

Fig. 10-3. Output dialog box.

You will find it easier to move just those fields you want to refer to in the final document, rather than all of the fields. Note that the order in which you move the field names to the right-hand list determines the order that the fields are placed in the resulting file.

When you have finished moving field names to the Output Order list, check the file type list (text, BASIC, SYLK, or merge). Which type you use will depend on which word processor you are going to use for the mail merge. Word is comfortable using the merge format, but MacWrite II is actually more comfortable with the text format. (For the sake of simplicity, from now on we refer to MacWrite II as MacWrite and Microsoft Word as Word.)

A Merge File

When you click Output to complete the Output command, FileMaker creates a new file on disk for you. You will want to check this file with your word processor to

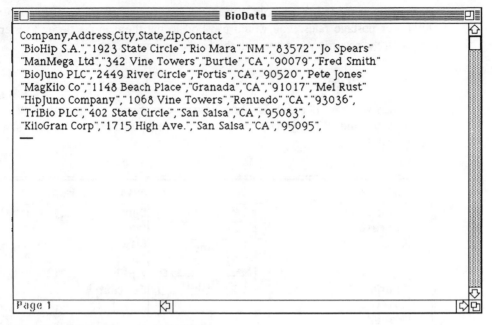

```
═▢═══════════════════════ BioData ═════════════════════▢═
Company,Address,City,State,Zip,Contact
"BioHip S.A.","1923 State Circle","Rio Mara","NM","83572","Jo Spears"
"ManMega Ltd","342 Vine Towers","Burtle","CA","90079","Fred Smith"
"BioJuno PLC","2449 River Circle","Fortis","CA","90520","Pete Jones"
"MagKilo Co","1148 Beach Place","Granada","CA","91017","Mel Rust"
"HipJuno Company","1068 Vine Towers","Renuedo","CA","93036",
"TriBio PLC","402 State Circle","San Salsa","CA","95083",
"KiloGran Corp","1715 High Ave.","San Salsa","CA","95095",
━
Page 1
```

Fig. 10-4. Merge file opened with Word.

make sure it came out right. In Fig. 10-4, you can see a merge format file opened by
Word.

The file consists of one line devoted to the field names, plus one line each for
every record you output. Note the commas between items on the first line. These separate the field names. Quotes as well as commas are used to separate field values
within each record.

If you have created a text file, you will find each record separated by a Return, as
in the merge file. But instead of commas between field values you will find tabs. In
Fig. 10-5, you can see a text file opened in MacWrite.

Note that a Text file does not contain any field name information. You might have
to add this in order to use the file in a merge operation. Also note that you can save the
Output settings in a script if you need to perform this operation on a regular basis.

Merge with MacWrite

Having created the data document, a text file output from FileMaker, you can
merge it with a form document in MacWrite (this is the fill-in-the-blanks document
that will be completed with information from the data file). However, you must first
modify the data file.

As we mentioned in the last section, you use a text file like the one shown in Fig.
10-5 as the data file for your merge in MacWrite. You first open the data file as a
"text" file within MacWrite. In order for MacWrite to recognize the fields in the form
document, you need to add a line above the records in the data document that lists the

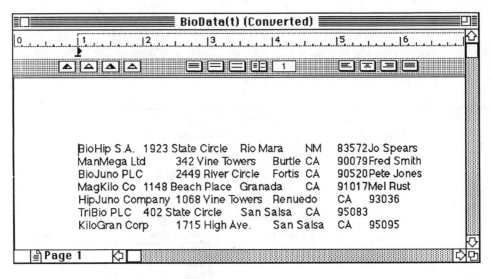

Fig. 10-5. Text file opened with MacWrite.

field names. These do not have to be the same names as the field names used in File-Maker. Place the edit cursor at the beginning of the first field of the first record and press Return. This creates a fresh line on which to type. Move the edit cursor back to the beginning of the document, ahead of the carrier Return, type the first field name, then press the Tab key. Type the second field name, then press Tab again, and so on, across the line. There must be a field name for each field but, as you can see in Fig. 10-6, the names do not have to line up over the field values.

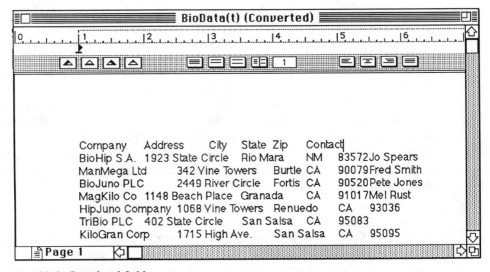

Fig. 10-6. Completed field names.

Now save the file as a MacWrite file using the Save As command. You might also want to print a copy of the data file for reference purposes, or at least print the first page. This will remind you of the field names you need to use. When you have done this, you should save and close the data file.

For the form letter, you can either create a new file or convert an existing letter. Type the text of the letter until you reach a point where you want to insert a piece of variable information from the data file. Now select Open Merge File, from the File menu. MacWrite will present a list of files. Select the data file and the Insert Merge Field menu appears, as shown in Fig. 10-7.

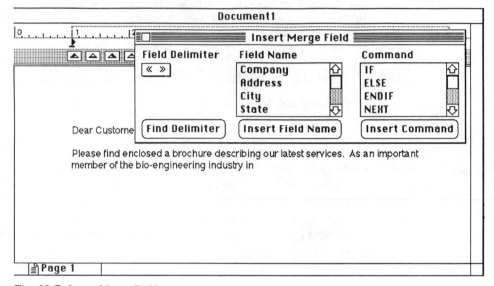

Fig. 10-7. Insert Merge Field menu.

Two lists, headed Field Name and Command, provide the information you need to insert field names in the text and create conditional statements (discussed later). The Field Delimiter box shows the characters that will be used to mark merge data fields in the text of the form document. These characters are placed on either side of the field name, as in «Company», to tell Macwrite to insert information from that particular field. Note that these codes are not simply two greater than or less than signs, but a special symbol. To insert a field in the letter, you highlight the field in the list and click Insert Field Name. For example, in Fig. 10-8, you can see the State field inserted with the delimiters automatically placed around it.

Once you have used the Open Merge File command, the Insert Merge Field menu remains available for further insertions. You can immediately bring it to the foreground with Command−I. In other words, this is a "sticky menu," one that does not go away until you click the close box. In Fig. 10-9, you can see the completed merge letter, with the fields correctly inserted to create an address as well as customized text.

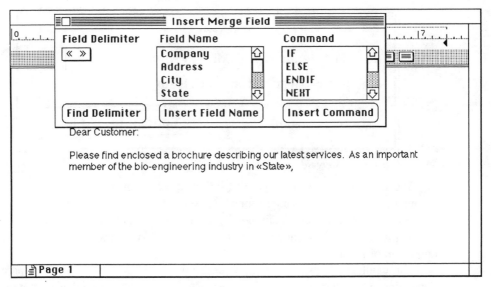

Fig. 10-8. Field inserted with delimiters.

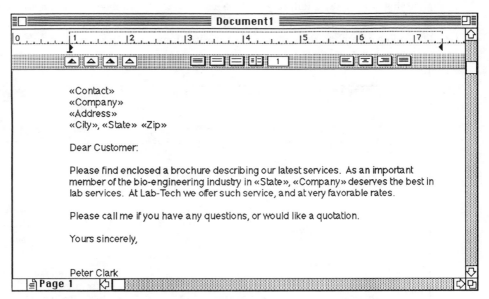

Fig. 10-9. Completed merge letter.

Note that appropriate punctuation must be included around the field names in the document, with punctuation marks added outside the field delimiters.

The document is now ready to merge with the data file. First save the form document in case something goes wrong during the merge operation. Then select Merge from the File menu. MacWrite presents the dialog box shown in Fig. 10-10.

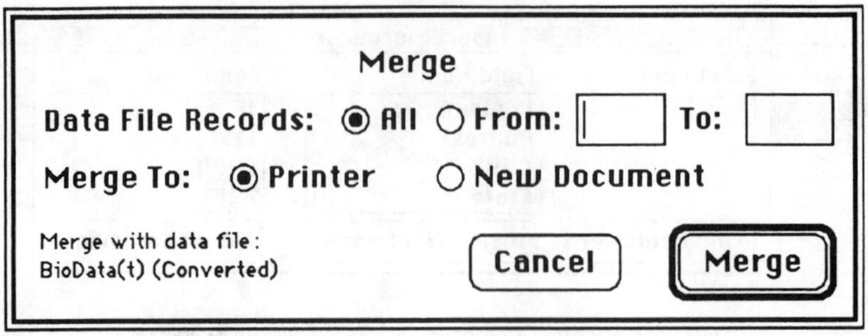

Fig. 10-10. Merge dialog box.

You can choose All to create a customized letter for each data record or enter record numbers to create letters for a limited series of records specified by record number (MacWrite automatically numbers records starting with 1). For a first merge, it is helpful to test the arrangement with a short series of records rather than the entire collection of records.

You can also choose to create the customized letters on the printer or as a new document. The latter is useful if you want to review the results before committing them to paper, or if you want to make further changes to one or two individual letters. Note that MacWrite is telling you the name of the current data file in the lower left of the dialog box. The current merge file is the one you open when you use the Open Merge File command. Having made your selections, you click Merge and the final letters are created. You can see the results of a completed merge to new document in Fig. 10-11.

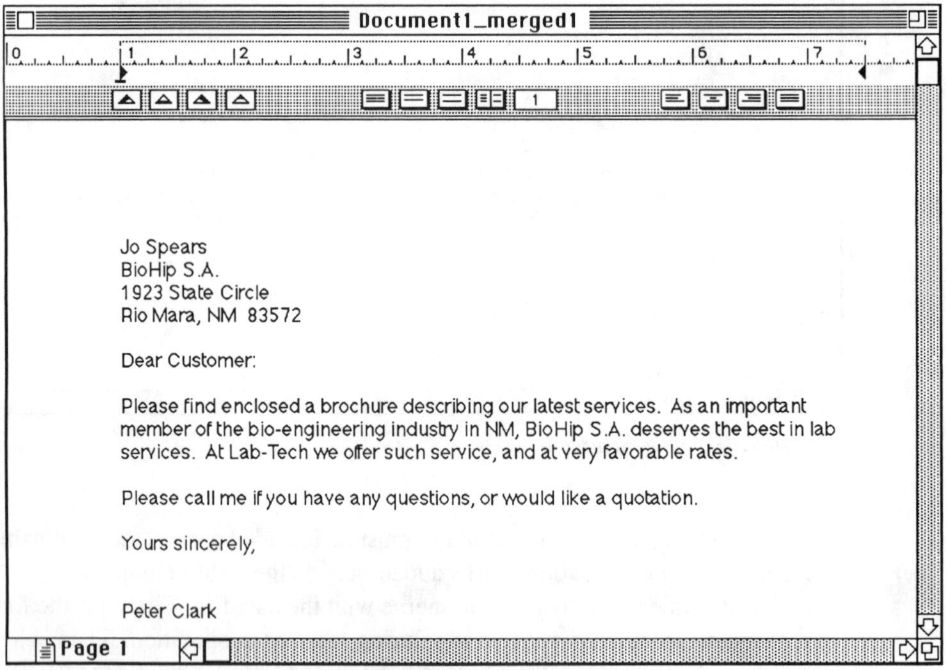

Fig. 10-11. Results of the Merge command.

Merge with Word

When you have used the FileMaker Output command to create a data document, using Merge as the file type, you can combine it with a form document created in Word. This is the fill-in-the-blanks document that will be completed with information from the data file. A merge data file requires no modification in order to work with Word, since the field names are already included in the file, as shown in Fig. 10-4. However, you might want to open this file within Word to check its contents and then save it as a Word document. You might also want to print a copy of the first page to make sure of the spelling of field names.

To create a form letter in Word, you enter field names within a letter, either creating the letter from scratch or converting an existing letter. You must enter the variables by hand, using the field names from the data file within delimiters, as shown in Fig. 10-12.

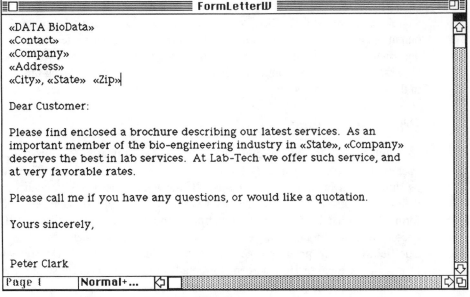

Fig. 10-12. Variables entered in a Word document.

Note that Word uses the same field delimiters as MacWrite. These are typed manually in the Word document using Option−for the opening symbol («), and Shift- −Option−for the closing symbol (»). Also note the first line of the document. This is a statement required by Word that defines data file to be used in performing the merge.

Unlike MacWrite, in which the data file must be opened by the Open Merge File command and remain open in order to perform a merge, Word makes the connection to the data file by requiring that you state the name of the data file at the top of the form document, as in Fig. 10-12. The format of the statement is «DATA FILENAME». Note that this document is in a different font from that used in the MacWrite form letter.

Font changes and other formatting have no effect on the mechanics of the merge. If you want to format merged text, you apply the format to the field name, including delimiters.

After you have created the form letter in Word and saved it to disk, you can select Print Merge from the File menu. Word presents the dialog box seen in Fig. 10-13, which has much the same set of choices as the one used by MacWrite.

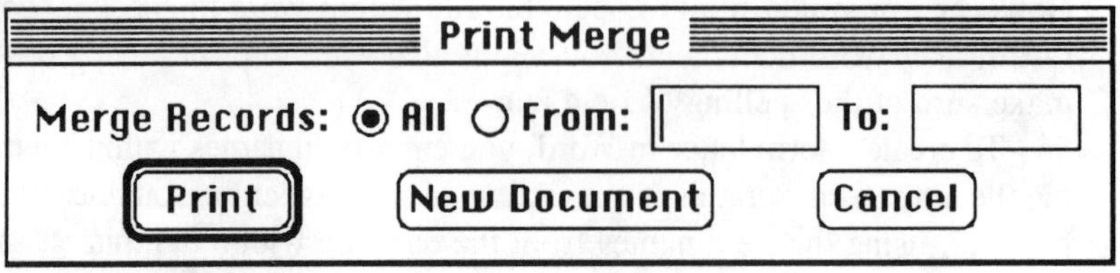

Fig. 10-13. The Print Merge menu.

You can merge to all records or just a selected series, such as 1 through 4. You can output the merge to a new document or the printer. Merge just a few records to a new document in order to test the merge without wasting paper. When you click Print or New Document, the form letter is filled in once for each record using the field values in the data file. The results are practically identical to those achieved in MacWrite.

Practical Merging

Both MacWrite and Word allow the use of conditional statements within merge operations. These perform useful tasks that further customize letters. These tasks can be summarized in statements, such as: "If the Middle Initial field contains an initial, then print Middle Initial, otherwise print nothing." This type of statement enables the form letter to handle a variety of situations. Another example might be: "If the Balance Due field contains a value, print Please remit Balance Due, but if the Balance Due field is empty, print Your account is completely up to date." Consult your word processor's manual or Help screens for details of how to construct such statements in your particular word processor.

After you have produced a bunch of letters using the merge process, you will probably want to mail them. This essential part of the operation is sometimes overlooked in accounts of mail merging but this can be where the process puts the biggest strain on your equipment and patience. Fortunately, most personal computer printers now do a better job of printing addresses directly on envelopes than they used to, and almost all can at least accommodate mailing labels which can then be stuck onto the envelopes.

Labels. One of the easiest ways to address envelopes is to put self-adhesive labels on them. The one-across pin feed labels can be handled by most dot matrix printers, even without a tractor feed option (the friction of the platen is usually enough to pull these labels through). Creating one-across labels from your name and address list is simply a matter of correctly informing FileMaker about the size and shape of your labels. The one-across pin feed labels are usually $1-1^1/_2$ inches deep and $2^3/_4-3^1/_2$ inches across.

Label stock that is pin-fed one-across is fairly easy to use if you avoid rolling it backwards with the platen. While you might be tempted to do this to utilize a few blank labels, the risk is that a label will get stuck on the platen requiring a tricky removal process. However, you might want to print labels two-across or three-across for faster results.

Whether you print labels with your word processor or with FileMaker will probably depend upon your level of comfort with the respective software and its handling of forms. Generally speaking, FileMaker is more adept at labels, particularly the two- and three-across variety, than most word processors.

Envelopes. Envelope feeding on some printers has to be done by hand. This is not actually as tedious as it sounds if the merge is limited to one or two dozen envelopes. Some printers have difficulty with the shortness of envelopes relative to regular paper. This is usually caused by a switch that senses the absence of paper as the envelope rolls through. You can cure this by putting a sheet of paper under the flap of the envelope, and so preventing the printer from thinking it is out of paper.

One option that is worth considering is continuous feed envelopes, regular envelopes attached to a backing that has pin feed holes. Many dot matrix printers can handle this stock and many stationers can order the envelopes printed with your return address. The main limitation here is going to be cost as these are a fairly expensive item.

Laser Printers. What about labels for people with laser printers? Well, this is a good news/bad news situation. Laser printers work a lot like photocopiers, and many are able to print on the self-adhesive label stock that puts 3 columns and 11 rows of labels on a 8.5" by 11" sheet.

Many laser printers can accept envelopes. These are usually fed and printed lengthwise, otherwise known as landscape mode. The most important step to setting up an envelope for the laser is to switch the Page Setup to "landscape" so that it prints at ninety degrees to the regular print. (The LaserWriter II takes envelopes from the manual feed very nicely.)

Quantity vs. Quality. Merge operations can generate large quantities of text from a small amount of input. In general, personal computers are more efficient at receiving input than their printers are at handling output. The main reason for this is that personal computer users have placed a strong emphasis on quality of output. They have been prepared to sacrifice speed in favor of results that "don't look like they come from a computer."

Earlier it was mentioned that many personalized sweepstakes letters are obviously the work of a computer—you can tell from the printing. If all large corporations cannot afford printers that generate typewriter quality letters by the million, it is only to be expected that not all personal computer users are connected to printers that can generate such output. However, the cost of "personal" laser printers continues to fall and other technologies, such as inkjet, are increasing in quality and speed.

The fastest personal computer printers are still the laser type. They produce 6 to 10 pages per minute. With a typical paper feed tray that holds 250 sheets, an 8 page-per-minute printer would need fresh paper in half an hour. This means that the effective printing rate would not top 500 pages per hour. A mailing to 3000 customers would take better than 6 hours. During that time the printer could not do any other work. It could not be left to do the work overnight because of feeding the paper. The computer that was running the merge program would be occupied for quite some time as well.

Merging to printer and merging to a new file both have their limits. Writing a 3000-page merge document to disk would require several megabytes of disk space. The ensuing background print would slow down work with the computer. Merging direct to the printer would occupy the computer until the printing was finished, unless you have print spooler such as TOPS Spool.

All this means that even if you have a laser printer and can spare the computer and an operator for six hours, you might want to think twice before tackling a merge with thousands of records. There is still the question of signing and folding the letters, stuffing the envelopes, not to mention the addressing of the envelopes. If you have a slower printer, the scope of operations must be adjusted accordingly. A letter-quality printer like the ImageWriter can turn out about a page per minute. With a sheet feeder holding about 60 pages at a time or a large stack of pin feed paper, the paper supply is not hard to handle, but eventually ribbon changes must be factored in, as must time to strip pin-feed paper down to single sheets. This means the six hours of computer and operator time could produce only about 500 letters.

Given these factors, it is important to be clear on the benefits to be gained from a merge mailing before investing the time and expense of entering the names and addresses and getting the letters out. Unfortunately, some people tend to think that because they already have a name and address list, perhaps from their accounting database or from another division of the company, that doing an in-house mail merge is almost free. In reality, factors such as expected response rate from a personalized mailing versus less expensive alternatives such as preprinted letters, should be weighed carefully before embarking on such a project.

Addressing. Whether you decide to send people a customized letter or a pre-printed piece, there is still the question of the mailing address. Earlier remarks about this process have indicated that it is not all smooth sailing. If your printer has a reliable envelope feeder, then printing direct to the envelope is a real possibility. Unfortunately such devices are not common enough at present. Many people will need to consider the mailing label alternative. Because these are usually about an inch long they feed very quickly through most printers making hundreds per hour a possibility even on slower printers.

To minimize the obviousness of the label on the letter consider using labels that match the envelopes (white being the most common shade of label, you might want to get company envelopes in white). Some office supply stores carry clear labels that don't do a bad job of lowering the profile of the label on the envelope.

Mailing labels have their own limitations. Small print is needed to get complete addresses on three-across labels. Pin-feed one-across label stock does not work well on a laser printer. However, it will work on printers with platens, even if they don't have pin-feed attachments. Most printers with platens can pull labels through fairly easily and keep them straight, although you will want to keep an eye on the printing process. Do *not* try to save labels or clear errors by rolling label stock backwards in the printer. This tends to stick labels to the platen (a fairly good remedy is to roll a stiff piece of card through, possibly using a little Liquid Paper Thinner to soften the glue on the label).

For some mailings, a very handy alternative to labels and envelopes is the continuous feed postcard. These are becoming more widely available and postage costs are substantially lower. If you use blank ones, you can run them through once for a personalized message on one side, and again for the address on the other. The results are different enough to catch attention, and they have the advantage of not requiring any opening.

One other alternative to the mailing label problem is to send letters and other mailing pieces in window envelopes. If you correctly position the recipient's address on the letter and fold the letter carefully, you can avoid separately addressing the envelope. Window envelopes can be ordered from a printer with your return address and are particularly useful for pieces of mail such as invoices where you can be flexible about the placement of the return address on the mailing piece.

A FileMaker Merge Tip

If you want to perform a mail merge within FileMaker, you must create a layout that simulates a letter. You can place fields where you want field values such as name and address to appear in the letter. The problem comes when you need several paragraphs of text in the letter. These are hard to create with layout text that does not wrap from one line to another.

One answer is to define a new text field and place it on the letter layout. Make this field as large as the body of the letter. In Browse mode, type the text of the letter as an entry in the new field. FileMaker text fields do word wrap and will rejustify text should you later decide to alter the size or shape of the field box. To place the same text in every record, you simply use the Replace command. This copies the text to all found records. One advantage of this approach is that you can alter the text of the letter in selected records if you want to.

SPECIAL CALCULATIONS

The range of functions and formats in FileMaker allows you to handle many calculations in fairly straightforward manner. However, some situations require special attention.

Time Calculations

In Chapter 6, you saw that FileMaker has several calculation functions that apply to dates. Together with the date field type and the Format Date command, these functions give you the ability to apply FileMaker to date-related databases. However, some filing and record-keeping operations need to deal with hours and minutes as well as days, that is, you need to do math with time in general rather than just dates. At first glance, it would seem that this would require a special set of field types and calculation formulas, and you have already seen that FileMaker has no special field types or calculation functions designed to handle time.

The lack of time fields/functions makes manipulating time with FileMaker less straightforward than just dealing with dates. Time calculations are very different from decimal calculations such as momentary transactions. In a momentary calculation, you can add 50 cents and 25 cents and get 75 cents. However, when you add 25 minutes to 50 minutes you get 1 minute and 15 minutes, or 1.25 hours. This difference in units can cause problems when you try to calculate and manage time, but these are not insurmountable. In a moment, we will examine how you cope with an example like the one in Fig. 10-14, where FileMaker needed to calculate the turn-around time on car repairs.

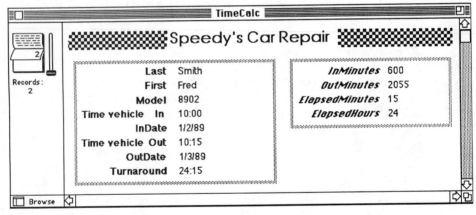

Fig. 10-14. Car repair database.

To perform a calculation on time FileMaker, you must first convert the time into a format that FileMaker can manipulate. You begin by splitting the time into separate elements, such as hours and minutes. When you have separated the information into these parts, you add the minutes together, add the hours together, carry the minutes greater than 60 over to the hours, and then assess the hours to determine days. This might seem burdensome, but once you establish the procedure, you will find it relatively easy to apply in FileMaker databases. We have provided an example of how to work with time in FileMaker that you can adapt to your own needs.

A Timely Example

To complete the database shown in Fig. 10-14, we needed to calculate elapsed time in order to track how much time was being spent on each car. The user is required to enter time data into two fields, the In field and the Out field. FileMaker then calculates the elapsed time between those two entries. The formulas and fields used are described in the following text and listed in Fig. 10-15, which is a printed report from FileMaker using the Field Definitions option on the Print dialog box.

Field Name	Field Type	Formula / Entry Option
Last	Text	
First	Text	
Model	Text	
InDate	Date	Auto-enter today's date
In	Text	
OutDate	Date	
Out	Text	
Turnaround	Calculation (Text)	= ElapsedHours & ":" & ElapsedMinutes
InMinutes	Calculation (Number)	= LEFT(In,POSITION(In,":",1)-1)*60+RIGHT(In,2)
OutMinutes	Calculation (Number)	= LEFT(Out,POSITION(Out,":",1)-1) * 60 + RIGHT(Out,2)+((OutDate-InDate)*24*60)
ElapsedMinutes	Calculation (Number)	= OutMinutes-InMinutes-(ElapsedHours*60)
ElapsedHours	Calculation (Number)	= int((OutMinutes-InMinutes)/60)

Fig. 10-15. Field definitions for time calculations.

The first step is to define the user entry fields for the times. These are of the field type Text because text functions will be employed to separate the hours and minutes. In the example, we defined text fields named In and Out. As prompted by the layout text, the user enters text into those fields in a 24-hour format. In other words, the A.M. hours are entered as HH:MM and the P.M. hours as (HH+12):MM. Thus, 2:30 A.M. would be entered as 2:30, and 2:30 P.M. would be entered as 14:30. This format is sometimes referred to as military or international time. Once the times are entered, they must be split into hours and minutes for the calculations to be applied.

The best way of manipulating the two different times would be to calculate the number of minutes that each time is from some base, such as midnight, and then compute the number of minutes between the two times. Once you know how many minutes are between the two times, you can easily convert the minutes to hours and minutes.

Stringing It Out

FileMaker has a number of text calculations that make it possible to manipulate strings of characters. The example uses the LEFT function and the RIGHT function. The LEFT function uses two parameters, the string with which you want to work, and the number of characters you want.

Unfortunately, because the time is entered in HH:MM format, it is difficult to say exactly how many characters you want. If the time is before 10:00 A.M., you need only one character; otherwise, you need two. Fortunately, you can use another string function, the POSITION function, to work around this problem.

The POSITION function uses three parameters: The string in which you are searching, the character for which you are searching, and the position from which to start the search. The function returns the position of the character for which you are looking. The time will be in the format HH:MM, so if you find the position of the colon (:) and subtract 1 from it, you will know how many characters you need for the hour portion of the time. Given this, the formula for the hours is:

    LEFT(In, POSITION(In,":",1) − 1)

Once you have the value for the hours, you need to find the value for minutes. Because you always enter two characters for minutes, finding this value is easier. The RIGHT function is the complement of the LEFT function. The RIGHT function uses the same two parameters, but returns a number of characters from the right side of the string. The formula for the minutes reads:

    RIGHT(In, 2)

Now that you have these two elements, you can create a calculation field that computes the number of minutes from midnight of the In. You create a calculation field, called InMinutes, with the formula:

    LEFT(In, POSITION(In,":", 1) − 1) * 60 + RIGHT(In, 2)

Although the LEFT function returns text as its result, FileMaker recognizes that a number is in the field and allows you to do the multiplication on it. Consider a couple of sample entries. If you enter 9:00 into the In field, the InMinutes field returns 540, the number of minutes 9:00 is from midnight is computed using the formula 9 hours × 60 minutes per hour = 540 minutes. If you enter 11:30 into In and InMinutes returns 690, the formula is 11 hours × 60 minutes per hour = 660 minutes, + 30 minutes = 690 minutes.

You can use the same theory to compute the value for OutMinutes from the Out field:

    OutMinutes = LEFT(Out, POSITION(Out, ":", 1) − 1) * 60 + RIGHT(Out, 2)

Once you have this, you should be able to calculate the difference between OutMinutes and InMinutes and have the solution, but it will not always be correct. Everything works correctly if the times are both on the same date, but if they are on two different dates, then the result will be wrong. To get around this problem, you need to use the same base for InMinutes and OutMinutes.

This means you need to define two date fields, InDate and OutDate, to correspond with the In and Out fields. You can then calculate the number of days between these two dates, compute how many minutes that will be, and add that value to the Minutes

Out field. Knowing this, the new formula for OutMinutes becomes:

LEFT(Out, POSITION(Out, ":", 1) − 1) * 60 + RIGHT(Out, 2) + ((Day Out Day In) * 24 * 60)

Once you have this formula, you can easily compute the number of hours elapsed and the remaining minutes elapsed.

ElapsedHours is a calculation field whose formula is:

INT((OutMinutes − InMinutes) / 60)

The INT function tells FileMaker to return only the integer portion of the quotient, not the fractional part. You divide by 60 because there are 60 minutes in an hour. To calculate the remaining number of minutes, all you need to do is find the number of minutes between OutMinutes and InMinutes and subtract the ElapsedHours field:

ElapsedMinutes = OutMinutes − InMinutes − (ElapsedHours * 60)

You now have all the formulas and figures you need to create a field called Turnaround that puts the results in an HH:MM format. To do this, you use the text concatenation feature of FileMaker. You can set up a calculation field called Turnaround with the formula:

ElapsedHours & ":" & Elapsed Minutes

This formula returns the proper value if the minutes value is equal to or greater than 10. For example, 9 hours and 15 minutes would read 9:15. If you had only 8 minutes, though, you would get 9:8, which is not quite right. To solve this problem, you add an IF function to check if the minutes value is less than 10 and adjust the results accordingly. Thus,

ElapsedHours & ":" & IF(ElapsedMinutes < 10, "0", "") & ElapsedMinutes

Remember that the result of this calculation is text, not a number. Once you have completed this formula, the defined fields should look like those shown in Fig. 10-16.

Note that this list includes two additional fields, InTime and OutTime, that are used to create A.M. and P.M. text in the layout, to help the user enter times more accurately. You can see these at work in Fig. 10-17, where the database is correctly calculating elapsed time even across a change in years.

The fields In, InDate, Out, and OutDate can be placed on layouts used for data entry, and the field ElapsedTime can be placed on the layout used to generate the result. In the layout in Fig. 10-18, you can see how all of the fields are arranged.

Now you can see how FileMaker can accommodate calculations it was apparently not designed to perform. Through use of time calculations like these, FileMaker becomes a useful time management tool. These formulas can be used in existing databases or in new ones. In addition, the techniques shown here can be adapted to other files, helping to make FileMaker more useful for you.

Field Name	Field Type	Formula / Entry Option
Last	Text	
First	Text	
Model	Text	
InDate	Date	Auto-enter today's date
In	Text	
OutDate	Date	
Out	Text	
Turnaround	Calculation (Text)	= ElapsedHours & ":" & IF(ElapsedMinutes < 10, "0","") & ElapsedMinutes
InMinutes	Calculation (Number)	= LEFT(In,POSITION(In,":",1)-1)*60+RIGHT(In,2)
OutMinutes	Calculation (Number)	= LEFT(Out,POSITION(Out,":",1)-1) * 60 + RIGHT(Out,2)+((OutDate-InDate)*24*60)
ElapsedMinutes	Calculation (Number)	= OutMinutes-InMinutes-(ElapsedHours*60)
ElapsedHours	Calculation (Number)	= INT((OutMinutes-InMinutes)/60)
InTime	Calculation (Text)	= IF (LEFT(In,POSITION(In,":",1))>12, "PM","AM")
OutTime	Calculation (Text)	= IF(LEFT(Out,POSITION(Out,":",1)) > 12,"PM","AM")

Fig. 10-16. Final field definitions.

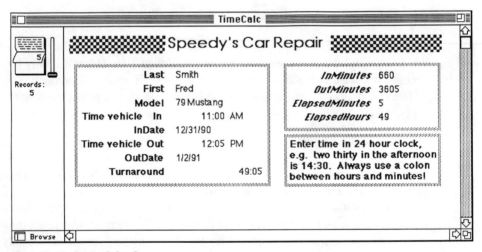

Fig. 10-17. Revised database.

A LITTLE HELP FROM FRIENDS

By now our enthusiasm for FileMaker and its versatility should be clear. Nonetheless, nobody expects one program to do everything. FileMaker is a tool, and as such it has its limits. As the old maxim goes, use the wrong tool for the job and it's likely to bite you. When you run into difficulties getting FileMaker to do what you want, consider turning to third-party software for assistance.

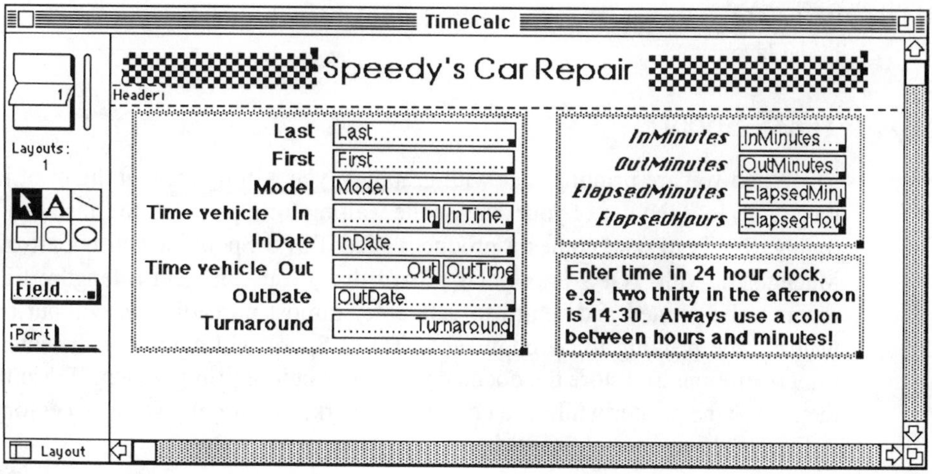

Fig. 10-18. Final layout.

Mail Merging

We have already considered the situation in which you have a lot of client names and addresses in a FileMaker database and you want to mail letters to these clients. The length and complexity of the letter and the degree to which you want it personalized should determine whether you write the letter as a FileMaker layout or you export the names and addresses to MacWrite or another word processing program to perform a mail merge. Often you will find a word processor works best for letters, while File-Maker handles the envelopes or mailing labels.

Charts

If the task at hand is a set of charts showing the sales of your mail order products by state, you cannot expect FileMaker to draw a chart from the FileMaker sales invoice database. Instead you should export the data from FileMaker to a spreadsheet such as Excel, where it can be statistically analyzed and graphed. The SYLK output format works well with Excel and other programs capable of generating graphs.

Graphics

Although FileMaker's drawing tools are very useful for enhancing forms and reports, nobody would suggest that they are a sophisticated graphics system. When you need complex images, it is best to create them in a specialized program such as MacDraw II from Claris and then import them to the Layout mode in FileMaker. We used Canvas 2.0 from Denaba Software as well as MacDraw II to design the company logos and other graphics used in our layouts, such as the one seen earlier in Fig. 10-2. To import a graphic, you select the image while working with the graphic file, issue the Copy command, and then load FileMaker database you want to enhance. When in the Layout mode, you issue the Paste command and the graphic is inserted as an object in the layout.

TOPS Spool

When you are printing files with graphics, you will notice that the print job takes longer. To lose the use of your Mac while waiting for a print job to finish can be frustrating. To the rescue comes a product called TOPS Spool, which is part of TOPS/Macintosh. With TOPS Spool and a hard disk, you can send a lengthy FileMaker report to be printed and return to data entry almost immediately, without having to wait for the printing to be completed. TOPS Spool will automatically intercept all print operations and store the documents on disk before printing them. Documents are then fed to the printer while you continue to work. You use the Desk Accessory shown in Fig. 10-19 to control TOPS Spool.

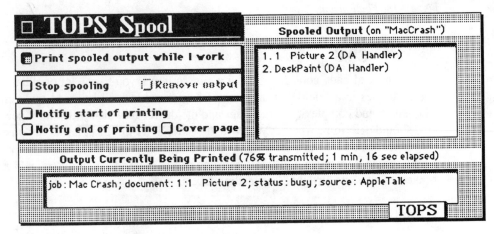

Fig. 10-19. The TOPS Spool DA.

Documents can be printed out immediately, or TOPS Spool can keep the document on disk to be printed at a later time. If someone else is using the printer, TOPS Spool will hold your document until the printer is free. TOPS Spool even remembers to print unprinted documents the next time you start your Mac. (You do not have to have a full-blown network to use or appreciate TOPS Spool. A single Mac connected to a LaserWriter can benefit from this software.)

TOPS Translators

Also included with TOPS/Macintosh is software known as TOPS Translators. This program overcomes some of the incompatibilities between file formats used on PC and Macintosh software. Using a format selection menu like the one in Fig. 10-20, TOPS Translators lets you translate files from WordStar, Multimate, WordPerfect, and dBASE III to popular Macintosh formats, including the SYLK format that FileMaker

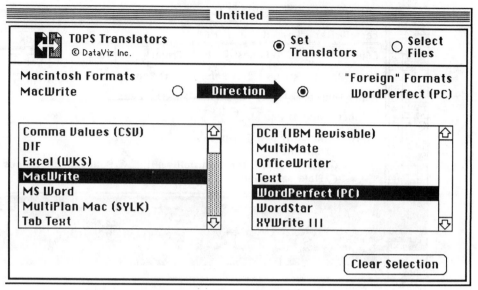

Fig. 10-20. TOPS Translators format menu.

reads. This increases your ability to load files from PC applications into Macintosh applications.

Screen Capture

You might want to capture all or part of a Macintosh screen for use in documenting a program or feature. The screen images used to illustrate this book were produced with the Capture program from Mainstay Software. This allows you to enclose a rectangle of screen and capture it to disk or to the Clipboard. You can "shoot" all of the screen or just part of it. You can use it when menus are pulled down, without affecting the menus. We usually captured the screen to the Clipboard and then used DeskPaint to print it. DeskPaint is a paint program that installs as a desk accessory. Published by Zedcor, DeskPaint actually comes with the HP ScanJet image scanner. We used this program to scale screens down for printing and to edit them, if required. You can see a familiar screen being edited in Fig. 10-21, where the normal text has been altered.

One handy feature of DeskPaint is that it always contains the same image as the Clipboard, so screens shot with Capture are automatically loaded into DeskPaint for printing. This combination makes a simple method of documenting Macintosh software.

THE STATIONERY STORE

These days many of us are working for ourselves rather than large corporations. This has meant a tremendous boom in the design and production of business stationery. Many personal computer owners have found that good printing stock, together

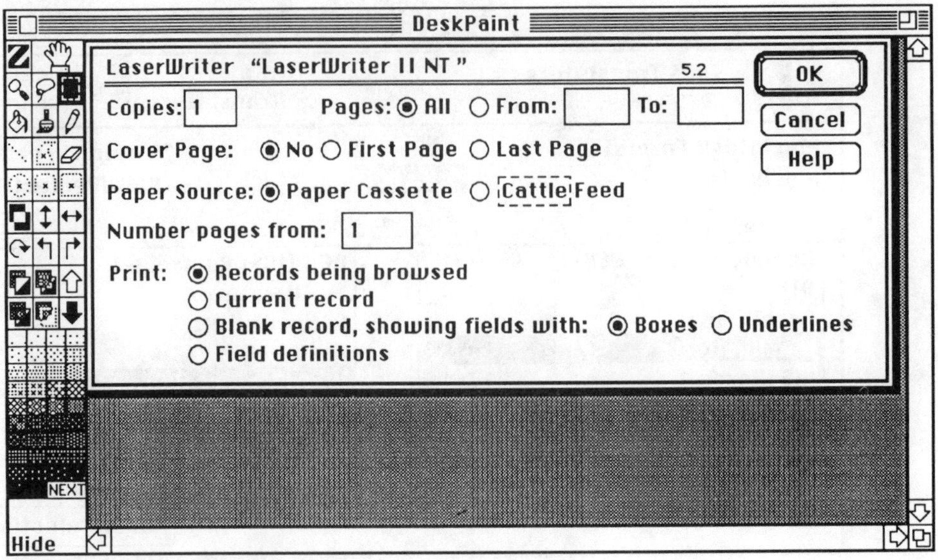

Fig. 10-21. Editing with DeskPaint.

with a laser printer, or even a high-quality dot matrix printer, can be used to turn out presentable letterhead on demand. This is an economical alternative to investing in large quantities of preprinted forms and envelopes, many of which go to waste because changes to name/address/phone number/logo render them obsolete.

We have found that a FileMaker database is a handy place to store stationery designs, including forms and envelopes. We use a database like the one shown in Fig. 10-22.

This database has very few records and is essentially a collection of different layouts. Some of the layouts have no fields at all and consist entirely of layout text and graphics. When we need a piece of letterhead, we just select the layout we want and use the Print command, selecting Current record. If we need several sheets, we use the Copies box to enter the number we need.

The Layout mode is a good report design environment, offering precise alignment tools and the handy Preview feature. You can quickly copy a design or layout and then edit the copy to produce needed variations on our basic stationery. For example, you can have a business letterhead that is customized for different employees or different aspects of the business. You could use a field called Division and enter one record for each division, thus allowing you to print sheets of stationery on an as-needed basis, rather than in bulk.

These days laser printers make light work of business size envelopes, and you can set up a layout like the one in Fig. 10-23 that includes your logo and return address. If you use name and address fields, you can use this design for casual envelope addressing, at the same time keeping records that allow you to print additional envelopes quickly to the same party for further correspondence.

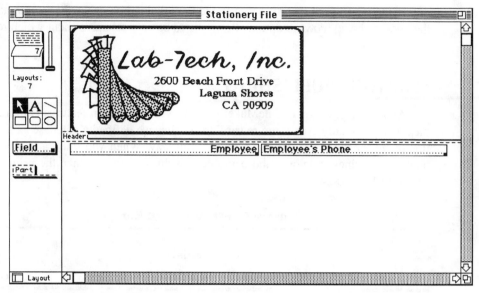

Fig. 10-22. A database for stationery.

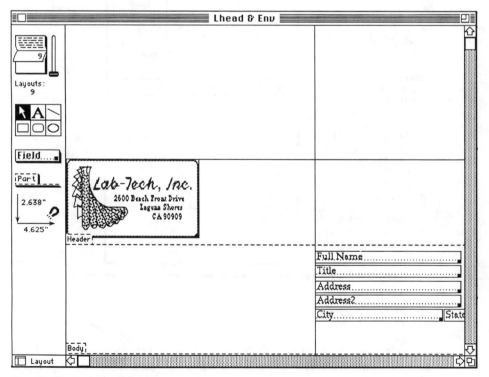

Fig. 10-23. Envelope layout.

Using the Current record setting in the Print dialog box or the Find command and the Records being browsed option allows you to be very selective about which records you print.

DATABASE PUBLISHING

Another application of FileMaker's extensive form design features is more complex, but potentially even more rewarding. Earlier we defined a database as a collection of information organized in a meaningful way. When you think about it, many books, magazines, catalogs, and pamphlets fit this definition. Take the printed page shown in Fig. 10-24.

Country Guest Houses of Europe

Inverdale

Peebleshire   Scotland

Tweedale Road
Near Peebles
Peebleshire
SCOTLAND,
ML13 2RT

U.K. 0721-34234

Fax/Telex   0721-43456

Season

Open early April to late
November

A delightful place from which to explore the Border region of Scotland, rich in history and folklore. The rooms are small but well-appointed with showers in most. The proprietor, Mr. Burns, is an amiable host and very attentive. Book early as this is a very popular venue, particularly during the Edinburgh Festival in late September thru early October.

How to get there:

Rates

40-50 per person per night
(Pounds Sterling)
VISA/MC

Pets	✗
Meals	✔
Kids	✔
Parking	✔
Pool	✗
Camping	✗
Sports	✔
Laundry	✔

Scotland   Page 33

Fig. 10-24. A book page.

This is a page from a guide to guest houses. It is also a record in a FileMaker database. Almost any type of publication that follows a consistent page layout can be organized and produced in this way. The use of graphic fields allows illustrations to be incorporated, and you can use graphic elements to dress up the page. The map and sketch in Fig. 10-24 were hand-drawn and then scanned into DeskPaint. From there they were Cut and Pasted into the picture fields in FileMaker.

In the example in Fig. 10-24, you could use icons instead of text to identify the fields in the lower right such as pool and parking. The check marks and crosses which are the entries in those fields are produced by using the Zapf Dingbat font.

The arrangement of fields and field text in a publication layout can be quite different from what would be appropriate for a more form-oriented layout. Many fields will not be identified by field text, as you can see from Fig. 10-25 which shows the layout used to generate the page in Fig. 10-24.

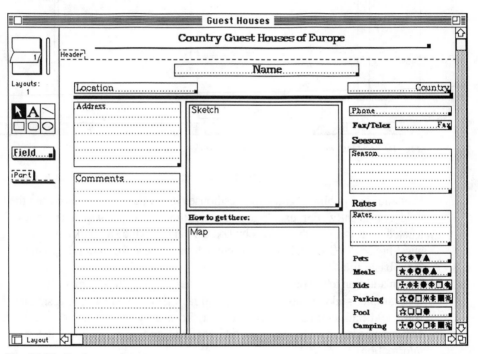

Fig. 10-25. Book page layout.

As you can see, such fields as the name and location are not directly identified as they are self-evident from their contents when a page is printed. You might want to use a data entry oriented layout for actually accumulating the entries and then rearrange for publication. This makes it clear for the person inputting the data which entries go where. You can see such a layout in Fig. 10-26.

In addition to simplifying the assembly of the data to be published, FileMaker allows you all manner of organization techniques. For example, suppose you have accumulated information on 250 guesthouses in 5 countries. You can sort the information by country to produce a country-by-country guide to guest houses. You can then use the Find command to group together all guest houses in one particular country, say

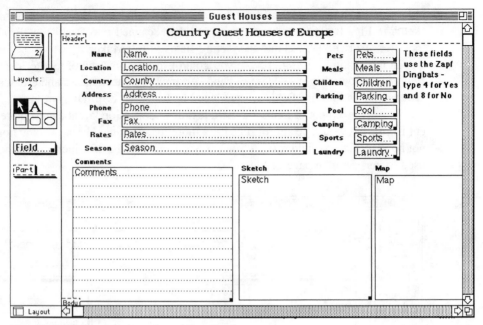

Fig. 10-26. Data entry form for publication data.

Scotland, and publish a guide to guesthouses in Scotland if you have used the Location field consistently. For example to record the county in which the guest house is located, you can sort the entries by Location and produce a county-by-county guide to guest houses in Scotland. You can publish numerous different compilations from the same basic file.

In addition to the page layouts, all manner of different summary lists are possible, for example, ranking entries according to facilities. If you were to assign a price code you could rank entries according to cost. To keep your publications up-to-date, you can create a merge file from the address field and send out form letters requesting information.

In short, by using FileMaker to organize your information, you have both a means of organizing and a method of publishing. You have the design features and presentation quality you need for publication, together with the ability to analyze and manipulate information that a good database provides.

CONCLUSION

Congratulations! If you've read this far without skipping too many pages, you now know most of what there is to know about FileMaker. Along the way, we have endeavored to be objective about the product and not gloss over its shortcomings. However, we can now let down our guard and say we really like this program. It can't do everything, and there are some important things it can't do, but it can handle a wide range of tasks quickly and to a level of detail that is exceptional. As the "presentation stakes" increase in business and professional organizations, leading to demands for higher and higher quality of appearance when presenting information, FileMaker has what it takes to not only manage your data, but also to present it professionally and with a touch of style. The latest version of FileMaker, called FileMaker Pro, expands on the themes of professional presentation and ease-of-use, and is described in detail in the next and final chapter.

11
Turning Pro

THIS CHAPTER SHOWS YOU how to take advantage of the improvements provided by FileMaker Pro, the latest version of the FileMaker program. The basic procedures for creating databases and organizing information with FileMaker Pro are the same as in earlier versions of the program. Almost all of the information in the previous chapters is directly applicable to all versions of FileMaker. However, File-Maker Pro provides some important new capabilities that allow it to take on a wider range of database applications, while making basic operations even easier for the inexperienced user. This chapter shows you how these new features work and how they can work for you, particularly if you are designing databases for others to use.

TIME TO UPGRADE

The streamlined operations, enhanced layout options, improved performance, and added functions of FileMaker Pro make it an important upgrade, and one that you should make as soon as possible. The main advantages of FileMaker Pro over previous versions are:

- Improved layout tools, with rulers, sizing, and full four-color and high-quality graphics, including TIFF and EPS files.
- Broader range of calculation functions plus a new field type for time values.
- Improved import/export capabilities with support for WKS, DBF, and DIF formats.
- Improved password control with Overview.
- Improved Preview with multiple zoom levels, hot-key, and menu access from both Layout and Browse modes.

- Pop-up lists, check boxes, and radio buttons for field entries.
- User-defined "buttons" on layouts to run commands and scripts.

FileMaker Pro automatically reads existing FileMaker databases, including all scripts, layouts, finds, and sorts. FileMaker Pro treats older files just as though they were created with FileMaker Pro. However, once an older database has been read into FileMaker Pro, it cannot be saved back into the older format (you can use the File Export command to transfer pure data back to an older version of FileMaker, but not layouts, scripts, and other important settings).

This one-way upward compatibility makes life complicated if all users within an organization do not upgrade to the latest version at the same time. We recommend that you make the change all at once and in an organized manner, removing older versions from your machines at the same time new versions are installed. At the end of this chapter are further notes on upgrading to FileMaker Pro.

You should find that there is very little learning curve involved in adopting File-Maker Pro, particularly because existing databases work just as they always did. Several of the new features in FileMaker Pro, such as the improved access to Preview and the layout switching in Browse mode, simplify operations without any changes to existing files. The bulk of this chapter is devoted to a review of the process of database creation and design, using FileMaker Pro. We point out differences between File-Maker Pro and previous versions and highlight situations in which the new features of FileMaker Pro make a difference.

CREATING A DATABASE WITH FILEMAKER PRO

When you start FileMaker Pro by clicking on the application icon, you are asked to choose either the Open command to load an existing database file or the New command to create a new database file. FileMaker Pro lists existing database files in the current folder, including files created by previous versions of FileMaker.

Preserving Old Versions

Before selecting a file created by an older version, you must decide whether you need to retain a copy of file in the original format. If you do, then you must use the Duplicate command in the File menu under Finder or MultiFinder to create a copy, before loading the older file into the new version of FileMaker. This is because File-Maker Pro does not have a Save As option to store files in the older format. The conversion of old files to the new format is automatic and one-way. FileMaker Pro warns you of this when loading an older file. This gives you a chance to cancel the File Open command and perform a File Duplicate before continuing.

Creating Fields

If you choose the New command from the File menu, either when launching File-Maker Pro or later, you are prompted to supply a name for the new database file, then asked to define the fields. The field definition procedure in FileMaker Pro is very similar to that in earlier versions, although the definition screen looks somewhat different, as you can see from Fig. 11-1. The field types remain the same, with the addition of the Time type, described later in the chapter.

As you can see from Fig. 11-1, a field called BookingDate has just been created, as the first field of a new database called BallonBookings. This database will be used by Ballonier, Inc., a company offering hot-air balloon flights, to track bookings.

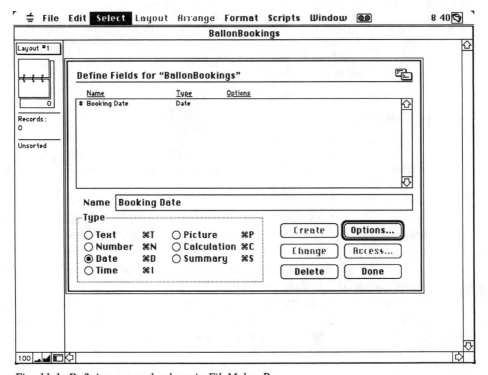

Fig. 11-1. Defining a new database in FileMaker Pro.

Auto-Entry Options

As you can see, the field type is Date and the user wants this field to reflect the date the record was created, which normally corresponds to the date the customer first calls to book a flight. The Options button is selected and the Entry Options screen appears, as in Fig. 11-2.

You can see that FileMaker Pro offers some useful auto-entry options. The Creation Date feature means that the field contains the date on which the record was created. In addition to Creation Date, you can select Modification Date. This automatically enters the date the record was created, but changes the date if the record is altered to reflect the day the alteration was made. If the field were of the Time type you could select Creation Time or Modification Time. If the field type were Text, you could select

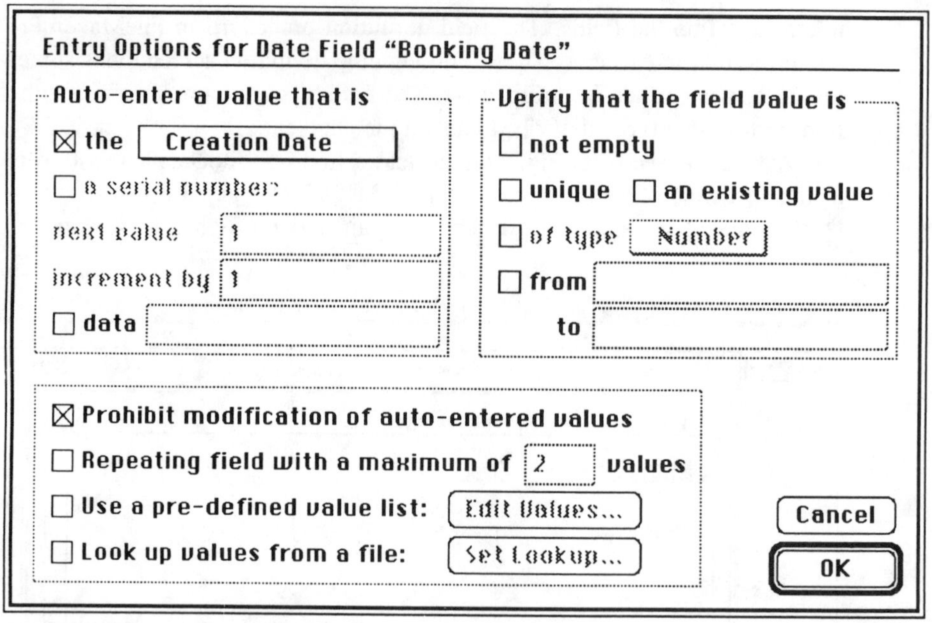

```
┌──────────────────────────────────────────────────────────────────┐
│                                                                    │
│  Entry Options for Date Field "Booking Date"                       │
│  ┌···Auto-enter a value that is ···┐  ┌···Verify that the field value is ···┐│
│  │  ⊠ the ┌ Creation Date ┐       │  │ ☐ not empty                       ││
│  │                                │  │                                   ││
│  │  ☐ a serial number:            │  │ ☐ unique  ☐ an existing value     ││
│  │                                │  │                                   ││
│  │  next value  ┌ 1 ┐             │  │ ☐ of type ┌ Number ┐              ││
│  │                                │  │                                   ││
│  │  increment by ┌ 1 ┐            │  │ ☐ from ┌          ┐               ││
│  │                                │  │                                   ││
│  │  ☐ data ┌          ┐           │  │    to  ┌          ┐               ││
│  └────────────────────────────────┘  └───────────────────────────────────┘│
│                                                                    │
│  ┌····································┐                              │
│  │ ⊠ Prohibit modification of auto-entered values │                │
│  │ ☐ Repeating field with a maximum of ┌ 2 ┐ values │              │
│  │ ☐ Use a pre-defined value list: ┌ Edit Values... ┐ │ ┌ Cancel ┐ │
│  │ ☐ Look up values from a file:   ┌ Set Lookup... ┐  │ ┌══ OK ══┐ │
│  └────────────────────────────────┘                   └──────────┘│
└──────────────────────────────────────────────────────────────────┘
```

Fig. 11-2. The Entry Options screen.

Creation Name or Modification Name. In this case, the name is that of the current volume, so if the hard disk on which you are running FileMaker Pro is called Paul and you select Creation Name, then Paul is automatically be entered into the field.

Note that the Entry Options screen allows you to prohibit modification of auto-entered values. This complements the verification options, such as not empty, unique, type, and range. The Entry Options is also where you create a Repeating field. This feature was previously located on the Format menu in the Layout mode. Moving the Repeating field feature to the Define field area makes it easier to access.

Another improvement is in the definition of serial numbers. You can now specify a string consisting of both letters and digits to be used as the initial value to increment from (for example B101, B102, and so on). You can increment by values other than 1 (for example 100, as in B100, B200). Note that you cannot increment text. Thus a starting or next value of 1A, incremented by 10, would lead to 1A, 11A, 21A, and so on. When you want a user to enter one of a limited number of set values into a field, you select the Use a pre-defined value list. This gives you a list box into which you can type the values. You then format the field in Layout mode with the Field Format command to implement one of the types of "pick a value" data entry methods, such as check boxes, radio buttons, or pop-up lists.

Calculating Fields

After the Booking Date field has been created, the user adds fields called Last, First, Address, and Phone to record details of the person making the booking. Then a Trip field records which trip the caller wants to book. The date of the trip is recorded in the Date field, which is followed by a field called Number which records how many people are in the party. As you can see from Fig. 11-3, a Cost per person field is added, followed by a calculation field called Total cost.

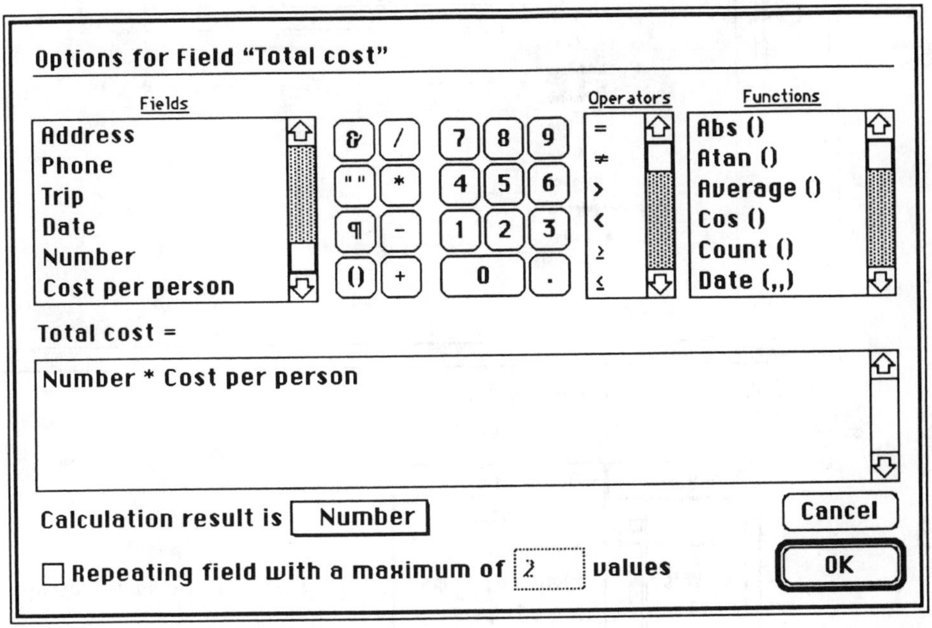

Options for Field "Total cost"

Fields		Operators	Functions
Address	`&` `/` `7` `8` `9`	`=`	Abs ()
Phone		`≠`	Atan ()
Trip	`" "` `*` `4` `5` `6`	`>`	Average ()
Date	`¶` `-` `1` `2` `3`	`<`	Cos ()
Number		`≥`	Count ()
Cost per person	`()` `+` `0` `.`	`≤`	Date (,,)

Total cost =

Number * Cost per person

Calculation result is | Number | Cancel

☐ Repeating field with a maximum of [2] values   OK

Fig. 11-3. Calculation options.

The definition of calculations in FileMaker Pro is very similar to that in earlier versions. There are more calculation functions, which are described later in this chapter, and the result type is easier to see. In this case the type is Number. Note that the calculation screen has a Repeating field option, to match that on the Entry Options screen.

Basic Layout/Browse

When you have defined all of the fields you think you need, you select Done from the Define Fields screen in Fig. 11-1. FileMaker Pro places you in Browse mode with the standard data entry layout, shown in Fig. 11-4. Note that the Booking Date has already been entered, a result of the auto-entry option.

While this looks a lot like earlier versions of the Browse mode, there are some subtle differences. Above the book icon is name of the current layout. This name box is actually a menu, as you will see in a moment. To begin with the first layout in a file is called Layout #1, but you can alter the name in Layout mode, using the Layout Options command.

If you have more than one layout, you can switch between them by clicking on the name box. This reveals a list of names, as shown in Fig. 11-5, an enlargement of a

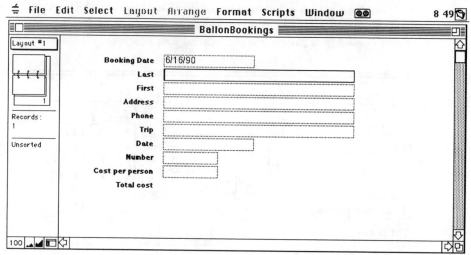

Fig. 11-4. The basic data entry layout.

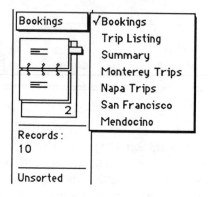

Fig. 11-5. Multiple named layouts.

more developed version of the bookings database. The current layout is indicated by a check mark. By dragging the highlight down to another name, that layout becomes the active layout in Browse mode, without having to enter Layout mode. This feature eliminates the need for a special script just to switch layouts from Browse mode. The use of layout names makes it easier for users to find the right layout.

Note that FileMaker Pro uses this style of pop-up menu in a lot of situations, especially for fields in dialog boxes. You can determine if a field is a pop-up menu if it has a shadow line around the bottom and right edges of the field box.

Also notice that the book icon has been changed slightly. You still click on the upper page to move to the previous record or the lower page to move to the next record. The current record number is still indicated (record 2 in Fig. 11-5). You can still edit the record number to move to a specific record (for example, replacing 2 with 5 moves you to record 5). A *book marker* replaces the slider control to allow you to move through records more quickly.

At the bottom left of the screen in Fig. 11-4, you can see several icons. The one closest to the horizontal scroll bar controls the display of the status area. You click on this icon to toggle between settings, turning on or off the display of the status area. A similar icon is used in the Layout mode to toggle display of the tools area. Next to the status area icon, in the lower left corner of Fig. 11-4, you can see the "Mountains" icons, similar to those in MacDraw II. These are used to activate the new Zoom command. This allows you to enlarge or reduce the active screen in any mode. The Zoom ratios are 25, 50, 100, 200, and 400.

You click on the smaller mountains to reduce the ratio, the larger mountains to enlarge. The current ratio is shown to the left of the mountains. Clicking on the current ratio box automatically switches you back to the normal ratio of 100. You can see a ratio of 200 in Fig. 11-6, where an enhanced layout is being shown.

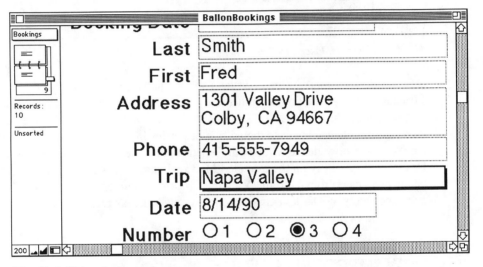

Fig. 11-6. Using the Zoom feature.

Note the Trip and Number fields in this example. These have been altered from the standard format. The Trip field is a pop-up menu, as indicated by the shadow line. The Number field uses radio buttons (the number of persons on each balloon trip can be 1, 2, 3, or 4). These two features are activated with the Field Format command in layout mode.

The use of Zoom in Browse mode can enlarge text to make it easier to see, or reduce large layouts so that the whole form is visible. The Maximum Layout Size in FileMaker Pro 96×96 inches, whereas the previous limit was 36×36 inches. In Layout mode, the Zoom feature makes designing much easier, particularly when dealing with detailed drawings or large layouts. The Zoom feature is also available when using the Preview mode.

As you can see from the Select menu displayed in Fig. 11-7, FileMaker Pro has made Preview a fully-fledged mode accessible from Browse and also from Layout. Preview has been assigned the keystroke Command–U.

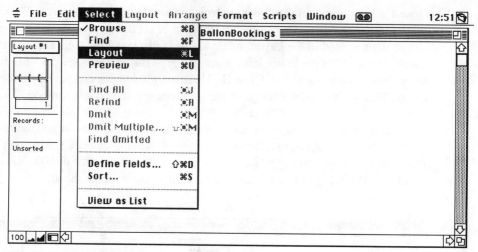

Fig. 11-7. The FileMaker Pro Select menu.

The Preview mode, illustrated later in the chapter, is more useful now, with the advantages of Zoom and more immediate access. Also note that the View as list is now a Select option, making it accessible in both Browse and Layout modes. Another subtle but useful change involves the editing of entries in fields and text used on the layout: You can now delete with both Delete keys. The Del key to the right of the Delete/Backspace key on the extended Mac keyboard now works in FileMaker Pro to pull in characters from the right. With the I-beam edit cursor in the middle of the word database, pressing Del four times produces data whereas pressing the regular Delete key four times produces base.

NEW IMPROVED LAYOUT

While the standard arrangement of fields and field text is serviceable, it is only a beginning. In Fig. 11-8 you can see what can be done with the basic data entry screen by using the tools and techniques available in the Layout mode.

The Layout mode in FileMaker Pro is where experienced users will notice the most improvement over previous versions. The entire method of operation has been streamlined, bringing it into line with conventions established in graphics programs like MacDraw II. New commands have been added to make the positioning of objects both easier and more precise. Pressing the Left, Right, Up, and Down arrow keys when an object or field is selected "nudges" the object, one pixel in the direction of the arrow. Any number of selected objects can be grouped so that any subsequent action performed to the grouped object works upon all objects that comprise the group. If grouped fields are of different types (number, date, picture, and so on), they need not be ungrouped to be formatted.

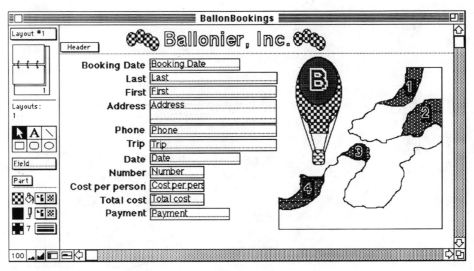

Fig. 11-8. An enhanced layout.

Laying Out Objects

All FileMaker layouts consist of a number of elements. The most basic are fields and field text. In addition it is common to add further text, to provide headings, instructions, and so forth. Shapes in the form of lines, rectangles, and circles can be added for decoration. Images or graphics created in other programs can be pasted into a layout to further embellish it.

Basic positioning of objects is accomplished by selecting objects with the mouse and then dragging them to the desired location. When you click on an object in File-Maker Pro, it is given *handles* just like in MacDraw II. These allow you to alter the objects size. An object that has handles can also be moved by clicking within the rectangle created by the handles and then dragging.

The rules for selecting objects have been changed in FileMaker Pro. Instead of dragging the select box so that it touches part of the object(s) you want to select, you now have to be more specific: You must enclose all of the object(s) for the select to work. For example, in the upper half of Fig. 11-9, you can see the select box has been drawn around a group of fields and field text. The effect of releasing the mouse button at this point is shown in the lower part of the figure.

Note that neither the Date field or the text Date are selected. This is because they were not entirely included in the select box. Also note that the text Cost per person is excluded for the same reason. While this approach to selection might take a while to get used to, it is more in keeping with other Mac programs, particularly drawing programs such as MacDraw II. The new approach is more precise when dealing with complex layouts. Remember that if you select more objects than you want, you can

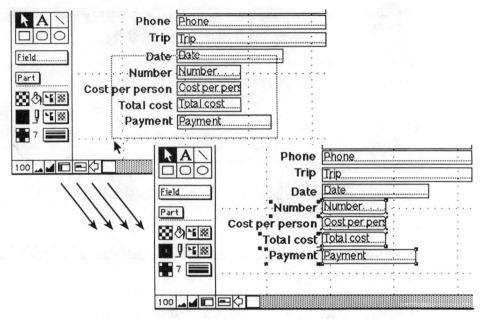

Fig. 11-9. Selecting objects in Layout mode.

deselect single objects by holding down Shift and clicking on the object you want to deselect.

In Fig. 11-10, you can see the main menu selections provided by FileMaker Pro in Layout mode. You can see that the Gadget menu has been replaced by Arrange. There are also changes to the Layout and Format menus.

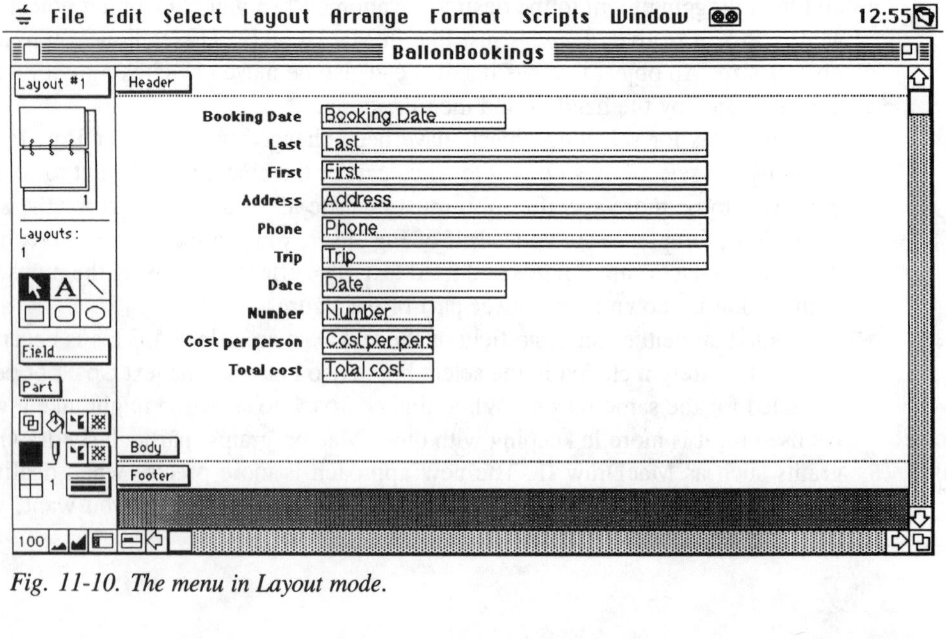

Fig. 11-10. The menu in Layout mode.

User-Definable Grid. While previous versions had an invisible grid that was of fixed proportions, the grid in FileMaker Pro is modifiable in inches, centimeters, or pixels. The Align to Grid command can be turned on and off from the Layout menu, as can Gridlines, Rulers, and T-Squares, which are now permanently magnetic. You can see the Layout menu in Fig. 11-11.

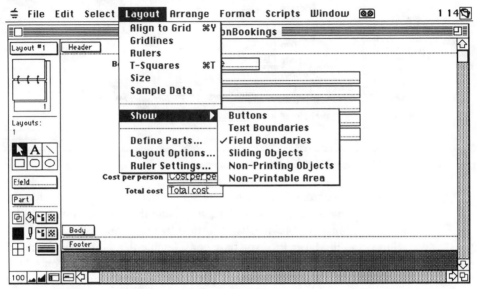

Fig. 11-11. The Layout menu.

Sample Data. When you turn on the Sample Data option, FileMaker Pro replaces the field names in the field boxes with data, placing text in text fields, dates in date fields, and so on. This allows you to see the effect of formatting options without going back to the Browse mode. You can quickly identify data that is improperly formatted or displayed.

Rulers. To make your layouts more accurate, you can display rulers along the vertical and horizontal axis in layout mode. The rulers can be in inches, centimeters, or pixels. You can see an enhanced layout displayed with Rulers in Fig. 11-12. Note that the upper left corner of the rulers shows the current unit of measure, in for inches. A shortcut for changing ruler divisions is by clicking on this area of the Layout screen, which rotates through the three options: in, cm, and px.

Note that in Fig. 11-12, the Gridlines option is on, as well as the Rulers option, and the new Size option. The Size option further aids the cause of layout accuracy by giving you precise location coordinates and dimensions for any object you select. In Fig. 11-12, the current object is the *map*, a drawing pasted from another program. You can see that this is 3.222″ high by 3.292″ wide. The top left corner is 4.431″ from the left edge of the page, and .986″ down from the top of the Body part (the bottom of the Header part). This type of detail makes it possible to achieve high levels of accuracy with relative ease. The measurements in the Size box change as you move

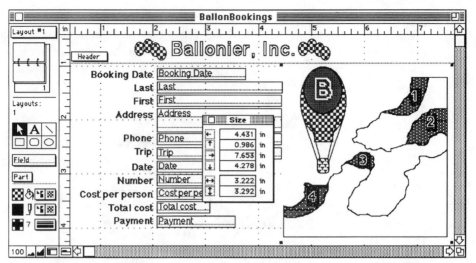

Fig. 11-12. Using Rulers and the Size command.

the selected object around. You can edit each measurement separately, for example, to make the map measure exactly 3.5″ square. Note that the Size option takes over the measurement functions previously performed by the T-Squares.

Show. In FileMaker Pro, you have considerable flexibility over what is displayed in a layout. The Show command, seen in Fig. 11-11, allows you to control the appearance of Buttons, Text Boundaries, Field Boundaries, Sliding Objects, Non-Printing Objects, and the Non-Printable Area. Of these items, both Buttons and Non-Printing Objects are new. Buttons are used to activate scripts or commands from icons on a layout, and are described in detail later in this chapter. While you might want to use these on a data entry layout, you might not want them displayed on a duplicate layout used for a report. Similarly, you might not want some graphics items to print out, although you would like to appear on-screen. Items in this category can be designated Non-Printing, using the Slide Objects command on the Arrange menu. The sliding of objects in FileMaker Pro is more sophisticated than in earlier versions, with any object being capable of sliding, as described later under the Arrange command.

Define Parts. You might have noticed in Fig. 11-11 that the appearance of the layout part identification tags (Header, Body, and Footer) have been improved slightly. The new design makes the parts easier to identify. You can also "flip" these tags vertically, which lets you see more view the entire layout area. This is shown in Fig. 11-13, which also illustrates the new Define Parts menu.

Note that the part tags are vertical. The special icon next to the Zoom icons and the status/tool area display icon is used to flip between vertical and horizontal display.

When a vertical tag does not have enough space for the full part name, it is abbreviated. For example, the top tag in Fig. 11-13 simply says T; this is short for Title Header, a body part that only appears at the top of the first page of a file. If you place the pointer on a vertical tag and hold down the mouse button, the full name appears until you release the button.

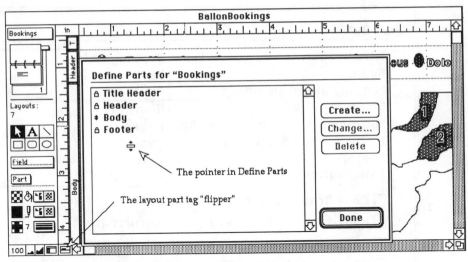

Fig. 11-13. Defining Parts.

When you select Define Parts from the Layout menu, you are shown a list of existing parts. Normally you begin with the basic three parts Header, Body, and Footer, and then add or subtract from there. To create a new part you simply click the Create button. To delete or change a part, you click on the part you want to alter and then click the appropriate button, which is ungrayed when an existing part is selected. Note that the pointer changes appearance in Define Parts. A number of menus with list in FileMaker Pro feature this type of pointer. This pointer indicates that the position of some items in the list can be changed. The items with small padlock icons cannot be moved, but those with up/down arrow icons can. You simply drag the item to a new position in the list.

When you choose Create or Change to make a new part or alter an existing one, the Part Definition dialog box appears, as shown in Fig. 11-14. This is a fairly straightforward dialog box that allows you to easily set up and alter parts such as Sub-summaries. FileMaker Pro gives you considerable flexibility when dealing with layout parts. Parts such as Sub-summaries and Grand Summaries are easier to reorder, using the define Parts dialog box.

In previous versions of FileMaker, the layout parts were often awkward to manage. For example, in order to reorder parts, certain parts had to be deleted, and then re-created in the new location. The facilities for altering a part in FileMaker Pro, such as what field a Sub-summary sorts by, are also useful. They avoid the need to delete the part then copy all fields over to the new part. Parts are now *objects* that can be highlighted and deleted with the Backspace key. Previous versions required unwanted parts to be Option-dragged over another part.

In Fig. 11-14, you can also see the new options for dealing with page breaks. These give you complete control over how records are printed and numbered relative to page length. For example, if you want a page break after every four records, you

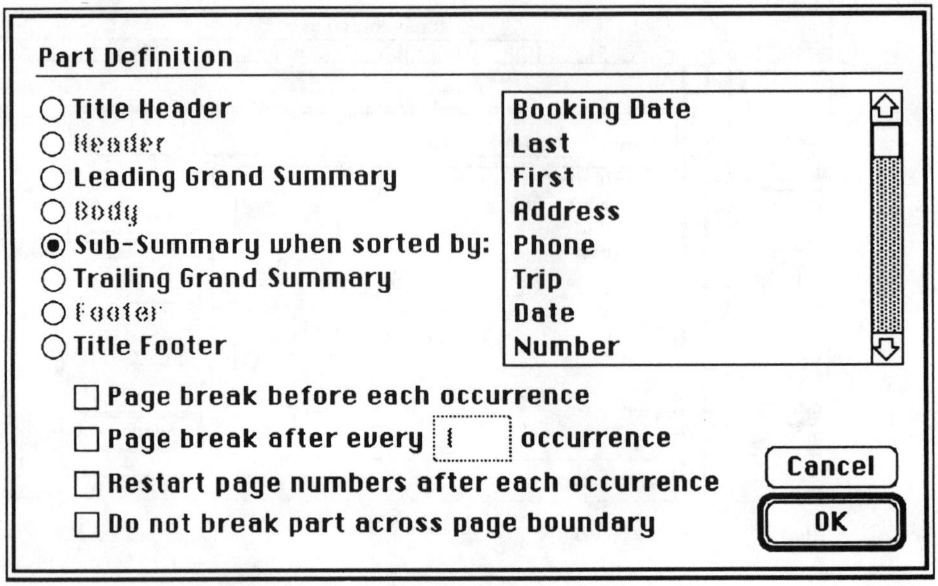

Part Definition
Title Header
Header
Leading Grand Summary
Body
Sub-Summary when sorted by:
Trailing Grand Summary
Footer
Title Footer
Booking Date
Last
First
Address
Phone
Trip
Date
Number
Page break before each occurrence
Page break after every 1 occurrence
Restart page numbers after each occurrence
Do not break part across page boundary
Cancel
OK

Fig. 11-14. Part Definition.

simply check Page break after every and enter 4 in the occurrence box. This is a good example of how FileMaker Pro has moved even closer to the goal putting the power of database management in the hands of nonprogrammers.

Layout Options. The commands needed to change the name of a layout, set up multi-column display, and assign passwords for the layout are all accessed from the Layout Options menu shown in Fig. 11-15. To name a layout, you simply type the desired name in the Name field. Columns are controlled by the Across and Down first buttons, the Display check boxes, and the field for the number of columns.

The Access button in Fig. 11-15 is used to manage passwords, an area of considerable improvement in FileMaker Pro. See the later section on passwords for more information.

Layout Options
Name
Trip Listing
Display in 2 columns
Across first
Down first
Access...
Cancel
OK

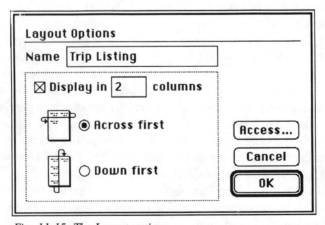

Fig. 11-15. The Layout options.

Ruler Settings. When you need to have precise control over the spacing of a layout, you might want to customize the rulers. The Ruler Settings option, shown in Fig. 11-16, allows you to specify the units for both the rulers and the gridlines. You can choose how coarse or fine to make the gridlines by altering the Grid Spacing.

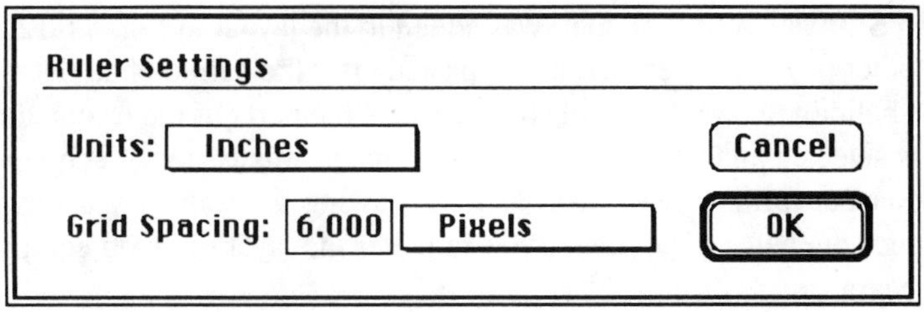

Ruler Settings

Units: [Inches]   (Cancel)

Grid Spacing: [6.000] [Pixels]   (OK)

Fig. 11-16. Ruler settings.

Making Arrangements

The new Arrange menu shown in Fig. 11-17 manages some useful commands for layout design. You now have the ability to group and lock layout objects, and alter their relative level, just as though the layout screen were a drawing program such as MacDraw II.

Arrange

Group	⌘G
Ungroup	⇧⌘G
Lock	**⌘H**
Unlock	⇧⌘H
Bring to Front	
Bring Forward	⇧⌘F
Send to Back	
Send Backward	⇧⌘J
Align Objects	⌘K
Alignment...	⇧⌘K
Slide Objects...	
Tab Order...	

Fig. 11-17. Arrange menu.

Group. When several objects need to be manipulated together, such as the drawing of a balloon in Fig. 11-12, you select the objects, then issue the Group command. This changes the multiple handles of the objects into a single set of handles. The balloon consists of several ellipses, a rounded rectangle, some lines, and a piece of text. Joined as a group, this object can easily be moved without fear of small parts going astray. If part of the balloon drawing needs to be altered, then the Ungroup command can be issued while the balloon is selected, and the drawing dissolves into its original parts.

Lock. Any selected objects can be *locked* so that objects can be pinned to an exact location on the layout. This prevents accidental alteration of objects. Locked objects can still be selected as sliding objects, and locking does not affect tab order. You can lock grouped objects. When an object is locked, its handles change slightly to indicate the locked status.

Shuffle. When the map was added to the layout in Fig. 11-12, it was pasted from another program. Because it was pasted after the balloon had been drawn, it obscured the balloon. The answer was to "shuffle" the parts of the layout. In this case, the map was selected and the Send to Back command was issued. Each new object created on the layout forms a new layer, as in a drawing program. By using the following commands on the Arrange menu, you can alter the layer of an object to achieve the desired appearance:

- Bring to Front   Places selected objects above all others.
- Bring Forward   Moves selected objects one layer closer to top.
- Send to Back   Places selected objects below all others.
- Send Backward   Moves selected objects one layer closer to bottom.

In the case of fields, the creation order is as follows: first field, first field text, second field, second field text, and so on. This corresponds to lowest level, next lowest, and so on. This means that the first time you come to use the Layout mode, the lowest layer will be the first field.

Align Objects. Using the Align Objects menu, you can automatically align and move fields in a variety of different ways (top to bottom, left to right, and so on). As you can see from Fig. 11-18, a sample display in the Align Objects dialog box accurately shows the manner in which selected objects are aligned.

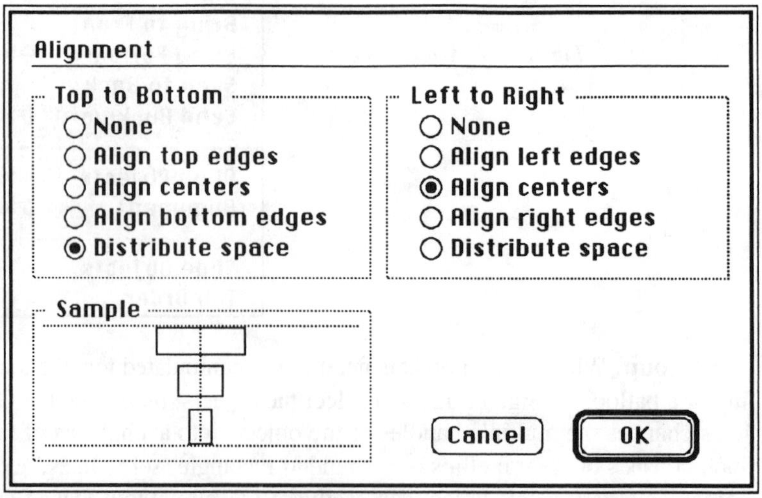

Fig. 11-18. The Alignment dialog box.

Slide Objects. When you want to remove blank spaces between objects during printing, for example to place the last name closer to the first name, you first select the objects that you want to move, then pick the Slide Object command from the Arrange menu. This is a big improvement over previous versions which slid all objects on the layout. In FileMaker Pro each selected object can slide up, left, or both. The individual alignment formatting of the objects (left, middle, right) does not affect sliding. Objects need no longer be precisely aligned to slide.

Non-Printing Objects. In the Slide Objects dialog box, you can elect to make selected objects non-printing. For example, you might have graphics and text that can assist while you are browsing but are not appropriate on a printed report. This option can help you avoid making extra layouts just to remove certain objects from reports. This is particularly useful when using the new "buttons" that are helpful while browsing to execute scripts and automate tasks, but which would not make sense on a printout.

The Formatting Options

As you can see from the menu in Fig. 11-19, FileMaker Pro has several new formatting options, plus a new method of accessing format commands. By double-clicking a field in Layout mode, you bring up the format dialog box appropriate to the field type (text, number, picture, and so on). If more than one field is selected, only the field that the pointer is on is formatted.

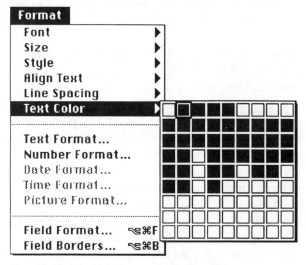

Fig. 11-19. The Format menu with Text Color.

Also different is the approach to setting Defaults. With no objects selected, the defaults chosen become the default choices for formatting options for the file. Previous versions of FileMaker used previous field selection to determine field default selections, which was often awkward.

Text Format. In addition to the Font, Size, Style, and Alignment options, FileMaker Pro now has Line Spacing and Text Color. As you can see from Fig. 11-19, this allows you to select the desired color from a palette box. The text styles available include Condensed and Extended. You can either set text options through the main Format menu or use the Text Format command to review all text settings at once, as shown in Fig. 11-20. Note the use of pop-up menus for easy selection, and the sample text displayed to show the effect of your selections.

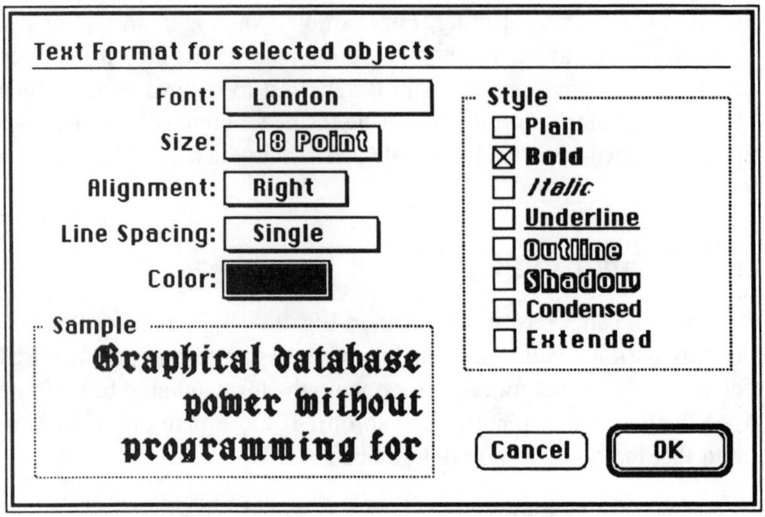

Fig. 11-20. The Text Format box.

Custom Font Size. You can now select a font of any whole point size using the Text Format dialog box. For example, you might want to use 13 or 17, rather than one of the standard sizes. When you use the Size dialog, you can see Custom below the regular sizes. Select Custom, and you can enter the point size you want. This then becomes an available option below Custom if you want to use the size again.

Number Format. Formatting numbers enables you to add currency units, thousands separators, and decimal places. The Default Number Format dialog box is seen in Fig. 11-21. Note the term Default, which means that the format you choose overrides any formatting you use when entering the number.

Note that you can customize the treatment of True/False or Boolean numbers. This allows zero to be formatted as No, while any other value is Yes. Alternatively, you could use False/Correct, Absent/Present, and so on.

As you can see in the lower-left corner of Fig. 11-21, you now have increased flexibility in decimal options and currency representation, with international formatting supported for custom currency symbol, thousands separator, decimal point, and leading/trailing orientation. This is arranged from the Decimal Options dialog box, shown in Fig. 11-22.

In fact, the number formatting allows a level of creativity which Excel users should recognize. For example, suppose you are working with a database of software. You want a field to contain a number that is kilobytes. By using Kb as the currency symbol, and trailing as the symbol position, you can have the field reflect 34 kilobytes

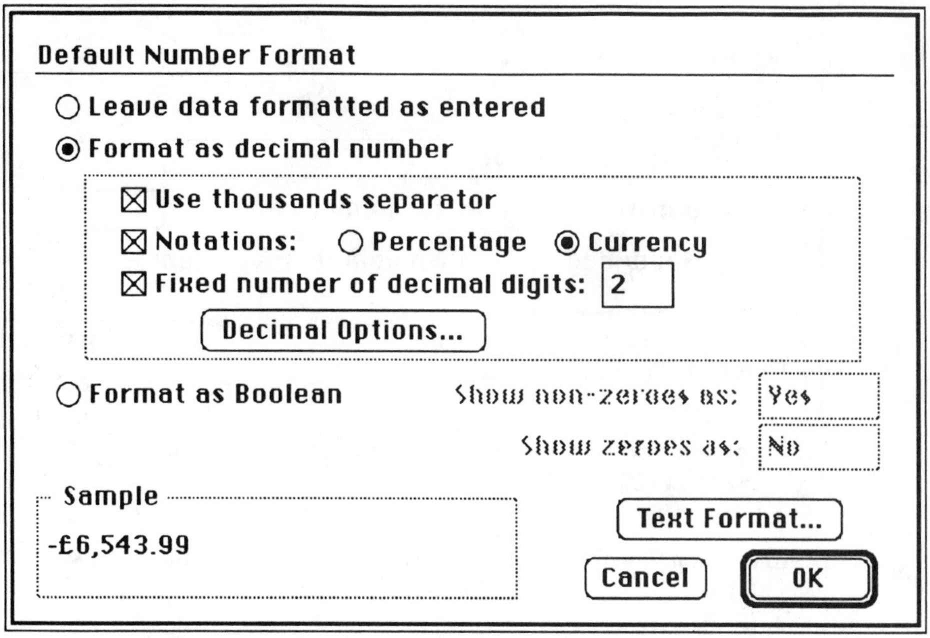

Default Number Format

○ Leave data formatted as entered
◉ Format as decimal number

    ☒ Use thousands separator
    ☒ Notations: ○ Percentage   ◉ Currency
    ☒ Fixed number of decimal digits: `2`

       [Decimal Options...]

○ Format as Boolean   Show non-zeroes as: `Yes`

                           Show zeroes as: `No`

Sample

-£6,543.99   [**Text Format...**]

                      [Cancel] [**OK**]

Fig. 11-21. The default number format.

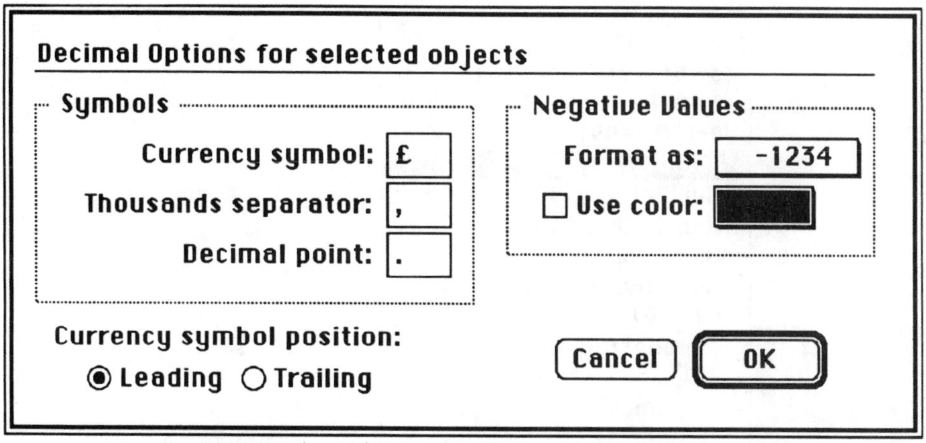

Decimal Options for selected objects

Symbols

    Currency symbol: `£`
    Thousands separator: `,`
    Decimal point: `.`

Negative Values

    Format as: `-1234`
    ☐ Use color: ▉

Currency symbol position:
◉ Leading ○ Trailing

    [Cancel] [**OK**]

Fig. 11-22. Decimal options.

as 34Kb. While there is a limit of three characters for the currency symbol, this still gives you considerable power to format numbers, avoiding the need for layout text position after the field.

Date Format. You can now customize date formats with a new variety of separator characters, leading zeros, and international order. You can see the date formatting menu in Fig. 11-23.

Note the sample date provided to show what the current format looks like. Also

Default Date Format

○ Leave date formatted as entered

◉ Format as: [October 31, 1991]

Separator character for numeric dates: [/]

☐ Show day and month numbers with leading zeroes

┌ Sample ─────────────────────────┐
│ October 31, 1991   │
└──────────────────────────────────┘

[Text Format...]

[Cancel] [OK]

Fig. 11-23. Date formatting.

note the option to include leading zeros. In numeric dates, this results in better alignment of date values. In Fig. 11-24, you can see the range of predefined date formats, which is extensive.

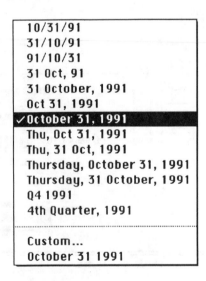

```
10/31/91
31/10/91
91/10/31
31 Oct, 91
31 October, 1991
Oct 31, 1991
✓October 31, 1991
Thu, Oct 31, 1991
Thu, 31 Oct, 1991
Thursday, October 31, 1991
Thursday, 31 October, 1991
Q4 1991
4th Quarter, 1991

Custom...
October 31 1991
```

Fig. 11-24. Available date formats.

Note that this includes continental date order, as well as a very useful quarterly option (this displays the quarter that a specific date falls in). If this list does not have what you want, you can choose the Custom option to create your own format using the menu shown in Fig. 11-25.

This gives you up to four parts for the date, with a choice of separator characters and extensive day/month/quarter/year options. Any formats you create with the Custom option are then added to the list of available formats.

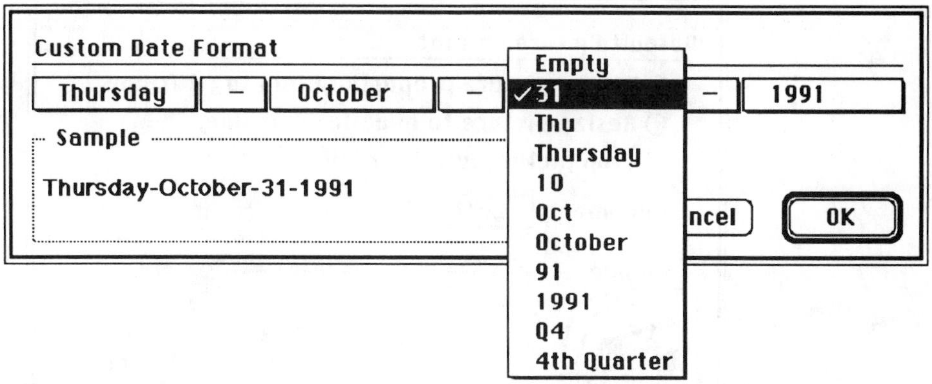

Fig. 11-25. Customizing the date format.

Time Format. To complement the new field type, Time, a special dialog box allows formatting of time values, with HH-MM-SS orientation, AM/PM suffixes, 24-hour or 12-hour time format, and user-selected separator characters. You can see the format options to the right of the menu in Fig. 11-26.

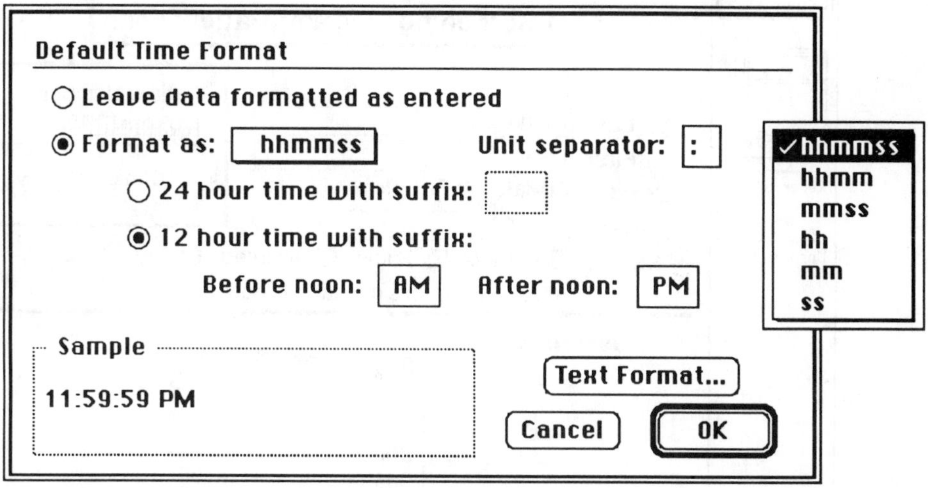

Fig. 11-26. Time formats.

Picture Format. You can format Picture fields with alignment: Left, middle, right. You can also resize pictures proportionally, to fill the frame, or crop to fit. As you can see from Fig. 11-27 a sample graphic shows how the format options you have selected affect an image.

Field Format. One of the most exciting improvements in FileMaker Pro is the implementation of check boxes and radio buttons for field entries (an example of radio buttons was shown earlier in Fig. 11-6). These options allow you to design data entry forms that are more consistent with the Macintosh interface. For example, suppose

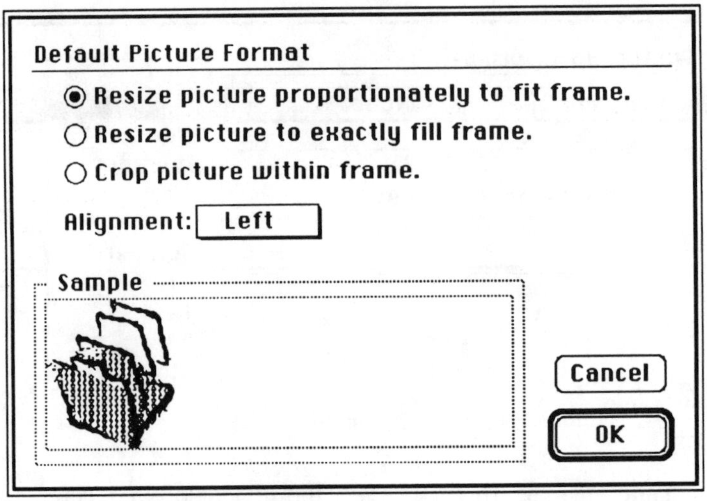

Fig. 11-27. The Picture Format dialog box.

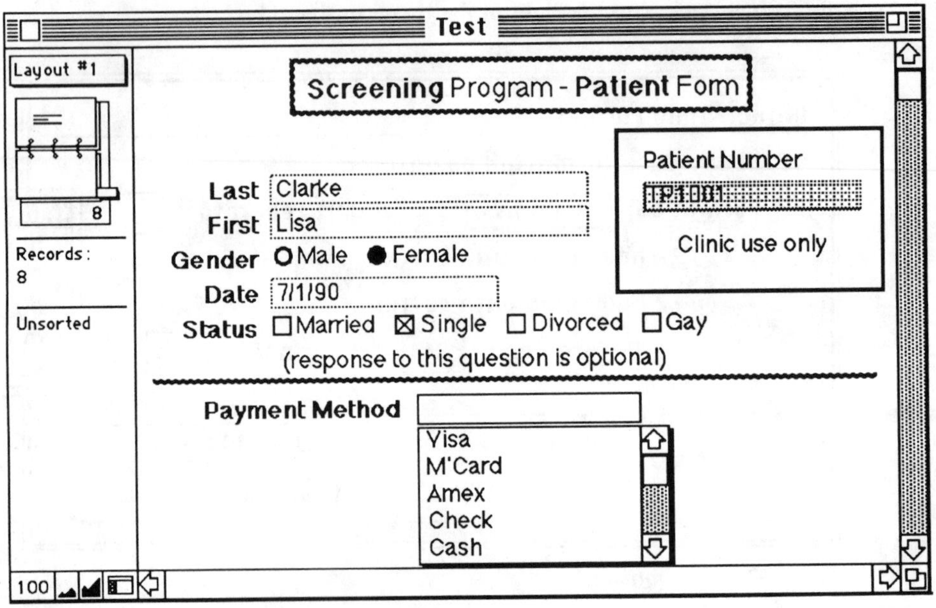

Fig. 11-28. A variety of field formats.

you have a medical form on which you need to record the patient's gender. Using radio buttons like those in Fig. 11-28, you make this as simple as possible.

To set this up you would choose the predefined list of values on the Entry Options when defining the Gender field. The two values Male and Female would be entered in the list. The Field Format command would then be selected from the Format menu in Layout mode. Shown in Fig. 11-29, the menu determines the way in which the value

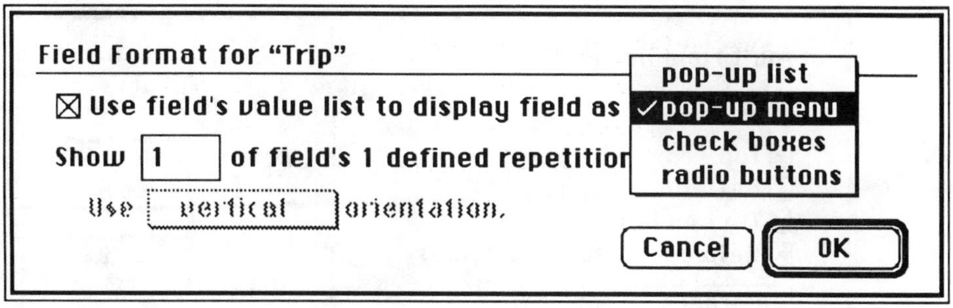

```
┌─────────────────────────────────────────────────────────────┐
│ ┌─────────────────────────────────────────────────────────┐ │
│ │                                      ┌──────────────────┐ │ │
│ │ Field Format for "Trip" ────────────┤   pop-up list    ├─│ │
│ │                                      ├──────────────────┤ │ │
│ │ ☒ Use field's value list to display field as │✓pop-up menu    │ │
│ │                                      │  check boxes     │ │ │
│ │ Show │ 1 │ of field's 1 defined repetition│ radio buttons  │ │
│ │                                      └──────────────────┘ │ │
│ │  Use │  vertical  │ orientation.                          │ │
│ │                              ┌──────────┐  ┌────────────┐ │ │
│ │                              │ Cancel   │  │    OK      │ │ │
│ │                              └──────────┘  └────────────┘ │ │
│ └─────────────────────────────────────────────────────────┘ │
└─────────────────────────────────────────────────────────────┘
```

Fig. 11-29. The Field Format options.

list is displayed. The pop-up list option actually appears like the list in Fig. 11-29. This is best for short lists.

The pop-up menu option appears like the Payment Method field in Fig. 11-28. This allows the user to scroll items in a longer list. The check box option works well where more than one response from a list is possible, as in the Status field in Fig. 11-28. Note that when you are completing a form with lists, check boxes, and buttons, the Tab key does not stop at these fields. To make sure that users select a value from these alternative format fields, you might want to use the Entry Options in Define Fields to require a value.

When you have defined a repeating field, you might want to use the Field Format command to alter the way the repeating field is handled on-screen. If you have defined the field to take 3 values, the message Show 1 of field's 3 defined repetitions appears in the Field Format dialog box. You can then alter this to determine how many field boxes appear, and, if more than one is to be shown, how they are to be organized, either vertically or horizontally.

Field Borders. A lot of time was spent by users of earlier versions of FileMaker trying to get boxes positioned around fields. FileMaker Pro allows you to specify the appearance of each field for both viewing and output. The Format Borders command offers new features for fields, including borders, with custom line width, shading, and color. This allows you to enclose fields in boxes and have them print that way. You can see boxes around the First, Last, and Date fields in Fig. 11-28. Text baselines can also be shown, and field boxes can be filled. This is useful for masking information, as in the Patient Number field in Fig. 11-28, which has an auto-entered number that the user does not need to see. The very compact Field Borders menu is shown in Fig. 11-30.

The check boxes determine where borders are drawn relative to the field box. The sample on the right indicates the effect. The pop-up list that currently says Borders in Fig. 11-30 indicates which part of the design is affected by the color, shading, and line format tools. The other parts are Fill and Baseline. When you have selected the part you want to alter you can then pick a color, a pattern, and a line thickness. The cross icon indicates the current thickness.

Note that you can assign borders between repeating values. The big advantage of boxing fields with the Field Borders commands is that the box automatically changes if

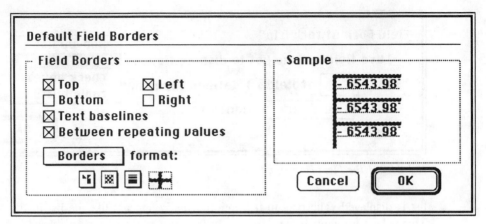

Fig. 11-30. Customizing field borders.

field dimension changes. You can also use the feature to simulate a list structure, with field borders forming a grid instead of layout lines and boxes.

Other Layout Changes

There are numerous subtle changes to working in the Layout mode. For example, a dotted border around the edge of the drawing area clearly shows the current paper margins. The size of the printable area and the overall paper size is based on selected printer and page setup. On color systems, the page margins are shown in off-white to further distinguish them from usable portion of the page. This feature simply allows you to see more distinctly the unprintable portion of the page, yet it does not alter the behavior of layout objects in any way.

The operation of the Tab Order command on the Arrange menu offers a significant improvement over previous tab order controls. You can change the order for an entire layout or for a selected group of fields. When you issue the Tab Order command each field is labeled, as shown in Fig. 11-31.

The original order of this layout had the Patient Number field as the second field. This was distracting for the user and so it was changed to the seventh. Other field numbers alter automatically when one of the numbers is changed. This approach, in which the order numbers are clearly visible, makes specific tab orders very easy to set up.

Sometimes you might want to paste text into a layout from another application. For example, you might have composed a letter in MacWrite II that you want to set up as a layout in FileMaker Pro for a mass mailing. FileMaker Pro accepts the entire text "in format" meaning that if the text is in Courier in MacWrite II, it is in Courier in the layout. In earlier versions of FileMaker, text could only be pasted one line at a time.

FileMaker Pro also allows you to apply different formats to the same piece of layout text. You select the characters you want to format from within a piece of text and then choose the Format command. This means you can mix sizes, styles, and even

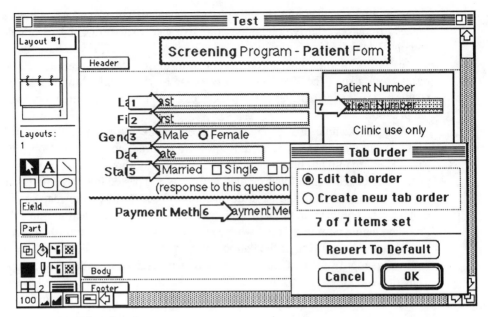

Fig. 11-31. Tab order changes.

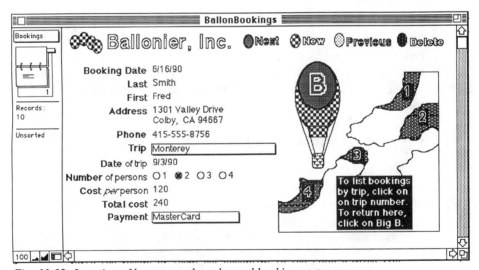

Fig. 11-32. Location of buttons on the enhanced bookings entry screen.

colors within the same piece of text. In Fig. 11-32, you can see a version of the bookings layout that uses this ability in more detailed field text.

Perhaps the most stunning change to the Layout mode is the one we cannot show here: The use of color. This transforms dull forms into appealing designs, and, when used judiciously, color can improve the accuracy of data entry and the effectiveness of reports. Bear in mind that your reports will not be in glowing color unless you have a color output device. When printing colored layouts on a black and white device, File-Maker Pro makes a fairly good attempt to give you what you want—a readable result without light colors fading away as shades of gray. However, if you have made extensive use of color on a layout, you might want to do a test printing to see what the results look like. (The Preview is in color and so does not show black and white results.) Avoid using dark text on a dark background as the text might not show up in the printout.

A good example of the improved Layout mode in operation is shown in Fig. 11-12. The Ruler option is activated, allowing accurate positioning of objects on the page. The Size tool has been activated and is currently showing the size of the map, a picture object. This object was created in Canvas and pasted into the layout. The Send to Back command from the Arrange menu was used to place the map in the background. The numbers on the four regions were added with the text tool in FileMaker Pro. The numbers were colored white, given a shaded background, then placed over the regions. The drawing of the balloon was created with the FileMaker Pro drawing tools. To simplify matters, the elements that make up the balloon were combined using the Arrange Group command. This allows the balloon to be moved more easily, and brought forward in the design using the Arrange Bring Forward command.

INTRODUCING BUTTONS

The enhanced version of the bookings layout shown in Fig. 11-32 features one of the most exciting additions in FileMaker Pro—*buttons*. These are areas of a layout that, when clicked, activate a command or script. In Fig. 11-32, the four small balloons labeled Next, New, Previous, and Delete have buttons. Also buttons are on the four numbers representing the areas covered by the four different trips offered by the balloon company.

Creating Command Buttons

Buttons can be placed in any layout part, including the header. Any layout object except a field can be a button. The Next button in Fig. 11-32 is in the header. Clicking on this button takes the user to the next record. The button actually consists of the text Next plus an oval drawing object. To turn these two objects into a command button they were selected in Layout mode, and the Define Button command was chosen from the Scripts menu. The Define Button menu is shown in Fig. 11-33.

You can see the button can either perform a script, issue a command, or switch to a layout. If you select Perform a script, you can select from existing scripts. This means that a script has to be created before it can be assigned to a button. If you choose Switch to layout, you can choose from a pop-up menu of existing layouts. If you choose Perform a command, you can select the command from a pop-up list. The choices available are listed in Table 11-1.

In the example, the Go To Next Record command was selected. When a command involves a dialog box, as in the case of the Print command, you can elect to skip the

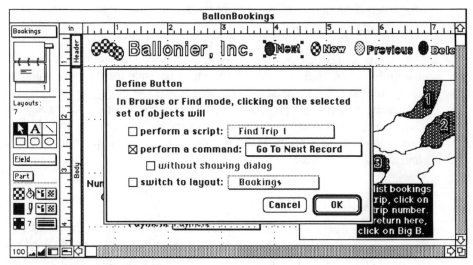

Fig. 11-33. The Define Button menu.

Table 11-1. Commands That Can Be Assigned to Buttons.

Close	Open
Define Fields	Page Setup
Delete Found Set	Paste Current Date
Delete Record	Paste From Index
Duplicate Record	Paste Current Time
Export	Paste From Last Record
Find Omitted	Preview
Find	Print
Find All	Quit
Go To Next Record	Refind
Go To Record	Relookup
Go To Previous Field	Replace
Go To Next Field	Save a Copy As
Go To Previous Record	Sort
Help	Spell Check Selection
Import	Spell Check Record
New Record	Spell Check Found Set
Omit Multiple	Toggle Status Area
Omit	Toggle View-As-List

dialog box. This allows you to create "instant action" buttons that work without pausing for confirmation.

When the button has been defined, you select OK to return to the layout. If you have selected multiple objects to act as the button, as in the case of the oval and the Next text, you should find that they have also been grouped. If you attempt to use the Ungroup command to separate the objects, FileMaker Pro warns you that this cancels the button definition. You might want to use the Slide Objects command to make the buttons nonprinting objects.

By assigning basic commands like "go to next record" to buttons, you can develop databases that even the most inexperienced of users can work with. You can even turn off the status area and let the user navigate the database without the book icon. However, you do need to give some thought to button actions. For example, if you create a button that takes the user to a different layout, you might want to make sure that another button can bring the user back to familiar territory. If you want the button to carry out a series of actions, then you probably will want to create a script and then assign it to a button.

Creating Script Buttons

Suppose that you want a button that lists all of the people who have bookings for a certain location. This can be accomplished in several ways, one of which would be to create a new list-style layout and then issue a Find command based on the name of the trip, such as Monterey. This action can then be used as the basis of a script. The scripting facilities in FileMaker Pro are much the same as in previous versions, with some improvements as described in the next section. Having created the script, you then select the layout object you want to trigger the script, and issue the Define Button command. So far, the process is fairly straightforward (for more on scripting, see Chapter 10).

What makes script buttons somewhat complex is the need to plan a series of buttons, so that users have a consist set of commands. For example, if you create a button on the main data entry screen that displays a list of trips to Monterey, you should provide a button that brings the user back to the data entry screen. If you are designing applications for others to use, then you should make sure that you do not create buttons that set off a string of events that confuses the user. As long as you bear these caveats in mind, you will find buttons a great help in making FileMaker Pro databases even easier and more "Mac-like" to use.

SCRIPTING

FileMaker Pro provides for scripts in much the same ways as earlier versions, although the commands are streamlined. You also have more options, as you can see from the screen in Fig. 11-34. Most of the options are provided in the form of pop-up menus. When switching to a layout, the layout name is shown, making correct identification much easier.

You can elect to pause a sort script during execution for the entry of sort criteria. You can also restore sort order, then pause to confirm or change. You can also elect to pause a script for find criteria with the option of restoring finds, then pausing to confirm or change.

A script can now be defined to perform any set or sequence of other scripts, without the linked scripts being modified. This means a more flexible combination of tasks

```
┌──────────────────────────────────────────────────────────────┐
│  ┌────────────────────────────────────────────────────────┐  │
│  │ Definition for Script:                                   │  │
│  │ "Monterey"                                               │  │
│  ├────────────────────────────────────────────────────────┤  │
│  │ ┌··When performing this script, automatically: ········┐ │  │
│  │ : ⊠ Switch to layout: │ Monterey Trips │               : │  │
│  │ : ⊠ Restore the Page Setup options                     : │  │
│  │ : ☐ Restore the import order and import from a file    : │  │
│  │ : ⊠ Find: │ Restore find requests and find │           : │  │
│  │ : ⊠ Sort: │ Restore sort order and sort │              : │  │
│  │ : ☐ Preview                                            : │  │
│  │ : ☐ Restore the export order and export to a file      : │  │
│  │ : ⊠ Print: │ without Print dialog │                    : │  │
│  │ : ⊠ Return to: │ original layout │                     : │  │
│  │ : ⊠ Perform a chain of scripts: │ Edit Chain... │      : │  │
│  │ └······················································┘ │  │
│  │                                                          │  │
│  │  ⊠ Include in menu              │ Cancel │  ║  OK  ║     │  │
│  └────────────────────────────────────────────────────────┘  │
└──────────────────────────────────────────────────────────────┘
```

Fig. 11-34. Defining a script.

is now possible. The previous versions required script #1 to trigger script #2, and script #2 to trigger script #3. Script #2 could then not be run in isolation without also executing script #3. Now you define a chain, using the Edit Chain dialog box, which lists scripts by number and name.

Further streamlining allows you to print from a script without pause to select OK from the print dialog box. This makes possible a *print button* that prints without any other input. You can also tell a script to return you to a selected layout after the script is run, which allows easier switching of layouts in scripts. Previously you could only return to the starting layout.

TIMES AND OTHER CALCULATIONS

Several improvements to calculation abilities in FileMaker Pro include several new functions and a new field type: Time. FileMaker Pro provides improved calculation speed and accommodates larger formulas. The limit is now 32K in size, allowing for more complex calculations, especially with regard to nested IF functions and text calculations. The previous limit was 250 characters.

The Time Type

FileMaker Pro has a new field type for time, plus appropriate formatting, to enable you to design databases incorporating time calculations, such as billing, and so on. This avoids the need for some of the complex time formulas described in Chapter 10. In Fig. 11-35, you can see an example of a database using the new time fields. Note the formatting of the time and date fields.

This database records the date and time that a patient enters the clinic. The Date and Time fields are actually auto-enter fields that record the time the record is created. The Released field shows the date the patient was released and the At field records the time of release. When only hours and minutes are needed, the time can be entered in 9:30 PM format. You can use a 24-hour format so that 21:30 would be entered instead of 9:30 PM. When greater accuracy is required, you can add seconds, as in 9:30:25 PM meaning 25 seconds past half past nine in the evening.

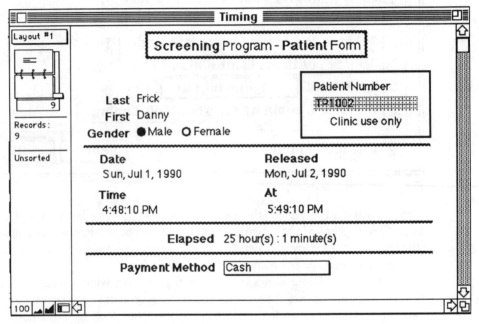

Fig. 11-35. Time-oriented database.

Time Formulas

When you come to manipulate time information for calculations you need to know that the basic measurement unit of time in FileMaker Pro is one second. FileMaker Pro considers one full day to be composed of 86,400 seconds ($24 \times 60 \times 60$). Within the same day, it is easy to perform time calculations such as clocking in and out. However, because date fields use a unit of 1 for each day, time math that extends past one day still requires some clever calculations. The easiest approach is to use a number of intermediate fields that convert days to seconds, or seconds to fractions of a day. Unfortunately, the ability to format values as time does not take care of the problems of combining different units of time. The Elapsed field in Fig. 11-35 uses the following formula to calculate the number of hours and minutes between Date/Time and Released/At:

NumToText (Int((((Released - Date)*86400) + ((At)-(Time)))/3600)) &
" hour(s) : " & NumToText(Round((60*(Mod ((((Released -
Date)*86400) + ((At)-(Time)))/3600,Int((((Released -
Date)*86400) + ((At)-(Time)))/3600)))),0)) & " minute(s)"

The result type is text. The heart of the formula is the following calculation which puts the difference between the two days/times into hours.

((((Released - Date)*86400) + ((At)-(Time)))/3600))

Note the use of the constant value 86,400 to turn days into seconds. The constant 3600 turns seconds into hours. The Int function gives you the number of complete hours (25 in the example). The following calculation uses the Mod function to find the fraction of an hour left over when the main formula is divided by the integer of its result:

Mod ((((Released - Date)*86400) + ((At)-(Time)))/3600,Int
((((Released - Date)*86400) + ((At)-(Time)))/3600))

By multiplying the result of this calculation by 60 and rounding to zero you get the number of whole minutes. All that remains is to use the NumToText functions and some text strings to flesh out the answer to a presentable form. Although FileMaker Pro allows larger formulas than previous versions, the full formula for the Elapsed field pushes the current limit. If longer field names were used, the formula could exceed the program's capacity.

Time Functions

A number of new functions are provided in FileMaker Pro to help you work with time values:

- Time   This function converts the numbers supplied into a valid time (remember that the units for time are seconds, allowing valid time values of $0-86,400$). Numbers greater than 86,400 are converted to the maximum time (24:00:00). The user must enter all three arguments or an error is returned.

- Second   This function takes the time supplied and returns the second that is contained in the time $(0-60)$. Zero is returned if the time is in the format hh:mm.

- Minute   This function takes the time supplied and returns the minute that is contained in the time $(0-60)$.

- Hour   This function takes the time supplied and returns the hour that is contained in the time $(0-24)$. Zero is returned if the time is in the mm:ss format.

Also, appropriate string conversion functions change text in time format to a time value (TextToTime) and to convert a time value to text (TimeToText).

Calendar Functions

In addition to the time functions, several calendar functions have been added to FileMaker Pro:

- MonthName   This function takes the date provided and returns the month in text form. For example, MonthName (11/15/91) returns November.

- DayName   This function takes the date provided and returns the day of the week (Monday, Tuesday, and so on). For example, DayName (10/10/90) returns Wednesday.

- DayofYear   This function calculates the actual day of the year (1−365). The first day of the year is January 1. Day order is computed based on the order in the international resource.

- WeekofYear   This function takes the date provided and returns the week number of the year in the range 1−54 where Monday marks the first day of the week (note that with 52 weeks per year plus the possibility of partial weeks at both the start and end of year means 54 weeks are possible).

Other New Functions

A number of other new functions expand the range of calculations possible with FileMaker Pro. They include new math and trigonometric functions.

Math Functions. FileMaker applications requiring heavy duty math capability have four more functions to call on: Exp, Log, Ln, Random, and Sqrt:

- Exp   This function raises the value of the natural logarithmic base (2.7182818...) to the power of the number in the function's argument. This performs the inverse of the Ln function. For example, Exp(1) = 2.7182818 while Exp(4) = 54.59815. Note that using Exp with any value greater than 23 produces an error.

- Log   This function returns the base 10 logarithm of the number supplied. Thus Log(100) = 2. If the value supplied is zero or less than zero, then the function returns an error.

- Ln   This function returns the natural logarithm of a number, so that Ln(100) = 4.60517. If the value supplied is zero or less than zero, then the function returns an error.

- Random   This function returns a random value between 0 and 1. The number is produced whenever a new record containing a calculation field using Random is created. Note that this function takes no arguments. While not everyone uses this function, it is very valuable for developers who need a large collection of data to test new databases. Using Random in a calculation field along with other functions you can produce realistic numeric values for fields like sales, salaries, and so on. For example, to create a collection of whole numbers between 1 and 50, you could enter the formula, Round((49-1)*Rand + 1),0) in a calculation field. Each record in the database will now show a number from 1 to 50 in this field. You can then turn the formulas into fixed values by changing the field type to Number.

- Sqrt   This function takes the argument provided and returns the square root. Thus Sqrt(16) = 4. This is useful in trigonometrical calculations, such as the calculation of the hypotenuse, or slope, of a triangle. For example, Sqrt(Base * Base + Height * Height) = Slope.

In fact, several new functions in FileMaker Pro cater specifically to trigonometric calculations. These are described in the next section.

Trigonometric Functions. Not everyone needs to calculate angles, curves, and areas, but when you do need to work with values of this kind, it is useful to have some basic functions to help you deal with calculations. FileMaker Pro adds the following functions:

- Atan   This function returns the arctangent of an argument or expression which has a value that is an angle in degrees.

- Cos   This function takes the argument or expression supplied as a number in degrees and returns the cosine of the number.

- Degrees   This function converts an angle specified in radians to degrees. Useful when working with other trigonometric functions.

- PI   This function returns the constant pi accurate to 17 decimal places (PI = 3.14159265358979324). This is useful when working with circles:

Area of circle = PI * Radius ^ 2
Circumference of circle = 2 * PI * Radius

Note that there is no argument for the PI function.

- Radians   This function converts an angle specified in degrees to radian. Useful when working with angles.

- Sin   This function takes the argument which is an angle in degrees and returns the sine of the number.

- Tan   This function returns the tangent of a number that is an angle expressed in degrees.

To put these new trig functions in perspective consider the diagram in Fig. 11-36.

Other Functions. A new function is provided in FileMaker Pro for use with repeating fields. The Last function returns the last value in a repeating field. Another new function, Summary, returns the totals in a summary field for all records with the same entry in break field. If the summary field is also used as the break field, this function supplies the Grand Summary.

THE SPELL FACTOR

While word processing programs have long supported the use of electronic spell-checkers, other applications such as spreadsheets and databases have had to make do

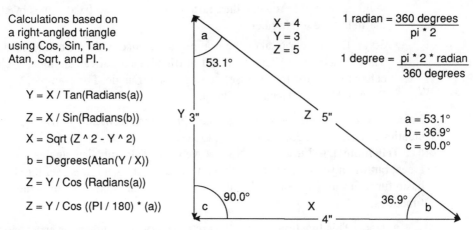

Calculations based on
a right-angled triangle
using Cos, Sin, Tan,
Atan, Sqrt, and PI.

X = 4
Y = 3
Z = 5

53.1°

$$1 \text{ radian} = \frac{360 \text{ degrees}}{\text{pi} * 2}$$

$$1 \text{ degree} = \frac{\text{pi} * 2 * \text{radian}}{360 \text{ degrees}}$$

Y = X / Tan(Radians(a))

Z = X / Sin(Radians(b))

X = Sqrt (Z ^ 2 - Y ^ 2)

b = Degrees(Atan(Y / X))

Z = Y / Cos (Radians(a))

Z = Y / Cos ((PI / 180) * (a))

Y 3"   Z 5"

a = 53.1°
b = 36.9°
c = 90.0°

90.0°   c   X   36.9°   b

4"

Fig. 11-36. Examples of trigonometric functions at work.

without. This used to be merely annoying, but now that many users are publishing reports directly from database and spreadsheet programs, the problem is more serious. As many FileMaker users know, it is all too easy to overlook a simple typo in a piece of layout text or even a field name, only to find the error duplicated a hundred-fold in a database. FileMaker Pro tackles this problem by providing a complete spelling facility that checks layouts and records, and even warns you of errors as you type!

Using the Spelling Checker

The spelling checker in FileMaker Pro is activated by the Check Spelling command on the Edit menu, shown in Fig. 11-37. The system works exactly like that in MacWrite II. In fact, FileMaker Pro can share dictionaries with MacWrite II. If you already know how to use the Spelling command in MacWrite II, then the Check Spelling command in FileMaker Pro is plain sailing.

As you can see from Fig. 11-37, you can check the spelling of text on a layout when in Layout mode. If you select a number of layout text objects you can select Check Selection. When in Browse mode, you can check the current record or the current set of found records. If you want to check the most recently typed word you can use the Spell Word command, which has a shortcut keystroke of Shift−Command−Y.

The FileMaker Pro spelling checker works by comparing the words in a layout or record with two lists of words. One list is a list of 100,000 words stored in a specially compressed format in a file called Main Dictionary. Additional words are stored in a plain text file called User Dictionary. If FileMaker Pro cannot find a word used in a record or layout in either of these files, it considers the word to be questionable and asks you to decide what should be done with the word. Your options are as listed in Table 11-2.

As you can see from Fig. 11-38, these options appear in the Spelling dialog box. The questionable word, in this case Compony, is actually highlighted in both the dialog box and the layout or record being checked (the highlighting does not appear in the

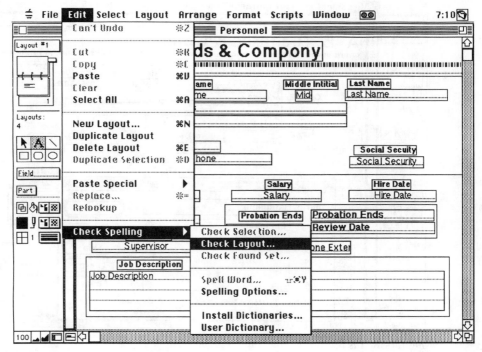

Fig. 11-37. The Edit Check Spelling menu.

Table 11-2. Options When Spell Checking.

1 Replace the word, giving you a chance to:

    a Edit the questionable word and then click on Replace to change this, and all other occurrences in the layout or record, to the corrected version.

    b Choose to replace the questionable word with a suggested alternative from the list provided, in this and all other instances in the layout/record (the number of instances is shown in the status area at the bottom of the spelling dialog box.

    c Accept the questionable word for this spell operation by clicking on it and then Replace.

2 Edit the word and then Check it again.

3 Skip the word, meaning that the word is acceptable in this instance, and all other instances in this record or layout.

4 Learn the word, meaning that it will be added to the list of words in the User Dictionary and thus no longer appears questionable in this and future sessions.

5 Cancel the spelling operation.

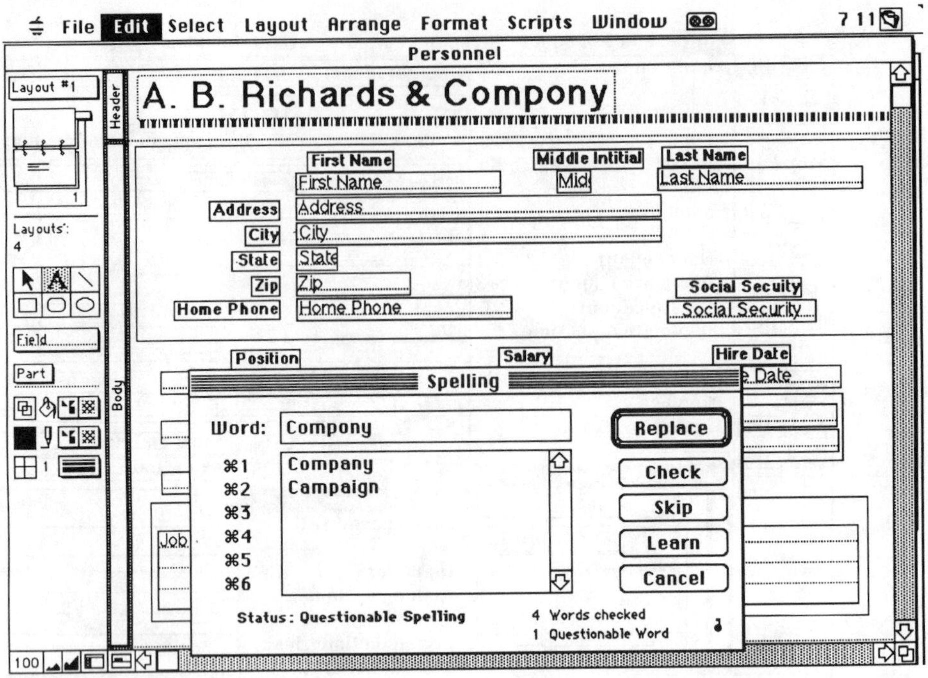

Fig. 11-38. The Spelling dialog box.

figure). The list below the questionable spelling in the dialog box shows possible alternatives.

The first alternative spelling in the list is normally highlighted for you. In this case, all you need to do is press Return or click Replace to correct the mistake. If you want to replace the questionable word with another of the words in the list you would click on that word, then click Replace (you can also use the Command–number option to select one of the words from the list).

If there is a valid reason for accepting the questionable word, for example, if it was a trade name or intentional misspelling, then you can either click on the Word box and then click Replace, or click on Skip. If you want to skip this questionable word in future spelling sessions as well, then you can select Learn, which adds the word to the User Dictionary file. This file is used for those special words that are correct as far as you are concerned, from fancy words like sphygmomanometer and gigabyte, which are correct but not in the dictionary, to trade names like FileMaker. You can always review the User Dictionary by using the User Dictionary command on the Check Spelling menu. This presents a simple dialog box, shown in Fig. 11-39, used for deleting, editing, or adding words.

Note that each variation on a word, including plural and capitalized forms, counts as a separate entry. As your User Dictionary grows it can become a valuable resource, speeding up successive spell checks. However, it is a good idea to review the file from time to time, particularly if you think you have added an incorrect word. Also, beware

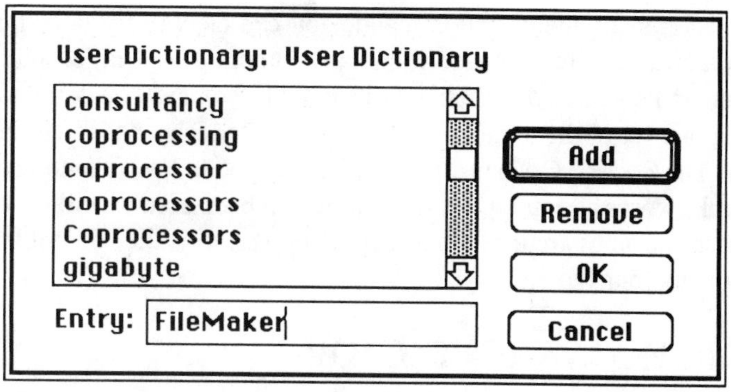

```
┌─────────────────────────────────────────────────────┐
│ ┌───────────────────────────────────────────────────┐ │
│ │ User Dictionary: User Dictionary                  │ │
│ │ ┌──────────────────────────┐ ┌─────────────────┐  │ │
│ │ │ consultancy            ⬆ │ │                 │  │ │
│ │ │ coprocessing             │ │      Add        │  │ │
│ │ │ coprocessor              │ └─────────────────┘  │ │
│ │ │ coprocessors             │ ┌─────────────────┐  │ │
│ │ │ Coprocessors             │ │    Remove       │  │ │
│ │ │ gigabyte               ⬇ │ └─────────────────┘  │ │
│ │ └──────────────────────────┘ ┌─────────────────┐  │ │
│ │   Entry: │FileMaker│          │      OK         │  │ │
│ │                              └─────────────────┘  │ │
│ │                              ┌─────────────────┐  │ │
│ │                              │    Cancel       │  │ │
│ │                              └─────────────────┘  │ │
│ └───────────────────────────────────────────────────┘ │
└─────────────────────────────────────────────────────┘
```

Fig. 11-39. The User Dictionary command.

of adding too many short words and acronyms that can be mistaken for common typos.

When the entire selection has been checked, the status message in the Spelling dialog box says Finished Spelling, and the Replace button changes to Done. You can click this or press Return to put away the dialog box. The dialog box will tell you the number of words checked and the number of questionable words, a feature that is perhaps more useful when using spell checking in word processing programs. The Check Spelling feature is a very welcome addition to FileMaker, but you must bear in mind that it does not really check spelling: It merely compares lists of words. This means that the following text is not called into question, even though it is wrong: Peas enter yaw add dress hear. Until context-sensitive spell checking technology is available, you will still need to proof read your documents yourself and have a colleague double-check for good measure. Use the Check Spelling command to help you find problems, but do not rely on it for word-perfect documents.

Configuring the Speller

If you install FileMaker Pro according to the manual's instructions you should be all set to use the Check Spelling command. If you select Check Spelling and get a message like Cannot find dictionary, then you need to check the location of your Main Dictionary and User Dictionary files, and make sure that FileMaker Pro knows where they are, using the Install Dictionaries command on the Check Spelling menu. File-Maker Pro automatically finds and uses files called Main Dictionary and User Dictionary if they are stored in the System folder or the FileMaker Pro folder. This is handy for MacWrite II users since MacWrite II also finds dictionaries in the System folder. Sharing the same dictionaries saves space, and can eliminate extra work adding special words to the User Dictionary file. If you keep the files elsewhere, you have to point out their location using the Install Dictionaries command, each session that you use the Check Spelling feature.

The Install Dictionaries command is also used when you want to work with a different dictionary. You can create a number of different user dictionaries for different projects, using the New command. You can elect to use a different main dictionary, perhaps a foreign language dictionary supplied by Claris. While you can have one main and one user dictionary as the default, you can check the same file against more than one set of dictionaries by using the Install Dictionaries command.

The Spelling Options command allows you to invoke automatic spell checking that checks words as you type. This feature can beep at misspellings or flash the menu bar. These warnings are useful and not too obtrusive as they do not stop you from continuing with your typing.

THE PASSWORD FACTOR

FileMaker Pro offers a more comprehensive password system than its predecessors. This is only appropriate as the added features of FileMaker Pro mean that it will be taking on increasingly important tasks involving what will at times be sensitive and confidential data.

Setting Up Passwords

The basic purpose of a password is to maintain the confidentiality of data stored in a FileMaker Pro file. When a file is first created, it has no password protection on it. This means that anyone who uses your computer can open the file. To place a password on your file, you deselect Exclusive on the File menu and then use the Define Passwords option on the Access Privileges menu, which is reached via File. As you can see from Fig. 11-40, this allows you to define one or more passwords for a file, each of which can have a variety of privileges assigned to it.

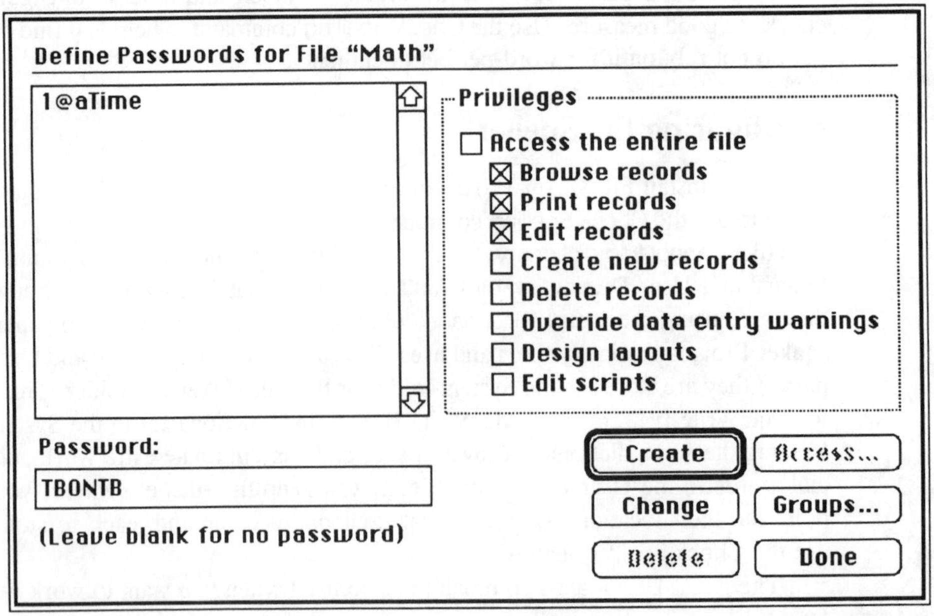

Define Passwords for File "Math"

1@aTime

Privileges
- ☐ Access the entire file
- ☒ Browse records
- ☒ Print records
- ☒ Edit records
- ☐ Create new records
- ☐ Delete records
- ☐ Override data entry warnings
- ☐ Design layouts
- ☐ Edit scripts

Password:

TBONTB

(Leave blank for no password)

Create | Access...
Change | Groups...
Delete | Done

Fig. 11-40. Defining a password.

The first password in a file should be one that can Access the entire file. If you are not connected to other users on a network, you only need one password. When you select Done from the Define Passwords menu, FileMaker Pro checks to make sure that you have at least one password that has entire file access, and makes sure that you know it, by presenting the dialog box shown in Fig. 11-41. Note that when you confirm the password by typing it, FileMaker Pro conceals what you type, to help keep the password confidential. The same "blind" typing is used when you supply the password upon opening a protected file.

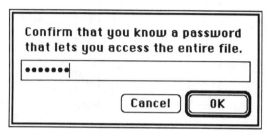

Fig. 11-41. Typing in the password.

Be warned that once you have assigned a password to a file you need to remember the password to be able to get back into the file the next time you come to use it. Without the password, the file is locked forever.

If your Macintosh is connected to others on a network, your FileMaker Pro files do not automatically become available to other users. As in earlier versions, File-Maker Pro gives you exclusive access to a file when it is first created and thereafter until you deselect Exclusive on the File menu.

Deselecting Exclusive makes the file available to others who have network access to your disk. You should not deselect Exclusive without selecting Access Privileges and defining a password. This limits the users who can access the file to those who have the password.

When allowing others to use your file, you might want to restrict what they can do to the file. As you can see from Fig. 11-40, you can do this by creating a password with limited privileges. A more detailed way to control access is to create a group. The Define Group command allows you to create a group that then has a password assigned to it. You can control access by group members down to specific layouts and fields. This is managed by the Overview option of the Access Privileges menu, as shown in Fig. 11-42.

As you can see by interpreting the icons, the Admin group has access to all layouts and fields. This is so that the file's manager can control all aspects of the file. A data entry operator would not need such broad access. In Fig. 11-43, you can see a modified set of privileges for the DataEntry group. Here there are some fields and layouts that are View-only.

As you can see, the pointer changes to a check mark when it passes over the selection column for any of the four columns in the screen. Using this new screen, you can

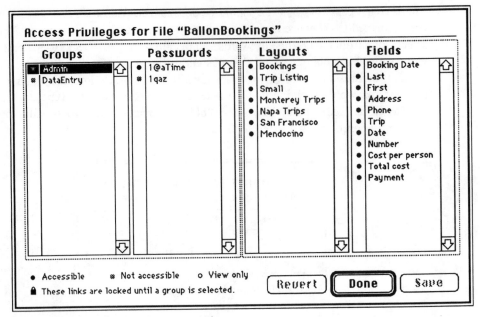

Fig. 11-42. The overview of access privileges.

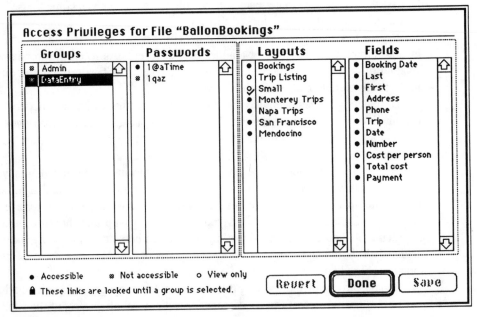

Fig. 11-43. Altered access privileges.

easily manage quite complex sets of privileges appropriate to any networking situation. Some of the more subtle changes in access privileges are the ability to prevent users from overriding dialog alerts that come up when entry option conditions are not met. You can prevent users from modifying scripts, allowing browse-only users to benefit from scripts without changing them. You can allow creation of new records without altering existing records. This is useful when clerical help is needed to enter data, as is the ability to prevent users from printing records, even though they might see records on screen.

You might see a couple of icons in FileMaker Pro while working on a network. The "double-headed crank arrow" sometimes appears to indicate that the window is being updated, typically by changes made elsewhere on the network. The "coffee-cup" icon appears when another user's request for data temporarily halts your access to a file.

IMPROVED IMPORTS AND EXPORTS

No single software program can do everything, so FileMaker Pro makes a real effort to get along with other applications, providing improved import/export features. The range of file formats that can now be read and written include: DBF, DIF, and WKS. These are primarily used by programs on the IBM PC. The DBF format was created by dBASE. The WKS format was created by Lotus 1-2-3, and although it is not the latest version of the 1-2-3 format it is a very useful "common denominator" format that can be read by a vast range of programs from Quattro Pro to Excel and from Paradox to 1-2-3/G.

Streamlined Menus

Apart from supporting a wider range of formats, FileMaker Pro has streamlined the import/export process, as you can see from the export field order screen in Fig. 11-44. The order of fields can be altered by dragging with the up/down pointer. By changing the order, you can ensure that the data is input correctly the first time, with less trial and error. The inclusion of fields is altered with the check-mark pointer that appears when the pointer moves into the select column.

As you can see, when exporting data, you can now choose to export the data unformatted or you can format the output using the formats of the current layout. This makes life easier for the recipient of the exported file. When you are using a File-Maker Pro format that has no corresponding format in the export format, for example when you send dates in October 31, 1991 format to the WKS format, then FileMaker Pro chooses something close, in this case, 31-Oct-91.

Notice that the File list in the Input From dialog box is filtered to show only those files of the type specified by the user. Another import improvement is the ability to scan data. As you can see from Fig. 11-45, Scan Data gives you the ability to see which data from the input file is going into what fields in the FileMaker Pro database. This makes life a lot easier!

In this case, the spreadsheet file being imported does not contain as many fields as the receiving file, but FileMaker Pro has successfully matched the fields. The "VCR" type buttons allow you to flip through records to make sure each one is correct.

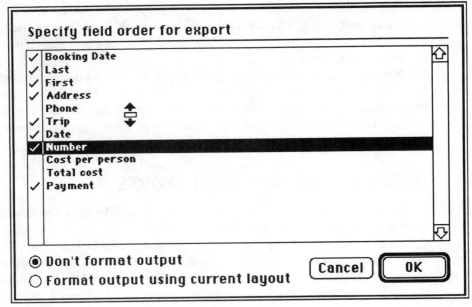

Fig. 11-44. Export field order screen.

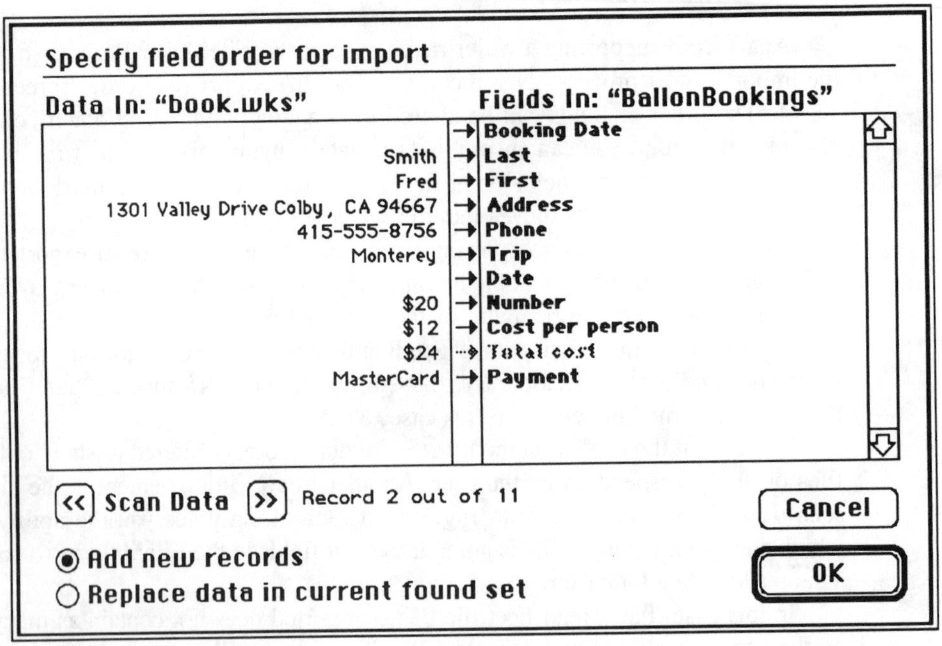

Specify field order for import

Data In: "book.wks"   Fields In: "BallonBookings"

	→ Booking Date
Smith	→ Last
Fred	→ First
1301 Valley Drive Colby, CA 94667	→ Address
415-555-8756	→ Phone
Monterey	→ Trip
	→ Date
$20	→ Number
$12	→ Cost per person
$24	⋯→ Total cost
MasterCard	→ Payment

〈〈 Scan Data 〉〉 Record 2 out of 11   Cancel

◉ Add new records   OK
○ Replace data in current found set

Fig. 11-45. Importing data.

Graphics Imports

Another aspect of importing with FileMaker Pro is the ability to read a variety of graphic file formats. Now images in TIFF and EPS graphic formats can be read directly into FileMaker Pro, either as entries in picture fields or as illustrations on layouts. This eliminates the need to use the Clipboard for transferring images and means you can use higher quality art. Previously, FileMaker could take only Mac-

Table 11-3. New Keystrokes.

Option−double clicking on a field in either Browse or Layout mode brings up the Field Definitions dialog.

Double−clicking a field name in Field Definition dialog brings up entry options.

Command−O for Open brings up Standard Open file dialog. Previously used to activate Omit.

Command−G for Group groups selected objects. Previously used to activate Find All.

Command−H for Lock locks selected objects. Previously used to activate Define Scripts.

Command−Y for Find Omitted finds omitted records. Previously used to toggle invisible grid.

Command−Shift−P activates Print without displaying dialog. Previously activated with Command−Option−P. Changed to avoid conflict with format, style, alignment dialog shortcuts.

Command−Shift−E deletes a record, request, or layout depending on active mode. Previously activated with Command−Option−E. Changed to avoid conflict with format, style, alignment dialog shortcuts.

Esc bypasses a pop-up list, hides the list, and leaves the cursor in the active field, allowing for easier manual entry when the pop-up list does not have the desired value for the field. Manual selection of field with Tab key or mouse was required in previous versions, slowing data entry and removing hands from keyboard.

Shift−Command−D brings up Field Definition dialog. No keyboard equivalent was available for this task in previous versions.

Shift−dragging items restricts horizontal/vertical movement. Changed from Option−drag for consistency with other applications.

Shift−drag constrains while objects are created or modified restricts as squares, circles, and straight lines. Previous versions used Option−drag to constrain tools.

Dragging the cursor to select multiple objects normally selects only objects completely enclosed within the area. Command−drag also selects any "touching" object as well. As in MacDraw II.

After highlighting a tool (line, ellipse, rectangle, etc.), choosing Select All selects all objects created with the particular tool. Same as MacDraw II.

Option−D duplicates a selected layout object (same as Duplicate Selection from Edit menu). Same as MacDraw II.

Paint, PICT, and PICT2 images, which had to be manually placed on the clipboard and pasted in. With the File Import option for reading graphics files, the size limit of 280K for graphic images is thus circumvented.

A BETTER PREVIEW

The terrific improvements to the Layout mode mean that FileMaker Pro can take on true presentation quality data publishing. To match the precision now possible in layouts, the Preview feature has been made a mode, available from the Select menu in Browse, Find, and Layout modes. With the Zoom feature, the Preview screen now offers both enlarged and condensed views of how your reports will look when printed. Switching in and out of Preview while working in Layout is particularly handy, giving you a quick check on the cumulative effects of your changes with the layout commands.

Other aspects of printing that have been improved include custom page dimensions. These are now integrated into Page Setup dialog (the feature is essentially unchanged, but moved from being a separate option in previous versions). You can now control page breaks from part definition dialog box. Previous versions of FileMaker simply inserted page breaks when needed, sometimes inconveniently in the middle of reports and records. Previous versions limited control to page breaks before leading Sub-summary and after trailing Sub-summary. You now have much greater control over where the breaks fall. Page numbering is also controllable from the Part Definition dialog box.

NEW KEYSTROKES AND SHORTCUTS

With a program upgrade, there are likely to be some subtle changes to command keystrokes. A number of new keystrokes and shortcuts can be found in FileMaker Pro. These are listed in Table 11-3.

CONCLUSION

The improvements in FileMaker Pro show that Claris and Apple are fully committed to making this program *the* database manager for the Macintosh. We hope that this book has helped you make the most of this powerful program.

Glossary

access rights Part of the control of files when networking, specifically, privileges given to a user to perform actions such as editing records and browsing records. Controlled by passwords. (See *password*.)

active window Also known as the current window, this is the desktop window that is on top and appears with a highlighted title bar. The active window is the window you are working in.

alarm clock A Macintosh desk accessory that displays the current date and time, and lets you set an alarm.

alert box A box that appears on the screen to give a warning or to report an error message. The warning is often accompanied by an alert sound.

alignment The lining up of FileMaker layout text and field contents by the left or right edge or middle. Used to make sure that you enter in fields or paste as layout text is consistently lined up.

Apple desktop bus (ADB) A way of connecting different components of your Macintosh system. A low-speed serial bus with connectors on the back panel of the computer to which you attach the keyboard, mouse, and other Apple Desktop Bus devices, such as graphics tablets and specialized keyboards.

Apple HD SC Setup A Macintosh utility program that you use to initialize and test SCSI hard disks.

Apple menu The menu farthest to the left in the menu bar, indicated by an Apple symbol. Use it to choose desk accessories, such as Control Panel and TOPS Spool. Can also be used to select from applications open under Multifinder.

AppleShare A network arrangement based on a dedicated file server. AppleShare allows users of other machines to work with files on the server's hard disk just as if that disk was directly connected to their own machine. (See *file server*.)

AppleTalk A network system that consists of the hardware and software to allow communication between Macintoshes. Encompasses network software and shared resources, such as printers. AppleTalk is built into Macintoshes and used in various implementations of Apple's communication networks. (See *network*.)

application A specific use of a program, for example, a mailing list is a typical application of FileMaker. Also short for application program.

application program A program that performs a specific task, such as database management (FileMaker), word processing (MacWrite), or graphics (MacDraw). Often called application for short.

arrow A tool used in Layout mode for moving objects, T-squares, and parts on the layout, and for selecting objects on the layout. When this tool is selected, the pointer is an arrow.

arrow keys   The four directional keys on the keyboard that, when pressed, move the insertion point when editing. Sometimes called cursor keys. (See *editing, insertion point.*)

ascending order   When sorting records, ascending order means alphabetical order for text or the text result of a calculation field, chronological order for a date or the date result of a calculation field, and lowest-to-highest numerical order for a number or the number result of a calculation field. (See *descending order.*)

ASCII   Acronym for American Standard Code for Information Interchange. A standard used to represent text inside a computer and to transmit text between computers or between a computer and a peripheral device such as a printer. Used to create text files, the most basic file format, it is readable by most application programs and easily transferable between computer systems.

auto-enter   A type of entry option which lets you specify values to be automatically entered in a field when you create a new record. Selected through the Define mode. (See *entry option.*)

background printing   A type of background processing that lets you print documents in the background while using the computer to perform other work. Background printing can be provided by utility programs such as TOPS Spool.

background processing   In multi-tasking environments, the operating system's ability to process lower-priority tasks while you perform other work on the computer.

Backspace key   A key that backspaces over and erases the previously typed character or the current selection. Its function is identical to that of the Delete key on newer Macintosh keyboards.

Backup   A spare copy of an application or a file. You make a backup of the application by copying it using the Finder. You can make a backup of a FileMaker database file using the Finder or the Save a Copy command.

baseline   A horizontal dotted line in a field that coincides with the bottom of each character, excluding descenders (such as the tail of a *p*). Used to make sure fields are level with each other and appropriate layout text.

BASIC file (commas)   A file format that can be created or read by programs written in the BASIC language. The format consists of a text only document with field values separated by commas and records separated by Return characters. File Maker can Output data to a BASIC text file and can copy data from a BASIC using the Input command.

binary   Characterized by having two different components, or by having only two alternatives or values available; sometimes used synonymously with binary system. Used by your computer to store information.

binary digit   The smallest unit of information in the binary system; a 0 or a 1. Also called a bit, a contraction of *binary digit.*

binary system   A numbering system in which each digit represents successive powers of two instead of ten, as in the normal numbering system, decimal. Binary uses only 0 and 1 instead of 0 through 9. For example, the binary number 101011 is 43 in decimal. Because the values 0 and 1 can be represented physically, as in the presence of absence of current, or a positive or negative voltage, the binary system is used extensively in computers and communications. A single binary digit 0 or 1 is called a bit.

bit   A contraction of *binary digit*. The smallest unit of information that a computer can hold. The value of a bit (1 or 0) represents a simple two-way choice, such as yes or no, on or off, positive or negative. (See *binary system.*)

bit-mapped display   A display like that used on the Mac, where the image is a representation of bits in an area of RAM called the screen buffer. With such a display, each dot or pixel on the screen corresponds, or is mapped, to a bit in the screen buffer. This system allows the screen to display more than a fixed set of characters. Images can be created and the shapes of characters changed.

body   The main part of a record layout. FileMaker prints one body for each record, placing as many as will fit on each printed page. (See *part.*)

book   A tool in FileMaker for turning to other records, to other layouts, and to other requests, one at a time. (See *slide control.*)

bridge   A device that lets you connect two or more networking systems together. (See *zone.*)

browse   A FileMaker menu command that lets you view, edit, add and delete records in the file. You can browse all the records in the file, or browse a subset of the records by using the Find command or the Omit Records command.

bus   A path along which information is transmitted electronically within a computer. Buses connect computer devices, such as processors, expansion cards, input devices, and RAM. (See *Apple Desktop Bus.*)

button   A pushbutton-like image in dialog boxes where you click to designate, confirm, or cancel an action. Used extensively in Macintosh applications such as FileMaker. (See *mouse button.*)

byte   A unit of information consisting of a fixed number of bits. A byte can represent any value between 0 and 255. The sequence of bits in a byte represents an instruction, letter, number, punctuation mark, or other character. (See *gigabyte*, *kilobyte*, *megabyte.*)

calculation field   A type of field in FileMaker that contains text, a number, or date computed from other fields within the same record, according to the calculation formula. (See *calculation formula.*)

calculation formula   An expression in a FileMaker calculation field that can contain field names, numbers, text, parentheses, operators (such as $+$, $-$, $*$, and $/$) and functions (such as MOD, INT, and PMT). Used to calculate values in a record, such as a loan payment.

calculator   A Macintosh desk accessory that works like a pocket calculator. Calculation results can be cut and pasted into FileMaker records using the Edit menu.

Cancel   When FileMaker is busy with an operation that can be canceled, the pointer changes shape to show you that you can stop the operation by holding down the Command key and typing a period (.).

Cancel button   A button that appears in a dialog box. Clicking it cancels the command.

Caps Lock key   A key that, when engaged, causes subsequently typed letters to appear in uppercase. Unlike the Shift key, Caps Lock applies only to alphabetic characters. On newer keyboards, the key has a lower physical profile when locked.

character keys   Any of the keys on a computer keyboard such as letters, numbers, symbols, and punctuation marks used to generate text or to format text; any key except Shift, Caps Lock, Command, Option, Control, and Esc. Character keys repeat when you press and hold them down.

check box   A small square box associated with an option in a dialog box. When you click the check box, you select the option. Check boxes are considered "checked" or activated when they contain an *X*. They differ from round radio buttons, which affect related options. (See *radio buttons*.)

chip   A term for integrated circuit, an electronic circuit entirely contained in a single piece of semiconductor material, usually silicon.

choose   To pick a command by dragging through a menu. You often choose a command after you have selected something for the application to act on; for example, selecting a file and choosing the Open command from the File menu.

chooser   A Macintosh desk accessory that lets you configure your computer system to print on any printer for which there is a printing resource on the current startup disk. If you are connected to an AppleTalk network system, you use the Chooser to connect and disconnect from the network.

click   To position the mouse pointer on something, and then to press and quickly release the mouse button. Some commands can be executed with a *double click*, which is two clicks in quick succession.

clipboard   The holding place for the last thing you cut or copied. When you paste, it is the contents of the Clipboard that are pasted.

clone   A copy of a FileMaker file that contains all the field definitions, layouts, and scripts, but not the records. To make a clone of a FileMaker file, choose the Save a Copy command from the File menu.

Close   To close a file or turn a window back into an icon choose the Close command or click the close box in the left corner of the window's title bar. Most Macintosh applications, including FileMaker, will not let you close a document without saving the latest changes.

close box   The small white box on the left side of the title bar of an active window. Clicking it closes the window.

code   The statements or instructions that make up a computer program like File-Maker.

Columnar Report layout   A FileMaker layout option that lets you specify the fields to be included in a new layout. FileMaker arranges the fields you specify in a row across the layout so that field values will appear in columns you print using the layout.

command   A word or phrase, usually in a menu, describing an action for the computer to perform.

Command key   A key that, when held down while another key is pressed, causes a command to take effect. The Command key is marked with a clover-leaf symbol.

On some keyboards, the Command key has an Apple symbol on it. In this book, we have used the term "Command" as in "press Command−C," which means press down the Command key and hold it down while you press C.

compatible   Capable of running without problems on a particular computer system. Applications are normally written to run on specific types of computers; File-Maker for the Macintosh will not run on an IBM. Applications that run on a computer system are said to be compatible with the computer.

compressed copy   A copy of a FileMaker file that contains all the contents of the original file but takes up less disk space. To make a compressed copy of a File-Maker file, choose the Save a Copy command from the File menu.

Concatenation   The ability to combine two or more pieces or strings of text into a single, longer string by joining the beginning of one to the end of the other in a text calculation. To join or concatenate text fields, use the ampersand (&) with the field name. To concatenate spaces or other text constants, enclose them in quotes, as in:

Full Name = First&" "&Last

Confidential layout   A layout that is available only to users with the proper access rights. If a user without the proper access rights tries to use a confidential layout, FileMaker displays the objects on the layout screen in gray, and the ability to add, edit, and view information on the Browse screen is not available. (See *access rights*.)

constant   A specific value that you type in a formula, such as the value .06 in this formula:

Sales Tax = Price * .06

Text constants must be enclosed in quotation marks in a calculation formula.

Control Panel   A desk accessory that you use to change the speaker volume, the keyboard repeat speed and delay, mouse tracking, and color display; to set the system clock; to create a RAM cache; and to set other preferences.

convergence   An adjustment you make with an RGB color monitor to ensure that its red, green, and blue beams are aimed correctly for the best color picture. You can test your monitor's convergence by using the Control Panel desk accessory.

Coprocessor   An auxiliary processor designed to relieve the demand on the main microprocessor by performing a few specific tasks. Coprocessors might favor a certain set of operations, such as floating-point calculations. Generally, coprocessors handle tasks that could be performed by the main microprocessor running appropriate software, that would be performed much more slowly that way.

copy-protect   To prevent disks from being copied without authorization, software publishers frequently copy-protect their disks. This discourages illegal duplication by software pirates. FileMaker is not copy-protected, but its use is restricted by the terms of the software licensing agreement.

current field   The FileMaker field you are working on. The current field is outlined with a solid border. If the current field is a text, number, or date field, you can type or paste information into the field at the insertion point, or replace or delete selected field contents.

current file   The file in the active window. FileMaker commands always work on the current file. You can make any open file the current file by selecting it from the Window menu.

current layout   The Filemaker layout that is displayed or that you last displayed before choosing another command. FileMaker always uses the current layout to display records on the Browse screen, display find requests, and preview or print records. You make a layout the current layout by choosing Layout from the Select menu and then using the book to display the layout you want.

current request   The Find request that is displayed or that you last used to find records.

current startup disk   The disk that contains the System Folder which your Mac is currently using. The startup disk icon always appears in the upper-right corner of the Finder desktop.

cut   To remove something by selecting it and choosing Cut from a menu. What you cut is placed on the Clipboard. In other editing applications, delete serves the same function.

data   Information, especially information used or operated on by a program. Data is actually the plural of datum, originally meaning a given, as in a given piece of information. Common usage is now to treat data as singular, as in "the data has been recorded" rather than "the data have been recorded" although the latter is technically correct.

Date field   A type of FileMaker field that holds a date. The date must be typed in a format like 7/30/86 or 7-30-1986, although FileMaker can display and print the date in any number of formats.

date stamp   A double slash (//) typed on a FileMaker layout. When you browse, print, or preview records, the double slash is replaced with the current date from the Macintosh's internal calendar.

default   Describes an assumption made by the computer, as in default setting, being the setting that a program uses unless you tell it otherwise. Many dialog boxes that offer a choice of actions like Cancel/OK have one marked as the default action, usually with a heavy outline. This action is the one performed if you press Enter.

Delete key   A key that moves the insertion point backward, removing the previously typed character or that removes the current selection. Its function is identical to that of the Backspace key on some Macintosh keyboards. (See *insertion point*.)

descending order   An order in which FileMaker records can be sorted. Descending order means reverse alphabetical order (Z to A) for text or the text result of a calculation field, reverse chronological order (latest to earliest) for a date or date result of a calculation field, and highest-to-lowest numerical order for a number or the number result of a calculation field. (See *ascending order*.)

desk accessories   Small applications, known as DAs, that are available on the desktop from the Apple menu regardless of which application you are using.

Examples supplied with the Mac system software are the Calculator and the Alarm Clock. Commercially available DAs include DeskScan for scanning images into a document, and BigCaps which displays font examples.

desktop   The Macintosh work environment including the menu bar and the gray area on the screen. The desktop displays the trash icon and the icons of any disks currently in the disk drives.

destination   The duplicate, as opposed to the original (or source), in making a copy of a document, folder, or disk.

dialog box   A box presented by a program like FileMaker that asks you for more information in order to complete a command. Can also present a warning. In these cases, the message is often accompanied by a beep.

dimmed command   A command that appears gray rather than black in a menu bar because that command is unavailable at the moment. For example, the Cut command is dimmed unless you have selected a piece of text or graphics to cut.

dimmed icon   An icon that represents an opened disk or folder, or a disk that has been ejected. You can select and open dimmed disk icons, but you cannot open the documents on them.

directory   A pictorial, alphabetical, or chronological list of the contents of a folder or a disk.

directory dialog box   A type of dialog box you use to work in the hierarchial file system from within an application. Such dialog boxes appear whenever you choose the Open or Save As commands from within FileMaker. (See *hierarchial file system.*)

directory window   A window that shows you the contents of a disk or folder.

disk   An information-storage medium consisting of a circular, magnetic surface on which information can be recorded in the form of small magnetized spots, in a manner similar to the way sounds are recorded on tape. Disks are either hard or floppy. (See *hard disk, floppy disk.*)

disk capacity   The maximum amount of data a disk can hold, usually measured in kilobytes (K) or megabytes (Mb). For instance, Macintosh 3.5 inch disks typically have a disk capacity of either 400K or 800K, although higher capacity disks are becoming more common.

disk directory   An index or list of the files on a disk, it holds the names and locations of every file on its disk.

disk drive   The device that holds a disk, retrieves information from it, and saves information to it. A hard disk drive has the disk permanently encased. A floppy disk drive requires that you insert a floppy disk.

document   What you create with a Macintosh application. A document contains information you can view, print, modify, and delete. A FileMaker document is also called a file.

double-click   To position the pointer where you want an action to take place, and then press and release the mouse button twice in quick succession without moving the mouse. Double-clicking is typically a quicker way of performing common tasks. For example, when you want to open a file, you can click once on the file, then click on the Open button, or simply double-click on the file.

drag   To position the pointer on a screen object, then press and hold the mouse button, move the mouse, and release the mouse button. This has the effect of moving or dragging the object. Used in Layout mode to position items such as fields and layout text.

duplicate   A criterion for finding FileMaker records that contain a value in a field that is the same as a value in another record. To specify a duplicate criterion in a request, type an exclamation mark (!) in a field. (See *request*.)

edit   Process of changing a string of characters, in a document, a FileMaker field, a field in a dialog box, or a desktop entry such as folder or file name. Editing takes place at the location of the insertion point. The standard Macintosh editing conventions are:

- The Backspace/Delete key removes characters to the left of the insertion point.
- The arrow keys move the insertion point through text without altering it.
- Text can be highlighted by dragging the insertion point through the text.
- Highlighted text is deleted when you press the Delete key.
- Highlighted text is replaced by the next character you type.

Pressing Enter/Return while editing can have one of two effects: It can add a new line to the text or confirm what you have typed. The effect of Enter/Return depends on the program you are using. (See *Enter, insertion point*.)

Enter key   A key that confirms an entry or sometimes a command. Also used to add a new line to text when typing. When you are presented with a dialog box in which one button is heavily outlined, pressing Enter accepts the action represented by the button, otherwise known as the default response. The Enter key is sometimes referred to as the Return key.

entry options   An option you can specify for a defined field to tell FileMaker to automatically enter information in the field, restrict what information can be typed in a field, or display a list of values. (See *auto-enter, lookup*.)

Ethernet   Ethernet is a widely used communications network, consisting of software plus a wiring standard that supports high-speed data transfer.

EtherTalk   A high-speed AppleTalk network system that uses Ethernet cabling.

exact match   A criterion in FileMaker for finding records that contain a value in a text field that exactly matches what you type in the same field in your request. To specify an exact match in a request, type an equals sign before a value in a text field. (See *request*.)

exclusive file   A FileMaker file that is restricted to only one user at a time. When creating a new file, FileMaker automatically checks Exclusive in the File menu.

expansion card   A circuit board that implements specialized functions not otherwise supported by the computer. Expansion cards are installed in expansion connectors or expansion slots such as those found in the Mac II.

expression   In a FileMaker calculation formula, a combination of field names, numbers, dates, text, operators, functions, and parentheses that calculates a result. Expressions can be used in any place in the formula that a constant or field name can be used. (See *calculation formula, constant, operator, function*.)

field   One component of a FileMaker record. A field can contain information such as a name, comment, birth date, dollar amount, or a calculation or summary value.

field name   A name you assign to identify a FileMaker field. You can change a field name at any time.

field type   The part of a field definition that tells FileMaker what kind of information you will put in the field. Field types include text, number, date, picture, calculation, and summary.

file   A document created by FileMaker. In general, any collection of information stored on a disk, including a document, a folder, a system file or resource, or an application.

file format   The internal organization of information within a file. Different applications use different file formats for their documents. FileMaker lets you input and output information to and from files in a variety of file formats.

file server   A combination of software and hardware, that allows users to share files and applications across a network. Typically includes a mass-storage device, such as a hard disk, to allow multiple users to store files centrally.

FileMaker Temp   A folder that FileMaker creates in your System folder as soon as you start running FileMaker. This folder holds temporary files created by FileMaker while you are running FileMaker. When you open a file, FileMaker creates a temporary file for that file. When you close the file, the associated temporary file is no longer needed and FileMaker removes it from the FileMaker Temp folder. (See *temporary file*.)

Find   A FileMaker mode in which you specify which record you want to find or which record you want to group together. This is done by entering criteria in the fields. Also, Find is a button on FileMaker's Find screen. Clicking the button tells FileMaker to find the records that match your request. (See *request*.)

Find File   A Macintosh desk accessory that lets you find any folder or file on a disk.

Finder   The application that maintains the Macintosh desktop and starts up other applications at the user's request. You use the Finder to manage documents and applications, and to get information to and from disks.

floppy disk   A flexible plastic disk for storing data magnetically. Those used in the Mac have a nonflexible plastic jacket and a metal shutter that moves aside when the disk is inserted into the drive, thus giving the drive access to the disk. The disks used in the Mac are $3^1/2$ inch in diameter.

folder   An area in storage used to group related documents, applications, and other folders on the desktop. Folders allow you to organize information to match your needs.

font   A complete set of letters, numbers, and symbols in one design, size, and style having a consistent appearance. Helvetica 12 point is an example of a font and size. FileMaker allows you to format fields and layout text with a variety of fonts.

Font/DA Mover   A utility program that comes with the Mac system software: It lets you add or remove fonts and desk accessories in your System file.

Footer   The part of a FileMaker layout that contains the bottom margin. Any text in Footer appears at the bottom of every printed page. (See *part*.)

format   The appearance of data. For example, you can format a number to be displayed as a percentage, text to be displayed in Helvetica 14 point, or a box to be filled with diagonal strips. (See *alignment.*)

found records   Many FileMaker commands apply to "found records," those that FileMaker locates when you issue the Find command. Found records are a subset of the complete set of records in a database, based on criteria you establish with the Find command. When Find is in effect, you see a count of the number of found records in the Browse mode.

function   An expression in a FileMaker calculation formula consisting of a function name followed by one or more values in parentheses, such as AVERAGE (Cost) or ROUND (PAYMENT,2). Filemaker obtains the result of the function by operating on the values within the parentheses. (See *calculation formula, expression.*)

gigabyte (Gb)   A unit of measurement equal to 1024 megabytes. Compare byte, kilobyte, megabyte.

Grand Summary   The part of a FileMaker layout that contains data summarizing all of the records you are browsing. FileMaker prints the Grand Summary before or after printing all of the records. (See *part, Sub-summary.*)

gray scale   Shades of gray on the screen that are created by varying the intensity of the screen's pixels, rather than by using a combination of only black and white pixels to produce shading. Can also refer to the use of gray in graphic images that are scanned into the computer.

greater than   A FileMaker criterion symbol (>) used for finding records that contain a value in a field that is alphabetically later, numerically greater, or chronologically later than the value you type in the same field in your request. Use > before a value in a request to specify greater than. (See *request.*)

greater than or equal to   A FileMaker criterion symbol (≥) used for finding records that contain a value in a field that is equal to or alphabetically later, numerically greater, or chronologically later than the value you type in the same field in your request.

guest   The second or any subsequent user to open a FileMaker file across a network. The file must first have been opened by another user, the host. (See *host.*)

hard disk   A disk made of metal and sealed into a drive or cartridge. A hard disk can store very large amounts of information compared with floppy disks.

hardware   In computer terminology, the machinery that makes up a computer system. (See *software.*)

Header   The part of a layout that contains the top margin, which appears at the top of every printed page. Text in a header is printed on every page of a report. (See *part.*)

hidden window   An open FileMaker file that is not displayed on the desktop. FileMaker lists a hidden window in the Window menu in parentheses. To display a hidden window, choose the file from the Window menu.

hierarchial file system (HFS)   A feature of system software that lets you use folders to arrange documents, applications, and other folders on a disk. Folders (analogous to subdirectories on IBM PC systems) can be nested in other folders to create as many levels as you need to organize your work.

highlight   To make something visually distinct from its background, usually done with the mouse, to show that the item has been selected or chosen.

host   The first user to open a FileMaker file in a network environment.

I-beam   A type of pointer used in entering and editing text. When the mouse pointer is an I-beam, you position it within text or elsewhere in a document and click the mouse button to edit the text at that point.

icon   A graphic representation of an object, a concept, or a message, usually used to represent disks, applications, folders, documents, and so on.

index   A list of all the values (words, numbers, or dates) that you have typed in a field in any FileMaker record. To see the index for the field that contains the insertion point, choose View Index from the Edit menu.

initialize   To prepare a disk to receive information. Initializing a disk divides its surface into tracks and sectors, which the operating system uses to keep track of the contents of the disk.

input device   A device that sends information to the microprocessor. The mouse and keyboard are the Macintosh's primary input devices.

insertion point   The place in a document where something will be added. You set an insertion point by clicking. It is represented by a blinking vertical bar.

Invisible Grid   This feature is normally active in the Layout mode to help you align objects during layout. If you turn the invisible grid off, you can drag objects in smaller increments. (See *point*.)

K   See kilobyte.

Key Caps   A desk accessory that shows you the optional character set available for a given font family.

keyboard shortcut   A keystroke that you can use instead of a mouse action to perform a task. For example, pressing the Command and the X keys at the same time is the same as choosing the Cut command from the Edit menu in FileMaker.

kilobyte (Kb)   A unit of measurement consisting of 1024 bytes. Often abbreviated as *K* (See *byte*, *gigabyte*, *megabyte*.)

Label layout   An option when creating a new layout that lets you specify the height and width and number of labels across the page and the fields to include a layout for the labels.

layout   A visual arrangement of fields, layout text, pictures, lines, and boxes that represents the way your records will look when displayed and printed. You can change any layout, create new layouts, or delete a layout whenever you like without affecting your data.

layout text   Text typed on a layout. Layout text can be column headings, descriptive notes, or whatever you wish. On the Standard layout that FileMaker creates for you, the layout text corresponds to the field names you have defined. You can replace, change, or remove any layout text using the text tool.

less than   A criterion indicated by a symbol (<) that is used for finding records that contain a value in a field that is alphabetically before, numerically less than, or chronologically earlier than the value you type in the same field in your request. Use before a value in a request to specify less than. (See *request*.)

less than or equal to   A criterion indicated by a symbol (≤) for finding records that contain a value in a field that is equal to or alphabetically before, numerically less than, or chronologically earlier than the value you type in the same field in your request.

line   A FileMaker tool for drawing straight lines on the layout. When the line tool is selected, the pointer is a cross.

local area network (LAN)   A group of computers connected for the purpose of sharing resources. The computers on a local area network are typically joined by a single transmission cable, and are located within a small area such as a single building or section of a building.

LocalTalk   A low-cost AppleTalk network system that lets you link up to 32 computers or devices together to form a local-area network.

lock   To prevent documents from being edited, discarded, or renamed, or to prevent entire disks from being altered. (See *write-protect*.)

lookup   An entry option telling FileMaker to automatically copy the value from a field in the lookup file into the field you specify. The lookup occurs when what you type in another field in the current file matches a value in a field in the lookup file. (See *entry options*, *lookup file*.)

lookup file   The file from which information is copied when FileMaker looks up values from another file. (See *lookup*.)

Macintosh Operating System   The combination of ROM-based and disk-based routines in the Macintosh that together perform basic tasks such as starting the computer, moving data to and from disks and peripheral devices, and managing memory space in RAM.

Macintosh User Interface   The standard conventions for interfacing with Macintosh computers. The interface ensures users a consistent means of interacting with all Macintosh computers and the applications designed to run on them.

magnet   An icon in FileMaker's Layout mode which shows whether or not the T-squares are magnetic. When moving objects on the layout, objects snap to the T-squares if the T-squares are magnetic.

main unit   The computer console, which contains the processor, memory, the built-in disk drive(s), the optional internal hard disk, and, on the Macintosh Plus and SE, the screen.

megabyte (Mb)   A unit of measurement equal to 1024 kilobytes. (See *byte*, *gigabyte*, *kilobyte*.)

memory   The place in the computer's unit that stores information while the computer is actively using it. Macintosh computers include a minimum of 1 megabyte of RAM (random-access memory) that you can use for your work and 256K of ROM (read-only memory) that stores certain system information permanently. Memory is distinguished from *storage*, which is permanent and usually on disk. (See *disk*, *RAM*, *ROM*.)

menu   A list of commands that appears when you point to and press the menu title in the menu bar. Dragging through the menu and releasing the mouse button while a command highlighted chooses that command.

menu bar   The horizontal strip at the top of the screen that contains menu titles.

menu title   A word or phrase in the menu bar that designates one menu. Pressing down the mouse button with the mouse pointer on the menu title causes the title to be highlighted and its menu to appear below it.

merge file   A file format used by applications such as Microsoft Word to store information for merging with another document to create form letters and other form documents. FileMaker can create merge files, making it easy to merge data in a FileMaker file with a form letter written in Microsoft Word.

Microprocessor   An integrated circuit on the computer's main circuit board. The microprocessor carries out software instructions by directing the flow of electrical impulses through the computer.

modem port   One of two serial communication ports on the back panel of many Macintosh computers.

mouse   The small mechanical device whose movement on your desk corresponds to pointer movements on your screen.

mouse button   The button on the top of the mouse. In general, pressing the mouse button initiates some action on whatever is under the pointer, and releasing the button confirms the action.

mouse keys   An easy access feature that lets you manipulate the pointer using the ten key numeric keypad instead of the mouse. See "Easy Access" in your Macintosh System manual.

Multi-launch   The ability of two or more people to use the same copy of an application simultaneously in a network environment. According to your FileMaker licensing agreement, in order for two or more people to use FileMaker simultaneously in a network environment, they must own the same number of copies of FileMaker as the number of people using FileMaker simultaneously.

multi-user   The ability of a network system or application to support several people using the same document at the same time. (See *network*.)

MultiFinder   A multi-tasking operating system for Macintosh computers that makes it possible to have several applications open at the same time, including background applications that let you perform one task while the computer performs another. FileMaker is compatible with MultiFinder and can be successfully operated "under MultiFinder."

nesting   Placing folders inside other folders when organizing files, or placing IF statements within IF statements in FileMaker formulas.

network   A collection of individually controlled computers connected together by hardware and software. A network allows users to share applications, documents, printers, and so on.

network button   A button on the FileMaker Open dialog box that lets you see the files you can open as a guest. To use this button, your Macintosh must be connected to an AppleTalk network.

notepad   A desk accessory that lets you enter and edit small amounts of text while working on another document.

number field   A type of FileMaker field that holds a number or a yes/no value. You can also type anything else in a number field, but only the number in the field is used for calculations and for finding. If you choose a number format on the layout, only the number in the field is displayed and printed. Data in number fields can only occupy one line, limited to 250.

numeric keypad   The set of keys on the right side of the keyboard that let you enter numbers and perform calculations quickly.

object   A field, line, box, piece of layout text, or picture on a layout. In general, a separate item on the screen.

open   To create a window from an icon so you can view a document or directory.

operating system   A combination of ROM-based and disk-based routines that together perform basic tasks such as moving data to and from disks and peripheral devices. An operating system acts as both a file manager and data flow manager, allowing applications such as FileMaker to concentrate on more specialized operations while the operating system performs housekeeping chores.

operator   In a FileMaker calculation formula, a word or symbol (such as + or −) that specifies an operation to be performed on the two values on either side of it.

Option key   A key used to give an alternate interpretation to another key you type. You use it to type international characters or special symbols.

output device   A device that receives information from the microprocessor. Your monitor and printer are output devices.

oval   A tool used for drawing ovals on a FileMaker layout. When the oval is selected, the pointer is a cross.

page break   An option that is available in the dialog box that FileMaker displays when you create a Sub-summary part on a layout. If you check the box next to page break, FileMaker puts the section symbol (§) in the part on the layout. If the Sub-summary part appears above the body, FileMaker starts a new page before printing each Sub-summary. If the Sub-summary part appears below the body, FileMaker starts a new page after printing each Sub-summary.

page number   Two number signs (##) typed on the layout. When printed or previewed, the number signs are replaced by the current page number.

parallel communication   A form of data communication in which the eight bits in each byte of data move along eight separate parallel lines inside a single cable.

part   A section of a FileMaker layout. A layout can have these parts:

- One Title Header.
- One Header.
- One Grand Summary before the body.
- One Sub-summary before the body for each Text, Number, Date, or Calculation field.
- One Body, One Sub-summary after the Body for each Text, Number, Date, or Calculation field.
- One Grand Summary after the Body.

- One Footer.
- One Title Footer.

password A word that you type to gain a set of access rights to a file, rights that have already been defined. Passwords let users control who can open a file and what action or actions can be performed. (See *access rights*.)

paste To put a copy of the contents of the Clipboard whatever was last cut or copied at the insertion point.

peripheral device A piece of computer hardware such as a disk drive, printer, or modem used in conjunction with a computer and under the computer's control. Peripheral devices are usually physically separate from the computer and connected to it by wires or cables.

picture An image that can be copied or cut from MacDraw, MacPaint, or another application or desk accessory and pasted onto a FileMaker layout or into a picture field. The picture is then displayed and printed in the appropriate place.

picture field A type of field that holds a picture. A picture can be copied or cut from MacDraw, Canvas, or other graphics program. Each record can display a different picture in a picture field.

pixel An individual dot on the screen. With a simple monochrome video display, a pixel is the visual representation of a single bit in the screen buffer (white if the bit is 0, black if it is 1). With color or gray-scale video displays, each pixel on the screen can represent several bits.

plain-text documents Documents consisting only of readable ASCII characters, without any formatting codes specific to a particular full feature word processing application.

point A unit of measurement used in layout mode. One point is approximately 1/72 inch. You can move layout objects in increments of one point, when using the layout with the Invisible Grid turned off.

pointer A small shape on the screen, most often an arrow pointing up and to the left, that follows the movement of the mouse.

port A socket on the back panel of the computer where you can plug in a cable to connect a peripheral device, another computer, or a network.

Power On key A key on the keyboard that starts the Macintosh.

press To position the pointer on something and then hold down the mouse button without moving the mouse. When applied to keys as in the statement "Press Enter," it actually means "tap" because some keys automatically repeat if you apply sustained pressure.

print monitor An application that monitors background printing and provides options intended to give you additional control over what happens to documents you are printing. (See *background processing*.)

printable area The area on a piece of paper in which a laser or impact printer can print images. The printable area changes according to the printer and paper size being used. When you create a layout, FileMaker takes the printable area into account.

printer port   One of two serial communication ports on the back panel of the computer.

printer resource   A file in the System folder that provides information the microprocessor needs to communicate with a printer.

question mark   A symbol that FileMaker displays in Number, Calculation, and Summary fields when the contents of the field will not fit in the space available. You can display the layout and reshape the field to be long enough to hold the field contents.

RAM   An acronym for random-access memory, the computer chips that store information temporarily while you're working on it. RAM can contain both application programs and your own information. Information in RAM is temporary, gone forever if you switch the power off.

RAM cache   This is a portion of RAM that you can designate to store certain information an application uses repeatedly. Using the RAM cache with some applications can greatly speed up your work, but it might need to be used sparingly or not at all with applications that require large amounts of memory, as is the case with FileMaker. Claris recommends you turn off the RAM cache when using FileMaker. Use the control Panel to adjust the RAM cache.

range   A criterion indicated by ellipsis (. . .) for finding records that contain values in a field that are alphabetically, numerically, or chronologically between two values in the same field in your request. Use this criterion between two values in a request to find records within a range, including the beginning and ending values. (See *request*.)

read-only memory   See *ROM*.

record   One component of a FileMaker file. Each record contains all the fields defined for that file. The information in one record can describe a transaction, a client, an inventory item, or anything else.

record number   Two at signs (@@) typed on the layout. When you print or preview records, the at signs are replaced by the current record number.

rectangle   A tool for drawing rectangles on a layout. When the box is selected, the pointer is a cross.

reformulate   An option in the Define dialog box that lets you edit a FileMaker formula for a selected calculation or summary field.

repeating field   A FileMaker field that has been formatted to let you store a number of distinct values in the same field within each record.

request   A set of criteria you specify to tell FileMaker to find records that you can then browse, edit, sort, print, delete, or copy into another file. If you type a value in a field on the request, FileMaker finds records which match the criteria. You can refine your request by using symbols with values in a request. (See *duplicate*, *exact match*, *greater than*, *greater than or equal to*, *less than*, *less than or equal to*, *range*, and *today's date*.)

reshape box   The small solid black box in the lower right corner of a field, line, box, or picture on the layout. Drag this box to a new location to change the size or shape of any of these objects.

resources Files contained in the System folder that provide information the microprocessor needs to communicate with devices attached to the computer system.

Return key A key that makes the insertion point move to the beginning of the next line. Sometimes used to confirm or terminate an entry or a command.

ROM An acronym for read-only memory, the memory chips that contain information the computer uses (along with system files) throughout the system, including the information it needs to get itself started. Information in ROM is permanent; as opposed to RAM, ROM does not vanish when you switch the power off.

rounded rectangle A tool used for drawing rectangles with rounded corners on a layout. When the rounded rectangle is selected, the pointer is a cross.

routine A sequence of software instructions. You can preserve routines in FileMaker by using the Script feature.

save To store information from RAM onto a disk. Some applications require you to issue a File Save to store the information you have entered. FileMaker constantly saves your work for you.

Scrapbook A desk accessory in which you can save frequently used pictures and text.

screen buffer A portion of memory in RAM from which the video display reads the information to be displayed on the screen.

screen width An icon that changes the width of the screen. The Screen Width icon hides or displays the status area.

script A named series of FileMaker commands that you can tell FileMaker to perform in a sequence. Scripts are useful for automating a series of commands you expect to perform frequently. You can always create, delete, or change any script.

scroll To move the contents of a window, or a list in a dialog box, by means of the scroll bar or scroll arrows.

scroll arrow An arrow on either end of a scroll bar. Clicking a scroll arrow moves the document or directory one line. Pressing a scroll arrow scrolls the document continuously.

scroll bar A rectangular bar that may be along the right or bottom of a window. Clicking or dragging in the scroll bar causes the view of the document to change.

scroll box The white box in a scroll bar. The position of the scroll box in the scroll bar indicates the position of what is in the window relative to the entire document.

SCSI An acronym for *Small Computer System Interface*, an industry standard interface that provides high-speed access to peripheral devices. Many hard disk drives and scanners are SCSI devices.

SCSI port The port on the back panel of the computer to which you connect SCSI devices.

sector A part of a track on the surface of a disk. When a disk is first initialized, the operating system divides the disk's surface into circular tracks, with each track divided into sectors. Tracks and sectors are used to organize the information stored on a disk.

select To designate where the next action will take place. To select, you click or drag across information with the mouse.

selection   The information affected by the next command. The selection is usually highlighted.

serial communication   A form of data communication in which the eight bits in each byte of data move single-file serially down one line inside a cable.

serial interface   An interface in which information is transmitted sequentially, one bit at a time, over a single wire or channel.

serial ports   The connectors on the back panel of the computer for devices that use a serial interface. (See *modem port, printer port*.)

Shift key   A key that, when pressed, causes subsequently typed letters to appear in uppercase, and causes the upper symbol to appear when number or symbol keys are typed.

Shift−click   A technique that lets you extend or shorten a selection by holding down the Shift key while you select (or deselect) something related to the current selection. For example, in FileMaker's layout mode, you can select several items by clicking on the first one, then Shift−clicking on the second, and so on.

SIMM   An acronym for single in-line memory module, a circuit board that contains RAM chips. SIMMs attach to SIMM sockets on your Mac's circuit board to expand RAM.

slide control   A FileMaker tool for turning to other records, layouts, and requests. The slide control is especially useful when turning to more than one record, layout, or request at a time. (See *book*.)

sort order   A list of the fields to be used when sorting the records. You can sort a file by values in as many Text, Number, Date, or Calculation fields as you need. (See *ascending order, descending order*.)

Standard layout   A layout that FileMaker creates, which you can then modify. The standard layout contains three parts: a Header, a Body, and a Footer. The Body contains all of the fields that you defined, plus layout text that corresponds to the field names. (See *part, layout text*.)

style   A visual variation to the characters in a font, such as bold or italic. On the Layout screen, you can change the style of any field or layout text. On the Browse screen, you can change the style of text entered in a text field.

Sub-summary   A part of the layout that displays and prints summary information when the records are sorted by a specified field. A sales report file that is sorted by the Salesperson field might have Sub-summaries of each salesperson's total sales and average commission. (See *part, Grand Summary*.)

Summary field   A type of field that holds a summary of all the values in a Number, Date, or Calculation field over a group of records. Summaries can be totals, averages, counts, maximums, minimums, or standard deviations of values in a field. A Summary field in a Grand Summary part displays the Grand Summary of all the records you are browsing.

SYLK (symbolic link)   A file format that stores data in cells (rows and columns). FileMaker can copy data from a SYLK file into a FileMaker file, and can copy data from a FileMaker file into a SYLK file.

tab group   The selected fields included in a tab order. A tab order is specified using the Tab Order command. (See *tab order*.)

tab order   The order in which you can tab through fields. To choose the tab order you specify a tab group using the Tab Order command. (See *tab group*.)

temporary file   A file that FileMaker creates in the FileMaker Temp folder containing information FileMaker needs to keep track of while a file is open. When you close a FileMaker file, the temporary file is removed from the FileMaker Temp folder. If you are unexpectedly interrupted while working in FileMaker and your open files are not closed properly, FileMaker does not remove the temporary files from the FileMaker Temp folder. You can remove temporary files from the FileMaker Temp folder by dragging them to the trash. (See *FileMaker Temp*.)

Text field   A type of field that holds anything you can type. Use text fields to hold names, addresses, comments, notes, memos, or any other text.

text file (tabs)   A text-only document that contains field values separated by tabs and records separated by Return characters. A text file contains just text; no formatting information, variation in fonts or styles, picture, page breaks, headers, or footers are stored. FileMaker can create a text file from data from a FileMaker file and copy data from a text file into a FileMaker file.

text tool   A tool for typing and editing text on the layout. When the text tool is selected, the pointer is an I-beam.

time stamp   A double colon (::) typed on the layout. When you print or preview records, the double colon is displayed with the current time from the Macintosh's internal calendar.

title bar   The horizontal bar at the top to a window that shows the name of the window and lets you move it.

Title Footer   The part of a layout that contains the bottom margin that appears at the bottom of the first printed page. (See *part*.)

Title Header   The part of a layout that contains the top margin that appears at the top of the first printed page. (See *part*.)

today's date   A criterion for finding records that contain a value in a date field or a calculation with a date result that is the same as the date in your Macintosh's internal calendar. To specify today's date as a criterion in a request, type two slashes (//) in a field. (See *request*.)

TOPS   A distributed file server that allows each computer on a network to function as a server. (See *file server*.)

track   A portion of a disk's surface. When a disk is first initialized, the operating system divides the disk's surface into circular tracks, with each track divided into sectors. Tracks and sectors are used to organize the information stored on a disk.

trash   An icon on the desktop that you use to discard documents, folders, and applications. Drag disk icons to the trash to eject disks.

Unsort   A button in the Sort dialog box that you click to undo the effect of sorting the records by returning the records to the order in which they were originally added to the file.

update folder   A folder on the System Tools disk, and on other application and system disks, that contains Read Me documents.

user group   A computer club where computer users exchange tips and information, usually about a particular brand of computer.

user interface   See *Macintosh user interface*.

user interface toolbox   Routines in ROM that provide application program developers with templates for windows, dialog boxes, icons, menus, and other standard elements of the Macintosh user interface.

utility program   A special-purpose application that alters a system file or lets you perform some useful function on your files. Examples are the Font/DA Mover, Capture, and PC tools for the Mac.

window   An area that displays information on the desktop. You view documents through a window. You can open or close a window, move it around on the desktop, and sometimes change its size, edit its contents, and scroll through it.

word wrap   The automatic continuation of text from the end of one line to the beginning of the next, word wrap lets you avoid pressing the Return key at the end of each line as you type. This is a feature that FileMaker text fields have in common with word processing programs. The last whole word and the insertion point is moved from the right edge of the field to the next line as you are typing.

wristwatch   The pointer that you see on the screen when the computer is performing an action that causes you to wait.

write-protect   To protect the information on a disk. You write-protect or lock a $3^1/2$ disk by sliding the small tab in the left corner on the back of the disk toward the disk's edge.

zone   A network in a series of interconnected networks, joined through bridges.

zoom box   The small box on the right side of the title bar of some windows used to expand or contract the window.

Index

Other Bestsellers of Related Interest

WRITING BETTER TECHNICAL ARTICLES
—Harley Bjelland

Publishing technical articles is a sure bet to enhance your professional career. With this unique new stylebook, you can develop the writing and editing skills needed to get published! This guide leads you through all the steps between the idea and the sale. The author targets the shorter technical article, but his techniques are equally well suited to all types of technical writing, including books, manuals, proposals, and letters. 208 pages, 40 illustrations. Book No. 3439, $12.95 paperback, $19.95 hardcover

BIT-MAPPED GRAPHICS—Steve Rimmer

This is one of the first books to cover the specific graphic file formats used by popular paint and desktop publishing packages. It shows you how to pack and unpack bit-map image files so you can import and export them to other applications. And, it helps you sort through available file formats, standards, patches, and revision levels, using commercial-quality C code to explore bit-mapped graphics and effectively deal with image files. 504 pages, 131 illustrations. Book No. 3558, $26.95 paperback, $38.95 hardcover

BUILD YOUR OWN MACINTOSH® AND SAVE A BUNDLE—Bob Brant

Building your own Mac is easy and much less expensive than buying one off the shelf. Just assemble economical, readily available components for your own catalog-part Macintosh, or "Cat Mac," with the help of this book. You can also upgrade a Mac you already own, add more memory, a hard disk, a bigger display, or an accelerator card to your existing systems—all at the best price. 240 pages, 113 illustrations. Book No. 3656, $17.95 paperback only

BAR CODING WITH EXCEL:
Covering Both IBM® and Macintosh™ Versions
—Irwin B. Galter

Here's the only how-to book available on installing and using bar coding systems with the spreadsheet Excel. Get a grip on product costs and raise the bottom line with the help of your personal computer. Low product cost and high product reliability are keys to survival in the world marketplace. This excellent manual will help you achieve these goals. 384 pages, 194 illustrations. Book No. 3302, $34.95 hardcover only

FoxBASE+™/Mac Simplified—Michael Masterson

Micro systems database expert Michael Masterson provides the advice and guidance you need to put FoxBASE+ through its paces for maximum data handling productivity, including how to write your own programs and create your own customized database. Includes alphabetical reference listings of commands, symbols, and functions and practical programming tips and techniques. 560 pages, 159 illustrations. Book No. 3187, $27.95 paperback only

THE FIFTH GENERATION: The Future of Computer Technology
—Jeffrey Hsu and Joseph Kusnan

The Fifth Generation presents a clear, readable account of applications, research, and technologies that make up the fifth generation. Authors Hsu and Kusnan cover each aspect of the subject in depth including fifth-generation research, parallel processing, vision systems, microchip technologies, speech processing, robotics, programming languages, natural language, and expert systems. 208 pages, 30 illustrations. Book No. 3069, $16.95 paperback only

MASTERING PAGEMAKER™: Macintosh®
Version 3.0—G. Keith Gurganus, M.S.

PageMaker introduced the world to desktop publishing (DTP). Still the top-selling DTP package, it continues to stretch the limits of personal computer capabilities with its latest release, Version 3.0. Packed with shortcuts, tips, and tricks, *Mastering PageMaker™: Macintosh® Version 3.0* can help you produce the kind of documents you've always imagined possible with desktop publishing. 224 pages, 143 illustrations. Book No. 3186, $16.95 paperback only

COMPUTER COMPOSER'S TOOLBOX
—Phil Winsor

Now you can discover the enormous creative and time-saving potential of computerized music composition. You'll find easy-to-follow programming guidance as well as an introduction to musical terms and trends. Included are 117 ready-to-use music subroutines to use in your own compositions. 272 pages. Book No. 3384, $19.95 paperback only